The Encyclopedia of the
Motorcycle

Bimotas were successful in endurance racing, the rider here being Charlie Williams

OPPOSITE: 750cc (46cu in) R11 BMW

The Encyclopedia of the
Motorcycle

Peter Henshaw

CHARTWELL BOOKS, INC.

ACKNOWLEDGEMENTS

The task of writing an encyclopedia and checking its contents just isn't possible without the help of many people. My thanks therefore go to Mike Jackson for reading the text, and Alan Cathcart who checked the Italian sections, any errors being mine, not theirs. Thanks also to Nikki Riley for her help with typing, and to Richard Stevens who allowed me to monopolize the office at weekends. Also to Zac Stevens, who spent hours in the *Motorcycle Sport & Leisure* archive searching out pictures and to Ian Kerr who supplied extra pictures. Stuart Lanning and the boys at *Scootering* magazine deserve a special mention for coming up with Lambretta pictures at short notice while Andrew Morland's extensive picture archive was invaluable and his sense of humour certainly helped keep me going. I'd also like to thank the team at Regency for taking the whole project on, not forgetting the authors of the books referred to who, like me, probably spent time staring out of windows wishing they were elsewhere. Finally, thanks to my long-suffering Apple Macintosh, and to Anna, for her patience through all those missed weekends.

The Publisher wishes to thank Andrew Morland, Garry Stuart and Peter Henshaw for supplying the bulk of the illustrations.

Published in 2008 by
Chartwell Books, Inc.
A division of Book Sales, Inc.
114 Northfield Avenue
Edison, New Jersey 08837
U.S.A

For all editorial enguiries please contact:
Regency House Publishing at
www.regencyhousepublishing.com

ISBN 13: 978-0-7858-2144-1
ISBN 10: 0-7858-2144-9

Printed in China

RIGHT: A Crocker with an Indian overhead-valve V-twin

FAR RIGHT: 1958 Matchless G12 650cc (40cu in)

CROCKER

INTRODUCTION

Humanity is capable of many wonderful things, but the art of making motorcycles is arguably not its greatest achievement. Throughout history there have been far more pressing needs than the desire to get from A to B more quickly and more pleasurably than anyone else. And yet, thousands of entrepreneurs have gravitated to the motorcycle industry; scratch any of them, and one will most likely find an enthusiast beneath the skin. Why else would anyone be willing to risk time and money in a business notorious for its glorious failures?

There are surely easier ways of earning a living. The product is a complicated one: it calls for skilled assembly, and if one is lacking the wherewithal to produce the more complicated parts in-house, they must to be bought in, expensively, from outside suppliers. Of those firms that were forced to obtain their engines from elsewhere, most eventually fell by the wayside. Some obtained virtually all of their components from outside sources and simply bolted them together.

Motorcycles have never been easy to produce and in addition have to contend with a highly competitive market in order to tempt conservative, yet fickle customers. That is why the successful, long-lived manufacturers have not, by and large, been great innovators; they simply made the best use of what was available and assembled it into an arrangement that people actually wanted to buy. Other, more idealistic producers tried hub-centre-steering, monocoque chassis, rotary engines and feet-forward layouts, only for them to be rejected on the showroom floor. But all these ideas (apart from the rotary engine, which now seems genuinely to have died a death) eventually made a come-back, and if the brave first-timer failed to make a success of them, then someone else eventually would once the world was ready for them.

Are we living in more hard-headed times? Brough-Superior, Vincent-HRD and Hesketh were all brave attempts (in the 1920s, '30s and '80s respectively) to produce big British V-twins, but all ultimately failed. Somehow, one cannot imagine the same fate befalling the many new motorcycle ventures of the 1990s. Production of bikes like the new Triumph, the Voxan and Excelsior-Henderson have been based on clear-sighted business plans. There is always an element of risk, of course, but these latest marques appear to have some indefinable extra on their side.

The last ten years of the 20th century has seen a renaissance in European and American motorcycling. Whether it is greater affluence or the arrival of well-off baby boomers at middle age (more than ever, this is a 40-something sport), or even the shift to motorcycling as a leisure activity, the older names are being reborn. In Italy, Ducati is enjoying a new lease of life, Cagiva is relaunching the MV Agusta name, while Laverda and Moto Guzzi are planning new-generation engines. BMW has expanded its range and, with Voxan, France has a motorcycle industry for the first time in decades. In America, Harley-Davidson's recovery has inspired a group of businessmen to bring back the Excelsior name and another to launch a new one, the Victory. Even Indian, subject to so many grand designs for relaunch in the past, may now finally be back in production. Similarly in Britain, one has seen John Bloor's Triumph as one of the first born-again marques, and Norton's chequered career keeps the motorcycle in the headlines.

Alongside all of this, powered two-wheelers (PTW is the current buzz-term) are enjoying a boom in the growing markets of the Third World, especially in China while, for different reasons, scooters are proliferating in Europe as our roads get ever more clogged and polluted. For the first time there is a dawning realization that the private car, as a means of personal transport, is rapidly becoming unsustainable in our modern cities. The challenge for today's PTW makers lies in building machines that can tempt commuters out of their cars and onto something more in tune with a world of finite resources.

On the subject of names: the naming of such emotive products as motorcycles is obviously important, so one can understand why the Whirlwind was so named, likewise the Eagle, the Express and the Joybike. But if there was a Panther and a Stag, why was there also a Rabbit? Silver Prince might possibly convince one to part with hard-earned cash, but what about Silver Pigeon? As for the Pouncy, the Autoflug and the Clément-Gladiator, one wonders what the inventors were thinking of at the time. Perhaps it is not surprising then, that the imaginatively named Génial-Lucifer lasted for over 20 years.

It only remains to say that a work of this nature does not claim to be definitive and almost inevitably will contain errors and omissions for which I apologize.

Peter Henshaw
St. Columb, Cornwall, England.

April 1999

The best-known make of all? The Harley-Davidson Duo Glide

A

ABAKO *Germany 1923–25*
A typical utilitarian bike for Weimar Germany, a 129cc (8cu inch) two-stroke.

ABBOTSFORD *Britain 1919–20*
An early scooter with a 1.5hp ohv four-stroke single.

ABC *Britain 1914–22*
There were several ABCs and this one, with Granville Bradshaw at its heart, concentrated on spare parts and design work after World War I. Meanwhile, Bradshaw's latest design had been taken over in 1919 by Sopwith, which had famously made aircraft during the war and now needed something new to sell. The bike it made was the definitive ABC, thought by many to be the predecessor of the first BMW, which it pre-dated by four years. It was a 398cc (24cu in) ohv flat-twin, with a 4-speed gearbox and chain-drive. It was certainly an advance on Bradshaw's early design, with automatic lubrication and rear suspension. Sadly, its advanced specification had not been sufficiently developed (a recurrent theme in the British industry) and its unreliability led to Sopwith's liquidation after just two years in the motorcycle industry.

ABC *Britain 1920–24*
No connection with Bradshaw's ABC, this one was assembled from bought-in components, notably Villiers engines of 247 and 296cc (15–18cu in).

ABC *Germany 1920–25*
Built amid the decadence of 1920s Berlin, there was little that was decadent about this 149cc (9cu in) two-stroke.

ABOVE and BELOW: The early ABC (1914) stayed with the flat-twin layout right to the end

ABENDSONNE *Germany 1933–34*
Georg Weissbinder's bike used two 98cc (6cu in) Villiers singles coupled together.

ABERDALE *England 1947–49*
A 98cc (6cu in) Villiers Junior-powered autocycle, having the luxury of drum brakes, lights and a speedometer.

ABE-STAR *Japan 1951–59*
Utilized its own 148cc (9cu in) four-stroke single.

ABINGDON/AKD *England 1903–33*
Used bought-in engines, notably from MMC, Minerva, Kerry and Fafnir, though soon developed its own 3.5hp singles, 5–6hp V-twins, and later 147–346cc (9–21cu in) four-stroke singles.

ABOVE: 398cc racing ABC of 1920

BELOW LEFT and RIGHT: Villiers-powered ABC Skootamota represented real minimalist motorcycling

ABJ *England 1949–54*
Autocycle and motorcycle with Villiers 98cc (6cu in) singles, plus a clip-on cyclemotor from 1952, with Miller's magneto.

ABRA *Italy 1923–27*
Began by assembling bought-in components (including DKW's 146cc/9cu inch single) but progressed to its own 132cc (8cu in) unit.

ACE *USA 1919–29*
Founded by Bill Henderson, having left the employ of Ignaz Schwinn, who had taken over the original Henderson concern in 1917. Produced a similar ioe 1229cc (75cu in) in-line four to the Henderson, but significantly lighter. Bill Henderson was killed testing a machine in 1922, and the company collapsed two years later. The company was eventually bought by Indian, which built developments of the four until 1942.

ACHILLES *Czechoslovakia 1906–12*
Bought-in engines (3.5hp singles and 5hp V-twins) from Fafnir and Zeus.

ACHILLES *Germany 1953–57*
Built 48cc (3cu in) mopeds and Sachs-powered scooters of 98 and 123cc (6 and 7.5cu in).

ACMA *France 1952–62*
Vespas of 123, 147 and 173cc (7.5, 9 and 11cu in) made under licence.

ACME *Britain 1902–22*
Used Minerva engines first, but not until 1918 did Acme make its own 348cc (21cu in) single and 997cc (61cu in) V-twin. Merged in 1922 with Rex.

ADER *France 1901–06*
Two-horsepower singles and 4hp transverse V-twins from this pioneer manufacturer.

ADLER *Germany 1900–58*
Despite its association with sporting two-strokes of the 1950s (not to mention typewriters), Adler was actually a pioneer, and even built its own engines from the start, ranging from 3–5hp. It abandoned motorcycles in 1907 but returned to the fold in 1949 with a 98cc (6cu in) two-stroke. A whole range of well-built two-stroke bikes followed, all of them using Adler's own power units. The air-cooled road bikes were well respected, but there were also water-cooled racing twins with up to 39bhp. They were successful in trials and motocross as well as circuit racing. But sales began to fade as an increasingly affluent Germany turned its attention to small cars. Adler was taken over by Gründig in 1958 which spelt the end of motorcycle production.

ADONIS *France 1949–52*
Scooters of 48 and 75cc (3 and 4.6cu in), powered by VAP engines.

ADRIA *Germany 1912–28*
Motorcycles were a sideline for Adria whose main business was making engines for cars and boats. They were side-valved singles of 276–346cc (17–21cu in).

ADS *Belgium 1949–54*
Assembler, using bought-in Sachs and Ilo engines of 98cc (6cu in). Low production.

ADVANCE *Britain 1906–12*
Notable for its low-slung frame, the Advance used its own 3hp singles and 6hp V-twins.

AEL *Britain 1919–24*
Actually a motorcycle dealer, it fitted bought-in frames to various engines.

AEOLUS *Britain 1903–05, 1914–16*
Unusual 492cc (30cu in) single with shaft-drive.

AER *Britain 1938–40*
Produced 246 and 346cc (15 and 21cu in) vertical twin two-strokes of its own design, after modifying Scott machines.

AERMACCHI *Italy 1948–78*
Aermacchi had been a well-known aircraft manufacturer before the war but, in a typical swords-into-ploughshares operation, added motorcycles after 1945. Its first prototype was actually electrically-powered, but the 123cc (7.5cu in) 125N finally reached production in 1950. This first on-sale Aermacchi was a cross between motorcycle and scooter, with a step-through frame but a dummy fuel tank. In the mid-1950s, the company launched the Chimera, a 172cc (10.5cu in) single with futuristic-looking full enclosure. It was a sales flop, though Aermacchi was partly able to redeem itself with new 50cc and 75cc speed records.

The company was by now in trouble, though in 1957 it did manage to launch 'naked' versions of its 175 and 250cc (11 and 15cu in) four-stroke singles, with their characteristic horizontal cylinders. Sales were improving, which attracted the attention of Harley-Davidson, who desperately needed a ready-made range of small bikes to sell, so decided to buy the company. Things were now looking up: the 175/250 singles were modern and lightweight, proving successful in competition, and went on selling right through to the early seventies. But the seed of a new two-stroke range was sown in 1967 with the M125 Rapido, which was to form the basis of a whole generation.

Such a success was the Rapido that Aermacchi expanded the two-stroke range (there was already a moped), but 90 and 100cc (5 and 6cu in) off-roaders followed, plus the much updated SX125 trail bike in 1973. There were also the RR250 and 350 two-stroke racers, which were very successful for a time. By now, the four-stroke single (known as the Sprint when wearing the Harley-Davidson badge) had grown to 344cc (21cu in) but was looking outdated next to the opposition. Aermacchi's response was to develop the two-strokes into 175, 250 and 350cc singles, in both road and trail form.

ABOVE: Aermacchi 350 single

BELOW: Like the 350 above, this 250cc racing Aermacchi carries the Harley-Davidson badge

The Aermacchi/Harley-Davidson four-stroke made a good racer as well

Although they looked the part, the SX/SST series lacked Japanese sophistication, and could not compete on price.

Unsold bikes were piling up in U.S. warehouses, and Harley-Davidson (itself now under new ownership) finally decided to pull out in 1978. The factory was sold to Cagiva, which initially continued production of the two-strokes. So despite a troubled final decade, Aermacchi's legacy was a good one, enabling the young and ambitious Cagiva to take its first big leap forward.

AERO-CAPRONI *Italy 1948–64*
Bought-in NSU two-strokes and own engines, including a 149cc (9cu in) flat twin.

AEROPLAN *Germany 1922–25*
Used DKW two-stroke singles in frames of its own design.

AEROS *Czechoslovakia 1927–29*
An interesting bike, the Aeros used 350 and 500cc (21 and 30cu inch) three-valve ohc singles from Küchen of Germany. The frame owed something to BMW.

AETOS *Italy 1912–14*
A 492cc (30cu in) V-twin, classed as a 3.5hp machine.

AFW *Germany 1923–1925*
Used bought-in Hansa ohv engines of 246cc (15cu in).

AGF *France 1948–56*
Scooters and motorcycles, all of which were powered by 123 and 173cc (7.5 and 11cu in) Ydral engines.

AGON *Germany 1924–1928*
Used a bewildering range of engines from other manfacturers, from 197cc (12cu in) Paqués to 996cc (61cu in) JAP V-twins.

AGRATI *Italy 1958–61*
Built mopeds until it merged with Garelli.

AIGLON *France 1908–53*
Used bought-in engines, among them Peugeot, Minerva, AMC and FMC units.

AIROLITE *Britain 1921–23*
110cc (7cu in) Simplex two-strokes powered these small commuters.

AJAX *Britain 1923–24*
Ajax buyers had the choice of Villiers two-strokes or a 346cc (21cu in) Blackburne sidevalve.

AJR *Britain 1925–26*
Named after its builder, A.J. Robertson (who also rode his own bikes in competition), all used JAP singles.

AJS *Britain 1909–74*
Harley-Davidson, Velocette, Matchless and AJS had one thing in common – all were set up by brothers enthusiastic enough to want to make motorcycles for a living. Harry, George, Jack and Joe Stevens (some sources say there were five brothers – take your pick!) were experimenting with petrol engines as early as 1897. Their father had owned an engineering works in Wolverhampton, so perhaps it was inevitable that his progeny should develop a similar interest, particularly at a time when the internal combustion engine was just taking off.

An early AJS V-twin, intended for sidecar work

Initially, the brothers sold engines to early makers of motorcycles, cars and cyclecars, and by 1900 were offering 2.25hp and 3.25hp singles in both air- and water-cooled versions, as well as frames. It was therefore a logical progression that they should turn their hands to producing a complete bike, though this didn't happen until 1909. At the same time they created the AJS company (Jack's initials – Albert John Stevens) and began selling motorcycles under their own name, though they also built bus chassis and radios among other things.

That first AJS used a little 2.75hp engine in a bicycle frame with belt-drive, typical of the time, and probably no better nor worse than most. But within a couple of years, they had progressed to a motorcycle proper, with a more substantial frame and a 298cc (18cu in) sidevalve engine plus three-speed gearbox (when most new bikes were sold with a two-speed hub or a fixed single-speed). Two were entered for the TT in 1911, though they could manage no better than 15th and 16th places. Better was to come, and a fast-revving (5,000rpm) 350cc (21cu in) chain-driven bike managed 9th in the 1913 TT.

But it was the following year that AJS's elusive TT success finally came to fruition. In the 1914 Junior, AJS 350s were 1st, 2nd, 4th and 6th, a victory which did a great deal to enhance the AJS image. As a result, the orders began to flow in, and the brothers Stevens were forced to move to a larger factory to keep up with the pace. War contracts taught them some useful lessons in the field of metallurgy which were put to good use in the first post-World War I TT,

Saddle tank, tank-drop instrument panel and knee-grips, all period features

in 1920. AJS won that TT, and the one after that *and* the one following. This was the glory period of AJS racing, and the bike which won those early TTs was the Single, an advanced piece of design with overhead valves set at 90 degrees to one another over a hemispherical combustion chamber. It is standard practice today, but then it allowed a great improvement in fuel flow as well as more space for larger valves. The gearbox had three speeds, but a two-speed clutch made this possibly the first six-speed motorcycle! It was light, and could run up to 121km/h (75mph); for its day, the Single was fast indeed.

AJS capitalized on this success with a large range of road bikes, which by 1925 included simple sidevalve singles for the commuter (250, 350 and 500cc/15, 21 and 30.5cu in), more sporting ohv jobs (350 and 500), and big sidevalve V-twins of 800 and 1000cc (49 and 61cu in). Ironically, racing success was proving more difficult to come by, and AJS hoped its 1927 ohc works racer would help turn the tide. It wasn't fast enough, though a couple of years' development did produce a second place in the Junior TT. Real competition success was to elude AJS until after World War II.

In the meantime, more serious matters were relegating race wins firmly into the background. Economic depression was just beginning to take hold and AJS, its glory

One of AJS's last V-twins, a 1938 AJS Colonial of 1000cc (61cu in)

days apparently behind it, was just not strong enough to survive on its own. A saviour came in the form of arch-rival Matchless. Based in Plumstead, London (away from the Midlands heartland of British bike makers), Matchless was owned and run by the Collier brothers. Together they formed Associated Motor Cycles (AMC) and were to swallow many more famous names before the entire group died a death in 1966. The first thing they did was move AJS down to Plumstead. From here on, the histories of AJS and Matchless were intertwined. Badge engineering on the road bikes was pursued with enthusiasm, to the point where the only difference between the equivalent AJS and Matchless was the colour scheme and the name on the tank. Whatever might be said in favour of badge engineering (it certainly made short-term production sense) is countered by its disastrous effect on brand loyalty: both AJS and Matchless discovered this the hard way.

All this, however, was still in the future as the mid-1930s brought economic recovery, while AJS's 350 and 500 ohv singles were popular machines. Like the Ariel Red Hunters, they probably represented the classic form of British single, with fine handling and a good four-speed gearbox and they did well in trials, a pointer towards AJS's main success after World War II. In fact, things were going well enough for the production of a very ambitious racing project. It was the V4, product of chief designer Matt

Wright. In a time when most purpose-built racers were singles, the V4 must have seemed an exotic beast indeed. It had overhead cams, of course, with twin carburettors and alloy cylinders and heads, but was perhaps rather ahead of its time. Two were entered for the 1936 Senior TT – both retired. AJS took 1937 out to develop it, and returned the next year with a supercharged version. Overheating was now the problem, so 1939 saw water-cooling as well. At last, the heavy V4 was able to show more of its speed, culminating in a battle with the supercharged Gilera four in the Ulster GP. The V4 pulled out a 19-second lead, and would have won if a front fork link hadn't snapped. Alas, it had no chance to prove itself again as the FIM banned supercharging after the war.

Singles & Porcupines

The 1939–45 conflict didn't leave much room for AJS, as AMC's contribution was the G3 350, which was badged as a Matchless throughout. However, 1945 saw a return of the pre-war 350/500s, now known as the Heavyweight Singles. They were little changed from the 1930s and, at least at first, that was all the market wanted, though as competition increased so even the faithful singles had to be updated here and there. The G3 had already introduced telescopic forks in 1943 (a first for AMC) and an alloy head arrived in 1951; a lighter, stiffer crankshaft came in 1954; higher compression and a stronger frame in 1956; AMC's own gearbox (replacing the long-serving Burman) in 1957; AC electrics and a less leaky primary chaincase came the following year and – the last big change – a duplex cradle frame in 1960.

Meanwhile, there had been a new, advanced AJS which owed nothing to Matchless – the Porcupine. It was a twin-cylinder racer, a simpler, less ambitious design than the pre-war V4, but unusual in that the engine was mounted horizontally, the fins sticking upwards like spikes (hence the name). Of almost 'square' dimensions, it had double overhead cams and sodium-cooled exhaust valves. At its 1947 TT debut, the Porcupine had to retire, but its heyday came in 1949 when it won for AJS both rider's and manufacturer's prizes in the 500 World Championship. And this in the face of the very fast Gilera four. In trials too, AJS was making a competition comeback, and Hugh Viney won the Scottish Six Days Trial three times in a row. While the Porcupine had been winning among the 500s, the 350cc 7R single became the definitive 350 racing machine and production 7Rs continued to sell well to clubmen who required a reliable, competitive bike for weekend racing.

However, AMC had not forgotten the lightweight market, which for AJS meant the arrival of the Model 14 in 1958. Named the Lightweight Single, at 154kg (340lb) for a simple 250 it was anything but, though still lighter than the 1930s-derived heavyweights. Notable for its circular gearbox (actually a separate item, though styled to look like unit-construction) it also had a cylinder axis set forward from the crankshaft axis, claimed to reduce piston slap and make better use of the power stroke. Did it make any difference? Who knows? In any case, the 250 managed a respectable 18bhp with its 7.8:1 compression ratio and sported a sensible full chaincase: this AJS was evidently aimed at commuters rather than boy racers.

ABOVE: AJS singles of the 1950s were solid but uninspired

BELOW: 500 Twin in Talmag Trophy trial

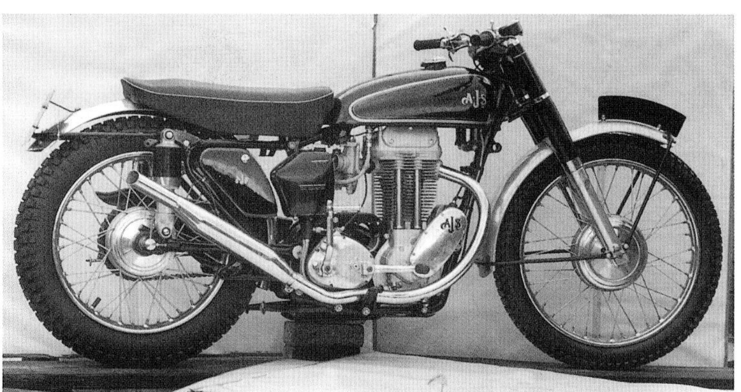

ABOVE: Big single in trials trim

BELOW: The AJS Twin lacked Triumph's style

A 350cc version followed in 1960 (a Model 8, if you insisted on the one with the AJS badge) to replace the 350 heavyweight single. But despite being a scaled-up 250, rather than a scaled-down 500, it still weighed a full 18kg (40lb) more than the equivalent BSA B40. Like the 250, it had to be worked hard to get it going. There was also a more sporting 250, the Model 14 CSR, with bigger carburettor, valves and higher compression: according to *The Motor Cycle*, it could manage 134km/h (83mph) flat out, but fast guys still preferred the Royal Enfield 250s. And as author Steve Wilson points out, the AJS Lightweight Singles were not really sporty enough for the tearaways, yet lacked the solid, plodding quality of the more deep-rooted Heavyweights. Not a success, then.

Singles were all very well, but like BSA, Norton, Ariel *et al*, AMC could not afford to ignore the great success of twin-cylinder road bikes. Its answer came in 1949 with a 500cc (30.5cu in) twin, designed by Phil Walker. Its chief difference from other British twins was that each cylinder had its own separate barrel and head, said to make maintenance easier, though in practice making the fitting of twin carburettors problematical, and AMC twins didn't get them at the factory until 1963. At the bottom-end, the crankshaft was

ABOVE: A 1954 AJS 7R3 of 350cc (21cu in) of which only three were ever made

BELOW: 1954 AJS 10R racing Twin

supported by three bearings instead of the usual two, which promised strength and vibration control. Again, in practice, the theory wasn't upheld – AMC 500s actually acquired a reputation for bad vibration at high speeds, and when the higher-powered 650s came along, had a habit of breaking cranks.

Still, they handled well, with the same Teledraulic forks as the singles, and at least gave both AJS and Matchless dealers something to sell against BSA. A 600cc (37cu in) joined the range in 1956 with more power (though still in a low state of tune). But the market (specifically, the U.S. market) wanted more power still, and AMC's answer was to lengthen the 600's stroke and turn it into a full 650, which for AJS purposes made it the Model 31. It could manage 174km/h (108mph) as a CSR, but it was soon evident that the AMC twin was nearing the limit of its own personal performance – use a CSR hard and cranks broke, cylinder-head gaskets blew, and the pistons, barrels and gudgeon-pins all behaved unreliably.

Back in 1952, AMC had bought Norton, a strong, sporting name but an ailing company. From 1964 AMC took badge engineering to its logical conclusion and began using certain Norton components on the AJS (and Matchless) range. Roadholder forks, wheels and brakes came first, and in 1965 the 750cc (46cu in) Norton Atlas engine gave rise to the AJS Model 33 CSR. It certainly looked good, with period swept-back pipes, alloy mudguards and slim seat; but all too late – the entire AMC group collapsed the following year. Out of the ashes came Dennis Poore's Norton-Villiers company but which built AJS-badged motocross bikes until 1974.

AJW *England 1926–57*
The company was founded in 1926 in Exeter, Devon by Arthur John Wheaton who bought in all his engines from outside – Villiers, Rudge, JAP and Anzani – all powered AJWs from time to time. By the time war broke out, the Exeter-built bikes were being distributed by the huge and well-known London dealer, Pride & Clarke.

Arthur Wheaton sold the firm in 1945 to Jack Ball, who transferred production to Wimborne in Dorset. Like Wheaton, Ball concentrated on utility machines using simple, proprietory engines. The Grey Fox used a JAP sidevalve twin of 494cc (30cu in), but was by no means outdated; telescopic forks and coil ignition featured. Still, it was hardly mass-produced, and only 70 were made over three years. AJW ceased manufacturing in 1957 when its engine supply dried up.

AKKENS *England 1919–22*
A short-lived beneficiary of Britain's post-World War I boom, the Akkens was a 292cc (18cu in) two-stroke.

ALATO *Italy 1923–25*
A 131cc (8cu in) two-stroke, built in Turin.

ALBA *Germany 1919–24*
Used its own small four-stroke engines.

ALBERT *Germany 1922–24*
A 183cc (11cu in) two-stroke.

ALBERTUS *Germany 1922–24*
Used a two-stroke which could run on crude oil after being warmed up on petrol. Lack of power (and reliability) killed it off.

ALCYON *France 1902–57*
Built fast V-twins before World War I, and a four-valve 348cc (21cu in) single. Produced mostly smaller bikes between the wars, up to 498cc (30cu in), some with shaft-drive. Post-1945, two- and four-strokes arrived, up to 248cc (15cu in).

ALDBERT *Italy 1953–59*
Produced two-strokes up to 173cc (11cu in) and four-strokes to 246cc (15cu in). The remarkable 174cc Razzo could top 150km/h (93mph).

ALECTO *England 1919–24*
Still used belt-drive, though an all-chain bike was introduced in 1923.

ALERT *England 1903–06*
Made by Smith & Molesworth of Coventry, with various Sarolea engines.

ALEU *Spain 1953–56*
198 and 247cc (12 and 15cu in) utility bikes, using in-house two-stroke engines.

ALFA *Italy 1923–26*
A splendidly Italian name, albeit using small English four-stroke engines from Norman, Bradshaw and Blackburne.

ALFA-GNOM *Austria 1926–28*
A 598cc (36cu in) ohc single.

ALGE *Germany 1923–31*
Used its own four-stroke singles of 173 to 498cc (11 to 30cu in) plus Villiers and Blackburne engines from 1928.

ALIPRANDI *Italy 1925–30*
Aristocratic Italian lightweights, with the choice of Swiss Moser, JAP or Sturmey-Archer power units.

ALLDAYS/ALLON *England 1903–24*
A real pioneer, building De Dion-engined three-wheelers from 1898. Renamed Allon in 1915.

ALLEGRO *Switzerland 1923–50*
Used various units of up to 348cc/21cu in (from Villiers etc.) but is better known for racing 175s. Later concentrated on mopeds.

ALLRIGHT *Germany 1901–27*
Utilized bought-in engines at first. Merger with Cito in 1922 brought the shaft-driven 500 single KG (Krieger-Gnädig), before Allright decided to concentrate on parts.

ALLSTATE *Austria 1953–56*
You could buy almost anything from Sears Roebuck, and Allstate was simply a re-badged Puch for the Chicago store.

ALLWYN *India c.1972–88*
Built 125–200cc (8–12cu in) Lambrettas after the Indian government bought Innocenti.

ALMA *France 1949–59*
Built mopeds and lightweights of up to 149cc (9cu in) only.

ALMORA *Germany 1924–25*
Like Albertus, another attempt to make use of the Löwy-designed crude oil engine.

ALP *England 1912–17*
Originally an off-shoot of Moto-Rêve, with small V-twins, plus a 199cc (12cu in) utility.

ALPHONSE THOMANN *France 1908–23*
98 to 173cc (6 to 11cu in) two-strokes.

ALPINO *Italy 1948–62*
Produced both two- and four-stroke engines, and broke 48cc speed records.

ALTEA *Italy 1939–41*
An advanced bike for its time, with a unit-constructed 198cc (12cu in) ohv engine.

ALTER *France 1955–56*
Made 49cc (3cu in) mopeds only.

AMAG *Germany 1924–25*
149cc (9cu in) Bekamo two-strokes.

AMAZONAS *Brazil 1978–90*
VW Beetle-powered behemoth, used by the Brazilian police and military, as well as by civilians.

AMBAG *Germany 1923*
Bought-in 155cc (9.5cu in) Gruhn singles in own frames.

AMBASSADOR *England 1947–65*
Ascot is more often associated with horse racing than with motorcycles, but this genteel town in rural Berkshire was home to Ambassador, founded in 1947 by ex-racer Kaye Don.

It began in a small way, but by the early fifties had progressed to making a 224cc (14cu in) single. Two years later, Ambassador's first 250s arrived, with single- or twin-cylinder Villiers engines and many other parts were bought in as well. It performed much the same as any other Villiers-powered lightweight of the time, but what the twin lacked in performance (it was mild-mannered with 15bhp) it made up for in reliability, and provided a top speed of just under 113km/h (70mph).

The Twin was later restyled with huge valanced mudguards, deep chainguard and 'bath-tub' rear-end. An electric-start version, the Electra 75, followed in 1961, using a 12-volt Siba Dynastart and two 6-volt batteries. Already, the enclosure fashion was on the wane, and a sportier Super S came in 1962, with flyscreen, lower handlebars and skimpier mudguards. Kaye Don also retired that year, which spelt the end of Ambassador as an independent manufacturer. However, DMW later bought the tooling and made Ambassadors for another few years.

AMC *U.S.A. 1912–15*
A 980cc (60cu in) ioe V-twin, with no connection to AMC of London (*see* AJS).

AMERICAN *U.S.A. 1911–14*
A 550cc (34cu in), 4hp single.

AMERICAN-X *U.S.A. 1910–30*
Really the Excelsior 996cc (61cu in) V-twin, but for export to Britain was renamed American-X to avoid confusion with the English Excelsior.

AMI *Germany 1921–25*
A 49cc (3cu in) four-stroke clip-on.

AMI *Switzerland 1950–54*
Two-stroke scooter, designed by Jaroslav Frei.

AMMON *Germany 1923–25*
Part-pressed steel, part-tubular frame, with bought-in two-stroke engines.

AMO *Germany 1921–24*
A 146cc (9cu in) two-stroke lightweight.

AMO *Germany 1950–54*
Berlin-built mopeds with in-house 48cc (3cu in) two-strokes.

AMS *Spain 1954–65*
Used bought-in Hispano-Villiers two-strokes, up to 247cc (15cu in).

ANCORA *Italy 1923–39*
Used Villiers engines until taken over by Umberto Dei, then produced 60–98cc (4–6cu in) lightweights.

ANDREES *Germany 1923–29*
Bought in engines from Bradshaw (oil-cooled flat twins), MAG and others. A new factory, its own engine and the Depression put an end to the company.

ANGLIAN *England 1903–12*
Various bought-in engines included units from De Dion and Sarolea.

ANGLO-DANE *Denmark 1912–14*
Well-named, being built in Copenhagen from British components.

ANKER *Germany 1949–58*
Ilo and Sachs two-stroke engines were used in these 48 to 244cc (3 to 15cu in) bikes, which Anker stopped making in order to concentrate on cash registers.

API LAMBRETTA *India c.1965–88*
Built 150/175cc (9/11cu in) Lambrettas under licence.

APRILIA *Italy 1973–*
Notable for its rocketing success in the 1990s, Aprilia was actually a bicycle producer right up to the early seventies and when Ivano Beggio took over the family firm it employed just 18 people. But unlike his father Alberto (a confirmed cyclist) Ivano preferred horsepower, and lost no time in producing Aprilia's first powered two-wheeler. There were mopeds at first, then 125cc (8cu in) trail bikes, all of which used bought-in engines from Minarelli, Sachs and Hiro. This practice of using bought-in engines became an Aprilia trademark, the only engines designed and built in-house being two-stroke GP racing units. Pure road bikes did not join the range until the early 1980s and by then Beggio had loftier ambitions in mind – namely Grand Prix racing.

In 1987, the Rotax-powered AF1 delighted the home crowd by winning the Italian 250 GP at Misano, ridden by Loris Reggiani. Three second places that season confirmed that this little-known Italian firm had a competitive machine. The company was astute enough to turn this new fame to commercial advantage, producing a run of Reggiani Replicas for the following season, not to mention painting the 125 road bike (also named AF1) in Reggiani colours. At the time, Aprilia's success on the home market encouraged Beggio to diversify, and in 1987/88 the company bought up companies involved in furniture and spectacle-making, as well as other products.

Unfortunately it was a disaster, draining Aprilia of capital at the very time it needed it most to fund the expansion of its bike business. (Although successful, Aprilia made only small machines, and needed to develop a complete range – preferably including a V-twin – in order to keep it flourishing.) It was actually near collapse, but credit from a group of banks saved it; Beggio lost no time in selling off the non-motorcycle interests, and Aprilia's recovery was so swift (it was already the top-selling marque in Italy) that he was able to repay the loan within two years. Production soared from 55,000 powered two-wheelers in 1992, to over 100,000 in 1994, 165,000 the following year and 200,000 the year after that. Between 1989 and 1998, turnover increased ten-fold. By the late 1990s, Aprilia was building a quarter of a million scooters, mopeds and motorcycles a year and looked like achieving its ambition of becoming the biggest European manufacturer. It had outgrown its original factories at Noale, in northern Italy, and opened a huge new plant at Scorze.

So what lay behind all this success? Small two-strokes were still Aprilia's backbone, aided by a booming scooter market in the mid-nineties to which the company added its upmarket Leonardo, powered by 125 and 150cc (8 and 9cu in) four-strokes, and a 250cc (15cu in) Yamaha-powered version was to follow. But the bike that really put Aprilia on the world stage was the RS250, the road-going replica of Max Biaggi's GP racer, on which he won the 250 Championship in 1994 (when Aprilia also bagged the 125 title).The RS used a development of the Suzuki RGV250 two-stroke V-twin, tuned to produce 70bhp. In an aluminium frame and with top-grade brakes and suspension, it was as close as one could get to a road-going racer at the time, and sold well. To capitalize on the success, a similar RS125 and even an RS150 followed, all doing wonders for Aprilia's image across Europe, and the 250 was actually a hit in Japan as well.

OPPOSITE: The RS250 capitalized on Aprilia's racing success and was close to a road-going racer
ABOVE: RSV Mille of 1998 was Aprilia's answer to Ducati

ABOVE: The Pegaso 650 single was versatile and fun to ride

The bike that did most to broaden Aprilia's market was the Pegaso, from 1993. Although it was styled to suggest off-road ability, the slim, handy Pegaso was a pure road machine, which succeeded in inspiring a whole raft of imitators. Its 649cc (40cu in) five-valve single-cylinder Rotax engine and long-travel suspension may have suggested rough going, but it was really more of a civilized supermoto, unlikely to get its tyres dirty. It was a huge success, bolstered by a ground-breaking agreement with BMW. Similar in concept was BMW's F650, which Aprilia built for BMW in the Noale factory. So when BMW sold as many F650s in the first year as it expected to in the first three, it was Aprilia which benefited.

Not that everything the ex-bicycle maker touched turned to gold. The Moto 6.5 will probably go down in history as one of motorcycling's greatest flops. Styled by international designer Philippe Starck, the egg-shaped Moto was intended to appeal to image-conscious urbanites. It was certainly distinctive, but a bit too radical for the buying public who stayed away, as the saying goes, in droves. A similar fate befell the Shiver, a V-twin concept bike with decidedly odd looks that did the rounds of the motorcycle shows in 1996. This time, customer clinics persuaded Aprilia that this was not the way ahead.

A V-twin had been part of Aprilia's plans for some time, though the financial problems had delayed it. When the RSV1000 was finally unveiled in 1998, it was as a sportsbike, underlining Aprilia's determination to compete in World Superbike racing. As had been known for some time, the Rotax-developed engine was a 60-degree V-twin, with liquid cooling and four valves per cylinder. Aprilia claimed 128bhp at 9,750rpm, for a top speed of around 274km/h (170mph). It would also herald, according to the company, a whole new family of V-twins, from 750–1200cc (46–73cu in), cruisers and sports tourers as well as the RSV. But first, Aprilia seemed more concerned with the 1999 World Superbike season, and late 1998 saw the RSV1000 SP announced. This would be the basis of Aprilia's factory racer, with a reworked engine (150bhp was claimed), new cylinder heads, an ultra-short stroke and rechipped fuel injection. There was also adjustable geometry (both rake and trail could be altered) and a drag coefficient of less than 0.30 Cx, seen for the first time on a road bike. It was all a far cry from those Minarelli-engined mopeds, and underlined the astonishing progress made by Ivano Beggio's Aprilia in the 1990s.

ARDIE Germany 1919–58
Arno Dietrich began making 305/348cc (19/21cu in) two-strokes, production continuing after his death in 1922, with a range of bought-in engines.

ARIEL *England 1902–71*
Singles, twins, fours and two-strokes, Ariel made them all. Yet despite being one of the more innovative British manufacturers, it faded away earlier than the other big names, perhaps more for boardroom political reasons than for any other. This was doubly ironic since Ariel's MD Jack Sangster had saved Triumph from extinction in the thirties, while Ariel's absorption into the BSA empire during the war was entirely voluntary.

The company's real strength lay in four men, each of them a key figure in the British industry's post-war success. Jack Sangster was the son of Charles, Ariel's founder, who was joint MD of the car and motorcycle division. Far from being the archetypical boss's son, the younger Sangster evidently had a keen business sense, well able to raise the cash to save Ariel from extinction in 1929, buy Triumph and make a success of it, and end up as chairman of the giant BSA group, to whom he had entrusted Ariel's future.

Around Sangster were three highly capable designers, who between them were responsible for many of the British industry's milestone designs from the thirties onwards. Val Page had come to Ariel from J.A. Prestwick, a classic production engineer whose talent lay in production-ready designs. He was behind the almost legendary Red Hunter single and Ariel's 500 twins, as well as a 650cc (40cu in) sidecar twin for Triumph. An 18-year-old straight out of college joined as one of his assistants in 1926 – Bert Hopwood.

The Ariel 500cc (30.5cu in) Red Hunter was the classic British single

Hopwood (as well as writing the fascinating book *Whatever Happened to the British Motorcycle Industry?*) was to spend his whole career in the industry, moving between Ariel, Triumph, BSA and Norton (where he designed the 500cc/30.5cu inch twin which formed the basis of Norton's entire post-war twin-cylinder range). Finally, and slightly senior to Hopwood in years, though then still a young man, was Edward Turner. Designer of the Triumph vertical twin (and thus arguably the inspiration behind all British post-war twins) and the unique Ariel Square Four, Turner was to dominate Triumph's fortunes in the 1950s. His forte was compact, good-looking designs and a flair for knowing what riders would find attractive.

So although not always regarded as one of the leading British makes (certainly post-war) Ariel contained four of the key figures who were to do much to shape the entire industry in the fifties and sixties.

Modest Beginnings

The company had begun modestly enough making three-wheelers from 1898 and motorcycles from 1902, the first being a conventional 3.5hp single, though within a decade the range had expanded to include a 498cc (30cu in) sidevalve single and ioe V-twin. Val Page came up with an overhead-valve 500 single in 1926, his first new design for the company. Having 20hp in a cradle frame, the sales team (headed by Vic Mole) conjured up the slogan 'Twenty horses in a cradle'. Some people were

A 1926 557cc (34cu in) Ariel. Despite the publicity stunts, bankruptcy was not far away

obviously impressed as the orders duly flowed in. In fact, Ariel at the time became known for publicity stunts; trials rider Harry Perrey rode his Ariel to the top of Mount Snowdon and, unforgettably, also across the English Channel on the 'Flotor Cycle', a standard Ariel equipped with floats.

None of which, unfortunately, was enough to prevent Ariel's parent company from going bankrupt in 1932. Jack Sangster bought the rights to the Ariel name (not to mention most of the essential tooling at knock-down prices) and very soon the new Ariel Motors (J.S.) Ltd. was up and running, with Edward Turner in charge of design and Bert Hopwood as chief draughtsman. Though they did not always see eye-to-eye (according to Hopwood himself) the careers of these two men would be linked for the next 20 years.

These must have seemed exciting times, designwise, for the Red Hunter singles were now coming on stream. Handsome ohv singles of 350 and 500cc (21 and 30.5cu in), they are for some the definitive British singles of their time.The 500 was fast (it could top 121km/h/75mph), reliable and a reasonably good handler despite the rigid rear-end. Although designed as road bikes, they went on to great success in all forms of off-road sport. After the war, Sammy Miller would achieve phenomenal success in trials with the famous GOV132. Yet, despite his advice, Ariel management refused to build a replica, which would surely have sold in great numbers.

Good though they were, the Red Hunters were actually refinements of a long-established form. The Square Four, on

Later Ariel MKII Square Four (the twin downpipes on either side are the giveaway). Designed as a sportster, it ended up tugging sidecars

the other hand, couldn't have been more different. With its four cylinders in a square formation, nothing had been seen like it before or since (recent two-stroke racers apart); Edward Turner wanted to build something with more power and smoothness than a twin, but not much more bulk. As a prototype, it was an ohc 500 which weighed little more than a single and had a tremendous power to weight ratio. Journalists favoured with a preview ride raved about its power, smoothness and speed. In production, it grew to 600cc (37cu in), then 1000 (61cu in) and gained a fair amount of fat on the way, turning Turner's revolutionary sportster into a tourer or sidecar machine. It certainly gained a following, as the Square Four remained a torquey, refined motorcycle quite unlike anything else; but it had lost the promise of that first super-sporty prototype. Still, it was part of the Ariel line-up right up to 1957.

During World War II, of course, Square Four production was suspended, Ariel concentrating instead on the ohv 350cc (21cu in) W-NG, of which 47,600 were supplied to the Forces. In 1945, the immediate priority was to get singles onto the hungry civilian market, and much of Ariel's production consisted of the VB sidevalve. Amazingly, this 557cc (34cu in) single could trace its basic dimensions back to the 1910 4hp model, though it was actually introduced in 1926. As a solid, reliable sidecar tug, this 17bhp single could haul the family along at a steady 72km/h (45mph). Meanwhile, there was still a market for sporting ohv singles, and the 350 and 500 Red Hunters kept going (the shorter-lived 250 was dropped), joined in 1952 by the alloy-engined VHA and progressing from rigid frames, to plungers,

The Square Four's engine layout remains unique among four-stroke road bikes

to Ariel's new swinging-arm frame in 1954. In some ways, the Red Hunters now represented the best of British singles. Fast enough for most riders, and with updated cycle parts, the 350 could exceed 75mph, the 500 137km/h (85mph), though was not over-tuned and temperamental.

Two-Strokes & Twins

But the 1950s, of course, was the time of the twins. Following the success of Triumph's Speed Twin, almost every British manufacturer felt obliged to come up with something similar, and Ariel's version was the KG/KH500. Designed by Val Page, it was a quiet engine which in KH form could manage 145km/h (90mph), though like most vertical twins of the time it was plagued by vibration at speed. However it was not a great success when compared to the Triumphs and BSA's A7, and lasted until 1957. The Huntmaster 650 was better regarded. It actually used BSA's 650cc (40cu in) twin, housed in Ariel cycle parts, but was none the worse for that. Against initial opposition from the loyal workforce, Jack Sangster had sold Ariel to BSA in 1943 and assumed a place on the BSA Board, so it was logical to use the well-respected A10 engine (a Hopwood design) to give Ariel dealers a modern 650 to sell. Some thought the Huntmaster was actually better built than the equivalent BSA, and it would certainly top 161km/h (100mph) and managed 19.5km per litre (55mpg), even when hitched to a sidecar, or 25km per litre (70mpg) solo. It was ironic that the Huntmaster turned out to be such a well-liked bike, as Sangster had always been against badge engineering (the practice of swapping badges between otherwise identical bikes). The idea was to cash in on brand loyalty, and although badge engineering made a great deal of sense from the point of view of production economics, in the long term it served only to erode those very loyalties from which it aimed to profit.

BELOW: This early Square Four could almost be mistaken for a twin

For good or ill, this was behind Ariel's model policy from 1959/60. Jack Sangster was now chairman of BSA, having replaced the flamboyant Sir Bernard Docker in 1956. He held that post for five years, so Sangster oversaw what happened to Ariel next. Now part of the BSA/Triumph stable, it made sense in a by no means booming motorcycle market to rationalize between these three makes, all of which had their own distinct ranges of four-stroke singles and twins. Since BSA and Triumph were better sellers, Sangster was faced with the prospect of putting the Ariel badge on those bikes or producing something completely different.

Not surprisingly, he went for the latter, and the two-stroke Leader couldn't have been more different. Ariel had long prided itself on producing what riders actually needed and its slogan, 'The Modern Motorcycle' (not to mention the decidedly modernistic prancing horse logo), reflected this. A market research programme was initiated in about 1955 and found that the growth market (as well as in big four-stroke roadburners) was in small commuter bikes. Scooters were in vogue, which meant weather protection and convenience. Many of the British manufacturers responded to the scooter boom with bikes that attempted to emulate the Vespas and Lambrettas. Ariel tried a different tack.

The BSA-engined Huntmaster twin was well-liked and economical

A later single, but Ariel was soon to abandon four-strokes altogether

The now-veteran designer Val Page came up with the Leader, which attempted to span that line between motorcycle and scooter. It wasn't a new idea – the Maico Maicoletta and others aimed to combine the convenience of a scooter with the performance of a small motorcycle. Not new perhaps, but a huge leap into the dark for Ariel: after all, its big four-strokes were gradually dropped in 1957–59 to make way for the Leader which was to become the sole Ariel from 1959 on. The name would undoubtedly sink or swim with it.

With fully enclosed bodywork, fairing and screen all as standard, the Leader claimed to be rideable in everyday clothing. This, it was hoped, would fulfil the goal sought by countless manufacturers down the years, the motorcycle for everyman, something that would break out of the limited enthusiast market into a much bigger demand for clean, convenient transport for the commuting hordes. Sadly, the Leader failed to achieve this nirvana; sales didn't make the big time, and it was dropped in 1965.

In a way though, the Leader and its naked cousin, the Arrow, deserved better. It owed nothing to previous bikes, was designed as a whole and Val Page and Bernard Knight took three years to develop it. The pressed steel frame housed the fuel tank under the seat which kept the centre of gravity down. Its 247cc (15cu in) two-stroke twin was based on good practice (owing something to the German Adler),

A 1957 Leader, brave but unsuccessful

with 'square' bore and stroke dimensions and 16bhp at 6,400rpm, enough to propel the Leader up to nearly 113km/h (70mph). And the bike positively bristled with convenience features: quick-release wheels, parcel compartment (in the dummy fuel tank) and optional panniers, clock and indicators. There was even a neutral gear light!

When it became clear that the Leader was a little too revolutionary for a conservative market, Ariel launched the cheaper, simpler Arrow – basically a Leader with all the bodywork stripped off. Unfortunately, this also exposed the sensible but by no means good-looking pressed steel frame, making the Arrow look a bit odd as a result. But it did actually sell, and things were starting to look good when a higher compression and bigger Amal endowed the sporting Golden Arrow with a

129km/h+ (80mph+) top speed. Arrows did well in competition as well. But that was all the development the parent company was prepared to give to its brave new two-strokes, apart from a cost-cutting Arrow 200 in 1964. Sales tailed off, and production ceased the following year.

It wasn't quite the end of the Ariel name, as BSA resurrected the badge for its hinged-in-the-middle 50cc (3cu in) trike in 1970. This sales flop, as has often been said, was just another nail in BSA's own coffin. In the 1990s, with 250cc (15cu in) scooters from Japan selling like hot cakes in Europe, it is tempting to think of the Leader as yet another opportunity missed.

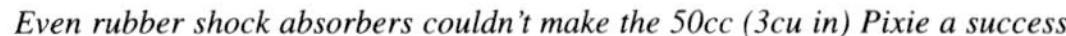

Even rubber shock absorbers couldn't make the 50cc (3cu in) Pixie a success

Weight-saving was vital to trials success

RIGHT: Lt. Hodgdon's Thunderchief did 1,400mph, his Ariel rather less

BELOW: Owners meeting, Isle of Man, 1982

ABOVE: *Two-stroke Hiro-engined Armstrong*

ARISTOS *Germany 1923–24*
Unusually, a low-seated, monocoque-framed, water-cooled flat twin.

ARLIGUE *France 1950–53*
Used French AMC and Ydral proprietory engines from 98cc to 248cc (6 to 15cu in).

ARMAC *U.S.A. 1911–13*
Its own 4hp single in 14 different models.

ARMIS *England 1920–23*
Used a wide range of bought-in engines from 269cc (16cu in) Precision two-strokes to 654cc (40cu in) MAG V-twins.

ARMOR *France 1910–34*
Two-strokes from 98cc (6cu in) and four-strokes of 173cc (11cu in) upwards, some with shaft-drive.

ARMSTRONG *England 1902–05*
Used 211cc (13cu in) Minerva engines.

ARMSTRONG *England 1980–87*
A maker of car parts which found its place in the motorcycle industry by buying Cotton and CCM. Used its expertise on a variety of track and off-road competition machines and a Rotax-powered bike for the army. In 1987 it pulled out, selling the rights to the military MT500 to Harley-Davidson, and CCM to Alan Clews.

BELOW: *Later Rotax-powered Armstrong*

BELOW: *Buying Cotton brought Armstrong into racing*

ARNO *England 1906–15*
Sidevalve singles of 294cc, 348cc and 498cc (18, 21 and 30cu in).

ARROW *U.S.A. 1909–14*
Lightweight motorcycles with own 1hp engines.

ASAHI *Japan 1953–65*
One of the longer-lived early Japanese makes. Most bikes used own 123cc and 173cc (7.5 and 11cu in) two-strokes.

ASCOT *England 1905–06*
Used Minerva and Antoine engines.

ASCOT-PULLIN *England 1928–30*
Advanced 498cc (30cu in) single with dry-sump lubrication and pressed steel bodywork and windscreen.

ASHFORD *England 1905*
Assembled machines with 3.5hp engines suplied by Minerva and Fafnir.

ASL *England 1907–15*
Most interesting feature was the pneumatic buffers for front and rear suspension. Used 3.5hp and 5hp engines.

ASPES *Italy 1967–82*
Built 49 and 123cc (3 and 7.5cu in) mopeds and lightweights, with Franco-Morini, Minarelli or own engines.

ASTER *France 1898–1910*
Supplied other manufacturers with engines, most of which had horizontally-split crankcases made of bronze; the 355cc (22cu in) single was popular.

A 1912 498cc (30cu in) Arno. The company, however, was short-lived

Druid Forks were fitted

ASTON *England 1923–24*
A 142cc (9cu in) two-stroke single with two- or three-speed gearbox and belt/chain transmission.

ASTORIA *Germany 1923–25*
Nuremburg-based, it was taken over by Nestoria when its 289cc (18cu in) two-stroke machines failed to make a profit.

ASTRA *Germany 1923–25*
Used a number of bought-in engines, the 293cc (18cu in) Bosch-Douglas flat twin, then JAP and Blackburne singles.

ASTRA *Italy 1931–51*
Utilized many Ariel parts, especially frames, and engine components for 498cc (30cu in) sv and ohv singles, also smaller 123–220cc (7.5–13cu in) models.

ASTRAL *France 1919–23*
A subsidiary of the Austral company, it concentrated on 98 and 122cc (6 and 7cu in) two-strokes.

ATALA *Italy 1925–34*
Built from bought-in components, including 174–496cc (11–30cu in) power units from JAP and Blackburne.

ATALA *Italy 1954–*
Made two-stroke scooters and mopeds of 49 to 124cc (3 to 8cu in). Moped production continues.

ATLANTA-DUO *England 1935–37*
An interesting machine, with low 19-inch Dunlopillo-padded seat, duplex steering, rear suspension, and weather protection. Used JAP engines of 248–746cc (15–45.5cu in).

ATLANTIC *Germany 1923–25*
A 193cc (12cu in) sv single.

ATLANTIC *France 1929–32*
Used bought-in engines from Chaise, Blackburne and others, up to a 497cc (30cu in) ohc unit.

ATLANTIK *Germany 1925–26*
A 173cc (11cu in) two-stroke which had limited production.

ATLANTIS *Germany 1926–32*
First used own 348/398cc (21/24cu in) two-strokes, but soon progressed to bigger four-strokes from Küchen, JAP and Blackburne, plus MAG's big V-twins.

ATLAS *England 1913–14*
492/496cc (30cu in) JAPs and Blumfields.

ATLAS *England 1922–25*
A 142cc (9cu in) two-stroke, notable for its forward-facing carburettor and belt-drive.

ATLAS *Germany 1924–29*
Used own 248cc and 348cc (15 and 21cu in) two-strokes, designed by Schleif who also rode these machines with success in hillclimbs.

ATTOLINI *Italy 1920–23*
Used 269cc (16cu in) Villiers two-strokes, plus rear suspension.

Blade-type forks

The Ascot-Pullin was unusual, advanced and short-lived

AUGUSTA *Italy 1924–31*
Fast overhead-cam singles, first a 348cc (21cu in) machine, then smaller versions designed by Angelo Blatto.

AURORA *England 1902–07*
Units used included MMCs and Coronets.

AURORA *Isle of Man 1919–21*
A 318cc (19cu in) two-stroke, one of just two bikes built in the IoM.

AUSTEN *England 1903–06*
2.25hp Kelecom engines were among those used.

AUSTRAL *France 1908–32*
Part of the Alcyon group, Austral started with 211cc (13cu in) two-strokes, and later used 246cc (15cu in) Zurcher and JAP engines.

AUSTRIA *Austria 1903–07*
One of the first clip-on motors, this one had 8hp.

AUSTRIA *Austria 1930–33*
Duralumin frames distinguished this Austria, plus a water-cooled Villiers unit on some models.

AUSTRIA-ALPHA *Austria 1933–52*
Concentrated on four-stroke racers before the war and two-stroke utility bikes afterwards. Later built parts only.

AUSTRO-ILO *Austria 1938*
Hitler's occupation of Austria put a stop to production of this 120cc (7cu in) Ilo-engined bike in its first year.

AUSTRO-MOTORETTE *Austria 1924–27*
Produced 82cc (5cu in) clip-ons, then a 144cc (9cu in) two-stroke twin and finally 173cc (11cu in) dohc racers.

AUSTRO-OMEGA *Austria 1932–39*
Used JAP engines of 348–746cc (21–45.5cu in) on a well-made machine.

AUTINAG *Germany 1924–25*
Small two-strokes and utilized a 496cc (30cu in) ioe single from MAG.

AUTO-BI *U.S.A. 1902–12*
Enclosed engines distinguished these Auto-Bi 1.5/2.5 hp singles.

AUTO-BIT *Japan 1952–62*
English-influenced 249cc (15cu in) single.

AUTO ELL *Germany 1924–26*
142cc (9cu in) Grade-powered two-strokes, designed by Max Ell.

AUTOFLUG *Germany 1921–23*
Scooter-like small-wheeler with step-through frame, usually with Bekamo two-stroke power.

AUTOGLIDER *England 1919–22*
Part of the first scooter boom, it had a 269cc (16cu in) Union two-stroke mounted above the front wheel.

AUTOMOTO *France 1901–62*
Both the company and its unexciting, though sturdy products were long-lived. Utilized a wide range of bought-in engines, latterly from AMC.

AUTOPED *U.S.A. 1915–21*
Unusual for an early scooter in that it had a four-stroke engine. Also built by Krupp in Germany under licence.

AUTOSCO *England 1920–21*
An early 180cc (11cu in) scooter.

AVADA *The Netherlands 1951–64*
Short-lived manufacturer of mopeds.

AVANTI *India 1982–93*
Built mopeds and an 150cc (9cu in) scooter, with help from Garelli.

AVENIR *Belgium c.1955*
49cc (3cu in) two-stroke utilities.

AVIS-CELER *Germany 1925–31*
Used Villiers engines at first, then added MAG singles up to 497cc (30cu in).

AVON *England 1919–20*
Unsuccessful with its 347cc (21cu in) Villiers-powered two-stroke.

AWD *Germany 1921–59*
Frames designed by August Wurring, who used a wide range of bought-in engines, and continued after the war with Sachs and Ilo two-strokes.

AWO *East Germany 1950–61*
Sophisticated small bike with unit-construction 246cc (15cu in) single and shaft-drive. Also produced larger racers including a dohc twin. Later built mopeds only, as Simsons.

AYRES-HAYMAN *England 1920*
A 688cc (42cu in) sv flat twin from Manchester.

AZA *Czechoslovakia 1924–26*
147cc (9cu in) lightweights, but also a more fearsome 996cc (61cu in) JAP V-twin.

AZZARITI *Italy 1933–34*
Fine engineering which anticipated Ducati's use of desmodromic valve gear in its 173 and 348cc (11 and 21cu in) ohc twins designed by Vincenzo Azzariti.

B

BAC *England 1951–53*
An early post-war British scooter (the Gazelle), with 98/123cc (6/7.5cu in) Villiers power. Also a 98cc lightweight.

BADGER *U.S.A. 1920–21*
The Badger's 163cc (10cu in) four-stroke engine was built into its rear wheel.

BAF *Czechoslovakia 1927–30*
Used a range of bought-in engines, from the 173cc (11cu in) Bekamo to 496cc (30cu in) Chaise.

BAIER *Germany 1924–30*
A range of two-stroke singles, some of unit-construction, though latterly a sole 492cc (30cu in) double-pistoned single.

BAILEUL *France 1904–10*
Bought-in Peugeot and Buchet engines.

BAJAJ *India 1961–*
Imported Vespas in the fifties, and licence-built them from 1961 with its own designs from 1971. Own 50–100cc (3–6cu in) step-throughs from 1980, and association with Kawasaki from 1986 led to Bajaj-built KB100s and ZZR 250s.

BAKER *France 1927–30*
Designer F.A. Baker had also worked for Cleveland and Beardmore-Precision before building these Villiers-engined lightweights.

BALALUWA *Germany 1924–25*
A forward-looking 346cc (21cu in) ohv single.

BALKAN *Bulgaria 1958–75*
Began with a Jawa-based two-stroke and went on to build mopeds and 73cc (4cu in) lightweights.

BAM *Germany 1933–37*
The BAM was really a Belgian FN but was assembled in the Berlin-Aachener-Motorradwerke to get around Hitler's ban on imported bikes.

BAMAR *Germany 1923–25*
Used bought-in 149/198cc (9/12cu in) engines from DKW, among others.

BAMO *Germany 1923–25*
Another DKW-dependent Weimar German brand.

BANSHEE *England 1921–24*
An interesting name, and one of the first bikes to use the 347cc (21cu in) Barr & Stroud sleeve-valved engine.

BARDONE *Italy 1938–39*
Designed its own 499cc (30cu in) unit singles as well as delivery trikes.

BARIGO *France 1992–*
France's only motorcycle maker for most of the 1990s, Barigo was founded by Patrick Barigault and is based at La Rochelle on France's west coast. With a background in 'supermoto' competition bikes, it seemed a logical step to produce a road-legal version. At that time in France there was a growing fashion for converting trail bikes into supermotos by fitting smaller wheels and road tyres.

The Supermotard roadster used a 600cc (37cu im) Rotax four-stroke single, with aluminium frame and quality cycle parts. Like all road-going supermotos, what it lacked in outright power it made up for in light weight, slim build and plenty of torque. It was, as journalists of the day never tired of pointing out, the ultimate stoppie and wheelie machine. Barigo followed up the Supermotard two years later with the Onixa, which used the same frame and engine with sportsbike cycle parts and bodywork.

BARNES *England 1904*
Used MMC and Minerva engines, but failed to survive for very long.

BARON *England 1920–21*
More an assembler than a builder, it utilized 269cc (16cu in) Villiers and 348cc (21cu in) Blackburne sv engines.

BARRY *Czechoslovakia 1932–39*
Started with racers, and a new 98cc (6cu in) two-stroke was killed by the war.

BARTALI *Italy 1953–61*
Small (all sub-200cc/12cu in) two- and four-strokes. Named after cycle racer Gino Bartali.

BARTER *England 1902–05*
The only bike in the world with the rear wheel driven directly by the camshaft.

BARTISCH *Austria 1925–29*
Good-looking overhead-cam singles of 348/498cc (21/30cu in), with either chain- or bevel-cam drive.

BASTERT *Germany 1949–55*
A range of mopeds, scooters and motorcycles of up to 247cc (15cu in).

BAT *England 1902–26*
BAT ('Best After Test') built mainly sporting bikes, from a 492cc (30cu in) ohv single upwards. Second in the 1908 TT.

BATAVUS *The Netherlands 1911–*
Prolific producer of mopeds, though in its early years also built motorcycles of up to 198cc (12cu in), with a variety of bought-in engines.

BAUDO *Italy 1920–28*
Used a bewildering array of bought-in engines, including JAP V-twins, Train two-strokes, 173cc (11cu in) Mosers and the Barr & Stroud sleeve-valve.

BAUER *Germany 1936–54*
Built mopeds before the war and small motorcycles afterwards, but pulled out to concentrate on bicycles after a novel 250 in 1952 (forward-facing carburettor) proved troublesome.

BAYERLAND *Germany 1924–30*
Used JAP engines, and a racing V-twin won the Grand Prix de l'Europe in 1927.

BAYERN *Germany 1923–26*
Produced a 293cc (18cu in) Bosch-Douglas flat twin, licence-built, then 498/988cc (30/60cu in) MAG V-twins.

BAYLEY-FLYER *U.S.A. 1914–17*
This intriguing flat twin had an automatic gearchange and shaft-drive.

BB *Germany 1923–25*
Used a 197cc (12cu in) Alba sv single.

BB *Italy 1925–27*
123cc (7.5cu in) two-strokes with horizontal cylinders, designed by Ugo Bocchi.

BCR *France 1923–30*
One of the first bikes to offer rear suspension. Power came from 98cc (6cu in) two-strokes to 498cc (30cu in) four-strokes.

BD *Czechoslovakia 1927–29*
A 490cc (30cu in) unit-construction bike, later sold under the Praga name.

BEARDMORE-PRECISION *England 1921–24*
Mostly used Precision engines up to 596cc (36cu in).

BEAUFORT *England 1923–26*
A 170cc (10cu in) two-stroke from a maker of invalid three-wheelers.

BEAU-IDEAL *England 1905–06*
Used bought-in Clément, Minerva and JAP engines.

BEAUMONT *England 1921–22*
Used the 269cc (16cu in) Wall or 348cc (21cu in) Blackburne. Named after its designer who went on to produce the Kendall 'people's car' in the 1940s.

BE BE *Germany 1923–27*
A 117cc (7cu in) two-stroke from an iron foundry.

BECCARIA *Italy 1925–28*
Mostly bought-in British components were used in this Italian lightweight.

BECKER *Germany 1903–06*
Used its own engines, or singles and V-twins from Fafnir.

BEESTON *England 1898–1910*
A real pioneer, thanks to owner Harry Lawson's ownership of the De Dion patents in England. Used a 346cc (21cu in), 1.75hp engine.

BEFAG *Germany 1922–24*
113cc and 176cc (7 and 11cu in) engines that could run on crude oil.

BEHAG *Germany 1922–26*
Built its own 218cc (13cu in) two-strokes, with a 348/490cc (21/30cu in) JAP option in a step-through frame.

BEKAMO *Germany 1922–25*
First bikes had wooden frames, though were actually more famous for their 129cc (8cu in) two-stroke engine with a pumping piston at the bottom of the crankcase. The engine was sold to, and built under licence by many rival manufacturers.

BEKAMO *Czechoslovakia 1923–30*
At first built German Bekamos under licence before becoming the sole manufacturer. Unusual frame with 8-inch diameter top tube to carry fuel and oil.

BENELLI *Italy 1921–*
Founded by the Benelli brothers, of whom there were six, it remained a family concern for half a century. Together, the brothers set up a small engineering workshop on the Adriatic coast, though it wasn't until after World War I that they built their first powered two-wheeler, a 98cc (6cu in) two-stroke attached to the front of a bicycle. Such machines were already outdated by then, and it wasn't long before the brothers designed a proper

The final incarnation of the six-cylinder Benelli was the 900cc (55cu in) Sei

The Benelli 250cc (15cu in) ohc single, which was fast and sporting

frame for the engine, and a two-speed gearbox. Benelli's first motorcycle was unveiled in 1921.

It soon grew to 147cc (9cu in), and the youngest brother, Antonio, raced it with great success, going on to do much for Benelli's profile by winning races all over Europe, and the company supported him with a succession of fast ohc four-stroke singles, being especially dominant in the 175cc (11cu in) class. Sadly, Tonino, as he was known, was killed while testing a bike in 1937. In fact, racing dominated the pre-war Benelli although its sporting road singles (particularly the ohv 175) sold well and the 250 Super Sport of 1936 showed an early use of plunger rear suspension; there was a 500 as well. Milestone Benelli racers at the time were the dohc 250 single and very advanced supercharged water-cooled four (also a 250 with a claimed 52bhp at 10,000rpm) which was launched at the Milan Show in 1939 but which fell foul of the FIM's post-war ban on superchargers.

A Benelli in sporting livery

The Benelli factory had been a target for Allied bombers during the war (it was making aircraft parts) so it wasn't until 1952 that Benelli launched its first really new post-war bike, the Leonessa 250 twin: it was mildly tuned but up-to-the-minute, with unit-construction, four-speed gearbox and swinging-arm rear suspension. More sporting was a new 175 single in 1959, with oversquare bore/stroke and 12bhp at 8,000rpm. Shortly afterwards, a 49cc (3cu in) two-stroke was launched – mopeds and minibikes were to be part of Benelli's range for years to come. In the late 1960s Benelli revealed its first big bike, the 650cc (40cu in) parallel-twin Tornado, which looked like an improved, updated version of the equivalent British twin.

It wasn't enough to preserve Benelli's independence, and in 1971 the company was taken over by Alejandro de Tomaso, who already owned Moto Guzzi; he was to

In the late 1990s, scooters brought a new lease of life to Benelli

oversee complete modernization of the range. There were 125 and 250 two-stroke twins from 1972 (they lasted for ten years, and the 250 sold well) and in 1973 the impactful 750 Sei (a six-cylinder superbike that predated Honda's CBX) and a smaller 498cc (30cu in) four, the 500 Quattro. Both bikes (especially the 500) owed a great deal to the contemporary Honda sohc fours. 'He who steals from a thief,' de Tomaso was quoted as saying, 'is a thousand times forgiven.' The 500 spawned 345 and 397cc (21 and 24cu in) versions, and Benelli followed it up with the delicate 231cc (14cu in) four in 1976 and a new 654 Sport (really 603cc/37cu in) soon after. Meanwhile, the Sei grew to 900cc (55cu in), but none of this really helped Benelli in the long term as its four-strokes were very similar to the Japanese opposition but far more expensive. So through the 1980s the company concentrated on small mopeds and scooters, plus from 1987 a water-cooled 125, which came in both sports and trail bike guises. But de Tomaso had had enough, and sold out to the Biesse company in 1989. Biesse originally intended to simply use up existing stocks of parts, but demand was strong enough to continue lightweight production into the 1990s. Benelli's fourth owner, Andrea Merloni, assumed control in 1997 and launched a range of aggressively styled 50cc (3cu in) scooters to take advantage of Europe's scooter boom of the late nineties.

BENOTTO *Italy 1953–57*
Used Ilo two-strokes up to 198cc (12cu in).

BERCLEY *Belgium 1905–09*
616cc (38cu in) vertical twin, one of the first in mass-production.

Engine detail of the 750 Sei which owed something to Honda

BERESA *Germany 1923–25*
198cc (12cu in) sv four-strokes.

BERGFEX *Germany 1904–09*
Built singles and V-twins with in-house or Fafnir engines.

BERGO *Germany 1924*
Utilized bought-in 145cc (9cu in) DKW two-strokes.

BERINI *The Netherlands 1949–81*
First produced a clip-on 49cc (3cu in) disc-valved two-stroke, then mopeds. The engines for the mopeds are still made in India and were exported to Europe from 1991 and sold under the Berini name.

BERLIN *East Germany 1958–65*
A 148cc (9cu in) MZ-powered scooter.

BERNARDET *France 1930–34*
Used 98–498cc (6–30cu in) engines from Chaise and Train.

Benelli K-1

BERNARDET *France 1949–57*
A leading French scooter manufacturer of the time, utilizing NSU engines.

BERNEG *Italy 1954–61*
Notable for its own tiny twin-cylinder engines of 159 and 174cc (10 and 11cu in).

BERO *Germany 1924–25*
A short-lived German lightweight with a DKW engine.

BERTIN *France 1955–58*
A manufacturer of mopeds.

BERWICK *England 1929–30*
Early use of shaft-drive with 246/346cc (15/21cu in) Villiers engines.

BETA *Italy 1948–*
Built bicycles from 1904, but made a range of mopeds and motorcycles up to 250cc (15cu in) from the 1950s, including a fast 173cc (11cu in) overhead-cam sportster. More recently Beta has concentrated on the off-road trials market, with various two-strokes up to 326cc (20cu in). The KR125 and 250 of the 1980s were typical.

BEUKER *Germany 1921–29*
Three-port two-strokes of its own design, up to 246cc (15cu in), powered the Beuker.

BEZDEZ *Czechoslovakia 1923–26*
Built 145cc (9cu in) four-strokes as clip-ons or as part of complete machines.

BH *Spain 1956–60*
Small moped manufacturer.

B&H *England 1923*
Built a 996cc (61cu in) V-twin machine for a short period.

ABOVE: Betas excel in indoor trials

BIANCHI *Italy 1897–1967*
Edoardo Bianchi was one of Italy's first motorcycle makers, being well-established by 1910. There was a 650cc (40cu in) V-twin in 1916, followed by a succession of singles and V-twins which added to Bianchi's enviable racing success. A powerful supercharged four-cylinder racer was killed by the war. After 1945, Bianchi still made exotic overhead-cam singles, though of smaller capacities of 123/248cc (7.5/15cu in) at first, and there were also more prosaic two-strokes. However, ohc vertical twins of 248/348cc (15/21cu in) were also developed. Bianchi 'celebrated' its 70th anniversary of making powered two-wheelers by ceasing production.

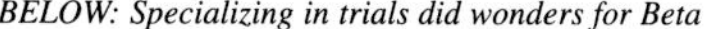
BELOW: Specializing in trials did wonders for Beta

BICHRONE *France 1902–07*
Early two-stroke manufacturer which sold its 2.25–2.75hp engines to other factories.

BIM *Japan 1956–61*
BMW-like sv flat twins up to 598cc (36cu in).

BIMA *France 1952–*
49cc (3cu in) two-strokes, made at the Peugeot factory.

BIMM *Italy 1965–80*
50–125cc (3–8cu in) mopeds and lightweights, including off-roaders. All engines bought in.

BIMOFA *Germany 1922–25*
Used sv Hansa engines on a bike designed by Gustav Kunstmann.

BIMOTA *Italy 1973–*
Bimota's existence relied on a truism – that in the seventies and early eighties the Japanese knew a great deal about four-cylinder engines, but not so much about motorcycle tyres, suspension and general dynamics. What Bimota (and other European builders) did was combine the best practice of European and Japanese engineering. Unlike most rivals, Bimota has survived (barring a few close calls with bankruptcy), even since the Japanese manufacturers have produced sportsbikes that handle as well as anything else.

Massimo Tamburini had already gained something of a reputation as a specials builder, but his Honda 750-engined racer of 1973 created so much interest that he decided to forsake his central heating business for motorcycles. Bi-Mo-Ta, incidentally, was derived from the names of the firm's three partners: Bianchi, Morri and Tamburini, though Bianchi had left when the bike era began. Their emphasis in the early days was on racing, and Tamburini, the engineer of the three, soon came up with another bike based around the Yamaha TTZ350 two-stroke twin. One of these actually won the 350cc world title in 1980. By then, Bimota was selling road-going frame kits for Japanese engines, and in 1977 unveiled its first complete road

Bimota profited from less than perfect Japanese cycle parts

Bimotas were successful in endurance racing, the rider here being Charlie Williams

bike, the Suzuki GS750-powered SB2.

The SB2 was far lighter than the standard Suzuki GS750 (a characteristic Bimota advantage), a good 32km/h (20mph) faster and naturally its handling was far superior. And it was more than just a reframed Suzuki; the rear suspension was by monoshock (years before this became commonplace) and the fuel tank was mounted underneath the engine, thus lowering the centre of gravity. The SB2 had only been on sale for a matter of months before another Tamburini creation was unveiled, this time with Kawasaki power. The KB1 came with a choice of 903cc (55cu in) or 1015cc (62cu in) Kawasaki dohc fours and its monoshock was mounted horizontally. The Kawasaki engine was mounted higher than the SB2's, and a spaceframe was used. Perhaps the most radical feature was variable steering geometry. By using eccentric upper and lower steering head bearings, the trail could actually be adjusted from 3.9 to 4.7 inches, to suit conditions.

Such chassis innovations helped establish Bimota as a forward-looking company with the real expertise that larger manfacturers lacked at the time. Its bikes were hand-built using the highest-quality suspension and brakes available. But it also meant that Bimotas were very expensive to build and buy, and the tiny concern often found itself overstretched. The end nearly came in the early 1980s, but Bimota managed to save itself with the back-to-basics DB1, powered by a Ducati V-twin. It was a success and put Bimota on a firmer footing through the 1980s as well as establishing a Ducati link that remains strong today. Racing continued to be an important feature, and Virginio Ferrari's Formula One title in 1987 (on a Yamaha FZ750-engined YB4) was perhaps Bimota's greatest racing success.

But despite the sales success of conventional bikes such as the DB1, there was still an innovative streak within Bimota. Nothing illustrates this better than the hub-centre-steered Tesi of 1991. Chief engineer Pierluigi Marconi (Tamburini had since left for Cagiva) had been working on the concept for ten years, mounting the front wheel on a twin-sided swinging arm working a single suspension unit. In theory, like all hub-centre systems, the Tesi improved handling by separating braking and suspension forces that conventional telescopic forks have to cope with on their own. In reality, the Tesi failed to live up to its promise, and was hampered by high price and teething troubles which confirmed the view of a conservative public that the Tesi was too clever by half. Fortunately for Bimota, its more conventional SB6 (Suzuki GSXR1100-powered) was selling well at the time.

Not that the Tesi deterred Bimota from thinking forward. Much money and development time in the 1990s was spent on the 500 V*due*, a 500cc (30.5cu in) direct-injection two-stroke V-twin. It was typically Bimota that its first in-house engine should be so radical, though the promise of 110bhp in an ultra-light chassis made everyone expect great things. But when the V*due* finally staggered into production in 1997, there were serious running problems with the fuel injection, and the bike was withdrawn (though in early 1999 it was still promising a relaunch). The weird-looking Mantra was

Not all Bimotas displayed Italian elegance

more successful and a departure for Bimota, with its naked bike looks. The sci-fi styling was a matter of taste, but it sold well.

Perhaps more to the point for Bimota's future, it was still able to sell more conventional sportsbikes like the 1100cc (67cu in) SB6 and the Yamaha 600-powered YB9, and when industrialist Francesco Tognon (fresh from saving Laverda) helped take over the troubled company in late 1998, he declared it would be returning to its roots. That was soon underlined by the DB4, using Ducati's 900SS engine, the Mantra's chassis and flowing sportsbike styling. It was soon followed by the SB8R, powered by Suzuki's 996cc V-twin and was 10 per cent lighter than Suzuki's own, and 10 per cent more powerful. Even if Bimota's original *raison d'être* had disappeared, it still seemed able to carve out a niche of its own.

ABOVE: *Ducati-powered DBZ Bimota*

BELOW: *Yamaha provided the YB8's engine*

ABOVE: *The hub-centre-steered Tesi was ultimately unsuccessful*

BELOW: *Bimota loved fully-clothed bikes*

BINKS *England 1903–06*
One of the first four-cylinder bikes, air-cooled and of 385cc (23cu in). Fitted both in-line and transversely.

BINZ *England 1954–58*
A Sachs or Ilo-powered scooter of 49cc (3cu in).

BIRCH *England 1902–05*
J.J. Birch produced his own engines mounted in triangular frames with built-in crankcases.

BIRMA *France 1949–late 1950s*
Used Aubier-Dunne 98cc (6cu in) two-strokes.

BISMARCK *Germany 1904–56*
Early bikes used massive bought-in V-twins. After a ten-year gap in production, Bismarck returned with motorized bicycles and, after World War II, small motorcycles.

BITRI *The Netherlands 1955–57*
Short-lived scooter manufacturer.

BJR *Spain 1953–61*
123/147cc (7.5/9cu in) two-strokes, and a 175cc (11cu in) ohv single.

BLACKBURNE *England 1913–21*
Cecil and Alick Burney bought the rights to Geoffrey de Havilland's engines, and went on to build their own designs and complete bikes with partner Major Blackburne. First was a 499cc (30cu in) sv single in 1913, though World War I put a stop to it. The company sold its motorcycle rights to the Osborn Engineering Co. (OEC) in 1919, thereafter concentrating on engines only.

BLACKFORD *England 1902–04*
211cc (13cu in) Minerva-engined bikes, named after their designer.

BLACK PRINCE *England 1919–20*
Used unusual 497cc (30cu in) flat twin two-stroke with just one spark plug housed in a pressed steel frame with rear suspension. A more conventional tubular-framed bike with a bought-in engine failed to save Black Prince.

BLEHA *Germany 1923–26*
Utilized a 247cc (15cu in) DKW two-stroke as well as its own 247cc sidevalve.

BLÉRIOT *France 1920–23*
There was a certain similarity between Sopwith in England and Blériot in that both aircraft manufacturer tried their hands at motorcycles after the war, using sv and ohv engines, but without success.

BLOTTO *France 1951–55*
123cc to 348cc (7.5 to 21cu in) two-strokes using bought-in engines.

BM *Italy 1928–31*
Used 490cc (30cu in) sv and ohv JAPs, in a partnership between Antonio Baudo and sidecar maker Meldi.

BM *Italy 1950–72*
A wide variety of small two- and four-strokes, notably its own unit-construction ohc singles of up to 174cc (11cu in).

BMG *Hungary 1939–44*
A wartime utility with its own 98cc (6cu in) engines.

BMW *Germany 1921–*
Few marques inspire such loyalty as BMW and there is good reason for this: the Bayerische Motoren Werke has used the same basic layout, from its first-ever complete motorcycle of 1921, right up to the present day. An air-cooled transverse flat twin is bolted to a car-type gearbox and shaft-drive. Other bikes might use elements of the whole, but no other manufacturer offers anything remotely similar. It is interesting that although there are many bikes built in the style of Harley-

BMW, the early years. Over 3,000 R32s were built from 1923–26

Davidson, no one has made a concerted effort to 'out-BMW' BMW – certainly none has succeeded.

As with Harley, of course, there have been some diversions: single-cylinder BMWs have come and gone with economic cycles; from the early eighties, liquid-cooled threes and fours were intended to replace the flat twins altogether; front suspension has shifted from leaf-sprung forks, to telescopics, to leading-link-type Earles forks, back to teles again, and finally to the current Paralever set-up. But through it all, the company has remained faithful to the basic concept of a shaft-driven flat twin. Neither is it just this layout which defines BMW. While most manufacturers have followed a greater or lesser obsession with performance, BMW's priorities have been different. Right from the start, the twin was designed to be reliable, practical and above all well made.

The company grew out of World War I when two engineering firms merged with the intention of building aircraft. Starting as BFW (it became BMW in 1917), the new firm was able to complete only 70 aircraft before the war ended. Forbidden from building more, BMW therefore had to find something which did not involve flight.

The eventual solution lay with the small engines BMW was making for the engineering firm of Otto, which had a factory next door. Otto was already building a little 148cc (9cu in) two-stroke motorcycle called the Flink, and requested BMW to build it a 500cc (30.5cu in) flat twin. The M2B15 of 1921 produced just under 6bhp and fitted fore-aft into Otto's Helios, though it was also bought-in by a number of other small motorcycle makers.

This fore-aft twin was actually made under a licence granted by Douglas, which had been using the flat-twin layout since 1907. BMW soon took over production of the Helios, which didn't please designer Max Friz. He was really an aircraft man, but fortunately for BMW, someone else realized that the company's future lay in two wheels.

They certainly got things moving, for only two years after the M2B15 was unveiled, BMW launched its first in-house motorcycle, the R32. Despite his reluctance, Max Friz had come up with an instant classic. All the elements of every single BMW twin since were there: an air-cooled flat twin, single-plate clutch, car-type gearbox and shaft-drive. Of 486cc

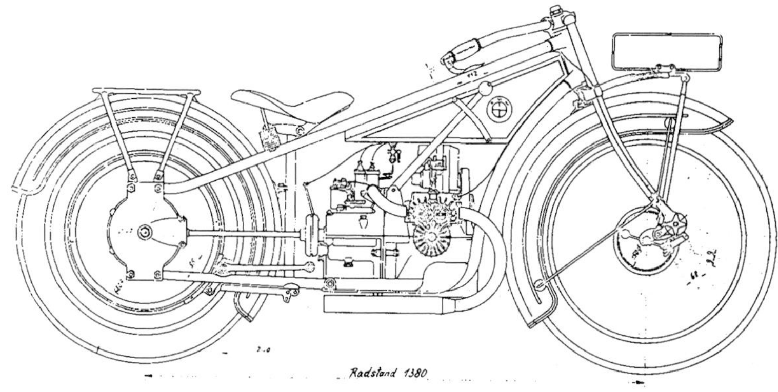

The first true BMW, the R32 of 1923 established the familiar layout which the company adhered to for decades. It was a transverse flat twin with shaft-drive

The pride of the Wehrmacht

(30cu in), it produced 8.5bhp at 3,300rpm, enough for a relaxed top speed of 97km/h (60mph), with the bonus of around 28km per litre (80mpg). Otherwise, it was up-to-the-minute stuff, with the three-speed handchange gearbox, automatic oil pump and magneto ignition (including electric lights); there was no front brake, but that wasn't unusual at the time! A racing version, the R37, followed in a couple of years whose overhead valves and higher compression were enough to almost double the power, though the ten special bikes built for works-supported riders were different again, with twin carburettors and light-alloy cylinder heads. The reward was a gold medal in the ISDT of 1926, which prompted Granville Bradshaw (designer of the ABC flat twin) to claim that BMW had simply copied his design! More recent research, however, found no evidence to support this.

Meanwhile, BMW was busy setting up another of its long-standing formats. The 250cc (15cu in) R39 of 1925 was the forerunner of a generation of BMW singles, every one of them sharing the same square bore and stroke of 68mm x 68mm. It had shaft-drive, of course, and because of its lightness was as fast as the R32. That original twin was updated as the R42 in 1926, and reflected the impact BMW had already made with sales of 7,000 in just two years, aided by the fact that it was cheaper than its predecessor. If Friz had any doubts about the motorcycle project, they must by now have been quelled. As before, there was an overhead-valve version, the R47 (though now more 'sporting' than 'racing', as sidecar gearing was an option). Long-stroke (but similar capacity) twins replaced these two in

ABOVE: R32 was the first of a long line

BELOW: 750cc (46cu in) sidevalve R11

1928 – the R52 and 57. Both also had BMW's infamous side-acting kickstart, frustrating to riders ever since.

Racing was a major part of BMW's policy at the time, as illustrated by the supercharged racer of 1927. It boosted power from 29 to 55bhp, enough to win the Targa Florio three years running, not to mention the German championship. In 750cc (46cu in) form, the supercharged BMW took the world motorcycle speed record in September 1929, at 216.05km/h (134.25mph). Apart from a couple of lapses, the record was to stay BMW's until 1951. That supercharger was something of an afterthought, but BMW followed it with a purpose-built 500cc supercharged racer in 1935 – the Kompressor. It was to win the Senior TT in 1939; but its international glory was short-lived as supercharging was banned soon after the war.

That earlier racer was BMW's first 750cc machine, but road versions soon followed, specifically the sidevalve R62 and ohv R63, with 18bhp and 24bhp respectively. The R63 was, unlike previous ohv BMWs, not just a conversion of the sidevalve, but had its own bore and stroke (83mm x 63mm) to help increase power. (Oddly, at 121km/h/75mph, it was only marginally faster than the R62.) Both 750s actually weighed little more than the existing models, being shoe-horned into the same tubular frames. In fact, it was the frame that next came in for major change. In 1929, BMW dropped it in favour of its pressed steel 'star frame'. The engine options were more familiar though, the sidevalve R11 and ohv R16 both having the same cylinder dimensions as the previous 750s, but with slightly lower capacities quoted. Both gained twin Amal carburettors

The BMW Kompressor used supercharging to good effect. This is a 1949 version

after a few years, as well as significant power increases, but retained the three-speed hand-change gearbox.

First with Hydraulics

Although its twins were becoming ever larger and more powerful, BMW had not forgotten that times were hard in Weimar Germany, and announced the R2 in 1931. Of 198cc/12cu inches (sub-200cc bikes were not taxed at the time) it was still expensive for its size, though built with the same attention to quality as its other bikes. This ohv single was to form the basis of all BMW singles since (F650 excepted, of course), and the innovative one-piece crankcase became a standard feature of the air-cooled twins as well. The price was partly justified by speed (97km/h/60mph) and economy (35km per litre/100mpg) that few could rival, though it still retained the leaf-sprung front forks that every BMW had used from the start. The R4 (398cc/24cu in) and R3 (305cc/19cu in) followed, with the same pressed steel frame; the expanding Wehrmacht (this was the mid-1930s) bought many of these.

There were more updates for the twins in 1935. Now known as R12 and R17, their most significant features were the hydraulically-damped telescopic forks, the first time these had been fitted to any production motorcycle. It was BMW's own work (sensibly patent-protected) and set the pattern for almost every motorcycle front suspension since (until BMW came up with its own new set-ups). Handling (especially on bends) was far superior to anything else, and extra weight was the only real disadvantage. One side benefit was that the new forks allowed equal-sized wheels, and typical of its practical priorities, BMW ensured that both were interchangeable, which remained a feature right up to 1969.

However, the R12/17 were really just updates of the much older machines, and the following year BMW came up with something all-new, the R5. It used the telescopic forks, of course (though still no rear suspension), but reverted to the more conventional tubular frame which enclosed the final-drive unit in a loop of tube to absorb the stress imposed by shaft-drive. The R5 also marked a return to the 500 class, but the 494cc (30cu in) ohv flat twin used a camshaft for each cylinder, thus shorter pushrods allowing higher revs and more power – 24bhp at 5,800rpm and a top speed of 140km/h (87mph). In fact, the R5 was something of a milestone, with positive-stop foot gearchange and coil ignition. It looked new as well, with a distinctive BMW style that was to take the company right up to the sixties.

A sidevalve 600 version, the R6, appeared in 1937, and both bikes were treated to plunger rear suspension the following year. In 1938 came the new performance flagship, the ohv 597cc (36cu in) R66, which could top 145km/h (90mph) but used the same cycle parts as the R51 (né R5). The same year saw the unveiling of something very different; the R71 was a development of the big sidevalve BMWs, and in its soft state of tune remained a favourite sidecar puller. The singles weren't neglected either, and when Germany's tax-free limit grew to 250cc (15cu in), so did BMW's little single, now with telescopic (albeit undamped) forks, while the 340cc (21cu in) R35 still sold well to the army.

The outbreak of war saw one of the company's most infamous bikes, the R75 sidecar outfit. As many as 20,000 of these monstrous machines were produced during the war, though as the factory was to disappear behind the Iron Curtain, the exact number is uncertain. Much of the company's output was dedicated to aero-engines, but the R75 was like nothing else before or since. Designed from scratch as an outfit (not as a solo motorcycle) it was intended to carry three hefty soldiers and a machine-gun. It also had to operate in locations as diverse as Siberia and North Africa, so came with knobbly tyres and two ranges in the four-speed gearbox, while the sidecar wheel was driven; there was a reverse gear as well. The whole thing weighed a not inconsiderable 420kg (925lb), so it was perhaps a good thing that the R75 pioneered hydraulic brakes on a motorcycle. Motive power came from a 745cc (45.5cu in) ohv version of the flat twin, giving 26bhp at 4,000rpm, top speed 95km/h (59mph). An interesting footnote: the American military was so impressed with the R75 as an adversary that it asked Harley-Davidson to build one; the Milwaukean XA was a straight copy of the BMW. But the R75, like the Allied sidecar outfits, had to contend with the Jeep.

It took a few years for BMW to get back to motorcycle manufacture after the war. Quite apart from the ruins from which the Munich factory had to rebuild, Germany was prohibited from making powered two-wheelers of any kind. Agricultural machinery, then an aluminium bicycle got the plant back in running order before 1948, when German manufacturers received the go-ahead to build bikes of up to 250cc. BMW actually had a 125cc prototype, a two-stroke flat twin, in the background, but the 250 limit allowed it to simply update the pre-war R23 single and reintroduce it as the R24, now with a four-speed gearbox and a little more power than before.

Meanwhile, George Meier (who had successfully raced the BMW Kompressor before the war) now went back to work, dominating racing in Germany from 1947

ABOVE: R51/3, the stalwart of the range

BELOW: R25/3 was a hard worker

ABOVE: R69S was BMW's sportster

to 1951. (The story goes that he hid the famous racer in a haystack for the duration!) Sidecar racing was proving fruitful for BMW too, with Max Klankermeier winning the German championship in 1949. It was a different story in international events where, with superchargers banned, the Kompressor lost its edge. An updated Rennsport in 1953 had fuel injection, swinging-arm rear suspension and a precursor of Earles forks at the front, none of which was enough to match the Nortons and Gileras. Sidecar racing was a different story, and here BMW-powered outfits dominated the world championship for 20 years.

The first road-going twin had re-entered production in 1949. The R51/2 was a development of its pre-war equivalent, though most of the changes seemed to aim at cost-cutting. BMWs had always been expensive bikes, and never was economy needed more than in those austere post-war years. The rear main bearing, for example, had previously had its own housing, but now ran directly in the crankcase; plain bushes replaced the rocker's needle-roller bearings; and the cylinder head was fastened down with four studs instead of five. Despite the changes, the R51 was still not bargain basement, though it sold well in its two-year run.

BELOW: The more modest R50 (1965)

That R51 was very much a modified pre-war design, but the new R51/3 and R67 of 1951 saw more fundamental changes. Fundamental that is, by BMW standards: the twin chain-driven camshafts reverted to a single spur-gear; the dynamo moved to the front cover, producing an impressive 160 watts (three times the norm) and coil ignition was dropped in favour of a magneto. Otherwise, power was unchanged, as were the cycle parts. As ever, there was a 600cc (37cu in) sidecar-biased version (the R67) tuned for torque rather than power. Despite their price, these early pre-war BMWs sold well; within five years of production restarting, 100,000 had been built.

The motorcycle market, after its early post-war emphasis on practical transport, was turning its attention to performance, and BMW responded in 1952 with the R68. Billed as 'The 100mph motorcycle', it was basically an R67 tuned to give 35bhp at 7,000rpm. Higher compression and larger Bing carburettors were the main changes, enough to make this the fastest road BMW yet. Unusually, as well as the standard road bike there was also an off-road version, with high-level silencer and wider handlebars. However, at 193kg (425lb), it was really rather heavy for serious mud plugging.

Revolution!

The year 1955 was of great significance. The European motorcycle market was over its post-war boom, and BMW was feeling the effects. Unlike the British manufacturers, BMW was not exporting many bikes to North America and despite being busy building aero-engines, bubblecars and sports cars, it actually faced bankruptcy in 1959. It was saved by banker Dr. Herbert Quandt who sold off the aero-engine interest and introduced two new cars (the 700, which used an enlarged flat twin, and 1500) which sold well and were profitable. All this was in the future when in 1955 big changes were made to the R26, R50 and R69, the most obvious of which was the installation of Earles front forks.

Designed by Englishman Ernie Earles, they were really a reversed swinging-arm arrangement, albeit truncated. More comfortable and effective than telescopic forks, although no other major manufacturer used them on a production bike, they became virtually a BMW trademark until 1969, and some enthusiasts consider the Earles-fork twins the best BMWs ever made. Engines (250cc/15cu inch R26, 500cc/30.5cu inch R50, and 600cc/37cu inch R69) were largely unchanged, though there was a new three-shaft gearbox and diaphragm clutch. A year later, the R69 had a small power increase and became the R60. These were the bikes that would see BMW right though to 1969. The only major change in all that time was the tuned R50S and R69S (35 and 41bhp respectively) and the R69S could top 175km/h (109mph) – still not as fast as the British vertical twins – but probably better mannered when doing so.

Say '1969' to a BMW enthusiast and he or she will croak 'Revolution' back at you. They are not referring to that era of social upheaval, but to BMW's biggest change to the twins since the very beginning. On the three new '/5' BMWs of that year almost everything was new. The twin now had a 745cc/49bhp version; the camshaft ran underneath the crankshaft, and there was a new high-pressure lubrication system. Earles forks were dropped in favour of conventional telescopics (which also meant the end of interchangeable wheels), and the new 12-volt electrics with 200-watt dynamo supported a standard electric start on the two larger bikes, plus indicators. There was even a choice of colours, and the front mudguard was made of plastic! Despite all the extra equipment, all three (the R50/5, R60/5 and R75/5) were lighter than before, though oddly they all turned out to be slightly slower as well. Of course, the price was still very much in the BMW tradition.

ABOVE: The R69S had an extra-long fuel tank

BELOW: The R90 was fast enough to race

As great a change as the /5 series was (and some traditionalists never recovered) it wasn't enough for BMW to keep up in the performance race. This was the age of the superbike: the Honda CB750, BSA/Triumph triples and Kawasaki Z1 had brought a new level of road performance off the shelf, and the R75/5 just wasn't in the same league. In 1973, the company revealed its answer.

The R90S was a new departure – the biggest, fastest BMW yet, with cockpit fairing and snazzy new 'smoke' colour schemes to emphasize the change. The basis of it all was an 898cc (55cu in) flat twin, with the familiar bottom-end (even the 70.6mm stroke was retained) but with a healthy 90mm bore to bring the desired capacity. With Dell 'Orto carburettors (lesser R90s stuck to the faithful Bings), the R90S produced 66bhp at 7,000rpm and could run up to 201km/h (125mph), then back down again thanks to twin front disc brakes. Helmut Dahne even won the Production TT on one in 1976. This was a new sort of BMW. It was a hit, and 24,000 were sold in three years. There was also a more conservative R90/6, in a lower state of tune and without the fairing, while the R60/6 and R75/6 acquired a five-speed gearbox and 280-watt generator. It is interesting to note, though, that the best seller of them all was the mild-mannered R60; it outsold the R90S two to one, which probably said much about BMW owners' priorities.

ABOVE: *R90S – the new generation*

The R90S might have been a giant leap forward, but its good-looking cockpit fairing gave little in the way of actual protection. In that, it was no better nor worse than any other seventies superbike, whose 193km/h+ (120mph+) speeds were only realistic with a rider lying flat on the tank. Now, of course, no serious sports tourer is sold without a fairing, and the bike which changed all that was the BMW R100RS. Its standard, full-size fairing was a milestone for road bikes, as its wind-tunnel design offered the elusive trilogy of fairing attributes: good aerodynamics, good weather protection and good looks. Unveiled in the summer of 1976, it allowed the RS rider to cruise at the 125mph top speed, and really took high-speed, long-distance motorcycling into a new era. Backing it up, the flat twin was bored out yet again, this time to 980cc (60cu in), which gave 69bhp at 7,250rpm. There was also a slightly detuned R100S and naked R100, not to mention the R60 and 75, all of which were now the /7 series. To go with the factory fairing, BMW also offered factory panniers which, like the fairing, were designed to fit the bike, not as an aftermarket accessory and, like the fairing, they were an innovation.

The following year, the R75 was replaced by the R80/7, a favourite of police forces the world over, and the year after saw a new R45/R65. The 473cc (29cu in) R45 was no ball of fire, particularly in 27bhp guise to take advantage of German insurance regulations, but the R65 was more of a true middleweight, with acceptable performance and good manners. At the same time, a new range-topper, the

BELOW: *R100RS was an aerodynamic milestone*

BELOW: *K100RS, BMW's four-cylinder revolution*

While faster and more complicated BMWs continued to appear, there was still a demand for the basic flat twin

R80GS heralded a new class of motorcycle

ABOVE: Monoshock R80ST

BELOW: K1100 luxury tourer

R100RT was launched, with a larger touring version of the sportier RS fairing. It became a favourite with long-distance riders for whom weather protection was a priority. A cheaper R80RT followed in 1982. More radical was the off-road R80GS of 1980. BMW had continued to compete in the ISDT, and the GS was a reflection of this. It was really another milestone bike, heralding a whole new class of 'adventure-tourers' with big softly-tuned motors, long-travel suspension and some nominal off-road capability. So it was with the GS, with new monoshock rear suspension, high-level silencer and wide bars. Although many GSs never ventured off tarmac, it became something of a cult bike, and a 980cc version soon followed. However, the ST road version using the same rear monoshock and alloy-barrelled engine was not a success.

The Brick

There had been rumours of an all-new liquid-cooled BMW for some time, so when the new K-series arrived in 1983, few were surprised. It was, the company claimed, impossible to adapt the air-cooled flat twin to forthcoming noise and emissions regulations without changing its nature. So at the time, the three- and four-cylinder K-series was seen as the twins' ultimate successor. Of course, it didn't turn out like that. But in 1983, the 987cc (60cu in) K100 looked very attractive to both BMW aficionados and those outside the fold. The dohc four-cylinder engine was mounted longitudinally laid on its side, which kept BMW's shaft-drive system intact and

R1100GS from 1993 used the new oil/air-cooled four-valve twin

The Rotax-powered Aprilia-built F650 was a real departure for BMW, and a highly successful one

ensured a relatively low centre of gravity. It was up-to-the-minute in design terms, with Bosch LE fuel injection and electronic engine management. In a modest state of tune it produced 89bhp, which drove even the unfaired K100 to over 209km/h (130mph). There were faired RS and RT models as well, with squared-off, angular fairings to suit the new look; the K-series soon became known as 'The Brick'.

The three-cylinder K75 followed a couple of years later, no more nor less than the K100 with one cylinder lopped off. Rather than use an extra shaft to balance out the triple, BMW simply fitted balance weights to the drive-shaft, which did the same job. In a slightly higher state of tune, the K75 produced 74bhp, though it was also a useful 10kg (22lb) lighter than the K100. Naked K75 and mini-faired K75S versions were offered. A K75RT tourer was to follow, but BMW's 1987 flagship was to be the K100LT, with every conceivable touring extra added to the RT. Perhaps more significant technically was the launch of ABS in 1988. BMW had been working on a practical anti-lock braking system for bikes for some time, and settled on a sophisticated though expensive electronic system. It worked well, and was eventually an option on all big BMWs, a true safety feature now offered by most of the major manufacturers.

Meanwhile, BMW had been forced by popular demand to bring back the R100. Reflecting its milder role these days (and the need to reduce noise and emissions) power was reduced to 59bhp, and in fact the other remaining flat twins – the R65 and R80 – were detuned as well. Very different was the radical K1, launched at the 1988 Cologne Show. Fully enclosed in bright red and yellow bodywork, it used a new 16-valve version of the K-series four, with 100bhp and a maximum speed of 241km/h (150mph). In image terms, it was a huge leap forward for BMW, and though the K1 was really too heavy to compete with the razor-sharp race-replicas coming out of Japan, it clearly signalled that the BMW was determined to break out of its traditional market.

In the early 1990s, BMW was riding high. Sales were increasing, and it was now hedging its bets by offering both air-cooled twins as well as the K-series. An enlarged 1092cc (67cu in) K1100 arrived in 1992, with both RT and RS versions.

However, the big news of 1993 was of an all-new flat twin. BMW, which had thought the twins would soon wither away, had been surprised by the continuing demand for them; as late as 1992 they were actually outselling the K-series. The all-new twin, codenamed R259, was its response. The familiar layout was still there, but just about everything else was new. Now cooled by oil as well as air, the new 1085cc (66cu in) twin had a camshaft in each head (driven by long chains from a jackshaft that also drove the oil pump) and four valves per cylinder, not to mention electronic fuel injection.

The new twin was a great success, and there was something heartening about it in the way that it applied new technology to an old concept while retaining what was different about BMW. But the engine was only part of it. The R1100's real innovation came in the Telelever front suspension. A

The 'naked' R850/1100R from 1994

single monoshock was hidden behind the headstock mounted on a massive strut which connected to the telescopic front forks: relieved of suspension duties, these were merely to keep the front wheel in line. There was no dive on braking and no fork twist and this patented system was a real step forward in motorcycle design. It was complemented at the back by Paralever (originally introduced on the R80GS) which again used a single damper, and allowed the driveshaft housing to act as a swinging arm.

Predictably, a whole range of variations on the theme followed: the sports touring R1100RS was soon joined by a new GS (albeit detuned to 80bhp). More than ever, BMW's GS was a comfortable tourer rather than a giant trail bike. Also in 1994 came an entry-level R850R, with the same 70.5mm stroke as the 1100, but a smaller bore and power was down to 69bhp. An identical-looking R1100R followed in 1995, as did a fully-faired tourer with the RT model name. This really confirmed that the new twins were BMW's mainstream product, with the K-series fours pushed upmarket as super-tourers.

If anyone had suggested, back in the old Earles forks days, that BMW would one day be selling a 650cc (40cu in) single with chain-drive, made in an Italian factory, their sanity would have been questioned. But, in the early nineties, BMW knew that it needed to broaden its range, but that a German-built small bike would cost too much. The answer lay with Aprilia, the Italian manufacturer, whose Pegaso was well-proven and of about the right size. It wasn't quite as simple as sticking BMW badges onto the Aprilia, though. The 652cc

The 125cc (7.6cu in) C1 scooter, for production in the year 2000

single (built by Rotax of Austria) was modified to BMW's specification (four valves in place of the Pegaso's five, for example), the new F650 Funduro having different bodywork, though most of its underpinnings were the same as the Aprilia. And although built in the same factory, it had its own production line, and BMW's own quality-control system was installed. The Funduro was a likeable bike, fast enough for moderate motorcycling, economical and comfortable. A more road-biased ST version soon followed, then the F650 became an established part of BMW's range.

A more radical move away from BMW's roots was the C1 scooter. Hawked around the motorcycle shows in the early nineties as a concept vehicle, journalists were invited to ride it in 1998, though the launch was still 18 months away. A 125cc (8cu in) four-stroke, it was like no other scooter then available in Europe, thanks to the roof which had built-in roll-over protection. The latter, said BMW, had persuaded the authorities to allow it to be ridden without a helmet. At the time of writing, the C1 is still under development.

But BMW had not forgotten the big bikes, and its fortunes continued to flourish in the late nineties, thanks to new variations. Although it had looked as if the K-series was being elbowed aside by the new twins, 1997 saw the K1200RS, which married a 1171cc (71.5cu in) version of the big four with the twins' Telelever/Paralever suspension set-up. It was actually a real-world version of the old K1, though now with a claimed 130bhp at 8,750rpm and

R1100RT (1995) was the touring flagship of the 1990s flat-twin range

K1200RS (1997) marked a new start for the four-cylinder K-series

with the emphasis on sports touring. There were new twins as well. The Harley-Davidson cruiser phenomenon was such a success that by now nearly every major bike maker was producing something along the same lines. BMW couldn't afford not to, but its R1200C managed to look quite individual, and certainly nothing like the Harley lookalikes. It used a 1170cc version of the twin, detuned to produce more cruiser-like power characteristics (61bhp and 72lb ft), but with the now-familiar Telelever/Paralever system and shaft-drive. In the summer of 1998 came the final variation to date, the R1100S, which showed just how far the market for sportsbikes had moved. Five years earlier, the RS had been perfectly acceptable as a sports tourer, but had been left behind by sportier rivals. The R1100S was BMW's answer, and with a 98bhp version of the 1100 twin, small fairing and lower bars it was really BMW's most sporting bike so far. But with alternatives like the C1 arriving, and the new twins well-established, it is unlikely that BMW will ever abandon its roots in well-made practical transport.

BNF *Germany 1903–07*
An early player, using mainly 2.75hp singles and 3.5hp V-twin Fafnir engines.

BOCK & HOLLÄNDER *Austria 1905–11*
3.5hp and 6hp V-twins.

BODO *Germany 1924–25*
147cc (9cu in) DKW engines were utilized by this small-scale assembler.

BOGE *Germany 1923–27*
Later better known for shock absorbers, it once built its own 246/346cc (15/21cu in) sidevalve machines.

BÖHME *Germany 1925–30*
Produced interesting two-strokes of up to 246cc, with water-cooling, double-diameter pistons and horizontal cylinders.

BÖHMERLAND *Czechoslovakia 1925–39*
Possibly the only three-seater motorcycle ever made, the Böhmerland was nothing if not different. Designed by Albin Leibisch, it had a very long wheelbase and twin fuel tanks mounted either side of the rear wheel (the wheels were of cast alloy). By contrast, the engine was a conventional 598cc (36cu in) ohv single. The production of a lighter 348cc (21cu in) two-stroke was cut short by the war.

BMW won the Granada–Dakar Rally in 1999

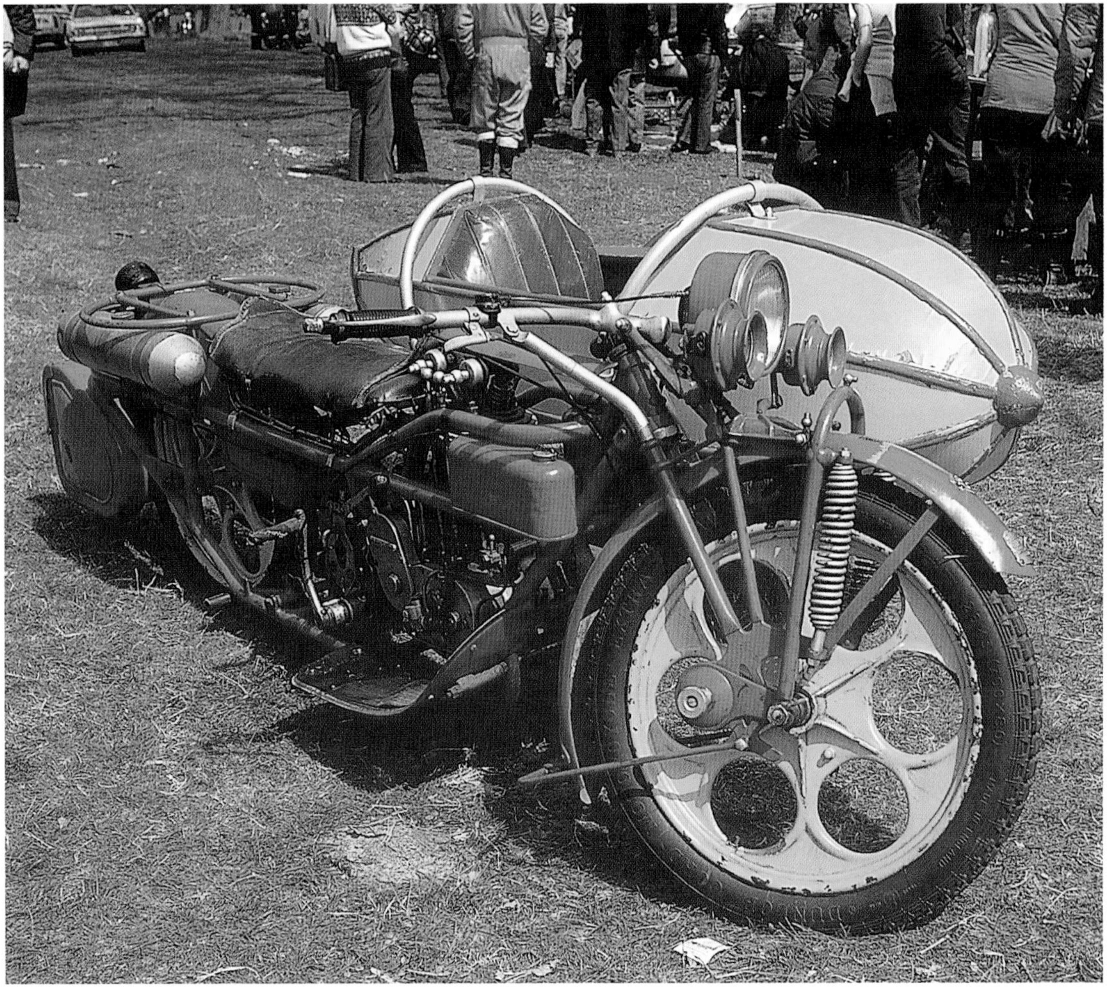

The Czechoslovakian Böhmerland could seat three

BOND *England 1949–55*
The first Bond product was a 98cc (6cu in) minibike with a pressed steel frame. More orthodox motorcycles with tubular frames had 98cc and 123cc Villiers and 123cc (7.5cu in) JAP two-stroke engines.

BOOTH *England 1901–03*
London-based pioneer, using De Dion and Minerva power units.

BORD *England 1902–06*
Another London-built bike, but with a 1.5hp engine.

BORGHI *Italy 1951–63*
Utilized the bought-in Ducati 49cc (3cu in) Cucciolo and BSA's 123cc (7.5cu in) Bantam engines for its own lightweights.

BORGO *Italy 1906–26*
The Borgo brothers pioneered several aspects of motorcycle design, building on their first range of big ioe singles (the biggest of which was 827cc/50cu in). Used aluminium pistons in 1911 and a variable-ratio belt-drive three years later. The 1920 497cc (30cu in) V-twin was of unit-construction, with oil-in-frame.

BORHAM *England 1902–05*
Fitted Minerva 2 and 2.5hp engines.

BOSS HOSS *U.S.A. 1990–*
Americans, so they say, like everything Big with a capital 'B'. Buildings, motor cars, open spaces ... and motorcycles. So it's hardly surprising that the largest production motorcycle in the world should be built in the United States. For many years, Harley-Davidson produced the largest-engined bike until pipped to the post by successively bigger Japanese machines such as the Kawasaki Z1300, Honda Gold Wing 1500 and Yamaha 1600cc WildStar. None of them, however, come anywhere near the Boss Hoss.

The innovative Bond Villiers (1951) gave way to more conventional designs

In 1990, Monte Warne had the idea of building a motorcycle powered by a Chevrolet V8 engine. He did so, and there was so much interest in the bike at Daytona Speedweek that year, that he went into production. At the time of writing, a thousand of the two-wheeled monsters have been produced, so the Boss Hoss is far from being a one-off special. Its basis is the well-known 5.7-litre Chevrolet engine which more usually powers a large car or pick-up. Several different rates of tune are on offer, ranging from 180 to 350bhp. The Boss Hoss weighs half a tonne, but is still a lightweight by V8 standards, so it needs only one gear and the engine is so flexible that one can ride it, clutch out, from tickover upwards, and accelerate away at a flick of the wrist. There is no neutral, though the bike does have a foot pedal which locks the clutch in. Not suprisingly, when Boss Hoss decided to offer an automatic version, most buyers opted for that. Final-drive was by toothed belt to a huge 215-section car tyre at the rear, which looked as if it would be incapable of leaning around corners, though in practice it could.

Even in one-gear form, the makers claim 0–60mph in 1.7 seconds, though the Boss Hoss's top speed is limited by aerodynamics (and how strong the rider's arms are) to around 201km/h (125mph). The company later launched a 'small' 4.3-litre

The all-American Boss Hoss is the only V8 motorcycle in current production

V6 version, with 195bhp at 3,500rpm and 250lb ft of torque (or four times the torque of a big Harley-Davidson, to put that in perspective). It is said to average 10.6km per litre (30mpg) and give a range of over 322 kilometres (200 miles) from the 7.5-gallon fuel tank. Both V6 and V8 are even being exported to Europe in 1999, and the V6 costs around £20,000 in Britain, depending on options. Whether you consider the Boss Hoss to be a pointless excess or the ultimate motorcycle, it is certainly the biggest.

BOUCHET *France 1902–05*
Powered by acetylene rather than petrol.

BOUGÉRY *France 1896–1902*
A pioneer bike, the engine was mounted between the pedalling gear and the rear wheel.

BOUNDS-JAP *England 1909–12*
Utilized bought-in 345cc (21cu in) singles and 492cc (30cu in) V-twins from JAP.

BOVY *Belgium c.1914–32*
Albert Bovy's motorcycles were English-influenced but utilized a wide variety of engines, makes and sizes from 98cc (6cu in) to 996cc (61cu in), from such manufacturers as MAG, Aubier-Dunne, and Blackburne.

BOWDEN *England 1902–05*
Frank Bowden used both his own and FN's 2/2.5hp engines.

BOWN *England 1922–24*
Bought-in engines from 147cc/9cu inch (Villiers) to 348cc/21cu inch (Blackburne).

BOWN *England 1950–58*
Produced a rebadged Aberdale 98cc (6cu in) autocycle, later adding small Villiers-engined motorcycles and a 49cc (3cu in) Sachs-engined moped.

BPR *Switzerland 1929–32*
Buratti, Ponti and Roch (hence BPR) fitted 347cc (21cu in) and 497cc (30cu in) single-cylinder Moser and Motosacoche engines into their own frames.

BRAAK *Germany 1923–25*
Used 129cc (8cu in) and 198cc (12cu in) Heilo and Namapo engines/frames.

BRADBURY *England 1901–25*
Oldham-based, and better known for quality rather than radical design, it made singles and V-twins to 871cc (53cu in).

BRAND *Germany 1925–30*
Used licence-built Bekamo two-strokes of up to 173cc (11cu in).

BRAVIS *Germany 1924–26*
The Munich-based marque used Bosch-Douglas engines, from 148cc (9cu inch) two-strokes, to 293cc (18cu in) flat twins.

BREDA *Italy 1946–51*
Another autocycle maker with its own 65cc (4cu in) two-stroke.

BRÉE *Austria 1902–1904*
A 1.5hp single-cylinder two-stroke designed by Théodore Brée.

BRENNABOR *Germany 1902–40*
Used mid-sized Zedel and Fafnir, as well as its own engines until 1912, when it concentrated on cars and bicycles. Also produced motorized bicycles from 1933.

BREUIL *France 1903–08*
Used mainly Peugeot and Zurcher engines in its own frames.

BRIDGESTONE *Japan 1952–67*
Now synonymous with tyres, the company built clip-on engines from 1952, mopeds from 1958 and lightweight motorcycles from the early sixties. Best remembered for its well made disc-valved two-strokes of up to 348cc (21cu in), which were advanced and fast for their time, it never produced on the same scale as the big four Japanese manufacturers, and no doubt found tyres more profitable.

BRILANT-ALCYON *Czechoslovakia 1932*
Aspired to being a 'people's motorcycle', with a 98cc (6cu in) two-stroke. However, few were made.

BRILLIANT *France 1903–04*
Used Peugeot and Zurcher engines.

BRITAX *England 1954–56*
Produced mini-scooters using Ducati's 48cc (3cu in) Cucciolò engine, and later a 49cc racer, the Hurricane.

BRITISH-RADIAL *England 1920–22*
Utilized three-cylinder radial sv engines of 369cc (22.5cu in), designed by J.E. Manes, built by C.B. Redrup and fitted to a Chater-Lea frame – unorthodox to say the least.

BRITISH-STANDARD *England 1919–23*
Despite its short life, it used a wide range of bought-in engines ranging from 147 to 548cc (9 to 33cu in).

BRM *Italy 1955–57*
48cc (3cu in) two-stroke machines.

BROCKHOUSE *England 1948–55*
Manufacturer of the 98cc (6cu in) Corgi folding scooter, it later bought Indian and produced the 248cc (15cu in) Indian Brave, with its own sv unit-construction single.

BRONDOIT *Belgium 1924–29*
248cc and 348cc (15 and 21cu in) two-strokes with external flywheels, later made a MAG-engined 498cc (30cu in) sportster.

BROUGH *England 1908–26*
The less famous Brough, founded by George Brough's father. First made singles and V-twins, later flat twins only, both sv and ohv, up to 810cc (49cu in).

BROUGH-SUPERIOR *England 1919–40*
'The Rolls-Royce of Motorcycles': it was said that officials from the makers of the 'Best Car in the World' visited George Brough's factory to check that his motorcycles justified the claim, and came away duly impressed. George's father, William, was in the same business, producing his first car in 1899 and a motorcycle a few years later. Father and son went into partnership but decided to part when it became clear that George would never be able to achieve his aim of producing the ultimate motorcycle unless he struck off on his own, which he did.

A friend suggested that the new firm be named Brough-Superior to avoid confusion with the father's company, which met with approval. George was quite clear in his wish to produce a high-priced, low-volume luxury motorcycle, which was exactly what the first production Brough-Superior of 1921 was. Powered by a 986cc (60cu in) ohv JAP V-twin, it was certainly fast, one of the few big V-twins in Britain available without the encumbrance of a sidecar, and contemporary road tests praised the handling and 8–80mph performance in top gear. It also established a Brough tradition of using bought-in components that was to stay with the firm: in addition to the JAP engine, Sturmey-

The Brough-Superior SS80, named after its guaranteed top speed of 80mph (129km/h)

Archer supplied the gearbox, Brampton the forks and Enfield the cush hub. Matchless, MAG and Austin engines were to be used as well.

The Brough-Superiors were certainly handsome machines, using nickel plating in abundance to set off the gloss black, and came with evocative names like 'Alpine Grand Sports'. In fact, one is reminded of the success of William Lyons' early SS sports cars, which also used curvaceous styling and bought-in components as a route to success. The difference is that the SS (later to become Jaguars) were good value, but Broughs were always expensive, the first one costing £175. A sidevalve SS80 followed with a guaranteed 129km/h (80mph), while 1924 saw the SS100 with the very latest 50-degree ohv JAP V-twin. As the name suggested, this one was guaranteed to reach 100mph (161km/h). Amidst all the speed machines, there were a couple of attempts at cheaper Broughs, notably a 750cc (46cu in) sidevalve in 1927 (with an alleged fuel consumption of 28.3km per litre (80mpg) and a 500cc (30.5cu in) ohv V-twin a few years later.

In 1932 George Brough unveiled something very different from his previous offerings. Brough-Superiors, with their large, torquey V-twins, had long been favourites for sidecar attachment, and the

ABOVE: Nearly all Brough-Superiors were V-twins

BELOW: Fast, exclusive, expensive

SS80 sidevalve V-twin

bike was designed specifically for that purpose, with a four-cylinder sidevalve Austin Seven engine. There was shaft-drive and twin rear wheels, and the use of the Austin gearbox meant a reverse as well, which must have been useful with such a heavy outfit. Meanwhile, the V-twins, too big to do well in road racing, were excelling at outright speed records. Bert le Vack had taken the world speed record with one in 1924, at 181.9km/h (113mph). Five years later, he raised it to 207.6km/h (129mph), only to see the record taken by a BMW in 1934 (215.6km/h/134mph). However, Eric Fernihough retook the record for Brough in 1937, at a whisker under 274km/h (170mph), but was tragically killed the following year when trying to beat his own record. Noel Pope set all-time lap records at Brooklands on a Brough, both solo and with sidecar.

Famous riders there were in plenty and famous customers too, or one at least. T.E. Lawrence ('Lawrence of Arabia') rode Broughs for years and owned several, being a personal friend of George Brough. His account of riding one on the bumpy, traffic-free open roads of the 1920s is a classic of motorcycle literature. Sadly, this enigmatic figure also met his death on such a bike.

George Brough had no intention of resting on his V-twin laurels, and his vision for the future was exhibited at the Earls Court Motorcycle Show in 1938. The Brough-Superior Dream used a 997cc (61cu in) flat-four engine, with unit-construction gearbox and shaft-drive. It may have heralded the dawn of a new era for the company, but war intervened and no more Brough-Superiors were made after 1940. In the motorcycle industry, like every other, 'might have beens' just aren't good enough.

ABOVE and BELOW: Brough-Superior SS100 belonging to T.E. Lawrence (Lawrence of Arabia)

BROWN *England 1902–19*
Used 348cc (21cu in) single-cylinder and 498cc (30cu in) V-twin sv engines, and adopted the Vindec name from 1919. (No connection with the German Vindec.)

BROWN-BICAR *England (U.S.A.) 1907–13*
Unusual in that the 3hp single and 5hp V-twin engines were fully enclosed. Was also built in the U.S.A. under licence, but was not a success.

BRUNEAU *France 1903–10*
From 1905 utilized a 498cc (30cu in) unit, one of the first vertical twins ever made. Used Zedel engines before that.

B&S *Germany 1925–30*
Brand & Söhne of Berlin used Bekamo-type two-strokes up to 173cc (11cu in).

BSA *England 1905–73*
If Brough-Superior was the Rolls-Royce of motorcycles, then BSA was the Ford, though some might argue that in its later years it bore a greater resemblance to the tottering giant, British Leyland. In the early 1950s though, BSA was at the height of its Ford days. It could rightly claim to be the biggest in the business, building 75,000 bikes a year at its peak (nearly as many as NVT (Norton-Villiers-Triumph) made in its entire ten-year existence). 'One in Four is a BSA' went the advertising slogan, and it was right. Its products weren't exactly cutting-edge, but they were solid, reliable and good value for money. Nortons won races; coffee-bar cowboys rode Triumphs; Dad went to work on a BSA. BSAs were exported by the thousand

and were supplied to armies and police forces the world over. The Small Heath works alone covered over one million square metres and employed over 12,000 people.

But despite its strength, its fall from grace was rapid: by 1963, Honda was building more bikes than BSA (in fact, more than the entire British industry) and ten years after that, BSA was to all intents and purposes dead. Contrary to popular belief, it wasn't lack of investment that brought the company to its knees; BSA actually spent a great deal of money on R&D and computer-controlled production in the sixties. What it didn't have was decisive leadership, sufficient organization and the right product.

The clue to BSA's origins lies in its name. The Birmingham Small Arms company was a joint venture by a number of small Birmingham gunsmiths. They progressed to bicycles as a means of smoothing out the troughs and peaks of a fickle firearms market. Motorized bicycles were a natural progression and in 1905 the company began producing strengthened frames and fittings to accommodate a 2hp engine, usually a Belgian-made Minerva. It wasn't until 1910 that the company unveiled its own all-BSA motorcycle, a 498cc (30cu in) sidevalve single with the then standard single-speed belt-drive, though a two-speed rear hub was offered within a year, and a proper three-speed gearbox soon after. A longer-stroke 557cc (34cu in) version appeared in 1913 (and was to remain in production for 20 years), with fully enclosed chain-drive. Although BSA continued to sell these bikes during World War I, and supplied some of them to the army, it returned to its roots in armaments for the duration.

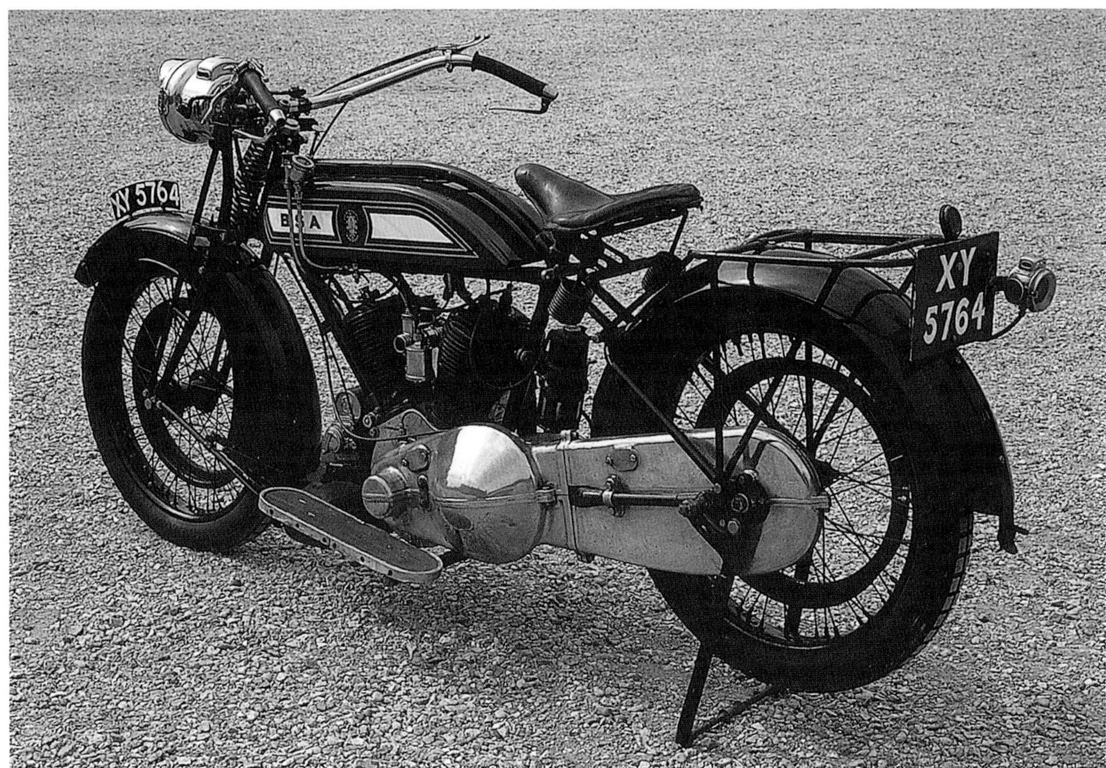

Not usually known for big bikes BSA, however, offered large V-twins up to 1940. This one dates from 1919

One project interrupted by the war was BSA's V-twin, which eventually surfaced in 1920. Intended mainly for sidecar work, it was a 770cc (47cu in) sidevalve with the cylinders at 50 degrees. The twin was designed for stamina rather than speed (it was all-out at 89km/h/55mph), which it certainly had, and was the first in a line of V-twins which were offered by BSA right up to 1940. There was soon an even larger alternative, the 986cc (60cu in) Model G, which produced 25bhp at 3,800rpm and goodness knows how much torque. It also proved its worth in 1926 when journalist John Castley and BSA salesman Bertram Cathrick set off on a two-year ride around the world mounted on heavy-duty 'Colonial' models (Empire-inspired terminology was common at the time, usually denoting higher ground clearance and sturdier suspension for uneven colonial roads). Twenty-three thousand miles later,

ABOVE and ABOVE RIGHT: 1932 986cc (60cu in) V-twin

they were back in Small Heath. In the early 1930s, BSA announced a different sort of V-twin, a revvier 500cc (30.5cu in) ohv unit, with a high-mounted camshaft to keep the pushrods short and stiff. Capable of 129km/h (80mph), and lighter than some equivalent singles, it was not a good seller and was dropped after three years, though a 748cc (46cu in) version followed.

Cheaper than Shoe Leather

Beloved though the V-twins were by some, it was the single-cylinder lightweights that were BSA's mainstay. The year 1924 saw two very different singles launched: the model L Sports was something new for BSA, a revvy sportster that could top 121km/h (75mph) with the optional 6.5:1 piston. The 'Roundtank', on the other hand, was in much more familiar BSA territory. So nicknamed because of its cylindrical fuel tank, the bike was a bargain basement sidevalve 250, which actually sold new for less than £40 in two-speed form. Despite the basic mechanics, it was good to ride and very popular; BSA sold 35,000 of them within four years, by which time the gearbox had three speeds and there were drum brakes at both ends. The Depression threatened to hit sales, so BSA responded with a pared-to-the-bone version which abandoned its sophisticated wet-sump lubrication (which had appeared in 1927) for the old gravity-fed system. Ready for the road, it cost £33 15s – shoe leather didn't come much cheaper than this.

It was its appearance that attracted many people to the Roundtank, and the

BELOW LEFT: Empire Star
BELOW: High-level exhaust, a period touch

same was true of the Sloper. With its 493cc (30cu in) ohv cylinder angled forward in the frame, the Sloper had a rakish look about it that was in tune with the times (announced August 1926). It was absolutely up-to-the-minute, with wet sump, saddle tank and a 90-degree valve angle. The Sloper wasn't particularly fast (it could top 105km/h/65mph) but it was quiet as well as good-looking, and one could always opt for a higher compression piston and racier cams. It was a real hit with the public, spawning 349 595cc sidevalve and two-port versions; some say that 80,000 were sold over the years.

No one could accuse BSA of resting on its laurels at this time. Despite the Sloper's success, it soon came up with an upright-

1939 350cc (21cu in) sidevalve

A 1949 B31 350

cylindered replacement, the W-series Blue Star. It wasn't as handsome as the Sloper but, with less weight over the front wheel, handled rather better. It soon gained a four-speed foot gearchange and, as ever, a handful of tuning parts were available, factory-fitted, to turn it into more of a sportster. Herbert Perkins and David Munro designed ohv and sidevalve versions, and within a few years the Blue Star was on sale in 250, 350 and 500 sizes. In latter ohv guise it produced a respectable 28bhp, enough for 129km/h (80mph). From 1936, there were also the Empire Stars (in honour of King George V's Silver Jubilee), basically twin-port versions of the 350 and 500, though the latter also had a different bore and stroke to the standard Blue Star, just to keep the partsmen on their toes.

As if that were not complicated enough, for 1935/36 BSA offered yet another single, the upmarket De-luxe. The idea was for a fully-equipped luxury bike with all extras included in the price. As well as full lighting and four-speed gearbox, the De-luxe single was advanced, with dry-sump lubrication (a preview of the post-war system) and high camshaft. Unfortunately, few buyers were convinced, and the De-luxe single didn't sell that well.

Its replacement was more of a success, certainly longer-lived. Val Page, one of the best known names in the inter-war industry, designed the M-series singles for BSA in 1936, and although they are most closely associated with the sidevalve sloggers that lasted right up until 1963, the M bikes started out as a complete range of five. The sole 350 was the M19 ohv and there were two ohv 500s, the M22 and M23 (which took up the Empire Star name). Sidevalve enthusiasts were served by the 500cc M20 and 600cc (37cu in) M21. All had dry-sump lubrication, the same very strong bottom-end, were very well made and endeared themselves to a generation of riders; they were also the first bikes to bear the Gold Star name. The latter came about when Walter Handley lapped Brooklands at over 164km/h (102mph) on a tuned Empire Star, winning the coveted lapel badge for covering the banked circuit at over 100mph – a gold star. There is nothing new about race replicas; Wal won his star in June 1937, and for the '38 season, BSA announced a tuned alloy-engined version of the Empire Star, the M24 (you've guessed it) Gold Star. In standard form, it could broach 145km/h (90mph), with optional 12:1 compression and running on dope, it was a genuine 100mph machine.

In fact, it was hard to believe that the M20/21 sidevalve sloggers came from the same family; with about 13bhp, but big, beefy flywheels, the workhorse BSA would, if not mount the side of a house, then at least pull unfeasibly large loads, whether it be a double-adult sidecar with wife, kids and luggage on board, or a massive tradesman's box. A pair of them won the Maudes Trophy for BSA (its second) in 1938. First they rode into Snowdonia for 20 climbs of Bwlch-Y-Groes; then down to Brooklands for 100

ABOVE and BELOW: A 1940 M20 of 496cc (30cu in) of which many thousands were built

OPPOSITE PAGE: Details from 1963 BSA sales brochures

laps of the banked circuit (average, 74km/h/46mph); then back up to Bwlch for another 20 pass storms; then (it wasn't over yet) back through London in the rush hour, with the gearboxes locked in top! BSA deserved its Maudes Trophy.

Although BSA was never much associated with the sporting side of things, it actually won more trophies than any other British factory. It even won first time out when Ken Holden rode a virtually standard 3½hp bike at Brooklands in 1913. Disappointing attempts at the TT led BSA to concentrate on trials and endurance events between the wars, and a whole string of successes followed in both domestic trials and the International Six Days. As well as Harry Perrey, riders like Bert Perrigo, Fred Rist, Majorie Cottle and Harold Tozer, to name but a few, helped bring BSA to pre-eminence in pre-war off-road competition.

All this had to be forgotten when war once again loomed over Europe. This time, BSA kept on mass-producing bikes, and supplied 126,000 M20s for the Allied effort. Despite limited ground clearance, the M20 was actually ideal for the thick of battle, being strong, reliable and easy to repair. Like Harley-Davidson's WLA, World War II gave BSA's own sidevalve slogger its moment of glory. Maybe it was all those ex-servicemen in the 1950s, with wartime memories and young families to transport, that kept the M20 in production for so long! BSA didn't have an easy war though – the Small Heath plant was easy to spot from the air and was devastated by Luftwaffe bombers, forcing the company to split production into what were known as dispersal factories, miles away from the Midlands blitz.

Singles & Tiddlers

In 1945, it was the M20 that led BSA back into civilian production, but it was soon followed by two more families of pre-war singles. The C-series 250cc (15cu in) singles were basic transportation; the 8bhp sidevalve could manage over 31.9km per litre (90mpg) while the flightier C11 would touch 97km/h (60mph). They were soon updated with telescopic forks in 1946, though riders had to wait another five years for an optional plunger rear-end, alternator electrics, four-speed gearbox and (finally) a swinging-arm frame. They were replaced by the C15 unit-construction 250 in 1958.

Another step up brought the 350cc (21cu in) B31 and B32. Val Page must have spent a busy couple of years at BSA, as his B-series singles were announced in the same year as the M family. Sold in 250 and 350 forms up to 1939, only the bigger version survived the war, with the 499cc (30cu in) B33 and B34 joining up in 1947. All were ohv, and took BSA's middleweight singles range right though the fifties. There were the updates you would expect – telescopic forks and plunger, then swinging-arm rear suspension; but really these were simple, solid singles in the BSA tradition. Mind you, each came in more sporting form, and the B31/32 had higher-level exhaust, more ground clearance and (later) alloy head and barrels.

These were really stepping stones to the full-house Gold Star, and were aimed at trials where the Gold Star dominated the circuits. In fact, the post-war Gold Star was to provide the consistent road racing success that had eluded BSA until then. The Goldie was certainly fast, but it was also affordable, and adaptable to a whole range of different events. The Clubmans TT in particular (designed for amateur riders on production bikes) became a virtual Gold Star benefit for a while. Although the Gold Star could be awkward to ride in traffic (it was, after all, built for speed), many enthusiasts did use them as everyday transport during the week, removing the lights at weekends to go racing. The DBD34 500 (though there were always 350s as well) of 1956 was perhaps the ultimate, the result of years of fine tuning and development with 42bhp, close-ratio gearbox and over 177km/h (110mph).

The Gold Star might have been BSA's most glamorous post-war bike, but there was another name from the other end of the scale just as famous – the Bantam. This too was a pre-war design, but not by BSA. The Bantam was really a DKW, the design having been offered to BSA as part of war reparations. (This applied to others among the Allies, which is why the Americans and the Russians also built suspiciously DKW-like lightweights after the war.) It couldn't have been simpler: a 125cc (8cu in) two-stroke with three-speed gearbox, housed in a rigid frame, though with the addition of telescopic forks. It may have only produced 4bhp, but the Bantam was reliable, and could in any case push its rider up to 76km/h (47mph) – quite sufficient for getting to work. So successful was it that BSA hardly changed the original layout (apart from capacity increases) throughout the Bantam's long life; the final D175 of 1969–71 boasted three times the power of the first Bantam, and a top speed of 105km/h (65mph), but it wasn't enough to frighten the Japanese opposition. When the Bantam was killed off (by a short-sighted management which ordered that all the jigs and tools be destroyed) half a million had been sold.

In fact, the Bantam was probably BSA's most successful post-war bike: but despite this, and the company's strong roots in building no-nonsense transport for non-enthusiasts, every other small bike it made after the war (with the possible exception of the unit-construction 250 single) was a failure in one way or another. The Winged Wheel, for example, actually looked clean and elegant, built into the rear wheel of the average bicycle (no aftermarket bolt-on this, but a designed-in package, which BSA either sold as a complete rear wheel to fit one's own or one of BSA's own cycles). Sadly, it didn't go on sale until 1953 when the autocycle boom was well past its peak. The design was sold to Raleigh. Next up (1956) was the 70cc (4cu in) Dandy, a sort of sub-scooter, but with bigger 15-inch wheels, clever two-speed pre-selector gearbox and four-stroke engine. In other

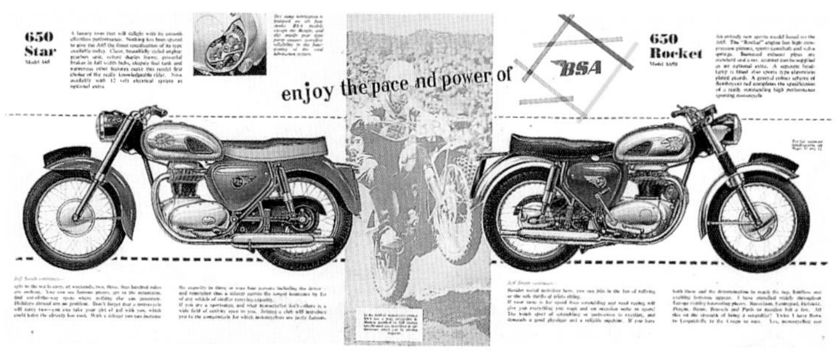

ABOVE and BELOW: The A10 Golden Flash was a well-mannered workhorse

ABOVE: An early Bantam in off-road guise

BELOW: Gold Star proved well adapted to all kinds of competition

words, a potential forerunner of the Honda stepthru. But to save money, someone specified a cast-iron barrel (designer Bert Hopwood, who had since left, wanted cooler-running alloy), so the Dandy overheated and seized on a regular basis. Two years on, and the BSA Sunbeam hit the streets: this was intended to meet Vespa and Lambretta head-on, and certainly looked the part. It was faster than the imports too, with a 175cc (11cu in) two-stroke or 250 four-stroke, not to mention many useful options including electric start. But here again, BSA missed the boat, the scooter boom being past its best by 1958, and of those buyers left, few wanted something as heavy and elaborate as a 250cc scooter, however fast it was. The Sunbeam (and the identical Triumph Tigress) were axed in 1964. A year earlier, BSA had tried again with the 50cc (3cu in) Pixie and 75cc (4.6cu in) Beagle, both four-strokes with pressed steel frames and impressive economy. But there were fundamental shortcomings in the Triumph Terrier-derived engines, all of which (plus the Sunbeam) were Edward Turner designs. There were few takers for either Pixie or Beagle – quite apart from the names, Honda's stepthru was now on sale.

Into the Mainstream

The story of BSA's early post-war twins makes for much happier reading. Like most British manufacturers, BSA had been shocked into action by the runaway success of Triumph's Speed Twin of 1937, and actually had an ohc prototype aimed at the 1940 season. War prevented it, of course, and when the new Val Page/Herbert Perkins A7 was announced in 1946, it was with an ohv twin with single camshaft and carburettor. By all accounts it was a willing, well-balanced bike, with its 26bhp enough for 137km/h (85mph) or so. There was also (from 1949) a twin carburettor Star Twin with 31bhp, though this added little to performance and served to dissipate some of the twin's sweetness.

Meanwhile, overseas dealers (particularly in the U.S.) and sidecar owners wanted more torque, which naturally meant a bigger engine. This was Bert Hopwood's first job at BSA, and his 646cc (39cu in) A10 was just the thing. Designed, built and prototyped in a very short space of time (three riders put 20,600km/12,800 miles on it in three weeks) the A10 was remarkably trouble-free. It was more than just an enlarged A7, as Hopwood splayed out the exhaust ports to improve cooling, specified a bigger, stronger crankshaft and an oil trough to give consistent lubrication to the camshaft. Even in its original mildly tuned Golden Flash form, the A10 gave an easy 35bhp at 5,500rpm; it could break the 100mph barrier, was economical, relaxed, and well within its limits. Soon after, a revised A7 was unveiled to incorporate the Hopwood A10 improvements.

A swinging-arm frame came to both bikes in 1954, and a beefier bottom-end for the A10 in 1958. The latter was just as well, as with the motorcycle market ever more performance-orientated, the pressure was on to squeeze out ever more power. The higher compression Road Rocket A10 (1955–57) produced 40bhp at 6,000rpm; the Super Rocket (1958–63) squeezed another 2bhp; finally, the Rocket Gold Star, which used Gold Star cycle parts and a super-tuned 9:1 compression version of the twin, managed 46bhp at 6,250rpm. The RGS, as it was known, was a real twin-cylinder alternative to the Gold Star, a child of the ton-up culture, but was only offered for the last two years of A10 production. Meanwhile, Lucas announced it was to stop making dynamos and K2F magnetos, which in turn meant the end of the A7/A10 in favour of the alternator-equipped A50/A65. Perhaps it was a reflection on BSA itself that it wasn't impending obsolescence that forced it to update its twin, but because Lucas had stopped making magnetos.

However, the company's other success story of the post-war era was well-entrenched in production. It was the 250cc (15cu in) C15, the replacement for the old pre-war C11/C12. Introduced in 1958, the C15 had immediate appeal. It was perky and free-revving (the 67mm x 70mm dimensions allowed an easy 7,000rpm) and light enough (127kg/280lb) to allow its

ABOVE: 1971 U.S.-specification Rocket Three

BELOW: Three cylinders, 58bhp

ABOVE: Superb shot of John Bank on a 500cc (30.5 cu in) scrambler

15bhp to have a reasonable effect, achieving 126km/h/78mph and 32km per litre/90mpg. It was well priced, too. Best of all, its unit-construction gave it a sleek, neat look quite different from that of the old pre-unit 250s. The C15 looked like a modern big bike in miniature.

A 343cc (21cu in) version, the B40, followed to replace the long-running B31, and with its stronger bottom-end was to become one of the most bullet-proof post-war singles. There were sports versions too, the Sports Star 80 and 90 (the numbers referred to top speed). But the 250 was always the better seller, particularly as Britain's new learner law restricted novices to a 250. However, BSA's small singles were under the same performance pressure as the big twins, and the C15 was replaced by the much more highly tuned C25 Barracuda in 1967, which claimed to be 'Britain's fastest production two-fifty'. Too fast, apparently, for the big-ends, and much the same was true for the B25 Starfire which replaced it the following year; 25bhp sounded a lot for an old-style 250, and it was just too much, made apparent by oil leaks and vibration. A 441cc (27cu in) version, the Shooting Star, was unveiled the following year, though offered little more performance than the 250.

In some ways, the A50 and A65 unit-construction twins were a sensible update on the A7/A10: alternator, coil ignition (plus 12-volt electrics from 1966), neater unit-construction, shorter wheelbase, lower weight. The new engines, though based on the general layout of the old ones, were freer-breathing, with more space for big valves and potential for tuning. However,

BELOW: DBD 34 Gold Star

BELOW: Small fuel tank and high bars indicated a U.S. specification

OPPOSITE: A 1971 BSA Rocket 3 of 750cc (46cu in)

BSA
ROCKET THREE

perhaps this was the very problem. The first A50 Star and A65 Thunderbolt were mildly tuned and docile, but as the decade progressed, so was there a familiar story of ever more highly-tuned versions, with an ever more highly-stressed bottom-end. It culminated in 1966 with the Spitfire. Twin Amal GP carburettors, 10.5:1 compression and 55bhp at 7,000rpm (a 45 per cent increase on the Thunderbolt) meant a claimed top speed of 193km/h (120mph). Ruined big-ends and fearsome vibration were even more likely.

The year after brought the bike that, had it been launched earlier, could have made all this over-tuning unnecessary. The Rocket Three was BSA's version of the three-cylinder 740cc (45cu in) Triumph Trident, and was identical to it apart from badging, different timing cover and tilted-forward cylinders. It was one of the first superbikes, with plenty of power (58bhp at 7,250rpm) and more performance in a road bike than anyone had seen before. It was heavy but very fast, and made a huge impact. Ironically, Bert Hopwood and Doug Hele had started work on their triple back in 1963, so it could have been launched three or four years earlier than it actually was. But with the faster, better-equipped Honda CB750 as a rival, it didn't stand much of a chance.

Last Stand

While all this was going on, BSA was approaching the slippery slope: profits were falling year on year as quality-control worsened and warranty costs increased. The Japanese, having coaxed America back to motorcycling, were now launching big bikes of their own, far in advance of

The unit-construction A65 was the final BSA big twin

anything produced by Small Heath. It was against this background, with company finances in a perilous state, that an ambitious, last-ditch attempt was made to relaunch the entire range for 1971. Virtually every BSA was changed in some way and central to the whole idea was a new oil-bearing frame for the twins, triples and B50 single. There was new styling across the board, and even indicators were fitted.

The Starfire 250 became the 250SS, with street scrambler styling, and the bigger single was enlarged again into the 499cc (30cu in) B50. Both were named 'Gold Stars' which must have seemed like heresy to veterans of the thirties and fifties. Neither lasted long, though the B50 actually enjoyed a brief success at endurance racing when run by Mead and Tomkinson. And even when BSA collapsed, the big singles didn't. Alan Clews bought up the remaining B50 parts stock and built them into CCM scramblers for the rest of the 1970s. But for the rest of the range, this was its last gasp; the new frame handled well, but was a good two inches too tall. In any case, it still housed the same old over-stressed twins and too-late triple. BSA/Triumph had spent valuable funds designing a new frame that it didn't really need, when the priority was a new engine. There was one new engine at the 1971 launch, the BSA Fury, with its dohc 350cc (21cu in) twin. It had been under development for some time, and several prototypes were running.

But it was not to be: BSA finances had reached the point where production of the new 350 was impossible. The company staggered on for another two years, though there were signs of a modest recovery, with Lord Shawcross replacing Lionel Jofeh at the head of the company. Indeed, Bert Hopwood (now head of engineering) had plans well in hand for an all-new up-to-date modular range of bikes from a 200cc (12cu in) single upwards. What they didn't have was the money to build them. The government of the day agreed to support what was left of the British motorcycle industry, but only if BSA/Triumph merged with the apparently successful Norton-Villiers under Dennis Poore. When that happened in 1973, it was effectively the end of BSA, though Small Heath went on building Triumph Tridents for another two years.

NVT itself rapidly downsized to what was virtually a cottage industry compared to the old days, though it did bring back the BSA name in the late 1970s. A canny mixture of Japanese and Italian components produced the BSA Brigand and Beaver mopeds, and the good-looking Tracker 125 and 175 trail bikes. The hope was that these would eventually finance a return to in-house design. They didn't. Ford, if the analogy can be stretched that far, had closed.

BSA *India c.1980–89*
The BSA name was used under licence for a range of Morini-engined sports mopeds. Later taken over by the Brooke Bond tea company, bikes then sold as Bonds.

BUBI *Germany 1921–24*
Short-lived motorized bicycle of 1.5hp.

BUCHER *Italy 1911–20*
Designed its own ohv singles and V-twins of 342cc to 568cc (21 to 35cu in).

BUCHET *France 1900–11*
Most notable for a 4.5-litre-engined machine for pacing cycle races.

BÜCKER *Germany 1922–58*
Always used bought-in engines, which over the years included units from Cockerell, Rinne, Columbus, MAG, JAP, Blackburne, Bark, Ilo and Sachs, ranging from 98cc to 996cc (6 to 61cu in).

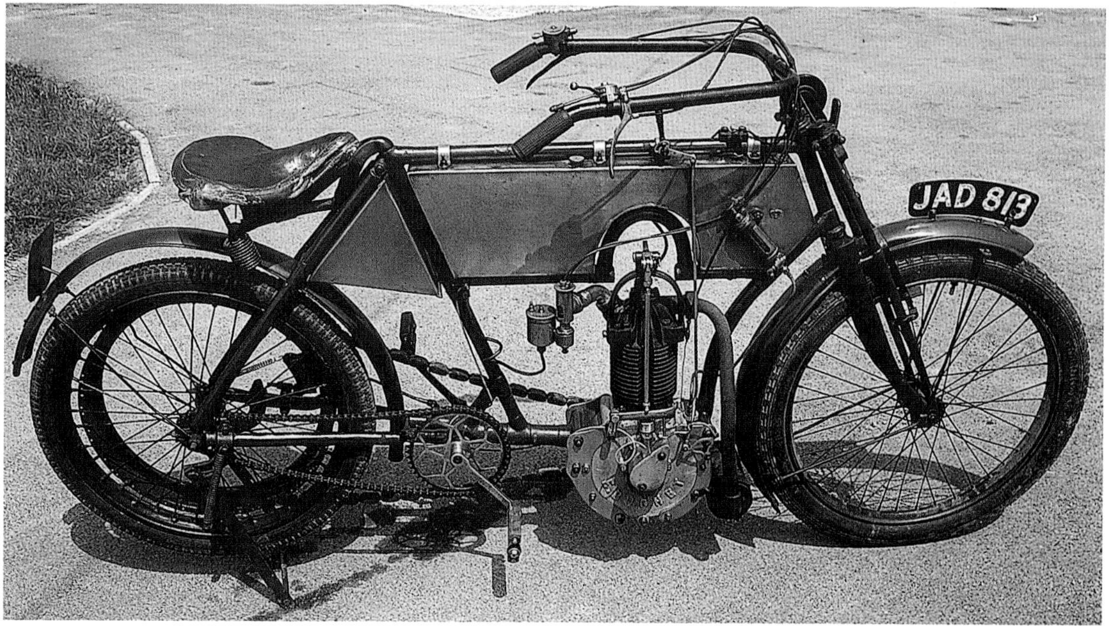

The 1903 420cc (25.6cu in) Buchet, one of its less fearsome offerings

BUELL *U.S.A. 1987–*
When Erik Buell left school, he was more interested in playing bass in a rock band than designing motorcycles. His day job was that of a bike mechanic, working in various shops around Pittsburgh, but the dream was to become a professional musician and Harley-Davidson is probably glad that he never did.

Instead of pursuing his dream, Buell enrolled at night school for an engineering degree, duly graduated, and landed a job with Harley-Davidson as a test engineer. At the time, though, he didn't own a Harley, preferring big Japanese two-strokes such as the Kawasaki triples and the Suzuki GT750. He later recalled that one of his jobs was to record how much oil contemporary Harleys were using; he reckoned it was more than the two-stroke Suzuki!

At 22 he began racing, after a serious off-road tumble, and discovered he had a talent for riding as well as engineering. Third in his first race, he was often in the top ten at national level despite being an unsponsored privateer. Good rider though he was, it was in chassis design that Erik Buell was to make his mark. Buell decided to build his own racer and chose as a basis the Barton Phoenix, a two-stroke square-four 750 built in Britain by Barry Hart. It was far more powerful than the equivalent Yamaha TZ750s, but needed a stronger chassis, which Buell designed and built.

The Buell RW750 was the result, and though Erik won some minor races on it, he decided to sell it to the American Machinists Union which continued to race it. In 1983 he also left Harley-Davidson to set up on his own to build the RW750. It was a brave decision, but soon seemed like the wrong one when the American Motorcycle Association (the sport's governing body) announced that Formula One was being replaced by World Superbike, which effectively made the RW750 obsolete overnight.

Then something occurred which changed the course of Buell's life. One of his ex-colleagues at Harley asked him to quickly put together a sort of American sportsbike for the future, for a dealer conference. The result owed much to the RW750: the RR1000 paid even more attention to aerodynamics, and used Erik's patented Uniplanar chassis design which all Buells use to this day. The latter uses the V-twin engine as an integral, stressed member of the chassis. That's nothing new now, but it was novel in the mid-eighties, especially when applied to a Harley engine. What makes the Buell version different is that it virtually eliminates vibration by suspending the engine from three rubber mounts, while four adjustable rods allow it to move in the vertical plane, but not laterally, thus taming the vibration while maintaining rear-wheel alignment and the chassis' integrity. Another Buell trademark – the underslung rear damper which works in tension rather than compression – was also a feature, and again is still used on modern Buells.

As for aerodynamics, the RR1000 was completely enveloped (even the front wheel was faired in) by rounded bodywork and looked more like a tennis ball on wheels than a motorcycle, let alone a Harley. Still, despite (or maybe because of) the looks and a high price, there was no lack of buyers for the bike, and 50 were made in 1987 and '88 until the supply of XR1000 engines dried up.

ABOVE: Sports touring Thunderbolt

OPPOSITE: Back-to-basics Lightning

There was obviously a market here for a sporting Harley-Davidson which had remained untapped. By this time, Harley's own Sportster had long since been overtaken in the performance race, but the Buell promised to close the gap once again, particularly in handling. Once again, Erik's factory contacts came good, securing him a supply of 1200cc (73cu in) Sportster engines to power a new generation of bikes. The RR1200 looked much the same as the 1000, but a more significant change was the RS1200, with most of the bulbous bodywork removed (save for a half-fairing); the RS marked Buell's move towards pure road bikes and away from its racing roots. There was even a dual seat, with an odd-looking hinge-up rear backrest. The otherwise similar RSS had a permanent solo seat and an oil cooler. There was no skimping on components, with WP forks and rear damper, plus Performance Machine six-piston front-brake caliper. Of course, it wasn't anything like as fast as a Japanese sportsbike (the Sportster engine had to be kept standard to meet EPA regulations) but it did provide a unique form of motorcycling; this was before the Japanese woke up to the attractions of V-twin sportsters, and began to build their own.

Sales grew, and Buell's success had not gone unnoticed by Harley-Davidson, which by this time had made a full recovery from the precipitous state in which it had found itself when

Buell

Erik Buell had left. Harley needed to broaden its market (specifically into sports and sports-touring bikes) and realized that through Buell it could do it. In 1993, it bought a 49 per cent stake (which left Erik in control) which allowed the move to a bigger factory at East Troy, an increase in production and cut prices. From building 100 machines a year, Buell was soon selling 800. The S2 Thunderbolt was unveiled the following year, with the same Buell chassis (tweaked here and there) and a 1200cc Sportster engine, but with all-new, more naked styling. Production was now high enough to justify tuning the V-twin, and the Thunderbolt had a 20 per cent power increase, thanks to better breathing. However, all Buells still suffered from the massive air cleaner box on the right-hand side of the engine, which did nothing for its looks.

The year 1995 saw the advent of the S1 Lightning, whose cut-down styling was its *raison d'être*. Mechanically identical to the Thunderbolt, the solo-seat Lightning typified the street fighter styling which was becoming popular, a reaction to fully-faired sportsbikes. The following year came a sports-touring version of the Thunderbolt, though the 'tourer' part was purely down to the addition of panniers and legshields. With the best will in the world the Thunderbolt, even with panniers, was still at heart a raw, gutsy sportster, without the sophistication and attention to detail of the Japanese and European tourers. There was also a cheaper Buell, the Cyclone, that year, cheaper mainly due to conventional Showa forks in place of the WP inverted type fitted to the rest of the range. Something else was making Buells cheaper though; the factory made 1,914 bikes in 1996, but over 4,000 the following year, when British customers enjoyed price cuts of £500 or more.

The S1 White Lightning was launched in late 1997, with 93bhp due to new cylinder heads, camshaft and flywheels. The year after, over 6,000 bikes were built and the fuel-injected X1 was announced, though it was still based on the Buell chassis and the Sportster V-twin. But perhaps the most exciting news was that Harley-Davidson had made the logical step and taken over Buell altogether, and Erik remained as chairman and chief technical officer. As the sporting arm of Harley-Davidson, Buell's future looks secure, and its founder is probably quite glad he took that engineering degree.

BULLDOG *England 1920*

Small assembler of orthodox lightweights, using bought-in engines from either Villiers or Coventry-Victor.

BULLO *Germany 1924–26*

Electric-powered motorcycle using a 0.7hp motor and 120-Ah battery. Not very many were made.

BÜLOW *Germany 1923–25*

Used own two-stroke engines of 2–3hp.

BULTACO *Spain 1958–83*

Francesco Bulto set up Bultaco after leaving Montesa. The company began with 124cc (8cu in) road and racing bikes, and the Sherpa trials bike in 1964, which won the World Trials Championship five times in the seventies. There were also Grand Prix successes in the late seventies, while road machines continued to sell on the home market. Closure was due to market decline.

Early Buell RS1200

The expert Sammy Miller on a Bultaco in 1965

Sales brochure for the Bultaco 350/250

BURFORD *England 1914–15*

Used 269cc (16cu in) Villiers and 496cc (30cu in) sv engines.

BURGERS-ENR *The Netherlands 1897–1961*

A reversal of the usual pattern; the company started with its own engines and went over to bought-in units, including Blackburne, JAP and Vitesse.

BURKHARDTIA *Germany 1904–08*

Pioneer two-stroke, with 165cc (10cu in) single and 244cc (15cu in) vertical twin made by Grade.

Bultacos represented state-of-the-art trials machines, but the company also built road bikes

BURNEY *England 1923–25*
Designed by Cecil Burney after leaving Blackburne, they were mostly 497cc (30cu in) singles, but there were also a few 679cc (41cu in) V-twins.

BUSI *Italy 1950–53*
A wide range of sporty two-strokes of 123 to 198cc (7.5 to 12cu in).

BUSSE *Germany 1922–26*
Utilized a whole range of bought-in engines, all under 200cc (12cu in), as well as its own power units.

BUYDENS *Belgium 1950–55*
Used Ydral and Sachs engines of 123cc to 248cc (7.5 to 15cu in).

BV *Czechoslovakia 1923–30*
Own engines, including 173cc (11cu in) two-strokes, 346/496cc (21/30cu in) singles and a 746cc (45.5cu in) sv V-twin.

C

CABTON *Japan 1954–61*
English-influenced bikes, from 123cc (7.5cu in) two-strokes to 648cc (39.5cu in) vertical twins, which proved unable to compete with the rapidly growing Big Four Japanese manufacturers.

CAESAR *England 1922–23*
Used a 269cc (16cu in) Villiers two-stroke.

CAGIVA *Italy 1978–*
Cagiva grew out of the ashes of the Aermacchi company when it was sold by former owner Harley-Davidson in 1978. Claudio and Gianfranco Castiglioni were businessmen with no previous background in motorcycles and their names were to become inextricably linked with the ups and downs of the Italian motorcycle industry over the next 20 years.

Like that other latecomer to the Italian industry, Aprilia, the Castiglioni started off making small two-strokes (mainly up to 125) for the home market, and evidently made a greater success of Varese than Harley ever did, with 40,000 bikes a year being built by the early 1980s. However, the brothers realized that to ensure long-term growth and stability they would need to sell bigger machines as well, and the quickest way to do this was to buy engines in from outside, a strategy that Aprilia was later to use to good effect.

Ducati was the obvious choice, with production at a low ebb and a desperate need to find another outlet for its V-twin engines. Cagiva signed a deal with Ducati's then-owners, the VM Group, to supply 6,000 engines for 1984, 10,000 for '85 and 14,000 in subsequent years. Production of Ducati-badged bikes would actually cease by the end of the first year. It didn't work out like that, of course, as Cagiva actually bought Ducati in 1985, realizing that the name itself was a sales asset (perhaps more so than Cagiva, which was still virtually unknown outside Italy). In fact, as Cagiva grew, it acquired other famous names: MV Agusta, Moto Morini, Husqvarna and CZ were all to come under Castiglioni control.

However, the planned range of Ducati-powered Cagivas got off to a slow start with the half-faired Alazzura, which failed to make much of an impact. Longer-lasting, and certainly more successful, was the dual-purpose Elefant 900. With its long-travel suspension and off-road styling the Elefant followed BMW's GS in pioneering a new class of 'adventure tourers' – large-engined bikes with some nominal off-road capability. Cagiva's version (it was also sold as a Ducati in the U.S.) used a detuned version of Ducati's 900SS air-cooled V-twin, producing 68bhp. It had monoshock rear suspension and plenty of ground clearance, and if you were tall enough (the seat was of stepladder height) could conceivably be taken down the odd rocky track; but really, the road-going Elefant was too big and heavy for serious off-road riding. Despite which, it sold quite well (aided by success in the 1984 Paris–Dakar race) and a 750cc (46cu in) version followed. The Elefant, named after Cagiva's elephant logo, remained in production right up to 1998.

Meanwhile, Cagiva wasn't neglecting its little bikes, the most notable of which was the 125cc (8cu in) Mito, launched in 1990. The Mito was the first mini-race replica, styled by Massimo Tamburini as a

BELOW: 125cc (8cu in) Roadster

BELOW: Low Rider

ABOVE: AR trail bikes near completion

road-going lookalike of Randy Mamola's 500cc (30.5cu in) Grand Prix racer. Technically, there was nothing particularly new about the Mito, with its 125cc (8cu in) reed-valved two-stroke engine and aluminium frame. What sold it were the authentic GP looks, not to mention a lower price than the equivalent Aprilia. It was also very fast; tuned to around 30bhp, it could push the lightweight Mito up to

172km/h (107mph). And it also had a seven-speed gearbox, which no doubt clenched the decision to buy for plenty of road-bound budding Mamolas. The Mito was later restyled to look like a miniature Ducati 916, ensuring its continued popularity.

Cagiva's mid-range bikes were less dramatic, a line based on the W16 trail bike, which appeared in 1988 with the company's own air-cooled four-valve single of 601cc (37cu in), the T4. There was an attempt to break into the commuter market with the River 600, a slim, sober, clean-looking bike designed for ride-to-work duties. A comfortable riding position and small panniers underlined the intention, but here again Cagiva seemed to have missed the mark. Much more of an eyeful was the Canyon of 1995, with the increasingly popular supermoto styling, a distinctive twin-headlamp front-end and trail bike-like riding position. Once again, power came from the T4 single. It was evidently more successful than the River, as Cagiva unveiled a scaled-up version using the 900cc (55cu in) Ducati engine – its name? *Gran* Canyon of course!

But all was not going smoothly at

ABOVE: Ducati-powered Gran Canyon
BELOW: Elefant opened up a whole new market

Ducati-powered trail bike

The Alazzura was also Ducati-engined

Alettas awaiting despatch

Cagiva. The company had overreached itself in the mid-1990s, and money was running short, forcing a pull-out from Grand Prix racing in 1995. But it had been a glorious era; Cagiva was the only European company to meet and beat the Japanese in 500cc GPs. The following year Claudio Castiglioni found a way out. He sold 49 per cent of Ducati (which was hived off as a separate company) to TPG, an American investment group, thus giving Cagiva the funds to pay off its debts and concentrate on new models. In 1998, TPG bought the remainder of Ducati, which further strengthened Cagiva's finances. In fact, it gave the company a new lease of life: the MV Agusta-badged four-cylinder bikes could finally go ahead, as could the much-delayed Cucciolo scooter. The latter was to have been built by CZ until Cagiva pulled out of the Czech Republic in 1997; the production Cucciolo used a Derbi engine instead. Meanwhile, a new factory at Cassinetta looked set to underpin Cagiva's expansion plans. It hadn't taken so long for the name 'Cagiva', to become very well known indeed.

CALCOTT *England 1910–15*
Used its own 249/292cc (15/18cu in) singles as well as White & Poppe engines.

CALTHORPE *England 1909–38*
Birmingham-based, the company used various bought-in engines before producing its own 348cc (21cu in) ohv and 498cc (30cu in) ohc singles in 1925. The 350s were a success and were produced in 250 and 500 sizes and with twin-port heads. Also used in the famous Ivory model of 1928, with sloping cylinder. But despite low prices (the basic 250 was listed at just £47 in 1938), the company hit difficulties and went into receivership. Bruce Douglas moved it to Bristol, and built a few Matchless-engined versions before the war brought an end to the business.

An early Calthorpe: note the vertical downpipe and belt-drive. The engine is from Precision

CALVERT *England 1899–1904*
Used Minerva engines as well as its own of up to 3.25hp.

CAMBER *England 1920–21*
Short-lived venture by a motorcycle dealer using 492cc (30cu in) Precision engines.

CAMBRA *Germany 1921–26*
In-house sv singles of 180/198cc (11/12cu inches) powered this Berlin-built bike.

CAMILLE-FAUCEAUX *France 1952–54*
Producer of 65cc (4cu in) mini-scooters.

CAMPION *England 1901–26*
Fitted a huge range of engine makes and sizes (147cc to 966cc/9 to 59cu in), and suppliers included Minerva, MMC, Fafnir, Precision, Villiers, Blackburne and JAP. Also sold its frames to other manufacturers.

CAN-AM *Canada 1973–87*
Off-road bikes built by Bombardier, whose roots were in snowmobiles. First produced 125/175cc (8/11cu in) two-strokes, later bigger two-strokes and 500/560cc (30.5/34cu in) four-strokes, all of which were built by Rotax, another subsidiary of Bombardier. Although successful in off-road competition there were also plans for a road-going 500 two-stroke twin. Increased demand for snowmobiles put an end to all Can-Am production.

CAPPONI *Italy 1924–26*
Used own 173cc (11cu in) three-port two-strokes.

CAPRIOLO *Italy 1948–63*
Ex-aircraft maker which produced a variety of small bikes, all under 150cc (9cu in). Some had pressed steel frames, some were tubular, and engines were two-strokes, ohv or ohc singles and a 149cc (9cu in) flat twin.

CAPRONI-VIZZOLA *Italy 1953–59*
Relied mainly on NSU for its engines of 173cc (11cu in) upwards; its last model, the Cavimax, was based on the NSU Max.

CARABELA *Mexico 1964–*
Large range of two-strokes of up to 450cc (27cu in), both road and off-road bikes. Some of the engines were bought in, some Carabela's own, while others were licence-built Jawas and Minarellis.

CARDAN *France 1902–08*
Early use of shaft-drive, with De Dion engine.

ABOVE: Campion bought in its engines

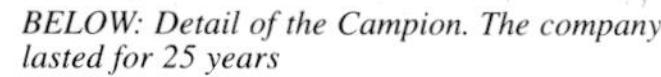
BELOW: Detail of the Campion. The company lasted for 25 years

BELOW: Can-Am Bombardier military machine

CARFIELD *England 1919–24*
Used a variety of bought-in engines from a 247cc (15cu in) Villiers to the 688cc (42cu in) Coventry-Victor flat twin. Notable for its sprung frame.

CARLEY *France 1950–53*
A mini-scooter powered by a flat-twin two-stroke.

CARLTON *England 1913–40*
A Villiers-engined lightweight, sold under its own name and that of a London dealer.

CARLTON *Scotland 1922*
Lightweights with 269cc (16cu in) Villiers engines. Limited production.

CARNIELLI *Italy 1931–80*
Teodoro Carnielli built bikes with bought-in engines up to 500cc (30.5cu in) before the war, and lightweights afterwards. The Graziella folding moped was produced from 1968.

CARPATI *Rumania c.1960s*
A moped maker, with own 65cc (4cu in) two-stroke.

CARPIO *France 1930–35*
Used 98/124cc (6/8cu in) Aubier-Dunne and Stainless two-strokes.

CARREAU *France 1902–03*
A 1.5hp pioneer.

CAS *Czechoslovakia 1921–24*
Built both scooters with miniature flat-twin engines and two-stroke motorcycles, all with disc wheels.

CASAL *Portugal 1964–*
First bikes used Zündapp engines, later Casal's own two-strokes, which included water-cooled 49cc (3cu in) and 27bhp (248cc/15cu in) units.

CASALINI *Italy 1958–*
Began with mini-scooters, now makes a range of mopeds.

CASOLI *Italy 1928–33*
Sporting lightweights, with Villiers and in-house engines.

CASTADOT *Belgium 1900–01*
1.5 hp Zedel-engined machines.

CASTELL *England 1903*
Used Minerva and Sarolea engines.

CASWELL *England 1904–05*
Strengthened bicycle frames with 2.5–3.5hp Minerva engines.

CAYENNE *England 1912–13*
A 499cc (30cu in) single, unusual in that it was water-cooled.

CAZALEX *France 1951–55*
Lightweight two-strokes of 49cc to 124cc (3 to 8cu in).

CAZANAVE *France 1955–57*
Briefly built mopeds and lightweights.

CBR *Italy 1912–14*
Produced a wide range, from small two-strokes up to 8hp bikes. Based in Turin.

CC *England 1921–24*
Charles Chamberlain ('CC') listed a large range of machines, from 147cc to 996cc (9 to 61cu in), but not many were made.

CCM *England 1971–*
A rebirth for the BSA four-stroke single in a succession of off-road bikes designed by Alan Clews, using first BSA parts then increasingly CCM's own. It was an Indian summer for the big four-stroke off-roader. Acquired by Armstrong in 1981, but bought back by Alan Clews in 1987, it now makes Rotax-powered off-roaders, and announced a return to the road market in late 1998.

CECCATO *Italy 1950–63*
A wide range of sporting two- and four-strokes, such as the overhead-cam 73cc (4.5cu in) Super Sport with 8bhp at 11,000rpm, which could exceed 113km/h (70mph).

CEDOS *England 1919–29*
Its in-house frames (then known as 'ladies' frames') housed 211cc (13cu in) two-strokes, as well as more conventional larger machines.

CEMEC *France 1948–55*
BMW-like 746cc (45.5cu in) flat twins, mostly sv but there were also some ohv 493/746cc (30/45.5cu in) versions.

CENTAUR *England 1901–15*
Included a 348cc (21cu in) V-twin, and also a 492cc (30cu in) single with silencer inside the frame's front downtube.

CENTAUR *Germany 1924–25*
1.5hp utilities with engines by Gruhn of Berlin.

CENTER *Japan 1950–62*
Unit-construction 149cc (9cu in) singles.

CENTURY *England 1902–05*
The lifespan of the company failed to match its name. Utilized Minerva and MMC engines.

CF *Italy 1928–71*
Made sporting ohc singles up to 248cc (15cu in) before the war, and was successful in racing. Bought by Fusi in 1937, it eventually (late sixties) built two-stroke mopeds.

CFC *France 1903–06*
1.5hp engines in beefed-up bicycle frames.

CHAMPION *Japan 1960–67*
Really made by Bridgestone, with 49–123cc (3–7.5cu in) two-strokes.

CHARLETT *Germany 1921–24*
Used own 195cc (12cu in) sv single.

CHARLKRON *Germany 1925*
Bought in the interesting Küchen ohc 3-valve engine.

CHARLTON *England 1904–08*
Used 402cc (24.5cu in) Buchet engines, which were originally made in France.

CHASE *England 1902–06*
The Chase brothers used various bought-in engines.

CHATER-LEA *England 1900–36*
Used a long list of proprietary engines over the years, even after it had designed its own singles and V-twins. Notable for an all-

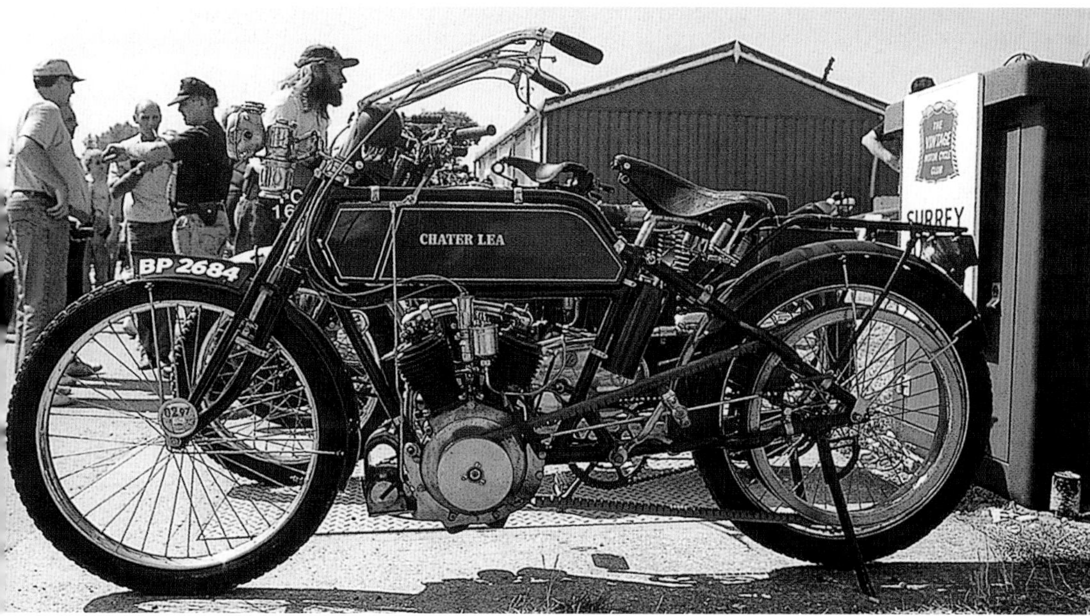

ter-Lea was a pioneer of chain-drive, though this early V-twin was belt-driven

n transmission as early as 1908 and its 545cc (33cu in) sv single. More ting was the 350cc (21cu in) face-cam ine, based on a similar Blackburne, ch won the Flying Kilometre record in 6.

ELL *England 1939*
cc (7.5cu in) Villiers-powered, but ited numbers were produced.

IORDA *Italy 1954–57*
-50cc (3cu in) bikes, first four-strokes, r Franco-Morini-powered two-strokes.

CHRISTOPHE *France c.1925*
Two-strokes of up to 248cc (15cu in) and four-strokes to 498cc (30cu in), including an advanced twin-port ohc unit-construction engine.

CIE *Belgium 1900–05*
3 and 4hp engines designed by M. Coutourier and Paul Kelecom.

CIMA *Italy 1924*
Short-lived attempt at a sporting bike with 247/347cc (15/21cu in) Blackburne engines.

CIMATTI *Italy 1949–84*
Built 49cc (3cu in) mopeds throughout its life, plus larger two- and four-strokes up to 173cc (11cu in) into the 1970s.

CITA *Belgium 1922–25*
Built own ohv singles of 173–348cc (11–21cu in) and triangular frames.

CITO *Germany 1905–27*
Used Fafnir singles and V-twins early on before designing its own three-port two-strokes. Later took over Krieger-Gnädig (advanced 500cc/30.5cu inch singles) before being taken over itself by Allright.

CITYFIX *Germany 1949–53*
Used 58cc (3.5cu in) Lutz engines (for a mini-scooter) and 98cc (6cu in) Sachs units for lightweight motorcycles.

CL *Germany 1951*
Not many of these 34cc (2cu in) mini-scooters were made.

CLAES *Germany 1904–08*
3.5/5hp Fafnir engines used, also sold as the Pfeil.

CLARENDON *England 1901–11*
Based in Coventry, it used its own 3hp unit as well as various bought-in engines.

CLAUDE DELAGE *France 1925*
Limited production – no connection with Delage cars.

CLÉMENT *France 1896–1935*
Various singles and V-twins from this pioneer of the industry, ending up with a unit-construction 63cc (4cu in) machine.

CLÉMENT-GARRARD *England 1902–11*
Charles Garrard fitted Clément engines into Norton frames for the British market.

CLÉMENT-GLADIATOR *France 1901–35*
A pioneer of rear suspension, which helped its racing record in the 1920s. Produced a whole range of 98–498cc (6–30cu in) road machines as well.

CLESS & PLESSING *Austria 1903–06*
Produced 2.75/3.5hp singles and 5hp V-twins, all in-house.

CLEVELAND *England 1911–24*
Used Precision engines (2.75/3.5hp singles).

CLEVELAND *U.S.A. 1915–29*
Began with 269cc (16cu in) two-strokes, then an ioe four-stroke, but was best known for its in-line fours, an alternative to the traditional American V-twin. The first was of 598cc (36cu in), which was unsuccessful, but a larger 737cc (45cu in) version in 1926 did better. Economic conditions forced Cleveland out of business, but not before the four had grown to 996cc (61cu in).

CLUA *Spain 1952–64*
Built Italian Alpinos and its own ohv singles.

CLYDE *England 1898–1912*
A real pioneer, using water-cooling as early as 1903. Used mainly JAP engines but also G.H. Wait's own.

CLYNO *England 1911–24*
Early bikes used Clyno's own variable ratio gear with Stevens engines. Later bought the rights to Stevens' big V-twin, and designed its own 269cc (16cu in) two-speed two-strokes.

CM *Germany 1921–23*
The Munich-built CM had a 110cc (7cu in) Cockerell two-stroke engine.

CM *Italy 1930–57*
The first CM was a little overhead-cam single, which set the pattern for what was to follow – mostly ohc sportsters up to 496cc (30cu in). It concentrated on smaller bikes after the war, the largest being a 250 twin.

CMM *England 1919–21*
Utilized a Union 269cc (16cu in) two-stroke in its own frame.

CMP *Italy 1953–56*
Produced mostly Ceccato two-strokes of 48–123cc (3–7.5cu in) though also used a 48cc Sachs and ohv Ceccato.

CMR *France 1945–48*
Very much based on the pre-war BMW, it was a flat twin of 745cc (45cu in).

COCKERELL *Germany 1919–24*
From the prolific designer Fritz Cockerell, who also created the radial-engined Megola. Cockerell motorcycles were small lightweights up to 170cc (10cu in), with water-cooling on the sportier versions.

CODRIDEX *France 1952–56*
49 and 65cc (3 and 4cu in) mopeds.

COFERSA *Spain 1953–60*
98–198cc (6–12cu in) two-strokes.

COLIBRI *Austria 1952–54*
Short-lived scooter, DKW-powered.

COLOMB *France 1950–54*
Built scooters and lightweights on a small scale.

COLUMBIA *U.S.A. 1900–05*
Pope-built single-cylinder and V-twin engines.

COLUMBIA *France 1922–26*
Both simple and open frames, with 197 or 247cc (12 or 15cu in) sv engines.

COLUMBUS *Germany 1923–24*
Maker of clip-on engines, its 248cc bike became the first Horex when the Kleeman family bought Columbus out.

COM *Italy 1926–28*
Typically Italian 123 and 173cc (7.5 and 11cu in) machines.

COMERY *England 1919–22*
Used 269cc (16cu in) Villiers power. Owned by racer Archie Cook.

COMET *England 1902–07*
Minerva engines with BSA cycle parts.

COMET *Italy 1953–57*
Well engineered little sports bikes, including a 173cc (11cu in) ohc twin.

COMMANDER *England 1952–53*
Notable for its partly enclosed engine (Villiers, of course) and square-tube frame.

CONDOR *Switzerland 1901–59*
Switzerland's second largest motorcycle maker, though it didn't produce its own engine until 1947. Early bikes used Zedel, MAG and Villiers, but Condor's own engine was a 597cc (36cu in) sv flat twin which later gained capacity and was used by the military. There was also a 348cc (21cu in) two-stroke twin from 1950 and an ohc 250cc (15cu in) single with shaft-drive, in prototype form.

CONDOR *England 1907–14*
Built one of the biggest singles ever (810cc/49cu in) and sold its engines to other manufacturers.

CONDOR *Germany 1953–54*
Scooter-like motorcycles using 48cc (3cu in) two-strokes.

CONNAUGHT *England 1910–27*
Built 293/347cc (18/21cu in) two-stroke singles with belt- and chain-drive. Four-strokes came later.

CONSUL *England 1916–22*
Used 247/269cc (15/16cu in) Villiers units.

COOPER *U.S.A. 1972–73*
Off-road bike, actually made in Mexico by Islo.

CORAH *England 1905–14*
Mainly used 498/746cc (30/45.5cu in) JAP engines, though alternatives could be fitted to order.

CORGI *England 1942–48*
Originally made for the British Air Force, the famous folding scooters were equipped with Sprite 98cc (6cu in) two-strokes. Made by Brockhouse Engineering who later owned the Indian company and produced the sv Brave.

CORONA *England 1902–24*
Early bikes had the engine mounted between saddle tube and rear wheel; later ones were more conventional, including a 346cc (21cu in) single and 493cc (30cu in) flat twin.

CORONA-JUNIOR *England 1919–23*
Very basic, cheap belt-driven bike, with 447cc (27cu in) sv single.

CORYDON *England 1904–08*
2.5/3hp singles and a 4.5hp V-twin.

COSMOS *Switzerland 1904–07*
Used Zedel and Fafnir engines in strengthened bicycle frames.

A 1910 499cc (30cu in) Corah gets a push

COSSACK *U.S.S.R. 1974–*
Flat twins from the former U.S.S.R. went under various names, and the Cossack was often sent for export. Built in both Kiev and Irbit.

COTTEREAU *France 1903–09*
One of the first car producers in France, Cottereau motorcycles used Minerva, Peugeot as well as in-house engines.

COTTON *England 1920–80*
Triangulated frames and excellent handling gave Cotton motorcycles their success. Designed by John Cotton, most used proprietory engines ranging from 147cc to 600cc (9 to 37cu in). This created an extensive range from Villiers lightweights to the four-valve Python-engined bikes of 498cc (30cu in), and included trials and motocross bikes. After the war, the company reverted to small two-strokes only, and was increasingly dominated by competition in the 1960s. There were new Rotax-engined racers in 1976, and it was taken over by Armstrong in 1980.

COULSON *England 1919–24*
Built 247 and 497cc (15 and 30cu in) sv singles and also 397cc (24cu in) ohv JAP V-twins.

COVENTRY-B&D *England 1923–25*
Limited production using a range of JAP engines, plus the Barr & Stroud sleeve-valve single, though also built the 170cc (10cu in) Wee McGregor two-stroke.

COVENTRY-CHALLENGE *England 1903–11*
Fafnir, Minerva and other engines were used for these strengthened cycle frames.

COVENTRY-EAGLE *England 1901–39*
A cycle maker which, despite a longish life, never built its own engines. Instead, it utilized a large range of 98cc–996cc (6–61cu in) units from Villiers, JAP, Sturmey-Archer, Blackburne and Matchless. Two bikes stand out: one with a pressed-steel channel-section frame (used various Villiers engines) and the Pullman of 1935, with rear suspension, pressed steel 'chassis' and enclosure. Last bikes used conventional tubular frames.

COVENTRY-MASCOT *England 1922–24*
Only ever sold 350s (21cu in), with engines by Blackburne, Bradshaw or Barr & Stroud.

COVENTRY-MOTETTE *England 1899–1903*
A 2.5hp engine designed by Turrell, based on a Bollée original.

COVENTRY-STAR *England 1919–21*
Used 269cc (16cu in) Liberty and Villiers engines.

A 1922 Coventry-Eagle of 249cc (15cu in)

COVENTRY-VICTOR *England 1919–36*
A devotee of flat twins, encompassing 499, 688 and 749cc (30, 42 and 46cu in), there was even a flat-twin Speedway bike, and other manufacturers bought the company's engines from them.

CP-ROLÉO *France 1924–39*
An interesting frame – part pressed steel, part cast iron – incorporating both petrol and oil tanks. All engines were bought in.

CR *Germany 1926–30*
172cc (10.5cu in) Villiers two-strokes.

CRESCENT *Sweden 1937–60*
Made 98cc (6cu in) Sachs-engined lightweights before the war, and the name was used by NV from 1955 until it was bought by MCB. An AJS7R-powered Crescent won the 1957 500cc Motocross World Championship.

A 1925 Coventry-Eagle of 1000cc (61cu in)

CREST *England 1923*
Used Villiers two-strokes or Barr & Stroud sleeve-valved engines.

CROCKER *U.S.A. 1933–41*
Began with a speedway machine, but after a couple of years unveiled its 45-degree ohv V-twin. Not many were made, but these 998cc (61cu in) and 1475cc (90cu in) twins were very fast for their time and perhaps could be described as American Vincents. Also built a few scooters towards the end.

CROFT *England 1923–26*
Fearsome 996cc (61cu in) V-twins with four or eight valves, and some with the 1078cc (66cu in) Anzani V-twin.

CROWNFIELD *England 1903–04*
Kerry and Givaudan small engines were fitted to step-through frames.

CRT *Italy 1925–1929*
Used Blackburne engines in a sporting chassis.

CRYPTO *England 1902–08*
Mostly used Peugeot or Coronet engines.

CSEPEL *Hungary 1932–75*
Built own Laszlo Sagi-designed two-strokes before the war and after it was nationalized, concentrated on two-stroke scooters and motorcycles under various brand names.

CUDELL *Germany 1898–1905*
Used De Dion engines of 402 and 510cc (24.5 and 31cu in).

ABOVE: A 1937 Crocker

BELOW: A very rare Crocker Speedway bike, of which there are only 20 known examples

BELOW: A Crocker with an Indian overhead-valve V-twin

ABOVE: Cushmanns were basic transport

BELOW: 1958 Cushmann Eagle, two-speed with Cushmann Husky engine

Later Cushmanns acquired motorcycle styling

CURTISS *U.S.A. 1903–12*
Glenn Curtiss built aircraft engines as well as single and V-twin motorcycles. Records were broken with a bike fitted with one of his air-cooled V8 aircraft engines.

CURWY *Germany 1923–31*
Produced own 348 and 498cc (21 and 30cu in) sv and ohv machines, and a few overhead-cam 350s as well. Later changed its name to Cursy.

CUSHMANN *U.S.A. 1936–65*
America had its own scooter boom, and Cushmann's leading contender used its own 'Husky' industrial four-stroke engine. It was supplied to the military as a parachutable bike and sold right through to the mid-1960s, when Honda's Cub showed how unsophisticated the Cushmann was.

CYC-AUTO *England 1934–56*
Moped with a strengthened cycle frame and a 98cc (6cu in) five-port Scott two-stroke.

CYCLE-SCOOT *U.S.A. 1953–55*
Scooter with a 2.5bhp ohv engine. Not successful.

CYCLON *Germany 1901–05*
Used DeDion, Werner and Zedel engines.

CYCLONE *U.S.A. 1913–17*
The first ohc V-twin on sale, which won many races until outclassed by the 8-valve Harley-Davidson.

CYCLOP *Germany 1922–25*
Used various bought-in engines up to 298cc (18cu in), including Kuriers and Namapos.

CYKELAID *England 1919–26*
1.25/1.5hp (133cc) engines, either as clip-ons or as complete lightweight machines.

CYRUS *The Netherlands 1952–71*
Offered choice of Villiers, Sachs or Ilo engines up to 148cc (9cu in).

CZ *Czechoslovakia 1932–93*
Began with a motorized bicycle, but soon progressed to 76cc (5cu in) lightweights, then a range of two-strokes up to 496cc (30cu in). After nationalization in 1949, linked up with Jawa and concentrated on bikes up to 250cc (15cu in), including the 175cc (11cu in) Cezeta scooter from 1959. All were two-strokes, apart from ohc racing bikes, and were very successful in motocross through the 1960s. Was sold to Cagiva in 1993, after the political changes in Eastern Europe.

Cyclone was the first to offer an ohc V-twin but was, however, shortlived

D

DAELIM *South Korea 1962–*
Built lightweights at first, plus licence-built Hondas from 1978.

DAK *Germany 1923–25*
A group of German car makers which between them built 117cc and 147cc (7 and 9cu in) Ilo-engined two-strokes.

DALESMAN *England 1969–74*
Successful off-road bikes with 98 and 123cc (6 and 7.5cu in) Puch as well as 123cc Sachs engines.

DALTON *England 1920–22*
Bought-in engines of 347/497cc (21/30cu in) from Blackburne or 688cc (42cu in) Coventry-Victors for these disc-wheeled machines.

DANE *England 1919–20*
Used Precision or JAP engines, with limited production in either case.

The 1998 Daelim 125 VT range-topper

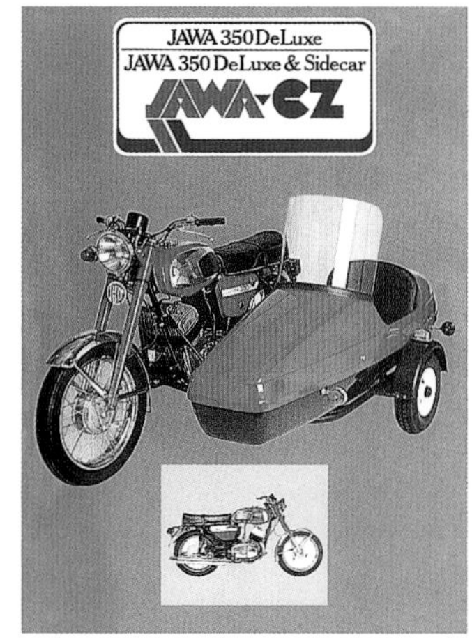

By the 1970s Jawa/CZ was firmly dedicated to utilitarian bikes, though there was the odd attempt to add glamour

DANUBIUS *Germany 1923–24*
198cc (12cu in) sv utility bike.

DANUVIA *Hungary 1955–63*
A 123cc (7.5cu in) two-stroke, designed by Csepel.

DARDO *Italy 1924–29*
Flat-twin two-strokes of 123cc and 174cc (7.5 and 11cu in).

DARLAN *Spain 1958–60*
A 94cc (6cu in) two-stroke, made in small numbers.

DARLING *Switzerland 1924–26*
Step-through frame with in-house 246cc (15cu in) three-port two-stroke.

DART *England 1901–06*
Used 2.5hp Minerva and MMC engines.

DART *England 1923–24*
Advanced overhead-cam 348cc (21cu in) machines designed by A.A.Sidney. Few were built.

DAVENTRY *Belgium 1951–55*
Puch, Sachs and other small two-strokes were used by this Belgian manufacturer.

DAVISON *England 1902–08*
Offered with choice of 2hp or 2.5hp Simms or Minerva engines.

DAW *England 1902–05*
Used a Minerva 2.75hp engine, made under licence.

DAW *Germany 1924–25*
An attempt at a fully enclosed motorcycle, with a 405cc (25cu in) two-stroke single and designed by Ernst Köhler.

DAX *France 1932–39*
98cc to 174cc (6 to 11cu in) two-strokes and unit-construction ohv four-strokes up to 498cc (30cu in).

DAY-LEEDS *England 1912–14*
Short-lived excursion into motorcycles by a maker of three-wheelers using its own 496cc (30cu in) ioe single.

DAYTON *U.S.A. 1911–17*
7hp, later 9–10hp V-twin Spake engines.

DAYTON *England 1913–60*
Production was in fits and starts for never more than a few years at a time with a 162cc (10cu in) clip-on from 1913–15; a Villiers-powered lightweight 1921–22; a 98cc (6cu in) autocycle 1938–39 and finally, Villiers-engined scooters from 1954–60.

DE-CA *Italy 1954–57*
Small (biggest was 98cc/6cu in) ohv singles and also a vertical twin, plus a 49cc (3cu in) clip-on.

DE-DE *France 1923–29*
A wide range of models using bought-in units from 98cc/6cu inch two-strokes to 498cc/30cu inch JAPs.

DE DION BOUTON *France 1926–30*
No real connection with the engine/car maker, this one built machines from 173cc (11cu in) upwards.

DEFA *Germany 1921–24*
Own 198cc (12cu in) sv engine was sold to many other manufacturers.

DEFY-ALL *England 1921–22*
Sprung frames, with Villiers or Blackburne power.

DEI *Italy 1906–66*
Built conventional four-strokes until 1914, then production stopped for 20 years to resume with Sachs-powered 78/98cc (5/6cu in) lightweights. Mosquito, Villiers and JAP engines were also used.

DELAPLACE *France 1951–53*
Used 173 and 247cc (11 and 15cu in) Ydral two-strokes.

DELIN *Belgium 1899–1901*
Thought to have used 1.5/2.5hp De Dion engines.

DELLA FERRERA *Italy 1909–48*
Advanced singles and V-twins, successful in competition, and an early user of rear suspension in the 1920s. Produced singles up to 637cc (39cu in) and twins to 996cc.

DELOMA *Germany 1924*
Used a crude-oil 142cc (9cu in) two-stroke designed by Löwy.

DELTA *Germany 1924*
Unusual, with full enclosure, rear suspension (leaf-spring) and a dual seat with 499cc (30cu in) two-stroke single.

DELTA-GNOM *Austria 1925–55*
All bought-in engines, apart from early 246cc (15cu in) two-strokes, and included a full range of JAPs (including a 996cc/61cu inch V-twin), Hans Pitzek 498cc (30cu in) singles and (after the war) various small two-strokes.

DE LUXE *U.S.A. 1912–15*
Made by Excelsior, with mainly V-twins from F.W. Spake of Indianapolis.

DE LUXE *England 1920-24*
In a bizarre kind of special offer, De Luxe gave everyone who bought its 350 single a sidecar frame, free of charge. Also sold a 269cc (16cu in) Villiers-engined machine.

DEMM *Italy 1953–82*
Built its own two- and four-stroke engines up to 173cc (11cu in), including a 145-km/h (90-mph) 173cc racer. Also sold engines to other manufacturers.

DENE *England 1903–22*
Despite its 19-year life span, Dene never built its own engines, which came from a whole variety of sources, and production was limited.

DENNELL *England 1903–08*
Notable for a 660cc (40cu in) three-cylinder model, with engine in-line, plus four-cylinder bikes with Franklin & Isaacsson engines.

DERBI *Spain 1949–*
A post-war survivor which has concentrated on two-strokes of up to 350cc (21cu in) in the 1950s but now produces mainly mopeds. Derbi's miniature racers won several world championships and were successfully ridden by Angel Nieto. Used bought-in 125/180cc (8/11cu in) Piaggio engines from 1999 for the Predator performance scooter.

DERNY *France 1949–57*
Unusual 123/173cc (7.5/11cu in) two-strokes and a 173cc scooter.

DERONZIÈRE *France 1903–14*
Powered by its own 282cc (17cu in) single as well as Zedel and Peugeot units.

DESPATCH-RIDER *England 1915–17*
The name suggests its intended purpose. Utilized 210cc (13cu in) Peco or 269cc (16cu in) Villiers power.

DEVIL *Italy 1953–57*
Two-strokes of up to 158cc (10cu in), and 123/173cc (7.5/11cu in) unit-construction four-strokes made at Bergamo.

DFB *Germany 1922–25*
Choice of 159cc (10cu in) two-stroke clip-ons or complete machines.

DFR *Germany 1921–33*
This ambitious factory built its own engines, first two-strokes, then sv and ohv four-strokes. Later raced a supercharged Bradshaw-engined machine and offered a 498cc (30cu in) Dresch-powered bike. It was ultimately taken over by Dresch.

DGW *Germany 1927–28*
Rebadging job for DKWs exported to Britain because of a dispute over trade names.

DIAG *Germany 1921–28*
Unusual in that the engine hung from the frame. Used various engines of up to 346cc (21cu in).

DIAMANT *Germany 1903–40*
This erratic producer first made Fafnir-powered bikes, but production stopped in 1908. Restarted 1926 with 496cc (30cu in) Gnädig-designed machines, then Opel used part of the factory to build its own bikes. Final two-wheelers were from 73–98cc (4.5–6cu in) mopeds.

DIAMOND *England 1910–38*
Used a wide variety of two- and four-strokes, including units from Barr & Stroud, Villiers and JAP, among others. Bought by Sunbeam in 1920. In 1969 a new Birmingham-based company offered Sachs-engined 123cc (7.5cu in) five-speed motorcycles.

DIETERLE-DESSAU *Germany 1921–25*
Interesting for its patented exhaust-injection system, with sv engines of 148–198cc (9–12cu in).

DIFRA *Germany 1923–25*
Mostly used 198cc (12cu in) sv Namapo engines.

DIHL *Germany 1923–24*
A Berlin-built 269cc (16cu in) single-cylinder two-stroke.

DKW RT125 spawned many post-war copies

DILECTA *France 1920–39*
Used a wide range of engine suppliers for capacities of up to 498cc (30cu in).

DJOUNN *Germany 1925*
Innovative 499cc (30cu in) single, but too radical to be a commercial success

DKF *Germany 1923–24*
Lightweights with 148cc and 198cc (9 and 12cu in) sv engines.

DKR *England 1957–66*
Villiers-engined scooters with 148–247cc (9–15cu in) single-cylinder and 244cc twin units.

DKW *Germany 1919–late 1970s*
There have been various explanations as to what the famous DKW initials stand for, but it is thought to be *Das Kleine Wunder* (Little Wonder). As this suggests, DKW's roots were in small bikes, and it only ever built two-strokes, the first being a 118cc (7cu in) clip-on. The first complete machine was the 122cc Golem scooter of 1921, with lightweight motorcycles the year after. Characterized by pressed steel frames and fan- or water-cooling, they were very successful and DKW claimed to be the largest motorcycle manufacturer in the world by the 1930s. Profitability was also aided by supplying engines to a vast array of smaller manufacturers. There were successful water-cooled racers, some with forced induction, and bigger two-strokes of 498cc and 598cc (30 and 36cu in). After the war, DKW moved from its Zschopau base (then taken over by MZ) to West Germany, and continued to make single- and twin-cylinder two-strokes up to 350cc (21cu in), notably the RT125, which was copied by BSA, Harley-Davidson and many others. A declining motorcycle market led to merger, then a takeover by Fichtel & Sachs in 1966, which used the name on a variety of Sachs-engined lightweights, including (in some markets) the rotary-engined W2000.

DMF *The Netherlands 1940–57*
Various utility two-strokes, the last using a 244cc (15cu in) Ilo engine.

DMG *Germany 1921–24*
Produced a 147cc (9cu in) clip-on, then a 198cc (12cu in) lightweight.

DMW *England 1945–71*
Mostly Villiers-powered two-strokes, though also used Velocette's flat twin and MAC units, not to mention its own prototype 498cc (30cu in) two-stroke. It was owned by ex-racing driver Kaye Don until 1962 when Arthur Frost bought it. DMW bought up Villiers stock when the engine maker closed, and now supplies spares.

DNB *Japan 1957–61*
Two-strokes of 123, 197 and 247cc (7.5, 12 and 15cu in).

DOBRO-MOTORIST *Germany 1923–25*
Used 145cc (9cu in) DKW and 346cc (21cu in) JAP engines in its own frames.

DOGLIOLI & CIVARDI *Italy 1929–35*
Limited-production sportsters, designed by Cesare Doglioli and powered by 170cc (10cu in) Norman engines. Later versions used 173–498cc (11–30cu in) JAP and Python units.

An early Dot single, photographed at Brooklands

DOLLAR *France 1925–39*
A large range, from 98 to 748cc (6 to 46cu in), the biggest of which was a four-cylinder model.

DOMINISSIMI *Italy 1924–28*
172cc and 248cc (10.5 and 15cu in) ohv singles.

DONISELLI *Italy 1951–61*
Used bought-in engines for Vedetta scooter and lightweight bikes.

DOPPER *The Netherlands 1904*
A long wheelbased, belt-driven 269cc (16cu in) single.

DORION *France 1932–36*
Lightweights with 98/123cc (6/7.5cu in) Aubier-Dunne two-stroke engines.

DORMAN *Hungary 1920–37*
Assembler using Villiers, MAG and JAP proprietory bought-in units of 172–499cc (10.5–30cu in).

DOT *England 1902–73*
Dot was formed by pioneer racer Harry Reed, and always used bought-in engines. Peugeot, Fafnir and JAP units were used at first, and later the oil-cooled 350cc (21cu in) Bradshaw engine, plus Blackburne power units. A long association with Villiers power began in 1928 with a whole range of bikes from 98–346cc (6–21cu in). However, Dot failed to survive the Depression and closed down in 1932. The name was revived in 1949, again

C.W. Baughn concentrating hard on a Villiers-powered Dot

Pat Lamper, another Dot rider

with Villiers two-strokes, and increasingly concentrated on off-road machines. It also imported Victoria and Guazzoni bikes and went over to Minarelli two-strokes when Villiers stopped supplying them. The end came soon after.

DOTTA *Italy 1924–26*
Piazza 173cc (11cu in) two-strokes were utilized by this assembler.

DOUE *France c.1903*
Utilized 1.5hp engines in bicycle frames.

DOUGLAS *England 1907–57*
There were no less than five incarnations of Douglas. In other words, it failed and was rescued several times in its somewhat chaotic 50-year history, which also saw it build cars, aero-engines and drain-covers. In spite of this, it enjoyed much competition success, both on-road and off, and helped establish the flat twin as a practical engine layout for bikes.

The Douglas story began with one J.F. Barter, who between 1902 and 1904 produced an eccentric single-cylinder machine (final-drive was taken from the camshaft) which prospective buyers found no difficulty in resisting. He then produced a 200cc (12cu in) flat twin, with some parts supplied by the Douglas Foundry Company based, like Barter, in Bristol. Neither a 300cc (18cu in) version nor an 800cc (49cu in) prototype were enough to stave off the inevitable, so Barter joined Douglas instead, with the intention of designing them a motorcycle.

Predictably, it was a flat twin, a 350 which only sold in very small numbers in 1907 and 1908. Despite automatic inlet valves (opened by atmospheric pressure rather than a camshaft), belt-slip, and poor mixture distribution, the fore-aft twin sold more in 1909, and better still the following year when a two-speed gearbox was added. Neither were sales harmed when Douglas managed 7th and 12th places in the 1911 TT and won it the year after. This, plus two team prizes in the Six Days Trial, secured Douglas a large contract for military machines in World War I and 25,000 were built.

After the war, the Douglas flat twins were gradually updated with overhead valves, all-chain drive and a lower frame. They were light and had a low centre of gravity, so continued to do well in competition and Tom Sheard won the Senior TT on one in 1923. At that time, you could still buy the basic military-style sidevalve 350 twin, plus a 600 sidevalve and 500 and 733 ohv models, all having the fore-aft flat twin and chain-drive. The new EW of 1924 looked very similar, but was actually substantially new, and was pared down to scrape below a 200-lb taxation class. An ohv version followed in

A 1914 348cc (21cu in) Douglas

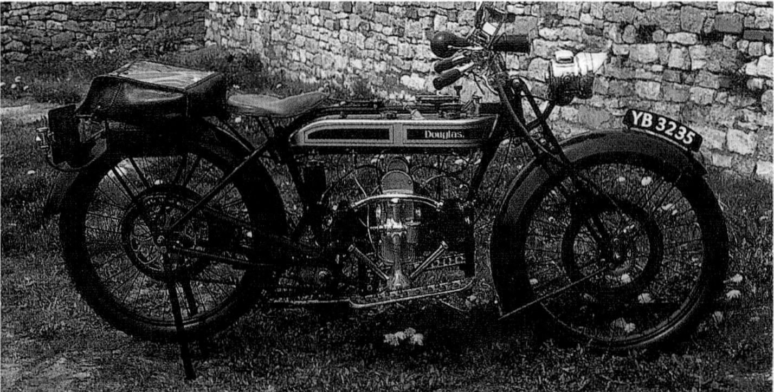

ABOVE: 1924 flat twin

1928, and dry-sump lubrication was added the following year.

The early 1930s saw more new ohv versions of the flat twin (Douglas produced a bewildering array of models in this period) and one of the company's many reorganizations, as well as a Villiers-powered lightweight commuter. There was also (in 1934) an ambitious 500 with alloy heads and barrels, though few were sold. Again the company collapsed, and again it was saved, and by 1937 the revived Douglas was again building its sidevalve 350, 500 and 600cc (21, 30.5 and 37cu in) twins, plus a 150cc (9cu in) two-stroke. There was no role for Douglas motorcycles in World War II, though once again the firm did well out of the aero industry.

In late 1945, it bounced back into the bike business with an all-new machine that was to take it right through the next decade. In some ways, the new ohv 350cc Douglas T35 was revolutionary. It broke with Douglas tradition in wearing its flat

BELOW: A very early Douglas

twin transversely, rather than fore-aft, but the real innovation was in the suspension. Where other British manufacturers were content to carry on with pre-war rigid frames, Douglas provided torsion bar suspension at both front and rear. The twin was of square bore and stroke dimensions (where contemporaries had wheezy long-strokes) and the sports MkIII could near 129km/h (80mph), faster than any equivalent 350. However, none of this prevented Douglas from going bust again within a couple of years. Douglas (Sales & Service) rose out of the ashes, and went on to build the 80 Plus and 90 Plus developments of the T85. Perhaps more far-sighted was the decision to licence-build the Vespa scooter from 1951, which did much to support Douglas for the next few years. By this time the company was owned by Westinghouse, which decided to cease two-wheeler production in 1957 (though Vespa assembly from knock-down kits went on for a while). This time there was to be no resurrection from the ashes and as a motorcycle maker, Douglas was dead.

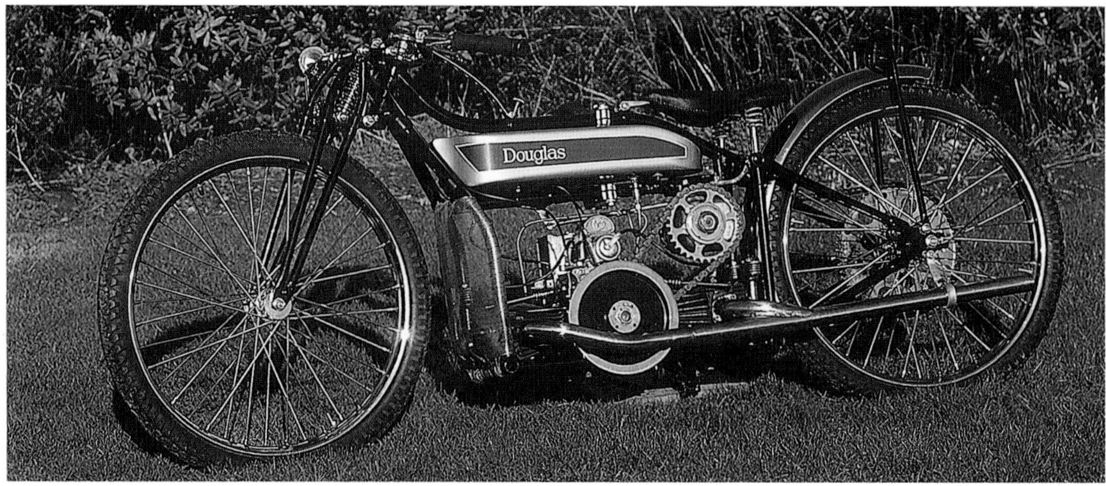

ABOVE and BELOW: Douglas did well in competition for a while, won the 1923 TT, and also enjoyed success in Speedway

D-RAD *Germany 1921–33*
First produced a 393cc (24cu in) flat twin, then a unit-constructed 498cc (30cu in) single, before being bought and closed down by NSU.

DREADNOUGHT *England 1915–25*
Utilized the 269cc (16cu in) Villiers engine.

DRESCH *France 1923–39*
A wide range of both two- and four-strokes up to 246cc (15cu in).

DREVON *France 1946–53*
A 173cc (11cu in) bike was the largest built by Drevon.

DS *Sweden 1924–28*
Used MAG 746cc (45.5cu in) engines, mainly for the Swedish military.

ABOVE: The 1958 Dragonfly, the final Douglas

ABOVE: Flat twin to the end

BELOW: Douglas 733cc (45cu in) at Brooklands

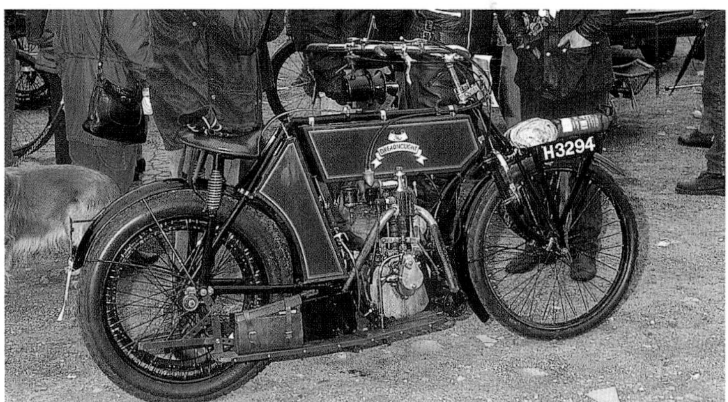

BELOW: Dreadnought

DSH *Austria 1924–32*
Started with Villiers power, and progressed to JAP and MAG engines up to 746cc (45.5cu in).

DSK *Japan 1954–62*
A 497cc (30cu in) flat twin was DSK's largest offering.

DS-MALTERRE *France 1920–58*
Utilized Ydral or French AMC engines of up to 248cc (15cu in).

DUCATI *Italy 1946–*
Ducati, one of the most evocative names in motorcycling, whose fast, exotic, temperamental V-twins respond to lavish care and attention. At least, that is most riders' conception of the bikes from Bologna. But until recently, the name was hardly known outside two-wheel circles. Success in World Superbike competition has brought this, the Ferrari of motorcycles, to mainstream attention. In the late 1990s, when it has already gained seven WSB Championships this decade and (for the first time for years) a firm financial footing, Ducati seems more secure than ever before. But far from being long-established, Ducati was a relative latecomer, particularly to the performance bikes with which everyone now associates the name. (Its first engine was unveiled in 1946, but Ducati's first V-twin wasn't announced until 1970.) It has been a rapid and chequered rise to the top.

Ducati's history, and much of its early success, were dominated by one man and one of his best ideas. Engineer Fabio Taglioni joined the company in 1955 and designed a whole string of sporting singles and V-twins through the fifties, sixties and seventies. Their magic ingredient was desmodromic valve gear, a positive means of valve closure which allows higher revs and consequently more power. This solution wasn't restricted to Taglioni; Mercedes had already used it in racing cars, but it seems that in practice his version was the most successful and long-lived.

However, we are a little ahead of ourselves. Adriano Ducati was a physics student, but his real interest lay in the expanding world of radio. With his two brothers, Bruno and Marcello, he had set up Società Scientifica Radio Brevetti Ducati in 1926, which rapidly expanded into optics and mechanics as well as electronics. All went well until late in the

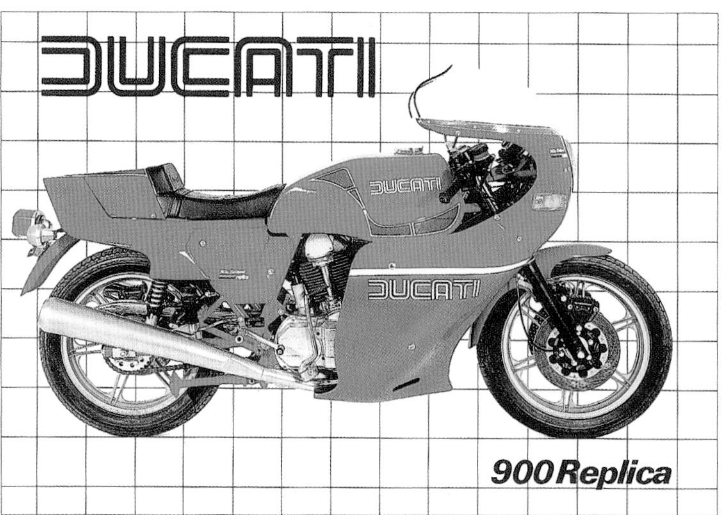

ABOVE and BELOW: The Ducati Mike Hailwood Replica was a celebration of 'Mike the Bike's' 1978 TT win

Sales brochure for the Paso 750

IL NOSTRO PASSATO HA UN GRANDE FUTURO

ABOVE: *The Paso 750 (1985)*

war when the German army commandeered the factory and promptly shipped most of the machinery back to Germany. Then what was left was virtually destroyed by Allied bombing!

It wasn't to be allowed to die, however. An unlikely liaison between the Italian government and the Vatican provided the finance to bring Ducati back to life in 1948, which enabled it to buy a ready-made prototype from the Siata company – the Cucciolo.

Low-Powered Start

Post-war Italy, like the rest of Europe (and Japan for that matter), was in desperate need of cheap motorized transport, and the simplest route was via tiny clip-on engines that could be bolted onto any bicycle. The Cucciolo ('Puppy') was a relatively sophisticated example of the breed being a 48cc (3cu in) four-stroke with a built-in two-speed gearbox. The Cucciolo produced about one horsepower, but Ducati's ambitions were clear: it broke the 12-hour 50cc speed record in 1951, at 67.16km/h (41.73mph). Although the Cucciolo began life as a clip-on engine, by the time it was dropped in 1956 it had been transformed into a true moped.

Well before then, however, Ducati was producing motorcycles proper. First was the 60 Sport, a 65cc (4cu in) four-stroke designed by Giovanni Fiorio, which was launched in 1950. Like the Cucciolo, the 60 was in a low state of tune (2.5bhp at 5,500rpm) but it formed the basis of a long line of pushrod singles. It soon grew into the higher compression 98, which in turn led to the 98 Sport of 1953. This could top 90km/h (56mph) and underlined a trend that was to take Ducati Meccanica far from

BELOW: *The original 864cc (53cu in) 900SS*

BELOW: *F1 was basically an enlarged Pantah*

its roots; it was not content to go on building cyclemotors.

This was where Fabio Taglioni entered the picture and assumed his pivotal role in Ducati's history. A graduate of Bologna University, he had gained valuable experience with the FB Mondial racing team (Mondial had won three world championships in succession) and Ducati's director, Giuseppe Montano, poached him in 1955. Montano's role was also crucial. He had decided that Ducati needed a new bike to win the prestigious Giro d'Italia race, took on Taglioni and set him to work. It was really these two men – Montano and Taglioni – who changed Ducati's direction in the way it was to develop for the next 30 years, from a maker of utility bikes, to a manufacturer of racers and sporting roadsters.

Taglioni's first contribution was the 98cc (6cu in) Gran Sport and Mariana, an all-new design with bevel-drive overhead camshafts which was to form the basis of Ducati's famous ohc singles. Hollywood scriptwriters couldn't have crafted a more dramatic debut for the Gran Sport: it was tested in February 1955, unveiled in March, and a few weeks later easily won the Giro d'Italia's 100cc class. The Gran Sport's engine was indeed advanced for its time: the bevel gear was expensive to make, but was the best engineering solution to reliable running at high engine speeds. The four-speed gearbox was in unit with the engine and the whole bike weighed only 80kg (176lb), which helped it exceed 129km/h (80mph) from just 9bhp.

But it was always envisaged that the Gran Sport would form the basis of future road and race bikes, and a 125cc (8cu in)

The 450cc (27cu in) Desmo was the ultimate Ducati single

version appeared in 1956 (12bhp at 9,800rpm) which duly won the Giro d'Italia outright. A 175cc (11cu in) came the year after and in the last Giro d'Italia (1957), Gran Sport Ducatis filled the first 12 places. It was the end of an era for these dangerous public-road races, but in three short years Ducati had made its mark.

It made sense to capitalize on this success by producing a detuned Gran Sport for the road, so that's what Taglioni did. Enclosed valve-springs, lower compression, and that was about the extent of the changes to the 175 Tour and 175 Sport (the latter could still break the 80mph barrier). Both 100 and 125cc versions were added in 1957, while the 175 soon grew into a 200, then a 250. Exports began, with the perhaps inevitable 175 Americano, complete with high-rise bars. These were road bikes, of course, but 1958 saw the introduction of the F3, an over-the-counter racer in the way the Gran Sport had been. Although it came in the same 125/175/250 sizes as the road machines, and looked superficially similar, the F3 was really completely different, with virtually no parts interchangeable. Notable was the 250 F3, which produced 32bhp at 9,000rpm and scored several successes in U.S. racing.

On the road, high points were the 250 Monza (touring) and Diana (sporting) which owed much to the F3 and mustered 24bhp in Diana form, though by the middle of 1963 it had developed into the Mark 3 Super Sport, which with 30bhp and a 10:1 compression was a real racer for the road. It was this bike that led to the almost legendary Mach 1, the first production 250 to claim a top speed of over 161km/h/100mph (though reality didn't always match the claims). The Mach 1 was raced, of course, and did well, but its real distinction lay in forming the basis of yet another capacity increase for this truly remarkable engine – the 250 Mach 1/S was the biggest Ducati yet, and with a twin-plug head almost scraped 40bhp.

While all this was going on, Ducati was also making a whole raft of less sporting bikes, notably 250GT and 350 Sebring ohc models, pushrod 125s and (in an attempt to get back to its utility roots) a range of two-stroke mopeds, scooters and 100/125cc bikes, the latter lasting right through the sixties. At the other end of the scale, Ducati's U.S. importer inspired the production of an extraordinary 1257cc (77cu in) V4, the Apollo. It was designed as a police bike, though both touring (80bhp) and sports (100bhp) versions were envisaged. Today, a 1200 V4 is nothing special, but in 1963 it was something else again. Unfortunately, the V4's period tyres couldn't keep up with its power, and the idea was shelved. A similar fate met two other 1960s ideas – parallel twins of 500 and 700cc (30.5 and 43cu in).

Desmo & Glory

All this tinkering with alternative bikes – the V4 and vertical twins – was no more than an aberration for Ducati, for the engineering principle that was to underpin its success for four decades had already been well and truly established. Here was Ducati's true core product and it lay in desmodromics.

The principle is simple: in a conventional engine, the valves are opened positively but closed by a spring, a perfectly acceptable set-up for most road vehicles. However, at high revs, the spring may be unable to close the valve quickly enough (we're talking many times per second here) and valve 'bounce' sets in, which limits engine speed and thus power. Fabio Taglioni's answer was to positively close the valve by means of a rocker, which in theory meant that the valve would close as reliably at 10,000rpm as it would at 1,000.

Ducati had decided to try Grand Prix racing, and had come up with a dohc 125cc (8cu in) single which was powerful but not quite up to the standard set by MV, Mondial and Gilera. In a few short months, Taglioni had designed, built and tested a desmodromic system for the Bialbero: at its debut (the Swedish GP in July 1956) it swept the board, lapping every other bike in the race. The new engine produced more power than the old one, and could rev to an unheard-of maximum of 14,000rpm plus. Taglioni's eight years of work had been vindicated, and Ducati (had it but known) had found its USP. It lost the 1958 125 GP championship by a whisker, and won all the home 125 championships. Mike Hailwood won his first Grand Prix on a 'desmo' 125 (his father had taken on the Ducati concession for Britain), but success thereafter was patchy despite that dream debut. Twin and four-cylinder racing 125/175s were also tried, without success.

They raced off-road as well – Xavier Baldet on a Pantah

Ducatis raced all over the world. This is Daytona, Florida

But the real glory years for Ducati desmos were to come. Taglioni dreamt of designing a desmo for the road, and in 1968 his dream came true with the wide-case 250 and 350 singles. They were raced for two years before the road bikes were unveiled, and revealed their potential with 45bhp (at 10,500rpm) from the 350. Both were followed in 1969 by a new, larger 450, the largest capacity that could be accommodated within the single's crankcases. The 250 could top 150km/h (93mph) – a match for the Japanese 250 two-strokes – and the 350 over 100mph. Wide, high touring handlebars were an option, but there weren't many takers. The 450 Desmo Superbike of 1970 (basically a replica of Bruno Spaggiari's race bike) claimed 40bhp and 193km/h (120mph). Alongside the Desmos, there were the more conventional 250 and 350 Mark 3s, but the more glamorous desmodromic-equipped bikes were always in the limelight. All the Ducati singles were dropped in 1974, having been overtaken by events. But for many they remain the ultimate sporting single – lightweight, quick-steering and slim.

A New Era

Fortunately for Ducati, it had already found a replacement – the V-twin. In the late sixties, the ever-larger superbike was becoming a reality. The Kawasaki two-strokes, BSA/Triumph triples, Honda CB750s – every year someone came out with something bigger and (supposedly) better than anything which had preceded it. In fact, when Fabio Taglioni made his first sketches for a big Ducati in March 1970, many of these were already on sale.

The unfaired Monster helped create a new market for Ducati – and its rivals

The first V-twin. This is a slightly later (1973) version of the 750GT

However, he worked so fast that Ducati had its new bike on sale little more than a year after that first sketch.

For Taglioni, the answer was obvious: use Ducati's experience of singles to create a V-twin. He chose to place the cylinders 90 degrees apart, which in many ways is the perfect format for a V-twin. It offers primary balance, better cooling for the rear cylinder and it is easier to keep the two inlet tracts at equal lengths. An engine was running within three months, and a complete bike was on the road in August. It didn't use desmodromics, but Taglioni had projected 80bhp at 9,200rpm, and desmo or no, everyone agreed that the original Ducati V-twin, with its shapely, flowing side covers (it was known as the 'round case') looked wonderful. It was oversquare (80mm x 74.4.mm) but with a lowish 8.5:1 compression ratio. Main bearings and gearbox were strengthened over the singles. But it wasn't designed with production economics in mind. The good-looking bevel drive to the camshaft needed very careful manufacture and assembly, and it took up to eight hours to build a single engine.

In June 1971, the first production 750GTs (complete with period metalflake paintwork in orange, green or blue) were unveiled but without immediate success; as one commentator has pointed out, the cylinder-head design owed much to the original Gran Sport (and there were no desmodromics on this one). Small 30mm carburettors stifled the engine and claimed power was a rather ordinary 55bhp. Still, the 750 Sport of 1972 (higher compression, freer breathing, bigger carbs) was much more like it, and displayed a little more of the potential of Ducati's new V-twin. And

BELOW: Twin exhausts of the 996

ABOVE: 916 limited-edition Senna

OPPOSITE: ST2 Supersport 900

both those first 750s shared superlative handling, thanks to a stiff frame based on a design by Colin Seeley, supported by substantial, good quality suspension (this was at a time when 'superbike' engines could outperform their handling).

But what really boosted the bike's image (not to mention sales) was its famous victory at Imola in April 1972. A 500cc (30.5cu in) V-twin had met with only limited GP success in the early seventies, but for the new Imola 200 race (designed for production-based 750cc/46cu inch bikes), it came up with a desmodromically-equipped 750. This was very different from the 750GT, which could rev no higher than 7,800rpm (the race bike would rev to 9,000rpm). Taglioni received the go-ahead for an all-out assault on Imola, where nine manufacturers were fielding teams, and obliged. From the start it was obvious that the Ducatis were suited to Imola. In

DUCATI
DUCATI SUPERSPORT 900

practice, veteran Ducati racer Bruno Spaggiari (well, he was 39-years-old) and F750 racer Paul Smart set the fastest times. The two of them led most of the race, with Smart coming home first. This tremendous win radically transformed Ducati's profile.

Softer & Smaller

It took Ducati two years to come up with a road-going replica of the Imola winner, but when it did, it was a very close replica indeed. Many manufacturers would have been content with some mild tuning and a race-style fairing, but the new Ducati 750 Super Sport had desmodromic valvegear, just like the racer, and even had conrods carved from solid billets, also like the racer. Once again, production economics were not uppermost! The first 200 were really homologation specials, built to satisfy production racing requirements, but they weighed only 180kg (400lb) and could manage 217km/h (135mph). All in all, a very different motorcycle to the 750GT, and the archetypal 'racer-with-lights'. It soon grew to 864cc (53cu in) as the 900SS (though a sleeved-down 750 was still available), a move originally inspired by the need to undertake Endurance racing, since two-strokes were rapidly taking over the shorter races. Gradually, the SS gained some fripperies, such as indicators, but at heart remained a raw sportster right up until it was dropped in 1981.

Meanwhile, the 'touring' side was being taken care of first by the 860GT (same capacity as the 900SS, but still with conventional valve springs and in softer tune than the 750). There was an electric-start GTE, and in 1976 the more European-orientated 860GTS. The 900SD (or Darmah) of 1977 was more of a concerted

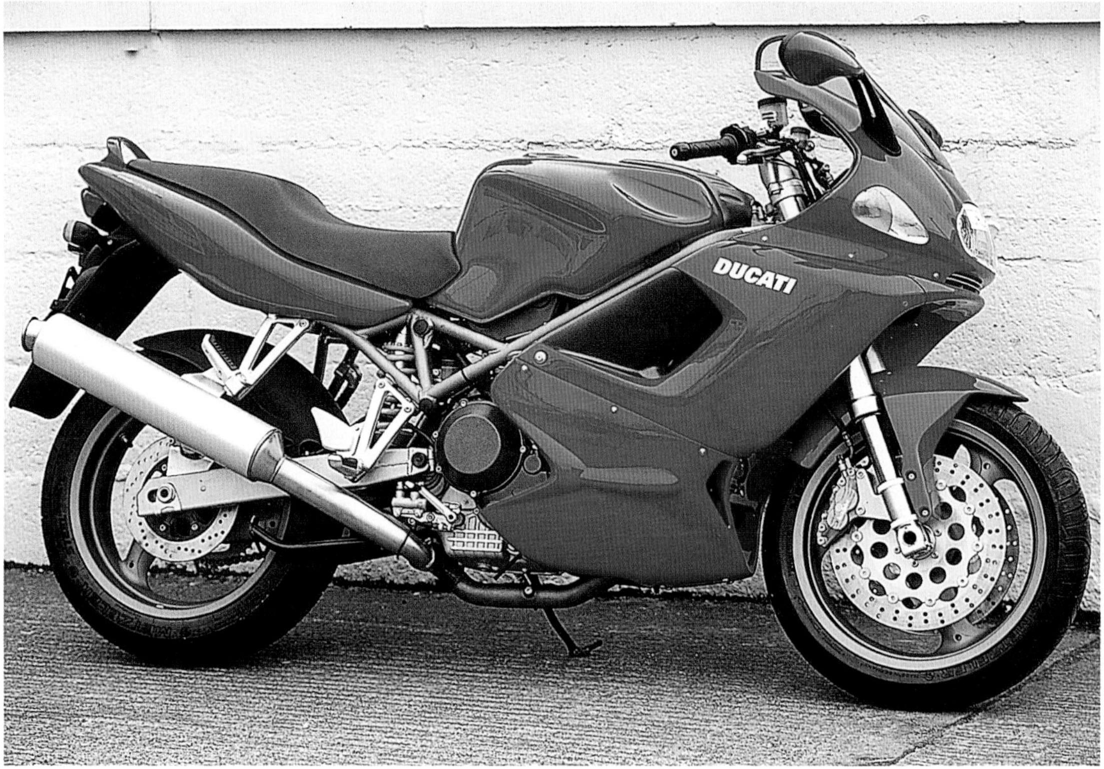

LEFT and ABOVE: The ST2 was Ducati's stab at the modern sports-touring market

1998 Monster Dark, a cut-price version of the standard Monster

step forward. Ducati, in a real effort to cure its traditional weakness of poor electrics, fitted an electric start and desmo cylinder heads, commissioned a modern styling job from Leopoldo Tartarini and managed to sell it at a price that could compete with the Japanese. The Darmah lasted five years and became Ducati's mainstream model.

Less successful was another attempt at mid-range parallel twins of 350 and 500cc (21 and 30.5cu in). Quite fast in 500 Super Sport desmo form, but unappealing to the *ducatista,* it was for some reason unable to appeal to other riders either. The Sport lasted until 1980, but by then a far more convincing Ducati 500 was making its debut. Typically, Taglioni had an answer to the failure of the parallel twins, a 500cc V-twin.

It was the Pantah, which for the first time abandoned the expensive bevel-drive cam gear for a quieter, simpler toothed belt-drive. The first prototype was built in 1977, but due to industrial troubles (the company was by now state-owned) it was two years before the bike was unveiled. This was a modern mid-range Ducati that owed less to the past: electric start, reliability and mechanical quietness all featured. Road testers liked the bike, which soon grew to a 600 (up to 61bhp at 9,100rpm by 1982) and overgearing seemed to be the only real criticism. In fact, the Pantah spawned a whole family of variations, like the less sporting 350XL and 600TL, though the ultimate was perhaps the 650SL of 1984–86.

While the Pantah was still in delayed prototype form, Ducati had enjoyed a victory on a par with that of Imola. Mike Hailwood, now 38-years-old (don't forget, he had won his first Grand Prix on a Ducati) had agreed to ride a 947cc (58cu in) TT F1 Ducati at the 1978 Isle of Man TT, not having raced there for 11 years. It was to be a fairy-tale return: Hailwood not only won the race but smashed Phil Read's Honda lap record at 178km/h (110.62mph), and this on a bike that had far less power than the Hondas and Kawasakis in the same race. This did Ducati a lot of good, and inevitably led to a Mike Hailwood Replica (really a 900SS with different bodywork and slightly more power). The MHR in itself became something of a cult bike, so much so that in 1998 Ducati showed the MK 900, a 1990s version of the same thing – or so the publicity of the time went.

As the big V-twin which had been ridden by Mike Hailwood found itself increasingly outclassed, Ducati turned to developments of the Pantah for racing: first the 600cc (37cu in) TT2 (which marked the company's official return to racing) and in 1984 the 750cc (46cu in) TT1, which enjoyed some success in both Endurance racing and the Battle of the Twins series. Once again, company politics delayed the introduction of a road-going version of the TT1 (this time, Cagiva was in the process of buying Ducati), but the 750 F1 was finally launched in 1985. Still very much a development of the smaller Pantahs (it still used 500-sized valves) the 750 produced 62.5bhp at 7,500rpm. Air-cooled Ducatis had long since been overtaken in the power game, but the F1 was compact and of course handled very well, able to make the most of its relatively limited bhp. In any case, it received a substantial power boost in 1986 (to 75bhp), not to mention fully adjustable front forks, though some thought the shorter-stroke Pantah-derived twin didn't have the same effortless feel as the earlier 750SS. The F1 was still winning races and, in the Ducati tradition, there were a handful of different race replicas.

Cagiva & Paso

The year 1985 was something of a turning-point for Ducati. The Italian government appeared to have no great interest in motorcycle production but that year sold out to Cagiva (which was already buying Ducati engines to power its own big bikes), which most certainly did. The Paso was the result. A complete departure for Ducati, it was more of a sports-tourer than a genuine sportsbike, with full bodywork that for the first time ever on a Ducati, hid the engine! The thinking was different: the new frame allowed easy access to the rear cylinder head to service the desmodromic valve gear; there was the latest sophisticated suspension, radial tyres, an hydraulic clutch and a large dual seat. As for the V-twin, it was still air-cooled, but the rear cylinder head was reversed to allow for the fitting of a single twin-choke Weber carburettor to serve both cylinders. This last change was a mistake and gave rise to endless fuelling problems that were never really rectified until fuel injection took over a few years later. Sadly, customers failed to be impressed by the new-found sophistication of the Paso, which was heavier and slower than the F1.

It was replaced by the 906 in 1989, which used various elements of the new four-valve 851 (notably water-cooled cylinders) with traditional two-valve desmodromic heads. This too was not a great success, though the 907IE which replaced it in 1991 was a great improvement: the Weber carburettor was replaced with electronic fuel injection and a 17-inch wheel improved the handling. Power was up to a claimed 90bhp at 8,500rpm, it could easily exceed 209km/h (130mph), and was actually a little lighter than the 906 into the bargain. Once again, sales failed to materialize, and the 907 was dropped after just two years.

The 748 looked almost identical to the 916 and used the same water-cooled, four-valve layout

Unfortunately, another Ducati of the mid-eighties was less than successful – the Indiana. Intended for the U.S. market, it married the 650 Pantah engine with custom cruiser styling. For the *ducatista*, this was simply a waste of a classic, desmodromic V-twin, and cruiser buyers didn't seem that impressed either.

However, Ducati was not about to forget its origins and, alongside the Paso, the lighter Super Sport remained. The F1 continued to sell well up to 1987, so it made sense to launch a new 750 Sport which encompassed elements of the Paso but the soul of the F1. In fact, it was really the Paso engine in a modified F1 frame. However, Ducati didn't use the water-cooled 906 engine in this bike, perhaps realizing that it was a little too radical for this 'traditional' Ducati. Instead, the new 900SS had an oil/air-cooled version of the two-valve twin, though still with the 851's crankcase and six-speed gearbox. It was less powerful than the 906, but significantly lighter.

In fact, this ideal of a simpler, lighter (and cheaper) Ducati became a permanent part of the range alongside the more complex four-valve water-cooled

Rare motocross Desmo single

machines. So in 1991, thoroughly revised 750s and 900SSs appeared. The Weber carburettor was discarded, but instead of fuel injection used two Mikuni carburettors, which improved throttle response and engine behaviour no end. In keeping with its position in the range (sporting, rather than super sports) the handlebars were higher and footpegs lower. These two bikes were staples of the Ducati range through the 1990s and sold well, although were overshadowed by the exotic 916. It should not be forgotten that there was also a 600cc (37cu in) version (from 1994) and, to suit certain tax classes, 350 and 400SSs as well.

Otto Valvole

Ducati's modern era, and the basis for its tremendous World Superbike success in the 1990s, was established in 1987 with the 851. It was still a V-twin, but with four-valve cylinder-heads (still desmodromic, of course), water-cooling, fuel injection and a six-speed gearbox. Early races confirmed that here at last was a Ducati that could match the speed of four-cylinder Japanese bikes, and in its racing debut it won the first round of the new World Superbike (WSB) Championship in April 1988.

Ducati had learnt its lesson by now, and road replicas of the successful race bikes were quick to arrive in the form of the 851 Strada and Superbike. Ironically, these first four-valve road bikes failed to live up to their promise, though better was to come. Meanwhile, the racer had grown to 888cc (54cu in), with 125bhp at 11,000rpm at the rear wheel and in 1990 Raymond Roche won the WSB Championship on one. The road version was the SP2 (now with the same 888cc as the racers) and there was a heavier, softer Strada with a dual seat as well.

At this time, the four-valve road bikes were building a very close association with the racers. The racing Ducatis were becoming increasingly dominant in WSB (helped by a lower minimum weight limit than for the four-cylinder bikes) and as they were developed year by year, so were the road machines. Naturally, the racing success rubbed off, and Ducati was riding high. The 888SPS of 1992, for example, was a true race replica, with carbon-fibre fuel tank, seat and silencers, gold series Brembo disc brakes and more power; in magazine tests it crested 260km/h (160mph). A divergence began to develop between the race replica SP (Sport Production) series and the 'softer' Stradas, a trend which continued with the 888's replacement, the 916.

The name '916' has become, in a few short years, as evocative as 'Mach 1' and 'SS' ever were. It was really a continued development of the 888, with a capacity increase to 916cc (56cu in). In SP form it had twin injectors per cylinder, titanium con-rods and a claimed 131bhp at 10,500rpm at the crankshaft. But for the road, the 916 Strada for 1994 was possibly more significant. There was more attention to ease of servicing, it had less fierce camshafts and, in 1995, a dual seat. However, for the really committed, Ducati continued to offer an SPS version. Without doubt, the 916 was the sportsbike of the mid-1990s, not least because of continued success in WSB. Now with a 955cc engine, and Carl Fogarty riding, the 916 dominated the 1995 season, which also marked the debut of the smaller 748

M750

OPPOSITE: The Monster 750 married 750SS engine to Monster running gear

ABOVE: Pantah 700cc (43cu in)

for the road. It was essentially the same as the 916, but of 748cc (45cu in) capacity. And it wasn't just V-twins: the Supermono 549cc (33.5cu in) single raced throughout the 1990s, though plans for a road version failed to materialize.

However, there was no danger of Ducati becoming too race-focused. Unhappy experiences with the Indiana and Paso had not diverted the company from new markets, and the Monster of 1993 was certainly that. It really was a new idea, owing something to the streetfighter style, something else to the Ducati ideal of a light, compact V-twin. However, there weren't many new parts on it, and it combined the 888 frame with the 900SS engine. And to underline the basic image, there was no rev counter! Such a success was the Monster, that 600cc and 750cc (37 and 46cu in) versions soon joined the 900.

But in 1996 it looked as if all this success might be thrown away. Cagiva, which had built itself into the largest Italian motorcycle manufacturer, now had financial problems of its own. Even suppliers were not being paid, and Ducati production fell while waiting lists rose. The answer came with yet another buyout of Ducati, this time by a group of American investors, the Texas Pacific Group (TPG). TPG had money, Ducati needed it, and a plan ensued to increase production substantially. Ducati built 12,500 bikes in 1996, but TPG was planning for 40,000 within four years.

To accomplish this, it was necessary to widen Ducati's market, though the basis for this had already been laid with the new sports-touring ST2, intended for launch in 1996. The ST2 owed much to the 907, with the same two-valve water-cooled engine, though bored out to 944cc (58cu in). The ST4 was a brave shot in a highly competitive but growing market, and received good, if not ecstatic press reviews. It was joined by a four-valve ST4 version in 1998, which really completed the renewal of the Ducati family for the 1990s: super sports 748/916 (which became 996 in late 1998), sports SS, 'naked' Monster and sports touring ST.

The year 1998 also saw the debut of the new Super Sport. Styled by Pierre Terblanche, it was more of a development of the old SS than an all-new machine, though the venerable oil/air-cooled twin had acquired fuel injection to produce 80bhp at 7,500rpm. Not everyone liked the new styling, but the half-faired version which followed was deemed better-looking – you could see the engine! With full order books and money in the bank (the company went public in March 1999), Ducati looks set for a new period of stability as the millennium approaches.

Dunelt 298cc/18 cubic inch J2, an interesting stepped piston two-stroke

DUCSON *Spain c.1950–80*
Mopeds and motorcycles up to 65cc (4cu in).

DÜMO *Germany 1924–25*
The same as the 198cc (12cu in) Autinag, but sportier.

DUNELT *England 1919–57*
A stepped-piston two-stroke single was made up to 1935, also a Rex-engined moped in 1957.

DUNKLEY *England c.1913*
Utilized bought-in engines from Precision, Peco and JAP.

DUNKLEY *England 1957–59*
Made mopeds and, unusually, built its own ohv engines.

DURAND *France 1920–23*
Used Zurcher engines.

DURANDAL *France 1925–32*
Used pressed steel frames for some bikes, all of which used bought-in engines up to 490cc (30cu in).

DUVAL *Belgium 1950–55*
Imported 123cc (7.5cu in) Royal Enfield two-strokes for its machines.

DUX *England 1904–06*
Minerva, MMC, Sarolea and others supplied the engines.

DUZMO *England 1919–23*
John Wallace designed these 496cc (30cu in) ohv singles and 992cc (61cu in) 50-degree V-twins.

DWB *Germany 1924–26*
195cc (12cu in) sv machines.

DYSON-MOTORETTE *England 1920–22*
Built a low-powered scooter-like bike with a 1.5hp engine.

E

EADIE *England 1889–1903*
Used De Dion, Minerva, MMC and other engines – also had Royal Enfield connections.

EAGLE *U.S.A. 1910–15*
Used bought-in Spake singles and V-twins.

EAGLE-TANDEM *England 1903–05*
Unusual De Dion-engined bike with a 'chair' in place of the saddle.

EBE *Sweden 1919–30*
First built 173cc (11cu in) clip-ons, then motorcycles with its own engines of up to 598cc (36cu in).

EBER *Germany 1924–28*
Began using Blackburne engines up to 497cc (30cu in), later Kühne and ohc Küchen units.

EBO *Germany 1924–30*
Utilized Precision and V-twin JAP engines.

EBS *Germany 1924–30*
Utilized a wide range of its own power units from 198 to 796cc (12 to 49cu in), though added a Villiers-engined machine in 1928.

EBU-STAR *Japan 1952–55*
A 248cc (15cu in) twin with a difference – one cylinder was vertical, the other horizontal.

EBW *Germany 1923–24*
Used Bekamo engines.

ECA *Germany 1923–24*
Limited production of 124cc (8cu in) two-strokes.

ECEKA *Germany 1924–25*
145cc or 173cc (9 or 11cu in) engines.

ECHELSDORFER *Germany 1929–31*
JAP-engined, but with the 198cc (12cu in) single, not the big V-twin.

ECHO *Japan 1958–60*
Built a 50cc (3cu in) two-stroke and the Pandra scooter.

ECKL *Germany 1923–26*
Started with clip-ons before making its own 198cc (12cu in) engine.

ECONOMIC *England 1921–23*
Aptly named at only £28.10s brand new, this was a 165cc (10cu in) twin-cylinder two-stroke with friction drive.

EDETA *Spain 1951–60*
147cc and 173cc (9 and 11) two-strokes.

EDMONTON *England 1903–10*
Used Minerva and Fafnir engines.

EDMUND *England 1907–24*
Fitted many different bought-in engines to its own frames, some of which incorporated leaf-sprung rear suspension.

EGA *Germany 1922–26*
Own 246/346cc (15/21cu in) three-port two-stroke engines.

EICHLER *Germany 1920–25*
Assembled utility bikes with DKW and Bekamo engines, and built DKW scooters under licence.

EISENHAMMER *Germany 1923–26*
Choice of DKW 206cc (13cu in) or own 225cc (14cu in) engines.

EISLER *Czechoslovakia 1920–26*
Produced both clip-ons and lightweight bikes with the same 148cc (9cu in) engine.

ELAND *The Netherlands 1955–59*
Mostly Sachs-engined two-strokes of up to 158cc (10cu in).

ELECT *Italy 1920–23*
Unusual 492cc (30cu in) flat twin with three valves per cylinder.

ELFE *Germany 1923–25*
Own 196cc (12cu in) three-port two-stroke with unorthodox frame.

ELF-KING *England 1907–09*
Its Minerva V-twin was equipped with a hand starter.

ELFSON *England 1923–25*
Used a Norman ohv of 170cc (10cu in) or its own 294cc (18cu in) two-stroke.

ELI *England 1911–12*
Precision-powered 3.5hp machines.

ELIE HUIN *France 1950s–early 1960s*
Used various French proprietary engines up to 248cc (15cu in).

ELIG *Spain 1956–59*
Utilized Hispano-Villiers engines of 123–198cc (7.5–12cu in).

ELITE *Germany 1923–40*
The company made cars until it merged with Diamant and built first a 1hp clip-on, then a range of Kühne-powered motorcycles. Also produced the Opel-powered EO from 1932.

ELLEHAM *Denmark 1904–09*
A step-through frame with a 2.75hp Peugeot engine.

ELMDON *England 1915–21*
269cc (16cu in) Villiers-engined.

ELRING *Germany 1924–25*
A rebadged ELFE two-stroke.

ELSTER *Germany 1924–26*
Own sv 197cc (12cu in) machine.

ELSWICK *England 1903–20*
Fitted Precision 348/498cc (21/30cu in) engines to its own frames.

ELVE *Belgium 1958–63*
Sachs-engined mopeds.

EM *Austria 1928–30*
A MAG-engined 497cc (30cu in) single was its sole offering.

EMA *Germany 1922–26*
Used a 145cc (9cu in) DKW engine with horizontal cylinder.

EMBLEM *U.S.A. 1909–25*
Typical early American singles and V-twins of up to 996cc (61cu in).

Emblem single in board-track trim, owned by Jim Lattin

ABOVE and BELOW: Emblem built both singles and V-twins, as did many American manufacturers of the time. This board-track racer had a Heitger carburettor

EMC *England 1947–52*
Ehrlich Motor Company began with its own 348cc (21cu in) double-piston two-stroke, but later used Puch engines. Joe Ehrlich built a few racing bikes in the early sixties, and 20 years later developed Rotax-powered racers with Waddon Engineering.

EMH *Germany 1924–29*
Step-through frames with overhead-cam Küchen singles.

EMMAG *Hungary 1924–27*
495cc (30cu in) singles and 670cc (41cu in) twins, all two-strokes.

EMURO *Japan 1957–58*
All two-strokes, from a 90cc (5.5cu in) single to a 494cc (30cu in) twin.

EMW *East Germany 1945–56*
Similar to a pre-war BMW, this was a 348cc (21cu in) single with shaft-drive and a pressed steel frame.

EMC's 348cc two-stroke used twin pistons in a common combustion chamber

EMWE *Germany 1924–25*
A 293cc (18cu in) two-stroke and welded box frame, all in-house.

ENAG *Germany 1924–25*
There were water-cooled barrels and air-cooled heads for these mid-sized two-strokes.

ENDRICK *England 1911–15*
Used a variety of bought-in engines, including Peugeots and Precisions.

ENDURANCE *England 1909–24*
Used Villiers two-strokes as well as its own engines.

ENERGETTE *England 1907–11*
Before he designed his own engines, James Landsdowne Norton's Energette used a licence-built Moto-Rêve unit.

ENGEE *Germany 1925*
Used a Kühne 348cc (21cu in) single.

EO *Germany 1930–31*
Short-lived combination of an Elite with an Opel ohc engine.

ÉOLE *Belgium c.1900–07*
Used Kelecom and Fafnir engines.

EPA *Germany 1924–25*
Fitted 293cc (18cu in) JAP sv engines to its own frames.

ERCOLI-CAVALLONE *Italy 1922–23*
An unusual format of engine – a 496cc (30cu in) two-stroke V-twin.

ERIE *U.S.A. 1905–11*
Used Minerva, Spake and Curtiss engines.

ERIOL *France 1932–39*
98cc (6cu in) two-stroke-powered lightweights.

ERKA *Germany 1924–25*
269cc (16cu in) two-stroke.

ERKÖ *Germany 1923–30*
Included an interesting 246cc (15cu in) two-stroke with double-diameter piston and rotary inlet valve. Later made four-strokes.

ERNST EICHLER *Germany 1924–25*
Pressed steel frames housed small two- and four-stroke engines.

ERNST-MAG *Germany 1926–30*
First used Küchen engines, later relying on MAG units of up to 996cc (61cu in).

ERR-ZETT *Austria 1938*
Lightweights using 98cc (6cu in) Sachs or Ilo engines.

ESCHAG *Germany 1923–25*
Belt-driven 298cc (18cu in) single.

ESCOL *Belgium 1925–38*
Imported various English engines, but last models had in-house 348cc (21cu in) two-strokes.

ETA *England 1921*
Three-cylinder radial-engined bike of 870cc (53cu in) with shaft-drive.

ÉTOILE *France 1933–39*
Aubier-Dunne-powered two-strokes of 98–198cc (6–12cu in).

EUROPA *Germany 1931–33*
Used both Villiers and the Berlin-built Schliha two-strokes.

EVANS *U.S.A. 1919–24*
A 119cc (7cu in) two-stroke lightweight, later made under licence by Stock in Germany.

EVANS-PONDORF *Germany 1924–25*
Advanced 496cc (30cu in) single with foot gearchange.

EVART-HALL *England 1903–05*
Started with 2.5hp engines in strengthened bicycle frames, and from 1904 produced a 385cc (23cu in) air-cooled four.

EVEREST *Germany 1925–26*
Own 496cc (30cu in) ohv single.

EVO *Germany 1923–25*
Used Ilo and in-house 146cc (9cu in) engines.

EVYCSA *Spain 1956*
A 173cc (11cu in) four-stroke with four-speed gearbox.

EWABRA *Germany 1921–24*
A 550cc (34cu in) single-cylinder sv.

EXCELSIOR *England 1896–1964*
There were four Excelsiors, of which the English company was the longest established. It began production by using a 1.25hp Minerva in its own bicycle frame

A do-it-yourself Villiers-engined Excelsior

and used bought-in engines from many sources, including an 850cc (52cu in) single. JAP-engined racers were successful in the twenties, as was the ohc Manxman (made in 248–498cc/15–30cu inch forms), Excelsior's most famous model. Contribution to the war effort was the 98cc (6cu in) Welbike. There were only two-strokes after the war, up to a 328cc (20cu in) twin. The company was taken over by Britax in 1964, who ceased production.

David Lee on an Excelsior Manxman. They are still raced to this day

ABOVE and BELOW: 1924 Excelsior V-twin

ABOVE and BELOW: The overhead camshaft Excelsior Manxman was a great success

EXCELSIOR *Germany 1901–39*
Like the English Excelsior, this one started out making bicycles and used a range of bought-in engines, including Minerva, Zedel, Fafnir, Bark and JAP units ranging from 198 to 496cc (12 to 30cu in).

EXCELSIOR *Germany 1923–24*
No connection with the earlier German Excelsior, this company built a simple 245cc (15cu in) two-stroke.

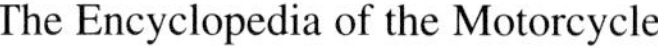

EXCELSIOR *U.S.A. 1908–31*

Part of Schwinn bicycles, it produced a complete range from a 269cc (16cu in) two-stroke, via 499cc (30cu in) singles to V-twins of 746 and 996cc (45 and 61cu in).

ABOVE: Excelsior-Henderson's legendary performance won the marque many hillclimb titles

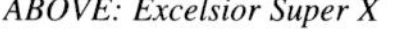

ABOVE: Excelsior Super X

EXCELSIOR-HENDERSON *U.S.A. 1998–*

It was the runaway success of Harley-Davidson in the late 1980s and 1990s that encouraged a number of entrepreneurs to attempt the production of an all-American rival. Brothers Dan and David Hanlon bought the name when Schwinn (who still owned it) ceased trading in 1992. A combination of local authority grants and investment banking financed the project. The 1386cc (85cu in) Super X was deliberately styled to ape the traditional American V-twin look that Harley had exploited so successfully. Unlike Harley's back-to-basics approach, though, the Super

BELOW: The 1999 Excelsior-Henderson Super X prototype

BELOW: Dave Hanlon cruises the Heartland on the prototype Excelsior-Henderson Super X

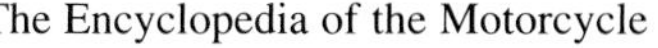

X had four valves per cylinder, dohc and electronic fuel injection. The engine itself was oil-cooled and rubber-mounted. Leading-link forks and exposed springs made for a very distinctive front-end. With Excelsior-Hendersons now entering production in the all-new factory, it looks as though the Hanlons' dream of producing an all-American rival to Harley-Davidson has become a reality.

OPPOSITE: Excelsior-Henderson 'four'

EXPRESS *Germany 1903–58*
There were three periods of production: Fafnir-engined bicycle frames to 1908; Sachs-engined mopeds and lightweights from 1933–39; use of Sachs, Ilo and own engines up to 250cc (15cu in) from 1949–58.

EYSINK *The Netherlands 1899–1956*
Began with bought-in engines, but later designed its own singles and V-twins up to 774cc (47cu in). Also a 702cc (43cu in) flat twin in the early twenties, though produced fitted four-valve Python singles as well, and built JAP singles of up to 198cc (12cu in) under licence. Only Villiers-powered two-strokes appeared after the war.

BELOW: Excelsior-Henderson engine detail

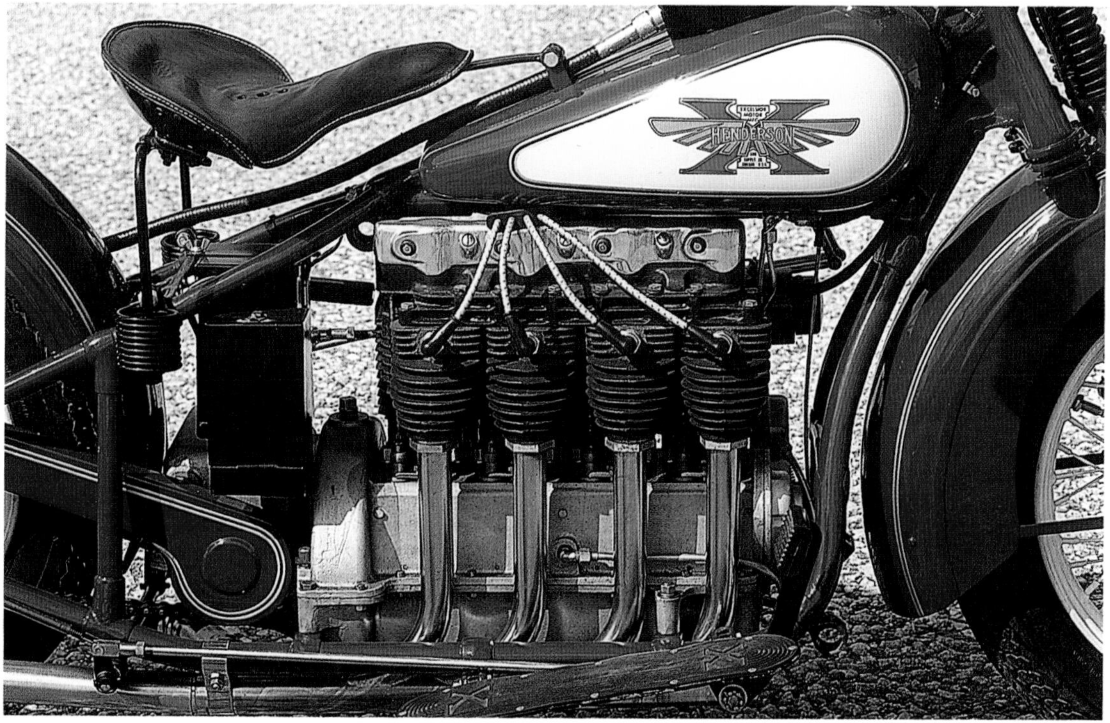

F

FABULA *Germany 1922–24*
A technically advanced unit-construction 246cc (15cu in) two-stroke with shaft-drive, designed by Nikolaus Henzel.

FADAG *Germany 1921–25*
A 118cc (7cu in) clip-on, and from 1923 an own-design 497cc (30cu in) single (though made for Fadag by Sarolea).

FAFNIR *Germany 1900–14*
Supplier of engines to countless pioneer manufacturers, but also made complete bikes from 1903.

FAGAN *Eire 1935–37*
Villiers-engined 123cc (7.5cu in) single.

FAGARD *Germany 1923–25*
Utilized a 145cc (9cu in) DKW engine – also known as FG.

FAGGI *Italy 1950–53*
Used exclusively Villiers engines to 147cc (9cu in).

FAINI *Italy 1923–27*
Made 108cc (6.6cu in) clip-ons and 198cc (12cu in) motorcycles.

FAIRFIELD *England 1914–15*
269cc (16cu in) two-strokes.

FAKA *Germany 1952–57*
Ilo-engined scooters of 147–197cc (9–12cu in).

FALCO *Italy 1950–53*
Used Sachs engines of 98 and 147cc (6 and 9cu in).

FALKE *Germany 1923–25*
Used Grade or DKW two-strokes of similar sizes.

FALTER *Germany 1952–63*
49cc (3cu in) mopeds.

FAM *Italy 1951–69*
Founded by one of the Benelli brothers, it made 115cc (7cu in) singles and 195cc (12cu in) flat twins.

FAMA *Germany 1923–25*
190cc and 420cc (12 and 26cu in) four-stroke singles.

FAMO *Germany 1923–26*
All used triangular frames and 127cc (8cu in) two-stroke engines.

FANTIC *Italy 1968–*
Fantic has concentrated on mopeds and small bikes, but has made its mark with a range of trials and motocross bikes as well as road machines. Most have used Minarelli or Franco-Morini engines, though some trials machines which have won championships use Fantic's own two-stroke unit. It is famous for the Caballero trail-bike range (the 124cc/8cu inch version produced 21bhp at 9,500rpm) and perhaps infamous for the Chopper. The latter, from the mid-1970s, was an early factory custom aiming to be a mini-custom bike complete with raked forks, high-rise bars and seat plus an eye-catching colour scheme. Buyers had a choice of 49cc or 124cc (3 or 8cu in) two-strokes. The author remembers being duly impressed, at an impressionable age, that Fantic's sports moped boasted *six* gears, when even five was considered exotic enough.

FAR *Austria 1924–27*
JAP-engined machines of up to 490cc (30cu in) from Franz and Anton Rumpler.

FARNELL *England c.1901*
2.75 hp Minerva engines in bicycle frames.

FAVOR *France 1919–59*
Built own two-strokes of 98cc (6cu in) upwards, but over the years offered bigger four-strokes from JAP and (after the war) AMC.

FAVORIT *Germany 1933–38*
A sidecar maker which also offered a 996cc (61cu in) JAP V-twin before concentrating on Sachs-engined lightweights.

FB *England 1913–22*
Built own two-stroke engines up to 411cc (25cu in) for sale, as well as complete bikes.

FB *Germany 1923–25*
Sometimes badged as Meteors, it produced 269cc (16cu in) two-strokes and later JAP and Blackburne-engined four-strokes.

FB-MONDIAL *Italy 1950–*
Built three-wheelers before the war but won the 125cc World Championship in 1949 and started making road bikes (ohv 125s) the following year. A succession of two-and four-stroke scooters and lightweights followed before the company was forced to close in 1979. A relaunch in 1987 did not last long, but the company tried again two years later with limited production of 125cc (8cu in) two-strokes and 600cc (37cu in) four-strokes.

ABOVE: Fantic 305 trials bike

OPPOSITE: Fantic later built state-of-the-art trials bikes

FBM *Italy 1950–55*
Mounted its horizontal single on the swinging arm. Capacity: 48–158cc (3–10cu in).

FECHTEL *Germany 1924–26*
Small assembler who fitted Hansa 198cc (6cu in) ohv engines into its own frames.

FEDERATION *England 1919–37*
Built in Birmingham for the Co-operative retail chain stores, bearing the Federal badge. Most models had the 147/269cc (9/16cu in) Villiers engines or 246/680cc (15/41cu in) JAP engines.

FEE *England 1905–08*
The Barter-designed sidevalve flat twins had engines of 198cc, 346cc and 676cc (12, 21 and 41cu in). Also known as the Fairy.

FEILBACH *U.S.A. 1912–15*
Operated in Milwaukee, but rather less successfully than Harley-Davidson. Produced singles and V-twins up to 1130cc (69cu in), with a shaft-driven option.

FEMINIA *France 1933–36*
Assembled lightweights with 98/123cc (6/7.5cu in) Aubier-Dunne and Stainless two-strokes.

12
FANTIC MOTOR
12

FERBEDO *Germany 1954*
Mini-scooter with a 49cc (3cu in) Zündapp unit.

FERRARI *Italy 1951–54*
No connection with Enzo, but produced two- and four-stroke singles and a 173cc (11cu in) ohc twin.

FERRARIS *Italy 1903*
2hp Peugeot engines in bicycle frames.

FERT *Italy 1926–29*
173cc (11cu in) ohv engines designed by Calamidas Fert.

FEW-PARAMOUNT *England 1920–27*
Unusual long-wheelbased bike with bucket seats and enclosed engines (up to a 996cc/61cu inch JAP). Few were built.

FEX *Germany 1923–24*
Tried with own 170cc (10cu in) two-stroke before utilizing DKW and Bekamo units.

FG *Germany 1923–25*
A rebadged Fagard.

FHG *Germany 1927–29*
Thought to be a French Grimpeur offered by its German importer.

FIAM *Italy 1923–25*
110cc (7cu in) clip-on.

FIAMC *Germany 1951–53*
123cc (7.5cu in) scooters and lightweights.

FIDUCIA *Switzerland 1902–05*
Used own 450cc (27cu in) single.

FIFI *Germany 1923–24*
Rebadged Eichler.

FIGINI *Italy 1898–1910*
Italian pioneer bike with single-cylinder mounted in the seat pillar.

FINZI *Italy 1923–25*
Advanced unit-construction V-twin of 598cc (36cu in), with enclosed chain and leaf-sprung saddle.

FIORELLI *Italy 1951–68*
123/173cc (7.5/11cu in) Ilo-engined lightweights, later mopeds.

FIT *Italy 1950–54*
123/147cc (7.5/9cu in) and Ilo-powered.

FIX *Germany 1922–26*
Used own 3hp two-strokes.

FKS *Germany 1921–26*
A 149cc (9cu in) engine mounted above the front wheel, and a 298cc (18cu in) flat twin – both two-strokes.

FLANDERS *U.S.A. 1911–14*
499cc (30cu in) sv single.

FLANDRIA *Belgium 1951–81*
Built its own engines, and apart from an early diversion into scooters and lightweights, all were of 49cc (3cu in). Also sold its engines to other manufacturers before closure in 1981.

FLINK *Germany 1920–22*
148cc (9cu in) two-strokes.

FLM *England 1951–53*
Designed by Frank Leach (ex-P&M) and used two-strokes up to 198cc (12cu in).

ABOVE and OPPOSITE: The 499cc Flanders single did not last very long

Flanders
4

FLOTTWEG *Germany 1921–37*
First produced 119cc (7cu in) clip-ons, later own four-stroke 183/246cc (11/15cu in) machines. Eventually sold out to BMW.

FLYING MERKEL *U.S.A. 1909–15*
Advanced bikes from the American industry's golden technical era. An early pioneer of gearboxes, sprung frames and electric starters.

ABOVE and BELOW: The Flying Merkel was a pioneer, but who remembers it now?

FM *Italy 1925–27*
MAG or Bradshaw 346cc (21cu in) singles in interesting aluminium-alloy frame with low-slung saddle.

FN *Belgium 1901–65*
Belgium's leading marque, famous for its pioneering use of shaft-drive from 1903, and a 360cc (22cu in) four-cylinder machine of 1904 (the first multi-cylinder motorcycle), though it started with a 133cc

OPPOSITE: A 1922 748cc (46cu in) four-cylinder shaft-driven FN

MN4911
7
MK 5651

ABOVE and RIGHT: Logo and engine details of the 1922 748cc FN

(8cu in) engine in a bicycle frame. The four lasted until 1926, but a new range of unit-construction singles were by then in production in both sv and ohv capacities of 350–600cc (21–37cu in) and were FN's mainstay until the 1950s. The company later concentrated on small two-strokes up to 200cc (12cu in), before two-wheeler production ceased in 1965. Also had racing and record-breaking successes between the wars, and designer Van Hout produced a supercharged ohc twin for FN in 1937.

FOCESI *Italy 1952–56*
Horizonal 49cc (3cu in) two-stroke, swinging-arm mounted. Used the Gloria badge.

FOCHJ *Italy 1954–57*
Used exclusively NSU engines.

FOLLIS *France 1903–60*
Always used bought-in engines from JAP, Python and Blackburne and later Ydral and AMC.

FONGRI *Italy 1919–25*
Sidevalve flat twins of 499/579cc (30/35cu in).

FORCE *Austria 1925–26*
A 346cc (21cu in) two-stroke.

FORELLE *Germany 1955–58*
Used various two-strokes of 140–246cc (8.5–15cu in).

FORSTER *Switzerland 1921–25*
2.5/3.8hp singles.

FORTUNA *Germany 1921–28*
External flywheeled two-strokes of 247 and 297cc (15 and 18cu in).

FORWARD *England 1909–15*
Built its own V-twins of 339 or 479cc (21 or 29cu in).

FP *Hungary 1924–25*
Own 346cc (21cu in) sv single.

FRANCE *France 1931–35*
Built own two-strokes of 98–245cc (6–15cu in).

FRANCHI *Italy 1950–58*
Used exclusively Sachs engines of 98–174cc (6–11cu in).

FRANCIS-BARNETT *England 1919–66*
Francis-Barnett was the result of a marriage. If he hadn't met Miss Barnett, Captain Gordon Francis would no doubt have joined his father's Lea Francis business, which built both bicycles and motorcycles. But his new father-in-law was building bikes too, under the Invicta name, and so the company was formed with capital from both Francis Snr. and Arthur Barnett, with Gordon Francis in day-to-day control. Francis-Barnett (or Fanny-B, as it was better known to most riders) never built its own engines, and the largest bike it ever sold amounted to 344cc (21cu in); but it did manage one or two innovations of its own.

The first production bike of 1920 was conventional enough, with a 292cc (18cu in) sidevalve JAP engine, two-speed Sturmey-Archer gearbox and belt- rather than chain-drive. It was aimed a little upmarket, with its alloy primary chain cover and little toe shields on the footboards. It was soon joined by a 292cc Villiers-engined alternative (two-strokes were to be Fanny-B's staple for the rest of its commercial life) and a 343cc JAP.

During the war, Gordon Francis had worked in a military transport repair shop, constantly frustrated by the number of despatch bikes with bent frames in need of straightening. Surely it would be easier, he reasoned, to bolt a frame together out of straight tubes when, if one or more were bent, you could simply unbolt them and replace them with new ones. In 1923, his original idea was finally unveiled to the public. By now, Francis-Barnetts were cheaper, and the basic two-speeder without clutch or kickstart cost just £27. As well as the pin-jointed frame ('Built like a Bridge', went the slogan), the front fork used a large clock-spring instead of the conventional coil; but it was the frame that attracted attention and had the added advantage of making the bikes easy to pack down small for assembly overseas.

Francis-Barnett wasn't a great one for competition, but three riders did scale Snowdon in July 1926: a year or so later, Glaswegian Drew McQueen made it to the top of Ben Nevis on his Fanny-B. That same year, the company introduced a 344cc in-line Villiers twin, but its real milestone came in 1933 with the Cruiser. The 250cc (15cu in) two-stroke Cruiser's frame was made of channel-section pressings, with deeply valanced mudguards, built-in legshields and enclosed crankcase and transmission. It was another attempt at wooing the non-motorcycling commuter onto two wheels, a theme that was to recur in the British industry until the Vespa and

BELOW: Francis-Barnett Falcon 87

RIGHT: Francis-Barnett 89 Cruiser

BELOW: The 1929 250cc (15cu in) Francis-Barnett provided cheap, basic motorcycling

Francis-Barnett police bikes were of limited use in pursuit duties

Lambretta did it properly.

Francis-Barnett was taken over by the Matchless-controlled Associated Motor Cycles in 1947, and thereafter became increasingly involved in badge-engineering, though it retained its own Coventry factory until nearly the end. Villiers two-strokes were now the sole power source until AMC came up with its own 150, 175, 199 and 249cc (9, 11, 12 and 15cu in) two-strokes, for which Francis-Barnett revived the old Cruiser name. As the Cruiser 84 in the early 1960s, it also retained the theme of extensive bodywork. Meanwhile, Bill King (who had actually designed the original Cruiser) was building the prototype 150cc Fulmer, complete with more bodywork, but AMC's financial problems put an end to all that.

FRANKONIA *Germany 1923–25*
Used a 145cc (9cu in) DKW engine, mounted horizontally.

FRANZANI *Germany 1923–32*
Used own 283cc (17cu in) two-stroke, later JAP and Küchen four-strokes.

FRECO *Germany 1923–25*
Bought in engines from DKW, Runge and (for racing) Blackburne.

FREITAL *Germany 1925–26*
A rebadged DKW.

FREJUS *Italy 1960–68*
Based in Turin, it produced mopeds and lightweights to 198cc (12cu in).

FRERA *Italy 1906–36*
Italy's largest manufacturer until 1930, it thereafter suffered a rapid decline in the face of Moto Guzzi's dominance. Built a large range of bikes over the years, all with in-house engines from 269cc (16cu in) two-strokes to 1140cc (70cu in) V-twins, though most were mid-sized singles. Was relaunched in 1945.

FREYER & MILLER *U.S.A. c.1902*
Pioneer of the rotation magneto, the engine was mounted behind the saddle.

FREYLER *Austria 1928–29*
Rotary valve 348cc (21cu in) engine designed by Adalbert Freyler.

FRIMO *Germany 1923–25*
Built by the Vis company using its own 246cc (15cu in) two-stroke.

FRISCHAUF *Germany 1928–33*
Used Blackburne, JAP and Küchen engines.

FRISONI *Italy 1951–57*
123cc/7.5cu inch (Villiers) lightweights and 160cc (10cu in) scooters.

FUBO *Germany 1923–25*
Used its own 170/269cc (10/16cu in) two-strokes, plus 247/347cc (15/21cu in) Blackburnes.

FUJI *Japan 1953–57*
49–249cc (3–15cu in) two-strokes and the Gasuden scooter.

FULGOR *Italy 1922–26*
143cc (9cu in) two-strokes.

FUSI *Italy 1932–57*
The FN importer, it used many FN parts, together with licence-built JAP engines. After the war, used its own 248cc (15cu in) ohc single.

FVL *Italy 1926–35*
Well finished ohv and ohc sporting singles up to 248cc (15cu in), designed by ex-racer Francesco Lanfranchini.

G

GA *Italy 1925–27*
Used Blackburne's 678cc (41cu in) ohv V-twin.

GABBIANO *Italy 1954–56*
123cc (7.5cu in) two-stroke, horizontally-mounted.

GABY *England 1914–15*
286cc (17cu in) three-port two-strokes.

GADABOUT *England 1948–51*
123cc (7.5cu in) scooter made by Swallow sidecars.

GAIA *Italy 1922–32*
Used bought-in engines, including the Rubinelli for its clip-on, 123/173cc (7.5/11cu in) Mosers, and the Ladetto & Blatto 173cc for its motorcycles.

GALBAI *1921–25*
Various two-stroke twins, plus MAG and Bradshaw-engined four-strokes.

GALBUSERA *Italy 1934–55*
Attracted attention with its supercharged two-stroke V8 prototype of 1938, plus a 248cc (15cu in) V4 of half the size; but its mainstay bikes used Python engines before the war, Sachs afterwards. The exotic two-strokes never made it into production.

GALLONI *Italy 1920–31*
Used a variety of engines from 249–746cc (15–45cu in), some in-house. Last model used a 173cc (11cu in) Blackburne.

GAMAGE *England c.1905–24*
Rebadged bikes sold by the Gamage retail stores, bought in from Omega, Radco and others.

GANNA *Italy 1923–67*
Bought in many different power units in its longish career, notably Blackburnes before the war and Puch, Sachs, Minarelli two-strokes post-1945. However, it did design its own 499cc (30cu in) ohc single in 1936.

GAR *Germany 1924–26*
A 499cc (30cu in) ohv single.

GARABELLO *Italy 1906–29*
Interesting designs were produced by Francesco Garabello, notably a water-cooled 984cc (60cu in) four from 1922, with shaft-drive. Later came a water-cooled 173cc (11cu in) single with rotary valves.

GARANZINI *Italy 1921–31*
Imported English engines only, from JAP, Villiers and Blackburne.

GARELLI *Italy 1919–*
A long-lived moped manufacturer, Garelli developed a successful 350cc (21cu in) two-stroke split-single, but interrupted production in 1935 in favour of military equipment. Returned to two-wheelers in 1945 with the Mosquito clip-on of 38cc/2cu inches (over 2 million made) and other lightweights. Merged with Agrati in 1961 and continued to produce a large range of two-strokes up to 125cc (8cu in). Returned to racing more recently, with 125 World Championship wins in the 1980s.

GARIN *France 1950–53*
49/98cc (3/6cu in) mopeds.

GARLASCHELLI *Italy 1922–27*
A range of lightweights of 65–173cc (4–11cu in).

GASUDEN *Japan late 1950s–late 1960s*
Rebadged Fujis.

GATTI *Italy 1904–06*
1.75hp De Dion engines in bicycle frames.

GAZDA *Austria 1926–27*
A 246cc (15cu in) two-stroke. Designer Anton Gazda also invented leaf-sprung handlebars.

GAZELLE *The Netherlands 1903–76*
Made short-lived use of Sarolea engines, but was more successful after a second attempt from 1932 with Ilo-engined 60/75cc (4/5cu in) lightweights. Continued with mopeds and lightweights to 1956, then mopeds only. Always used bought-in power units.

GAZZI *Italy 1929–32*
173cc (11cu in) ohv machines.

GB *England 1905–07*
Utilized 3.5 to 5hp Minerva engines in long-wheelbased frames.

GD *Italy 1923–39*
Built own two-strokes and a 173cc (11cu in) ohc single, which had great racing success.

GECO-HERSTAL *France 1924–28*
Own 173cc to 346cc (11 to 21cu in) sv singles.

GEER *U.S.A. 1905–09*
Pioneer, with own singles and V-twins.

GEHA *Germany 1920–24*
In-house 1.5hp two-strokes.

GEIER *Germany 1934–54*
Exclusively produced small two-strokes with Ilo engines before the war, plus Sachs units after production resumed in 1950.

GEKA *Germany 1924–25*
173cc (11cu in) DKW engines.

GE-MA-HI *Germany 1924–27*
Used a wide variety of bought-in engines for its own frames, including units from Grade and Esbe.

GEMINI *Taiwan 1970–*
Licence-built Yamaha two-strokes.

GEMS *Italy 1921–23*
269cc (16cu in) two-strokes.

GÉNIAL-LUCIFER *France 1928–56*
This company with the intriguing name bought in two-strokes to 246cc (15cu in).

GENTIL *France 1903–04*
A horizontal cylinder was used on this short-lived pioneer.

GEORGES RICHARD *France c.1899*
Used various engines, later taken over by Unic.

GEPPERT *Germany 1925–26*
147cc (9cu in) Grade and DKW-engined two-strokes.

GÉRALD *France 1927–32*
Used 98/173cc (6/11cu in) Aubier-Dunne and 248cc (15cu in) ohc Chaise engines.

GERARD *England 1913–15*
Used 269cc (16cu in) Villiers engines.

GERBI *Italy 1952–53*
Utilized Sachs engines of 98–173cc (6–11cu in).

GERMAAN *The Netherlands 1935–1966*
Later owned by Batavus, the company had a history of various lightweights with Sachs and Ilo, as well as Hungarian Csepel engines.

GERMANIA *Germany 1901–08*
A trade name for the Laurin & Klement machines, built under licence by a Dresden firm.

GEROSA *Italy 1953–75*
Started with its own small four-stroke singles before switching to Minarelli engines.

GERVO *Germany 1924*
Limited production of 198cc (12cu in) sv and 173cc (11cu in) DKW-engined two-strokes.

GH *Czechoslovakia 1924–25*
Used Villiers power and also built Sirocco and Velamos machines.

GIACOMASSO *Italy 1926–35*
Well-made bikes, at first with 174cc (11cu in) Mosers, later with Giacomasso's own ohv and ohc singles and twins.

GIGANT *Austria 1936–38*
Used JAP engines up to a 746cc (45.5cu in) V-twin, plus a Husqvarna-engined racer.

GIGUET *France 1903*
Used De Dion or Minerva engines.

GILERA *Italy 1909–*

Giuseppe Gilera founded a company that was to earn an excellent competition record. His first bike used a 317cc (19cu in) ohv single with belt-drive, though sv engines were also offered later. Gilera enjoyed something of a turning-point in 1936 when it bought the rights to the Rondine four-cylinder racer. It was very advanced for the time, with water-cooling, dohc and supercharging, and Gilera developed it into one of the fastest racers of the era. Race wins and record-breaking (some achieved by Gilera himself) followed. Meanwhile, the road bikes were more prosaic sv and ohv singles to 498cc (30cu in), though some had rear suspension, and the famous ohv sporting Saturno appeared in 1939. After the war, new air-cooled four-cylinder racers continued Gilera's competitive track career, notably in the hands of Geoff Duke, who was 500cc World Champion, Gilera-mounted, three times in a row, while the public was offered a variety of four-stroke singles and twins up to 500cc (30.5cu in). In 1969 Piaggio took over the company, which saw the introduction of smaller two-strokes, though the four-stroke singles were not neglected, with a new 350 in 1985. The latter was later expanded to 558cc (34cu in), in which guise it powered the café racer-style Nuovo Saturno of 1990, which was originally intended for the Japanese market but proved successful in Europe as well. It was also used for the trail-style Nord West (really a pure road bike) with the big single producing 52bhp. Piaggio closed Gilera's Arcore factory in 1993, but has since reintroduced the name on a range of performance scooters, the Runner 50, 125 and 180.

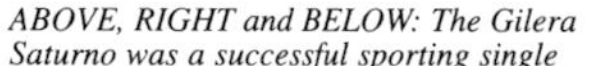

ABOVE, RIGHT and BELOW: The Gilera Saturno was a successful sporting single

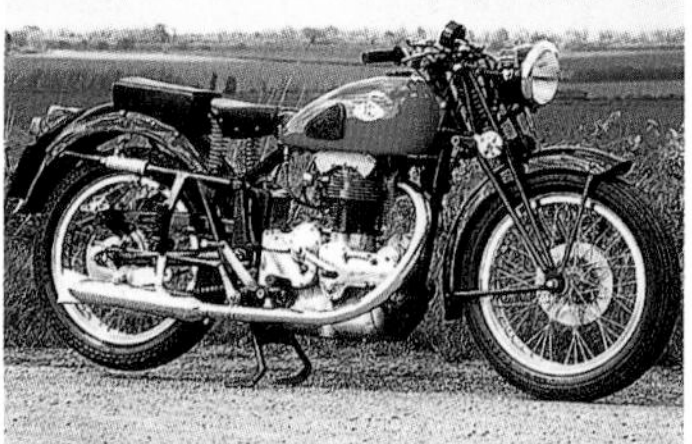

Gilera Nord West

Geoff Duke, in contented retirement, seated on a Gilera at Daytona

GILLET-HERSTAL *Belgium 1919–60*

One of the Belgian big three (with FN and Sarolea). Its first bike was its own rotary-valve 300cc (18cu in) two-stroke, with ohv singles from 1926 and a new range of inclined singles from 1930, the latter of 250–600cc (15–37cu in). Post-1945, it produced mainly two-strokes, and merged with FN and Sarolea in 1955 in an attempt to survive. Production ended five years later.

ABOVE, LEFT and RIGHT: A typical post-war Italian single from Gilera

BELOW: The Runner scooter kept the Gilera name alive

ABOVE: Gilera RC750

ABOVE: Gilera Nuovo Saturno

GIMA *France 1947–56*
Used Ydral, AMC and other bought-in engines to 148cc (9cu in).

GIMSON *Spain 1956–64*
49 and 65cc (3 and 4cu in) mopeds.

GIRARDENGO *Italy 1951–54*
Produced its own two-strokes of 123–173cc (7.5–11cu in).

GITAN *Italy 1950–85*
Used its own two- and four-stroke engines to 175cc (11cu in), later concentrating on mopeds.

GITANE *France c.1947–80*
Engines by Ydral, VAP and Sachs, plus a 49cc (3cu in) Testi in the 1970s. Taken over by Renault in 1980.

GIULIETTA *Italy 1957–80*
49cc (3cu in) Minarelli-engined mopeds, built by Peripoli.

GIVAUDAN *England 1908–14*
Used singles and V-twins by Precision, Villiers *et al.*

GL *France 1919–21*
Built from mainly English imports, including JAP, Sturmey-Archer and Binks.

GLENDALE *England 1920–21*
Used 269cc (16cu in) Villiers and 346cc (21cu in) Blackburne engines.

GLOBE *England 1901–11*
Minerva and Sarolea engines were used.

GLORIA *England 1924–25*
Assembled a 173cc (11cu in) two-stroke engine by Train into a frame by Campion.

GLORIA *England 1931–33*
Actually made by Triumph and was Villiers-powered.

GLORIA *Italy 1948–55*
A 48cc (3cu in) two-stroke, mounted on a swinging arm.

GN *Italy 1920–25*
Used bought-in 346cc (21cu in) two-stroke units.

GNÄDIG *Germany 1925–26*
A 350cc (21cu in) ohv machine designed by Franz Gnädig.

GNOM *Germany 1921–23*
A 63cc (4cu in) clip-on.

GNOME et RHÔNE *France 1919–59*
More famous for its aircraft engines than motorcycles, it started out with a licence-built ABC flat twin, mounted transversely, and introduced its own single-cylinder engines from 1923 (306, 344 and 498cc/19, 21, and 30cu inch sv and ohv), which were well received. From 1930, it produced BMW-inspired flat twins as well, again with sv or ohv, pressed steel frames and capacities of 495 or 745cc (30 or 45cu inches). After the war, concentrated on its own small two-strokes of up to 200cc (12cu inches), used extensively by the French police.

GOEBEL *Germany 1951–79*
49cc (3cu in) Sachs-powered mopeds.

GOETZ *Germany 1925–35*
Built just 79 machines in a decade, all to order, ranging from a 246cc (15cu in) Villiers to a 796cc (49cu in) Columbus ohc vertical twin.

GOGGO *Germany 1951–54*
Range of scooters to 173cc (11cu in), later dropped in favour of Goggomobil minicar.

GOLD-RAD *Germany 1952–81*
Producer/importer of mopeds.

GOLEM *Germany 1921–23*
Built by DKW, which produced a scooter-like 122cc (7cu in) machine. The rights to it were later bought by Eichler.

GOLO *Austria 1923–25*
JAP 346/490cc (21/30cu in) and Bradshaw-engined 347cc singles.

GORI *Italy 1969–83*
Started with uprated Bimm motocross bikes, and from 1971 built 50–245cc (3–15cu in) bikes using Sachs, Franco-Morini and Rotax power. Taken over by SWM in 1980, then dropped.

GÖRICKE *Germany 1903–59*
Intermittent production was over three phases: 1903–12, typical pioneer singles and V-twins with belt-drive; 1928–33, a new range, with MAG, Blackburne and Villiers engines; 1949–59, Sachs and Ilo-engined two-strokes to 247cc (15cu in).

GORRION *Spain 1952–55*
Sachs-engined mopeds and lightweights up to 174cc (11cu in).

GOUGH *England 1920–23*
Used 293cc (18cu in) JAP and 548cc (33cu in) Blackburne engines.

GOUVERNEUR *Germany 1903–07*
Used 3.5hp GN engines.

GR *Italy 1925–26*
Headed by Count Gino Revelli, the company had only limited production.

GRADE *Germany 1903–25*
Exclusively two-strokes, with successful 118 and 132cc (7 and 8cu in) machines. Also sold its engines to other manufacturers.

GRANDEX-PRECISION *England 1910–16*
The 'Precision' tag was due to the early use of Precision engines, dropped when the factory began offering a wide range of JAPs as well.

GRAPHIC *England 1903–06*
Utilized De Dion, Minerva and MMC engines.

Greeves 350cc (21cu in) single

Greeves was famous for its trials bikes (LEFT) but also sold road machines (ABOVE)

GRASETTI *Italy 1952–65*
123/148cc (7.5/9cu in) two-strokes.

GRATIEUX *France 1919–21*
Interesting two-stroke radial engines.

GRAVES *England 1914–15*
Actually built by New Imperial, with a 292cc (18cu in) JAP unit, on behalf of the mail order catalogue Graves.

GREEN *England 1919–23*
Charles Green was an early pioneer of water-cooling, mostly in small singles.

GREEVES *England 1951–77*
Two men were the driving force behind Greeves, and soon after they retired the company closed. Bert Greeves was a draughtsman and natural engineer, while his cousin, the ebullient Derry Preston-Cobb, possessed a shrewd business mind and aptitude for salesmanship. Preston-Cobb had also been paralyzed from birth, and the two men went into business as Invacar Ltd., making small Villiers-powered invalid carriages.

But Bert Greeves had ridden a Norton before the war and before long a prototype machine with rubber-in-torsion suspension both front and rear was up and running. Of course, it used a Villiers engine, while the rubber suspension (claimed to be impervious to weather and self-damping) gave 5 inches of movement at the front, four at the rear. Development was aided by the fact that Invacar's works manager, Frank Byford, was a keen scrambler rider, which itself was to have a strong influence on the company's direction. In 1953, the new bikes were finally unveiled: three- and four-speed roadsters, plus a scrambler, all using the

ABOVE and BELOW: Scramblers kept Greeves afloat in its later years. Note the H-beam frame

197cc (12cu in) Villiers. They also shared the unusual frame, which used a cast-alloy H-section beam in place of an orthodox front downtube. There was also a twin-cylinder roadster, powered by a 242cc (15cu in) British Anzani two-stroke (Greeves never built a four-stroke bike) and a few years later, the Fleetstar, with a 322cc (20cu in) version of the Anzani twin.

However, not everyone could cope with the avant-garde frame and the company soon began to offer a conventional tubular one as an alternative, while the rear rubber-in-torsion suspension was soon changed for conventional Girling spring/damper units. The front suspension was to change to hydraulic dampers as well, but conventional telescopic forks did not arrive until 1968, and then only on the competition bikes. But Greeves was becoming increasingly competition-orientated, especially after the arrival of new development engineer Brian Stonebridge, fresh from the BSA competitions department. He was the brains behind a new 197cc scrambler, on which he famously challenged Britain's top riders on their own big works bikes. On the little Greeves, he won the 350cc race easily, and was second in the 500. In honour of the venue, the new bike was named the Hawkstone.

More success followed when the talented young Dave Bickers joined as works rider, and Bert Greeves designed a new square-finned 246cc barrel for the engine. But the Villiers had reached the limit of its potential, in both engine and gearbox, and Greeves and Stonebridge began to increasingly develop their own solutions. Dave Bickers won the 250cc European Championship two years running, but more power was always needed to keep up with the big names. Greeves' answer was the Challenger of 1964, an all-new scrambler and a Greeves-designed engine which, in road-race form, produced 30bhp at 7,500rpm. Typically, a Challenger barrel found its way into Derry Preston-Cobb's Invacar!

The company was still offering road bikes, encouraged by a few police contracts, but the range had been slimmed down to a 197cc (12cu in) single and 249cc (15cu in) East Coaster twin. Villiers ceased production in 1968 which spelt the end for these, plus the trials model (which now used a Challenger top-end on Villiers crankcase). But the serious scramblers continued, and in 1967 offered telescopic forks for the first time, while the famous H-beam made way for a conventional tubular frame the following year. The Challenger had already grown into a 364cc (22cu in) twin-port version, then 390cc (24cu in). In the 1970s, the Greeves Griffon, with its 380cc engine, part-developed by Dr. Gordon Blair of Queens University, Belfast (who also collaborated with Silk) was the only motorcycle on offer. In April 1977 Derry Preston-Cobb retired, followed by Bert Greeves, and the company they had founded ceased trading soon afterwards.

GREYHOUND *England 1905–07*
Powered by Minerva, MMC and Fafnir.

GREYHOUND *U.S.A. 1907–14*
Used Thor's 4.5hp single.

GRG *Italy 1926–27*
A vertical twin produced from two 174cc (11cu in) Della Ferrera singles coupled together.

GRI *England 1921–22*
G.R. Inshaw designed his 348/496cc (21/30cu in) engines with a single valve. How it worked is a mystery.

GRIFFON *France 1902–55*
Built own singles and V-twins as well as using bought-in engines. Was taken over by Peugeot in 1927, and became a rebadged Peugeot after the war.

GRIGG *England 1920–25*
Used various small engines of its own (1.75hp scooter and 181cc/11cu inch ohv) and larger bought-in units, including a 990cc (60cu in) B&H V-twin.

GRINDLAY-PEERLESS *England 1923–34*
This former sidecar manufacturer fitted a wide range of proprietary engines, from the 147cc (9cu in) Villiers to the 996cc (61cu in) JAP via mid-sized singles from Python or JAP.

GRITZNER *Germany 1903–62*
Used Fafnir singles and V-twins in its early days and, like many German and French makes, concentrated on small two-strokes after 1945, in this case with Sachs engines of 98–174cc (6–11cu in).

GRIZZLY *Czechoslovakia 1925–32*
At first, produced a 246cc (15cu in) two-stroke, adding larger MAG-engined models in 1929.

An early Gritzner, Fafnir-engined

GROSE-SPUR *England 1934–39*
Built by Carlton with the 123cc (7.5cu in) Villiers for the London dealer Grose.

GROTE *Germany 1924–25*
Modular motorcycling – the basic 305cc (19cu in) two-stroke single could be doubled or tripled up to 614 or 921cc (37 or 56cu in).

GRÜCO *Germany 1924–25*
Used 346cc (21cu in) Kühne ohv engines in its own frames.

GRUHN *Germany 1920–26*
Hugo Gruhn's Berlin-based company mainly concentrated on building frames for other manufacturers as well as producing its own 198cc (12cu in) Alba-powered motorcycles.

GRUHN *Germany 1921–32*
Built a few machines before World War I, with full production beginning in 1921. Used proprietary engines to 246cc (15cu in), and later its own shaft-driven 198cc (12cu in) single.

GRUTZENA *Germany 1925–26*
Used a Kühne single. Limited production.

GS *Germany 1920–24*
A 129cc (8cu in) two-stroke, offered as a lightweight or a clip-on.

GS *Germany 1923–25*
Of 145cc (9cu in) and Gruhn-powered.

GSD *England 1921–23*
Flat twin with 496cc (30cu in) and shaft-drive. A shaft-driven 342cc (21cu in) single was also offered.

GUARALDI *Italy 1905–16*
Used both Fafnir and Sarolea engines up to 550cc (34cu inches).

GUAZZONI *Italy 1935–79*
Built Calthorpe-engined bikes before the war, sub-250cc/15cu inch two- and four-strokes afterwards, including successful disc-valve racers. Concentrated on mopeds in the 1970s.

GUIA *Italy 1950–54*
Assembler of 98–147cc (6–9cu in) two-strokes.

GUIGNARD *France 1933–38*
Mainly 98/123cc (6/7.5cu in) two-strokes.

GUILLER *France 1949–56*
Built Italian SIM scooters under licence, and bought in a range of engines to power its own machines.

GUIZZARDI *Italy 1926–32*
Own 124/174cc (7.5/11cu in) singles, including an ohc unit.

GUIZZO *Italy 1955–62*
Produced 48cc (3cu in) mopeds and 149cc (9cu in) scooters.

GÜLDNER *Germany 1925*
Produced a 490cc (30cu in) ohv single, very close to the equivalent Norton.

GUSTLOFF *Germany 1934–40*
98cc (6cu in) Sachs-engined mopeds.

G&W *England 1902–06*
Used Minerva, Peugeot and Fafnir bought-in engines.

H

HACK *England 1920–23*
An unflattering name for a 103/110cc (6/7cu in) mini-scooter.

HADEN *England 1920–24*
A 347cc (21cu in) Precision two-stroke.

HAGEL *Germany 1925*
Produced its own 247cc (15cu in) three-port two-strokes.

HÄGGLUND *Sweden 1972–74*
Developed for the Swedish army, with monocoque frame, single-sided suspension, 24bhp (345cc) Rotax power and automatic transmission. Sadly for this interesting bike, Husqvarna won the order, and the Hägglund never got beyond the prototype stage.

HAI *Austria 1938*
With an unusual cast frame, which included the fuel tank, it was powered by a 108cc (7cu in) two-stroke.

HAJA *Germany 1924–25*
Used a Hansa 198cc (12cu in) sv.

HAKO *Germany 1924–25*
Identical to the equivalent HRD, including the 348/490cc (21/30cu in) JAP singles.

HALUMO *Germany 1923–26*
147cc (9cu in) two-strokes, later producing its own small four-strokes to 298cc (18cu in).

HAM *The Netherlands 1902–06*
Used a 2hp Altena single.

HAMILTON *England 1901–07*
Sold its singles (2.25–4hp) and V-twin (4.5hp) to other manufacturers.

HAMPTON *England 1912–14*
A T.D. Cross engine of 492cc (30cu in) powered the Hampton.

HANFLAND *Germany 1920–25*
Hanfland and Kurier-badged bikes powered by Hanfland's own 147cc (9cu in) two-strokes.

HANSA *England 1920–22*
Used 269cc (16cu in) Arden and 346cc (21cu in) Blackburne sv engines.

HANSA *Germany 1922–26*
Made two- and four-stroke singles of 148–246cc (9–15cu in), the last being a 246cc ohv engine with horizontal valves.

HARLEY-DAVIDSON *U.S.A. 1903–*
It was by a series of happy coincidences that the Harley family from Manchester, England and the Davidsons from Scotland both emigrated to North America in the late 19th century, and settled in Milwaukee. And that two of their sons, Bill Harley and Arthur Davidson, should end up working at the same engineering establishment, become firm friends, and begin experimentation with the internal combustion engine.

Arthur was the outgoing one, a patternmaker who developed into a natural salesman. Bill Harley was more the technician, a draughtsman who designed not only the first Harley-Davidsons but a whole generation of them. Arthur had two brothers: Walter was a machinist by trade who helped build the first machines, though he soon took responsibility for the administration and became the first-ever president of Harley-Davidson Inc. William, the eldest Davidson, came in later; an experienced toolmaker and foreman, he was the obvious choice for works manager in the rapidly expanding factory.

These were the four founder members of Harley-Davidson, and the fact that they succeeded where countless others failed was down to basic character traits that were to stand them in good stead in the turbulent years to come: those of practicality, commonsense and innate caution.

But it was Arthur Davidson and Bill Harley who set the ball rolling, building a single-cylinder motor to power their fishing boat. Keen to do things properly, they first read around the subject, then were given a head start when a draughtsman named Emil Kroeger lent them a set of drawings for the basic De Dion four-stroke engine. The third

ABOVE: The Hampton was belt-driven

BELOW: A 1915 Harley-Davidson V-twin of 61cu in (1000cc)

LEFT: A 1923 Model J with overhead inlet, side exhaust valves

ABOVE: Harley kept on making singles. This is a 1929 500cc (30.5cu in) Model C

prototype was powerful enough to push the boat along, but fortunately for four generations of motorcyclists, the two friends were also keen cyclists, so a motorized bicycle was a natural progression. Like most machines of the time, their first prototype was no more than a heavy-duty cycle frame with the little 160cc (10cu in) motor bolted on. It worked, but needed more power, so they came up with a larger 410cc (25cu in) version, which was enough to give the re-engined prototype a 72km/h (45mph) capability. Typical of the time, it was air-cooled, with an overhead inlet/side exhaust valve (ioe) set-up, driving the rear wheel through a crude single-speed leather belt. Then it was ridden until something broke (and things did) when they would go back to the workshop and design, build and fit a stronger part, and set off again: frame, wheels, hubs – just about everything was strengthened to transform the prototype from a cyclemotor into something like a real motorcycle.

So they had a working machine, but it was still more part-time hobby than serious business proposition. But by late 1903, several things caused the project to take a new turn. After riding the bike, Walter Davidson threw over his machining job in Kansas and took another back in Milwaukee; that way, he could work on the bike in the evenings. Meanwhile, William C. Davidson (father of the boys) built a 3 x 4.5m (10 x 15ft) shed in the back garden – their first factory. But most significant of all, they received their first order and the 'Harley Davidson Motor Company' was in business.

Rapid Growth

For many budding young entrepreneurs, this would have been the cue to rush into production, but the founders were prepared to take things slowly at first. Two machines were built in 1904, while Bill Harley went off to the University of Wisconsin to work for an engineering degree. Slowly, more orders began to trickle in as word got round that the new Harley-Davidson was one of the more reliable motorcycles. Eight bikes were sold in 1905, and Walter gave up his day job to work full-time in the shed, which had to be doubled in size. Within a year it was outgrown again, and a well-to-do Scots uncle named James McLay lent them the money to buy a plot of land on Chestnut Street (later renamed Juneau Avenue). A new factory went up, which produced 49 machines in its first year, then 154, then 450, then over 1,000 and 3,000 in 1911. When the war in Europe broke out three years later, there were just two contenders for the title of largest U.S. motorcycle manufacturer: Indian and Harley-Davidson. So from a shed in the back yard to (almost) a leader of industry in less than ten years – it was an astonishing feat.

Meanwhile, the market was also moving on, with buyers demanding more power. Bill Harley took the quickest, simplest route, one followed by many manufacturers at the time, by turning the single into a V-twin. This theoretically allowed the use of many existing parts (or at least very similar ones based on existing experience) such as crankcase, cylinders, barrels, heads and cycle parts. Harley's first prototype was shown as early as 1907, but it wasn't a success as the atmospheric inlet valve arrangement (sucked open by the descending piston) couldn't cope with the demands of two cylinders. Only when the F-model appeared in 1910, with a proper pushrod-operated inlet valve, was the Harley-Davidson V-twin truly practical. Of 799cc (49cu in), it had enough extra power to justify a tensioner for the drive-belt, but grew to 997cc (61cu in) – a familiar Harley size – in 1912.

ABOVE: A 1933 VL sidevalve V-twin

OPPOSITE: A 1934 VL 'E'

Harley-Davidson claimed that the new twin would reach 105km/h (65mph), but its real advantage at the time was as a sidecar machine, and Harley-Davidson lost little time in offering this as an option. There were commercial sidecars with van bodies as well, and the F model was approved by the mail service, which opened up a huge market. At the peak (1919) it was selling seven sidecars for every 10 bikes before Ford's Model T got cheap enough to offer a more comfortable alternative, and the American motorcycle became more an enthusiast's machine than family transport. But there were important technical innovations going on as well: chain-drive with a practical clutch; three-speed

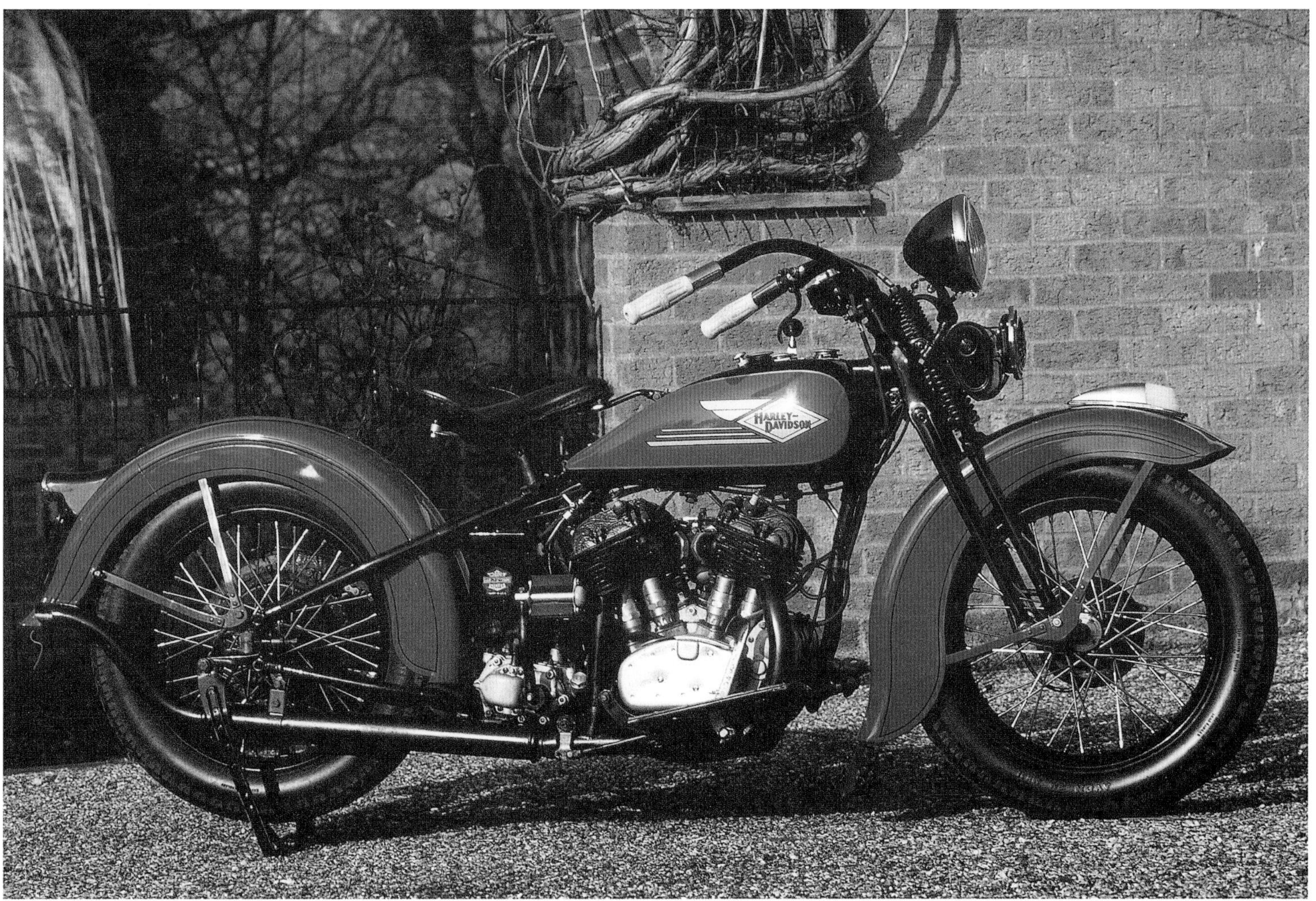
HARLEY-DAVIDSON

HARLEY-DAVIDSON

gearbox; full magneto electrics (the mag-equipped Harley was the J model); automatic oil pump. The years 1911–16 were in fact a brief period of innovation when American motorcycles led the world in technology, though the situation didn't last.

Harley's position vis-à-vis Indian was greatly strengthened by World War I. In a fit of patriotic zeal, Indian offered most of its production to the government at a low price. Canny Harley-Davidson, on the other hand, reserved half its output for the civilian market. This resulted in many disgruntled Indian dealers with no bikes to sell, dealers which Arthur lost no time in recruiting to the Harley-Davidson camp. This marked the start of serious rivalry between the two firms that often went beyond normal competition. It included ruthless undercutting by both sides and the development of a tribal mentality which segregated riders into separate clubs. In reality, the top management of each side met once a year to fix prices, but there was no love lost.

Still, Harley-Davidson received enough encouragement in the immediate post-war boom to borrow $3 million to double capacity and buy the latest machine tools. And there was an all-new bike, completely different from the existing singles and V-twins. Owing much to the English Douglas, the Sport Twin was a quiet, well-mannered flat twin of 588cc (36cu in) and was a brave attempt at broadening Harley's market with a European-style machine. Alas, both this and the ambitious expansion were bad moves as in 1921 the U.S. economy went into depression and Harley sales slumped to 10,000, the lowest for a decade. The new enlarged factory had the capacity to make 35,000 bikes a year, and it would be many years before it could be fully used for the purpose. As for the Sport Twin, it lacked the vitality of Indian's faster Scout V-twin, and in any case cost only $15 less than a Model T. The Sport was dropped after four years. More successful was an enlarged 1200cc (73cu in) version of the J model and its extra performance was rumoured to be much appreciated by illicit booze runners in those prohibition days. Faster still was the Two Cam, which used separate inlet and exhaust cams for significantly more power (the 74-inch JDH could top 137km/h (85mph). Little wonder that Harley belatedly introduced front brakes for 1928. Some riders thought the Two Cams the best bikes Harley ever made.

OPPOSITE: A 1939 61E 'Knucklehead'

ABOVE: 1939 Harley-Davidson Knucklehead 61cu in (1000cc)

BELOW: The sidevalve V-twin evolved into a reliable machine

Depression & Recovery

No one escaped the effects of the Wall Street Crash of 1929, and Harley-Davidson was no exception. Like everyone else, it saw its sales slump from a peak of 28,000 in 1920, 17,000 by the end of the twenties, to 10,500 in 1931, then 7,000 the following year. The low point came in 1933 when just 3,703 Harleys were sold in America. With the whole world at a low economic ebb, there were very few export sales to add to that, and it is hardly surprising that the talk at boardroom level was of closure. It says something for Bill Harley and the three Davidsons, all of whom could have sold up and taken a comfortable early retirement, that they chose to battle on. But closure would have been an admission of defeat: they had created the company through their own efforts and had sons who would follow them (Harley-Davidson was to remain a family affair right up to the 1960s), and of course they employed a huge workforce which needed jobs.

So as well as a general tightening of belts, there were new bikes aimed at diversification away from big V-twins (the original single having been dropped), notably 350cc (21cu in) singles and a 750cc (46cu in) V-twin. Just as significant, Indian was building successful versions of both, and such was the rivalry between the two firms that Harley felt obliged to meet them head-on. So the little 'Peashooter' single was a direct response to the 350cc Indian Prince. Available in both sidevalve and overhead-valve form, it was cheap, and apart from a few reliability problems proved to be quite a success. It did well in competition too, as the American Motorcycle Association (by now Harley-dominated, it has to be said) set up a 350cc class which the Peashooter duly dominated. A competition version was even built, and the bike attracted the near-genius of Joe Petrali to the Harley fold. A tremendously gifted rider, he was also an excellent development engineer and proved instrumental in bringing more racing success to the company. Less successful was the C model, a 500cc (30.5cu in) sidevalve single that appeared to have little to recommend it.

Harley's new 750 V-twin of 1928 didn't appear very promising either. A response to Indian's lively sidevalve Scout, it was quite heavy and underpowered and one dealer found that even after careful running-in, it could only manage 90km/h (56mph). It did come good in the end as the slightly more powerful W-series (which formed the basis of the wartime WLA) and was at least reliable. Additionally, of course, the bike formed the basis of the famous three-wheeled Servi-car, introduced in 1932 and a faithful servant to generations of garages and police forces: it actually survived in production until 1974.

But none of these bikes provided Harley's bread and butter, which continued to be the big twins. Once again Indian had forced the pace with good-performance sidevalve V-twin Chiefs of 61 and 73 cubic inches (1000 and 1200cc). Harley-Davidson's answer was the new V and VL (the 'L' denoting higher 4.5:1 compression) which claimed 30 per cent more power than the long-running ioe V-twin. However,

ABOVE: A 46cu in (747cc) WLA in RAF colours

BELOW: A 1946 Knucklehead. Telescopic forks were fitted later

OPPOSITE: A fully-equipped WLA in U.S. Army trim

once bikes arrived at dealers, this was seen to be hopelessly optimistic. Light flywheels gave good acceleration from low speed, but did little to enhance the lugging capability expected of a big V-twin. The new bike also weighed about 45kg (100lb) more than the old one, which certainly didn't help. Putting this right meant a new flywheel, crankcase and frame, and 1,300 bikes had to be completely rebuilt. It was an expensive lesson though, like the 750 twin, the V/VL did develop into a reliable machine and spawned a 1340cc (82cu in) option in 1935. Another of Harley-Davidson's favourite engine capacities had arrived. Needless to say, Indian was also in the process of making one.

Every motorcycle manufacturer has a milestone bike, and Harley's is the 1936 Knucklehead. It was significant in so many ways. It was Harley-Davidson's first overhead-valve road-going V-twin (though there had been an 8-valve racer years before), its first with a modern dry-sump lubrication system: cycle parts and styling were all new; more importantly it marked the final victory over Indian (which had been overtaken in the sales war and had nothing comparable), and it was a mark of faith in the future, given the go-ahead when both Harley-Davidson and the U.S. economy were at their lowest ebb and

A civilianized WLC. Harley's 'small' sidevalve twin was a reliable, if unglamorous performer

This 1948 WLC is loaded with all the necessary touring accessories

Modernization was a gradual process. A 1949 Hydra-Glide

production was cut back to a minimum.

Still, the 61E (its official title) or Knucklehead (some thought the rocker covers looked like knuckles) failed to make its projected 1934 launch date despite work starting on the project three years earlier. In fact, the first engine wasn't complete and in a frame until May of that year. Immediately, it proved to have serious oil leaks from the top-end, partly due to the large number of joints in the design. The engineering department argued for a pilot run of 200 bikes to test the water before the commitment to a main launch and big production run. In the event, they compromised, and the final launch in 1936 was a low-key affair, with dealers informed that this was a limited-production flagship.

None of this did any good, as the first all-new Harley for years was eagerly anticipated by both dealers and customers alike. And when the Knucklehead first arrived they were not disappointed. With a bigger bore and shorter stroke than the existing V-twin, it revved harder and produced more power (40bhp at 4,800rpm from the EL) than any previous Harley. It looked good too, somehow compact and business-like, with that beautiful teardrop tank with the speedometer on top. It was a hit, and 1,900 were sold in the first year. Naturally, as was now traditional with Harley, there were teething troubles: the oil leaks continued, exacerbated by the new lubrication system, which over-delivered to some parts and starved others; valve springs broke (until a new supplier could be found); and the all-iron engine was subject to overheating if pushed too hard. Nearly 100 modifications were hurriedly made in the first year.

Still, the Knucklehead was fast, glamorous and desirable, and Joe Petrali capitalized on this by setting a new measured mile speed record of 136.18mph (219.15km/h) on one. Petrali's bike was well tuned, with twin carburettors, higher compression, higher lift cams and gearing that allowed a theoretical 257km/h (160mph). What it didn't have was the smart, supposedly aerodynamic bodywork, which nearly caused Petrali to lose control at 100mph. He ordered its removal, and the record was taken without. With Knucklehead as sportster of the range, the big sidevalve twins could relax into their natural role as solid, heavy, reliable tourers, though they were dropped soon after the war. A 1200cc (73cu in) version of the Knucklehead (the FL) in 1941 indicated the way things were going.

Meanwhile, Harley-Davidson was contemplating more wartime work, which was to bring the glory years to the 750 twin, known as the '45'. What had been an unloved gap-filler in peacetime had its finest hour in time of war. The company built 88,000 bikes for the war effort, and the vast majority were 45s. In military specification it became the WLA, which meant the lowest optional compression, enlarged cylinder-head finning to aid cooling and a bigger air cleaner. There was a skidplate under the crankcase, a more substantial luggage rack, black-out lights and a gun scabbard. Never a sparkling performer in civilian dress, the militarized WLA could barely scrape 50mph with all this equipment on board. Still, unless you were been chased by Germans on BMWs, this hardly mattered. What mattered more was the WLA's absolute reliability, which endeared it to thousands of GIs. Although there were many other wartime experiments at Milwaukee, notably the BMW-based XA shaft-driven flat twin, the WLA became America's definitive army bike.

The 1940s also saw changes at the top of the company. Some said it was overwork, the sudden demand to maximize production, that caused Walter Davidson's death in Feburary 1942, though he had been suffering from a liver disorder for some time. Bill Harley followed him in September 1943, and as the elder Davidson had passed away five years earlier, that left just Arthur of the original four founders. He and his wife were to die in a car crash after the war. However, there was a whole new generation waiting in the wings, underlining Harley-Davidson's status at this time as a family controlled and run company. William Harley Jnr. took over his father's job of vice president/engineering, while his younger brother John ran the parts department. William Davidson's elder son (William A.) became president in 1942, while Walter's sons (Walter C. and Gordon) were vice president/sales and vice president/manufacturing, respectively. It was some time before the two families could be persuaded to relinquish their grip.

Business as Usual

In 1945, when GIs were beginning to return from all over the world, Harley-Davidson seemed set fair for a new period of

The Panhead (from 1947) introduced hydraulic tappets

prosperity. Many of these men had learnt to ride during the war, while at home there was a pent-up demand for consumer goods while everyone had been working rather than spending; and the bikes were known and well proven. Indian, the only domestic rival, was a shadow of its former self, and imported British motorcycles represented (as yet) a tiny portion of the market. Yet, despite all this, the company was forced to go public in the 1960s to raise cash before submitting to a *de facto* takeover. What went wrong?

There was actually little amiss with the big V-twins, selling in their traditional market. The trouble was that the market was shrinking, and not until 1957 did Harley-Davidson have a true rival for the bigger imported bikes. However, all this was in the future when the Panhead (rocker covers like baking pans) was unveiled in 1947. It certainly looked like a substantial update with its hydraulic tappets, aluminium heads and internal oilways. Unfortunately, the oil pump now had to force lubricant up through a cat's cradle of oilways, which also supplied the tappets as well. This meant erratic oil pressure which upset the tappets, which in turn altered the valve timing and could lead to snapped rocker arms. Part of the eventual cure was to move the tappets from the top to the base of the pushrods – at least if oil pressure did vary, it wouldn't now upset the timing as much. However, the alloy heads were a genuine advance and once again, once the engine was sorted out after the first year or so, it proved fine.

Meanwhile, the running gear came in for some much needed updates. Telescopic front forks came in 1949 (with the bike

ABOVE: A 1956 Panhead with sidecar

lacked any fundamental development apart from capacity increases. More ambitious was the Topper scooter, which used a 165cc (10cu in) version of the Hummer engine with automatic transmission. Like the British, Harley came to the scooter market late, and when it did just couldn't match the flair of the Italians. The Topper was not a success.

But it was in the middleweight class that imports from BSA, Triumph and Norton (among others) were making inroads and all Harley had to offer was the 750cc WL. This bike, with its hand gearchange and top speed of 113km/h (70mph) simply failed to be serious competition for the light, nimble 500/650 imports, most of which could top 90–100mph. There was actually a proposal for a thoroughly modern

renamed Hydra-Glide) and a foot gearchange/hand clutch three years later (though you could still have the hand-change if you insisted); swinging-arm rear suspension came in 1958 for the Duo Glide.

But what was Harley doing about the foreign imports, which by 1950 were taking 40 per cent of the market? It actually tried to persuade the U.S. Tariff Commission to slap extra import duty on them, but was rebuffed. It already had the 125cc (8cu in) Hummer to sell against the lightweights. This was really a DKW, offered to Allied manufacturers as part of war reparations (BSA also made it as the Bantam). It was actually quite successful for a time as it was simple in the extreme and able to top 80km/h (50mph), but

BELOW: The Harley-Davidson Hummer was derived from a pre-war DKW. This is a 165cc (10cu in) version

middleweight to meet the imports head-on, but nothing came of it. What Harley offered instead, from 1952, was the K-series, which on paper looked bang-up-to-date with unit-construction, foot gearchange, telescopic forks, swinging-arm rear suspension and a sidevalve V-twin. This now-obsolete engine layout seriously restricted power (though a later capacity increase to 897cc/55cu inches did help a little) and the K-series did not sell well.

Not until 1957, when an overhead-valve top-end was added, did Harley finally have the middleweight competitor that it needed. It was the XL series, the Sportster, which was really another milestone, simply because it was such an advance on what had gone before. Bored out to 883cc/54 cubic inches (another famous capacity) it produced 40bhp at 5,500rpm and was a genuine 161km/h (100mph) motorcycle. Here at last was a Harley that could outrun a Triumph, at least in a straight line, and more power followed in 1959. As it happened, the Sportster was to be overtaken in the horsepower race as the sixties progressed, but it did wonders for the company's image and formed the basis of a whole new family of Harleys. What it didn't do was sell in vast numbers or make a great deal of money for in 1965 Harley-Davidson held a mere 6 per cent of its home market and was again running short of cash.

Buy-Ups & Sell-Outs

Part of the reason for the lack of funds was Harley-Davidson's takeover of the Italian manufacturer Aermacchi. Finally convinced that it needed something other than the ageing Hummer in the lightweight class, Harley bought a controlling interest in

Electra Glide in touring trim

A 1968 Electra Glide

Aermacchi, which had an 80mph 250cc (15cu in) single and a desperate need of working capital. The idea was to sell it in the U.S. with Harley-Davidson badges on the tank, giving the company an up-to-date small bike at a competitive price. And apart from some headaches over the quality of Italian electrics, the whole scheme worked rather well. The Sprint (as it was called in America) was fast, light and easy to ride, and it sold at a steady 4–6,000 a year through most of the sixties and early seventies; it actually outsold the Sportster two to one in 1967. It gained more power (not to mention the world 250cc speed record in 1965), was enlarged to 350cc (21cu in) and even gained an electric start in 1973. Towards the end, it was looking outdated next to the Japanese bikes, but Aermacchi had an answer to that.

A whole range of two-strokes came

ABOVE: *1974 Harley-Davidson Aermacchi 350cc (21cu in)*

ABOVE: *Harley-Davidson Aermacchi 250cc racer*

BELOW: *The first Sportster was a fresh attempt at rivalling smaller imported bikes*

over from the Varese factory as well: the Rapido 125 (solid commuter), the M50 moped, and finally a range of two-stroke trail bikes of 125, 175 and 250 sizes that had most of the accoutrements to compete with the Japanese, if not the sophistication. These also sold well for a while, but like every other post-war small Harley, they ultimately lacked development and a forward model plan. In 1978, the company sold its interest in Aermacchi and decided to restrict itself to V-twins and it has continued to do so ever since.

Meanwhile, the FL/FLH big twins, despite their increasing obsolescence, continued to sell steadily, and there were occasional updates, notably the electric start Electra Glide in 1965 and the Shovelhead engine (the rocker covers looked like – you've guessed it!) the following year. The latter heralded no fundamental change, producing no more power than the Panhead and with the same familiar layout, though it was to stay in production right up to the early eighties. The Sportster too was updated, with better brakes, 12-volt electrics and electric start, but was beginning to look a little elderly.

Once again, Harley was running out of cash, and this time a share issue just would not suffice. Instead, it sought a merger with a stronger partner, which turned out to be AMF (the American Machine and Foundry Company). AMF is often castigated as an asset-stripper, or at least accused of running Harley-Davidson down; but in reality it invested a great deal of money into plant. Its mistake (with hindsight) was to try and recoup the expense in double-quick time with a massive production increase. Quality nose-dived and the bikes earned a bad name. But on the product front, it wasn't all bad news. The 1970 Super Glide, although largely a mix of existing parts, was a new idea (the first factory custom) and Harley has been doing well out of it ever since. Some glassfibre bodywork and a lower, longer look transformed the bike, and it sold well. The same couldn't be said of the XLCR ('Café Racer') whose European looks and matt black finish were just too much for the traditionalists.

However, Harley hit the nail on the head with the 1977 FXS Lowrider. It was no more than a restyled Super Glide, with low seat, flat bars and a Fat Bob tank, but the buyers loved it and nearly 10,000 were sold in 1978. Harley-Davidson was beginning to realize that a Harley was expected to look a certain way, whether it be a stripped-down Sportster, a custom bike, or a fully-dressed cruiser. From the mid-seventies on, its range split into these three families. Buyers didn't want a

ABOVE: The Topper scooter

BELOW: The Servi-car served two generations of riders

BELOW: The 45cu in (737cc) KR racer stuck to sidevalves

OPPOSITE: The XR750 racer had a long, successful career

Micah Stevenson
Harley Davidson
Micah Stevenson
T-M MOTORSPORT
FT.WORTH, TX
92
DRS Darcy Racing Specialties

modern-looking Harley and Harley fully realized this important fact just in time. By the end of the decade, the company appeared to be on a happier footing: production had settled down to an achievable 45–50,000 a year and an all-new family of bikes was on the distant horizon, while the FL series saw the return of the 1340cc (82cu in) capacity. The trouble was that by the end of the seventies, AMF had had enough.

A New Start

This time, the answer was a management buy-out. In 1980, AMF had already decided to sell, but there were no takers, so a group composed of senior management, led by Vaughn Beals and backed by finance from Citibank, rose to the challenge. Negotiations dragged on through 1981, but eventually it was all agreed and Harley-Davidson was independent once again. After the initial euphoria (owners and dealers across America rejoiced that the AMF era was over), Harley-Davidson was forced to face up to some unpalatable facts. It was losing money, market share was continuing to slide and the problem of poor quality was becoming endemic.

However, it wasn't all bad news, as even through the late seventies AMF had continued to invest in new models. Most ambitious was the long-term NOVA programme to produce a family of liquid-cooled engines of 500–1300cc (30.5–79cu in), developed by Porsche. It is often forgotten that these actually got to the running prototype stage, and were even shown to dealers, though that was as far as they did get. Work was also well in hand on a final major update of the V-twin which

ABOVE: The new-generation XR1000 racer

BELOW: Sportster with XR paintwork

BELOW: The XR750 in its element

The 1992 Fat Boy. Who else but Harley-Davidson could get away with a name like that?

ABOVE: The 1995 Road King dropped the handlebar fairing

BELOW: On Daytona Beach

OPPOSITE: 1993 Electra Glide

ABOVE: The Classic

was seen as an interim project to keep things competitive until NOVA was ready. And 1980 saw more immediate benefits. The FXB was a standard Lowrider apart from the replacement of both primary- and final-drive chains with toothed rubber belts. This was the first motorcycle in the world to use belt-drive for both primary and final, and it was so successful that there have been belt-driven Harleys ever since. Cleaner, quieter and less maintenance-intensive than a chain, it was a real step forward. Another significant new model was the FLT Tour Glide of the same year which used rubber mountings to quell the V-twin's vibration, and introduced a five-speed gearbox.

Further good news came from the Tariff Commission, which finally agreed to place a temporary (five-year) tax on imported bikes over 700cc, giving Harley-Davidson a crucial breathing space. It made good use of the time, working hard to improve both quality and productivity, where great strides were made. So much so, that the company was held up to others as a shining example; it was apparently possible for an American concern to be as efficient and quality-conscious as a Japanese.

But the biggest event of the eighties was surely the launch of the Evolution V-twin in 1983. It said a great deal about the firm's new mindset that it was preparing to tackle existing warranty problems. Here was one new Harley engine that put reliability at the top of its priorities, and one that would be right first time with no hurried modifications or sudden recalls.

1996, and the Evolution V-twin was still the mainstay of Harley's range

Like every other Harley-Davidson V-twin since the Knucklehead, it was an evolution (hence the name) rather than a new concept. The bottom-end and the bore/stroke dimensions were unchanged, and though it was still air-cooled, with two pushrod-operated valves per cylinder, everything from the cylinder barrels up was new. There were alloy barrels and heads, a narrower valve angle, easier porting and a lighter valve train. In short, the Evo, as it was known (the nickname 'Blockhead' just didn't catch on) was 10 per cent more powerful than the Shovelhead, produced 15 per cent more torque and was 9kg (20lb) lighter. It was oil-tight and well-mannered. It worked.

At first, it came only in 1340cc (82cu in) guise, though the Sportster 883 Evolution came later, followed by 1100 and 1200cc (67 and 73cu in) versions. Having got the engine right, Harley-Davidson was able to concentrate on those styling quirks which it knew would sell. First off was the Softail of 1984, which gave the appearance of a genuine pre-Duo Glide hardtail rear-end, but with the suspension units cunningly hidden beneath the gearbox and in its first year the Softail was Harley's best-seller. After years of having to contend with accusations of producing obsolescent bikes, Harley now found that bikes with a retro appearance were exactly what some people wanted to buy, as long as they started on the button and didn't leak oil. Consequently the Heritage Softail (1986) hid its Showa forks in huge shrouds that mimicked the first Hydra-Glide, while the Springer Softail (1988) actually reintroduced the springer front fork. Forty years after it was abandoned as outdated, the same basic fork that Bill Harley introduced in the first decade of the century was back in production (albeit redesigned).

By now, Harley-Davidson was becoming something of a success story, so much so that when it returned to the stock exchange in 1986 to raise capital, there was no lack of backers and ever since it has been finanicially secure. In the early nineties, when it was selling everything it could make, things went a little quiet as far as new models were concerned. There was the Fat Boy in 1990 (a smoother, sleeker FXR with solid wheels), the new Dyna Glide frame with two-point rubber mounting the year after, and the first use of fuel injection. But it wasn't until 1998 that Harley unveiled its V-twin for the next century, the Twin Cam 88.

Despite the name, this latest V-twin did not have twin overhead camshafts. In fact, like every other Harley V-twin since the Knucklehead (sidevalves aside) it had two pushrod-operated valves per cylinder, the cylinders being air-cooled and set at a 45-degree angle. And yet Harley claimed that only 21 parts had been carried over from the Evolution, 'most of them screws'. What was new was the 1450cc (88cu in) capacity with a bigger bore and shorter stroke than before plus of course the twin camshafts, though in the traditional position. There were deeper fins to improve cooling, new ignition and breather systems, plus a new combustion chamber. Like its predecessor, the Twin Cam came with either carburettors or fuel injection but offered significantly more power and torque – around 19 per cent and 15 per cent respectively. Harley, it has to be said, was keeping half an eye on two new home-grown rivals, the Victory V92C and the Excelsior-Henderson, both of which were due to go on sale in 1999, and both of which promised more performance than any Harley-Davidson.

And so, despite the prospect of growing competition, Harley-Davidson can confidently look towards the new century. Its future is by no means assured, but it looks more secure than it has for a very long time. Perhaps it has simply rediscovered something that the four founders knew from the beginning – that you succeed by giving the customers what they want.

HARPER *England 1954–55*
Scooter with 198cc (12cu in) Villiers power.

HARRAS *Germany 1922–25*
Built Bekamo two-strokes under licence for use in its own frames.

HASCHO *Germany 1923–26*
Used DKW, then Villiers two-strokes.

HASCHÜT *Germany 1929–31*
172cc (10cu in) Villiers engines.

HASTY *France 1930–34*
Used 98cc (6cu in) Aubier-Dunne two-strokes.

HAVERFORD *USA 1909–14*
This small American factory built 4hp single-cylinder machines with automatic inlet valves.

HAWEKA *Germany 1921–26*
English-influenced machines with JAP or MAG engines.

HAWKER *England 1920–23*
Built own 293cc (18cu in) two-strokes designed by aircraft pioneer Harry Hawker.

HAXEL-JAP *England 1911–13*
A 293cc (18cu in) JAP sv engine was used for a limited production run.

HAZEL *England 1906–11*
Began using V-twin Peugeot engines, later a 393cc (24cu in) JAP.

HAZELWOOD *England 1905–23*
Now a forgotten marque, though many were exported. Production was split between machines with JAP singles and Hazelwood's own 499–998cc (30–61cu in) V-twins.

HB *England 1919–24*
Simple well-made machines with 346cc and 498cc (21 and 30cu in) sv and ohv Blackburne engines.

HEC *England 1922–23*
247cc (15cu in) Villiers-powered two-strokes.

HEC *England 1939–55*
Very early autocycle, with in-house 80cc (5cu in) two-stroke.

HECKER *Germany 1921–56*
Started with own two-strokes, though later bought in a full range of JAP and MAG four-strokes. Sachs-engined lightweights were added from 1931 and after 1945 it used only Sachs and Ilo engines to 248cc (15cu in).

HEIDEMANN *Germany 1949–52*
98/123cc (6/7.5cu in) Sachs-engined lightweights.

HEILO *Germany 1924–25*
Produced a 348cc (21cu in) three-port two-stroke single and also experimented with supercharging.

HEINKEL *Germany 1952–62*
Range of two- and four-stroke mopeds and scooters, built in the former aircraft factory.

HELI *Germany 1923–25*
Advanced 246cc (15cu in) two-stroke, water-cooled, with unit-construction, leaf-sprung fork, though still belt-driven.

HELIOS *Germany 1921–22*
Forerunner of BMW, using a proprietory flat twin. It was unsuccessful, which encouraged BMW to proceed with its own all-new design.

HELLA *Germany 1921–24*
Horizontally-mounted two-strokes of 147/183cc (9/11cu in).

HELLER *Germany 1932–26*
Used the same 493cc (30cu in) flat twin as the Helios, and from 1924 the similar MJ 746cc (45.5cu in) unit.

HELO *Germany 1923–25*
A Bekamo-type two-stroke of 149cc (9cu in).

HELYETT *France 1926–55*
Sold a complete range over the years from 98cc–996cc (6–61cu in). One interesting variation was a JAP V-twin mounted transversely to allow shaft-drive, with the gearbox in unit. After the war, concentrated on small two-strokes up to 123cc (7.5cu in).

OPPOSITE and ABOVE: The Henderson was perhaps the best-known American four

HERCULES *Germany 1903–*
Despite rarely building its own engines or offering any great innovation, Hercules grew to be one of the largest German manufacturers in the 1950s. It began with a belt-driven machine in 1904, and in the 1920s used bought-in engines from JAP, Sachs and others. After World War II, production resumed in 1950 using Sachs and Ilo two-strokes of 100–250cc (6–15cu in). Bought up by Fichtel & Sachs in 1966, it merged with the Zweirad Union (DKW, Express and Victoria). Since then, the Hercules name has been chiefly used on mopeds, though 1974 saw the W2000, the first rotary-engined motorcycle to reach production. It was of 294cc (18cu in), air-cooled, and produced 27bhp at 6,500rpm for a top speed of just over 145km/h (90mph). Unfortunately, there was a lack of confidence from a conservative public (this was the time of NSU's troubled Ro80 car) and less than 2,000 were built.

HENDERSON *U.S.A. 1911–31*
Said by some to be the best of the big American four-cylinder bikes, the Henderson was also one of the first. William Henderson's version was air-cooled, with 1068cc/65cu inches (later 1301cc/79cu inches) and unit-construction. The gearbox had three forward speeds and one reverse! Development continued up to 1931 when Ignaz Schwinn, whose factory it was, decided to pull out of the motorcycle market.

HENKEL *Germany 1927–32*
Paul Henkel took up production of the KG motorcycle, a 503cc (31cu in) shaft-driven single with unit-construction which had been built by two companies before. Henkel added a 198cc (12cu in) Blackburne-powered lightweight as well.

HENLEY *England 1920–29*
Always used bought-in engines, the first being the 269cc (16cu in) Villiers, then the 497cc (30cu in) Blackburne, with other Blackburne and JAP models following. Became New Henley in 1927, and began to offer bigger V-twins.

HERBI *Germany 1928–32*
Choice of 198cc (12cu in) Blackburne-powered machines or 498cc (30cu in) three-valve Küchens.

BELOW: A Hercules single of the 1980s

HERCULES *England 1902*
MMC, Minerva and White & Poppe engines were used.

HERDTLE-BRUNEAU *France 1902–14*
One of the first to use an ohv engine. Also produced a water-cooled 264cc (16cu in) vertical twin.

HERKO *Germany 1922–25*
Built its own 122/158cc (7/10cu in) two-strokes and a 198cc (12cu in) sv, and sold both engines and frames to other manufacturers.

HERKRA *Germany 1922–23*
Used own 141cc (9cu in) two-strokes.

HERMA *Germany 1921–24*
Produced a 148cc (9cu in) clip-on that would fit either wheel.

HERMES *Germany 1922–25*
Similar to the English Cockerell, with a 124cc (8cu in) two-stroke.

HERMES *Germany 1924–25*
Step-through frame with choice of 348 or 678cc (21 or 41cu in) JAP power.

HERO *India 1978–*
Licence-built Peugeot mopeds, and a 98cc (6cu in) ohc Honda from 1985. The following year brought tooling from Puch of Austria, and since 1988 the company has built two-strokes under the Hero-Puch name.

HEROS *Germany 1921–29*
Made its own two- and four-stroke engines up to 247cc (15cu in), not to mention gearboxes.

OPPOSITE and ABOVE: The Hesketh V1000 – handsome but flawed

HEROS *Germany 1923–24*
Another Heros, made by a Berlin-based factory which used 142cc (9cu in) DKW two-stroke engines.

HERTHA *Germany 1924–25*
Used a 142cc (9cu in) DKW unit.

HESKETH *England 1980–82*
Hesketh, the new British superbike, was announced to a delighted press and public in April 1980. They were delighted because, deep down, almost everyone wanted to see a new British bike. There were one or two sceptics, such as the national daily which described the new V-twin as just another folly of the English aristocracy, but they were in the minority. Two years later, when the whole enterprise collapsed in a highly public and embarassing manner, there was no shortage of critics.

It was like something out of a novel. The plump Lord Hesketh had inherited the family seat at the age of five. At 23, he was running a successful Formula One racing team; now he was going to build a bike to beat the world. As the plot was revealed, so the more promising it seemed. The Hesketh V1000 was to be a one-litre V-twin, full of character, relatively light and simple by eighties standards, but with all the modern conveniences of a luxury superbike. Engine design was to be by Weslake, well-known for its race-winning speedway singles, with styling by John Mockett. They were aiming, according to Hesketh, at a two-wheeled Aston Martin – fast, superbly made, and of course all-British. And according to the press (based on brief rides on hand-built

Lord Hesketh's dream was to kick-start the British motorcycle industry

prototypes) they had managed to do it.

So it was a great pity when everything went wrong. When the V1000 eventually went into production, the press reports were very different. On bikes intended for sale (as opposed to those carefully assembled prototypes) the gearchange was slow, clonky and obstructive, and there was bad transmission snatch. Even worse, the engine, the beautiful 90-degree V-twin with its four-valve heads and racing heritage, lacked torque at low revs and rattled like 'two skeletons in a dustbin' as one road tester put it. After around 170 bikes had been built, the receivers called a halt, though Lord Hesketh did buy back sufficient tooling to maintain production in a very small way back at the family seat at Easton Neston.

HESS *Germany 1925*
Germany's only four-cylinder, of 799cc (49cu in) and air-cooled.

HEXE *Germany 1923–25*
Produced 142cc (9cu in) clip-ons and 269/346cc (16/21cu in) lightweights.

HIEKEL *Germany 1925–32*
348cc (21cu in) three-port two-stroke with low seat.

HILAMAN *U.S.A. 1906–13*
475cc (29cu in) singles and 950cc (60cu in) V-twins with chain-drive.

HILDEBRAND & WOLFMÜLLER
Germany 1894–97
The first motorcycle ever made for commercial sale may also have been the first commercial failure. Designed by Heinrich Hildebrand and Alois Wolfmüller, with mechanic Hans Geisenhof, its 1488cc (91cu in) flat twin was water-cooled, the radiator forming the rear mudguard. It produced 2.5hp at 240rpm and drove the rear wheel directly via long cranks (the wheel also acted as flywheel). It had total-loss lubrication and a surface carburettor. Unfortunately, the company failed to develop it, and this pioneer was soon overtaken by faster-running engines at home and in France. The H & W ceased production within three or four years.

HINDE *The Netherlands 1899–1938*
Briefly offered 2hp De Dion clip-ons and the name was used again in the 1930s for an autocycle and two lightweights.

HIRANO *Japan 1952–61*
49/78cc (3/5cu in) mini-scooters and 123/173cc (7.5/11cu in) lightweights, all two-strokes.

HIRONDELLE *France 1921–26*
Produced 198cc (12cu in) sv singles, among others.

HIRSCH *Germany 1923–24*
Offered its own 128cc (8cu in) two-stroke or DKW's 142cc (9cu in) equivalent.

HJ *England 1920–21*
Utilized 269cc (16cu in) Liberty and Villiers engines.

HJH *Wales 1954–56*
One of the few Welsh motorcycles, built in Neath with Villiers power to 247cc (15cu in).

HKR *Germany 1925–26*
A continuation of the HRD-like Hako, with little changed.

HMK *Austria 1937–38*
Another English-influenced make, using JAP engines.

HMW *Germany 1923–28*
Produced 3hp singles, with own sv engines.

HMW *Austria 1949–64*
Produced the 49cc (3cu in) Fuchs clip-on, then a range of mopeds and lightweights.

HOBART *England 1901–23*
An example of how complex the early industry could be. Hobart sold its engines, frames and other parts to other assemblers, built its own bikes but bought in proprietory engines as well. Also built the McKenzie motorcycle.

HOCHLAND *Germany 1926–27*
Limited production of a 496cc (30cu in) ohv flat twin.

HOCKLEY *England 1914–16*
Utilized 296cc (18cu in) Liberty and Villiers two-strokes.

HOCO *Germany 1924–28*
Used a wooden frame and (on some) a fully enclosed engine such as the Nabob two-strokes or the 346cc (21cu in) JAP sv.

HODAKA *Japan 1964–78*
Was an established engine maker, which only diversified into complete bikes when its main customer closed down. Hodakas were mainly trail bikes, aimed at the American market (they were never sold in Japan) and used its own 90, 100 and 125cc (5, 6 and 8cu in) two-strokes; a 250 was added in the final years.

HOENSON *The Netherlands 1953–55*
Used 147cc (9cu in) Sachs and 198cc (12cu in) Ilo engines.

HOFFMANN *Germany 1949–54*
As well as the usual Sachs/Ilo-powered lightweights, Hoffmann made the Vespa under licence and an upmarket 246/298cc (15/18cu in) flat twin, a sort of mini-BMW.

HOLDEN *Germany 1898–1903*
English pioneer, with a water-cooled 3hp four-cylinder engine driving the rear wheel direct.

HOLLEY *U.S.A. 1902–late 1910s*
Rearward-facing 2hp engine in strengthened cycle frame.

HONDA *Japan 1947–*
Coca-Cola, McDonalds ... and Honda. There are few companies almost guaranteed worldwide recognition, but Honda is one of them. Wherever you go, however remote the area, someone will have heard the name, even if they've never seen its products. It is a remarkable story, all the more so because Soichiro Honda was a self-taught engineer who did not

The little-known Hodaka was aimed at the United States

build a powered two-wheeler of any kind until after World War II. Neither was it a smooth path: the fledgling Honda Motor Company came close to bankruptcy in 1952, and when Soichiro Honda first visited the TT in 1954, he was shocked at just how far ahead the Germans and Italians were. Few could have guessed that six years later this curious little man would be back, and beating them all. Not only that, but by 1959 Honda was out-producing the entire British motorcycle industry.

Honda wasn't the only Japanese motorcycle manufacturer to arise from the ashes of the war. In the early 1950s there were over 100 of them, all sharing the same advantage of a massive home market in need of cheap personal transport, protected from imports by a substantial tariff war. That Honda succeeded where so many failed was down to a reliable product, a nationwide dealer network (many of the companies sold only within their own provinces), and a willingness to risk large-scale investment.

Soichiro Honda was born in Komyo near Hamamatsu in 1906, the eldest son of the village blacksmith. From an early age he was more interested in matters mechanical than academic, and at 16 left school and home for Tokyo, where he became an apprentice car mechanic. He learned fast, and after six years returned to Hamamatsu to set up his own repair shop. The business did well in a rapidly industrializing Japan, so well that Soichiro was able to race cars part-time and a love of racing was to remain with him for the rest of his life until a serious accident put an end to his racing career. Piston rings were his next venture, and with the help of

Honda's original CB750 led to a whole family of road-going fours. This CB650 was one of them

the local technical college (where Honda studied metallurgy), he discovered the correct material and went into mass-production. It soon became clear that Honda's talent lay not only in practical design, but also in *production* design for high volumes which was to form the basis of his success.

Honda's company went on making piston rings throughout the war until the factory was damaged by bombing in 1944 and an earthquake finished it off the following year. He sold up what was left, and in October 1946 set up the grand-sounding Honda Technical Research Institute, which was really no more than a medium-sized wooden shed. He also realized that cheap transport in a war-devastated Japan constituted a huge market just waiting to be tapped. What really gave him a head start was coming across 500 war-surplus two-stroke engines. Bolted to a standard bicycle, with belt-drive to the rear wheel, they became the first Hondas. It was a slow, crude device that ran on a mixture of petrol and turpentine, but it worked, and the 500 engines were all used.

Rather than attempting to design a new engine from scratch, Honda simply built his own A type by copying the ex-army one. Of 50cc (3cu in), it produced 1bhp at 5,000rpm, had a flywheel magneto, slide carburettor and a crankcase valve to aid induction.

At first, the A was simply bolted into a standard bicycle, but Honda soon came up with a purpose-built frame, still with pedals, but stronger, longer and lower, with a sprung front fork. In 1948, a B model followed, a load-carrying three-wheeler with the little engine stretched to 89cc (5cu in). Inevitably, the bigger engine found its way into another two-wheeler, the C, which looked more motorcycle-like than ever, though still with a crude belt-drive.

The following year, however, saw Honda's first true motorcycle. Named the model D, or Dream (a favourite Honda name for years to come), it utilized Honda's own channel steel frame; there was a proper two-speed gearbox and chain-drive, and power came from a 98cc (6cu in) two-stroke. In looks it owed much to pre-war German thinking, but for Japan in 1949 it was one of the best machines available, and sales began to mount.

Despite the success, the little company was still on shaky ground (most of its outlets were small bicycle shops that were often slow to pay their debts, or collapsed altogether); but an answer came in the form of Takeo Fujisawa, an excellent accountant, good at chasing money and recruiting dealers. Not only did this allow Honda to concentrate on design, but it gave the company a nationwide network of dealers, all of whom stocked Honda spares, which was a great advantage over smaller concerns restricted to selling to their own locality. The strategy paid off, and by 1950 Honda was by far the largest manufacturer in the country, producing nearly half its entire output. This stood the company in good stead when a price war ensued in the early fifties.

ABOVE: Racing at the TT

Expansion

The range continued to expand, with two significant bikes in 1952, one indicating Honda's interest in technical advance, the other its commitment to cheap, basic transport which brought the money in. The E model Dream was Honda's first four-stroke, a 146cc (9cu in) single that was technically interesting in having three valves per cylinder (two inlets and one exhaust), with twin carburettors to supply the twin inlet ports. It produced 5.5bhp at 5,000rpm and drove through a two-speed gearbox, while most of the frame and cycle parts were transferred from the D model. It failed to handle that well and tended to drink oil, but the E was something of a milestone for Honda. The F model Cub was just as significant. Although Honda's natural inclination may have been towards technically advanced machinery, he also knew that, with the Japanese market still recovering, basic transport would be the foundation of the company's fortunes. So the Cub was a bolt-on 50cc (3cu in) two-stroke for bicycles, fitting low on the left-hand side of the rear wheel. It produced 1bhp at 3,000rpm, added only 6kg (13lb) to the weight, and it was a hit. Within six months, production was up to 6,500 a month, and the Cub was accounting for nearly three-quarters of Honda production.

Once again, increased production meant lower prices, which in turn allowed Honda to undercut and outsell its dwindling competitors. But it wasn't out of the woods yet. Soichiro knew that to consolidate its success the company needed to expand, so he went on a

BELOW and OPPOSITE: Honda's original CB750 set new standards for high-speed convenience

HONDA
HONDA
HONDA
HONDA
494
595
94
CHEVY VAN

shopping trip to Europe and the United States, ordering over $1 million-worth of machine tools in the process. With an economic downturn at home, this produced a financial crisis at Honda which was only overcome by forward-looking officials at Honda's bank who realized that in the long term the company would have no trouble paying off its debts. A hostile takeover from Mitsubishi was rebuffed, and Honda was on its way.

Meanwhile, the bikes kept on improving, and the J model of 1953 was Honda's first really up-to-date machine. It was very similar to the contemporary NSU, with its pressed steel frame and 89cc (5cu in) ohv engine. The gearbox was three-speed, with a positive stop footchange and there were telecopic forks and torsion-bar rear suspension. In fact, the company continued to closely examine foreign machines. (Honda took a trip to the 1954 TT, not to take part but to watch, and came back with a number of components to study.) At the time, the Japanese government had banned the importation of foreign motorcycles, though if a home producer wanted to buy one for study there were ways and means. Perhaps it was this that led to jibes about Japanese 'copies', but this was an over-simplification; what they were really doing was studying, learning, then invariably doing it better.

Another design milestone came in 1955 with Honda's first overhead-camshaft engine, the Dream SA. Showa had already attempted this, but was troubled by oil leaks and broken camchains. Honda learned from this domestic experience as well, with the result that the 246cc/15cu in SA was largely trouble-free. It was of unit-construction, with a clean modern appearance, and there was also a 344cc (21cu in) SB, Honda's biggest machine yet. They received more power and new forks in 1957, and became the M series.

By this time, Honda was firmly established as market leader at home, and had begun tentative exports. But the bike that transformed it into the most successful manufacturer in the world, and played a central part in transforming the image of motorcycling as well, was about to be launched – the step-thru. Unveiled in August 1958, the Super Cub C100 was a masterstroke in all sorts of ways. First, it was just what the market was ready for; most countries were beyond post-war austerity, but not yet affluent enough for mass car ownership, so a 90cc (5.5cu in) scooterette was about right. Second, the C100 combined the weather protection and ease of use of a traditional scooter, but was better balanced and easier to ride due to the bigger wheels and centrally mounted engine. Developing countries with unmade roads preferred bigger wheels, but everyone appreciated the automatic clutch. Third, the 49cc (3cu in) four-stroke engine was quiet, economical and could push along at 64km/h (40mph) – just fast enough to keep up with city traffic. Finally, like most Hondas to date, the step-thru was a quality product, well built and reliable. Not having been built down to a price, it wasn't the cheapest on the market, but it would almost guarantee trouble-free running. Selling to people who wanted no more than to fill it with petrol and go – this was a big plus. The C100 was clean and neat, with an enclosed chain and decently covered engine – and it always started. It was no wonder that 24,000 were sold in the first five months. From 1960, Honda could depend on half a million sales every year, and by 1983, with no sign of demand declining, 15 million had been built. Today, the step-thru (visually very similar to the first C100) is still selling well all over the world. Without doubt, it is the most successful powered two-wheeler of all time.

It was this success that encouraged Honda to begin an export drive. By now, the Japanese market was just about saturated and the only way for the company to expand was to sell abroad. American Honda was set up in 1959, with European importers over the next few years. It was considerably helped by an ingenious advertising campaign emphasizing that Honda was aiming, not at enthusiasts but at people with no idea of a what it was like to ride a powered two-wheeler. Motorcycles were noisy, anti-social things with hairy, smelly riders. A Honda step-thru, on the other hand, was different: 'You meet the nicest people on a Honda', went the slogan, and it was bang on target. As a result,

BELOW: Phil Read leaps Ballaugh Bridge at the Isle of Man TT

OPPOSITE: Racing four-strokes brought Honda to the world's attention

Shell
NGK
HONDA
54

step-thrus sold in their thousands to the U.S. and Europe, as well as to South-East Asia, helping to rekindle a new interest in powered two-wheelers in general. Sales in the U.S. in particular boomed as never before and other manufacturers had much to thank Honda for.

There were of course variations on a theme. The pushrod C100 gave way to the overhead-camshaft C50 in 1967, and there were bigger variants – the C70 and C90 – which provided enough performance for out-of-town commuters. The C110 was a motorcycle-style version, with the C100's engine suspended from a pressed steel frame. Different again, but with the same mechanics, was the CZ100 of 1960, better known as the Monkey Bike. The idea was to squeeze C100 engine and transmission into the smallest possible package and the Monkey utilized diminutive 5-inch wheels and a rigid frame and forks. In bright colours, it was a cheeky little number that gave rise to a curious inverted snobbery and even attracted a virtual cult following. The Monkey Bike is now made by the Chinese, and there is at least one firm in Britain still offering tuning parts.

In time, all these small Hondas came to use ohc engines, and the pioneer was the CS90 of 1964. It was an 89cc (5cu in) single which produced 8bhp at 9,500rpm, with the cam driven by a chain on the left-hand side. Both head and barrel were of light alloy, the cam itself ran directly into the head, while the barrel was placed close to the horizontal; this basic ohc layout was to power the small Honda singles for years to come.

ABOVE: Motocross introduced two-stroke Hondas

BELOW: The FireBlade set new standards of excellence

BELOW: The high-tech NR750 used oval-shaped pistons

ABOVE: *André Malherbe enjoyed motocross success on the CR500*

Motorcycles Proper

Honda launched its first road-going twin in 1957, a natural result of Soichiro's trip to the TT in 1954, where he was impressed by the twin-cylinder ohc NSUs. It was the C70, of 247cc/15cu inches (with 'square' bore and stroke of 54mm), built of aluminium with an 8.2:1 compression ratio, 360-degree crankshaft (so the pistons rose and fell together) and central chain to drive the cam: power was 18bhp at 7,400rpm. It drove through gear primary-drive and an engine-speed clutch to a four-speed gearbox and enclosed chain. Honda still preferred leading-link forks to telescopics which, with the deeply valanced mudguards, added to the cobby Germanic look of early Hondas. It would be a few years before Hondas began to look genuinely sporting.

Different versions sprouted with each passing year: the electric start C71 in 1958 and the CS71 that same year, tuned to produce 20bhp at 8,400rpm thanks to a higher compression of 9.0:1. There was also an RC70 scrambler, with high-level open pipes, the 20bhp engine and no lights, whose main difference was a tubular frame (the other twins used the more familiar pressed steel). There were new capacities as well. The C90 was a miniaturized 125cc (7.6cu in) version of the C70, with 11.5bhp at 9,500rpm and the option of standard or sportier looking CB90 guise (the engine was the same). Similarly, the C95/CB95 used a 154cc (9.4cu in) version of the twin, with 13.5 or 16.5bhp. At the top of the range, the 250

BELOW: *Tom Herron riding an 810cc (49cu in) racer at the TT*

BELOW: *The 1998 VFR800, a class-leading sports tourer*

was bored out to 60mm to give 305cc (18.6cu in), powering the C75 and CS76. (Happily, Honda was to change its model names to reflect capacity a few years later.)

All of these early twins were something of a revelation in Europe, offering the apparently exotic features of ohc and all-aluminium power units at a reasonable price. Not only that, but they were reliable, did not leak oil and appeared to thrive on high revs. No wonder they made an impact. The handling, with softish suspension reflecting imperfect understanding of motorcycle dynamics lacked the precision of European bikes, but not enough to deter many buyers.

The 250s received a power increase as the C72 in 1960, to 20bhp, and 24bhp at 9,000rpm for the sportier CB72; the twin was converted to wet-sump lubrication at the same time. The CB was in fact quite different to its 'touring' counterpart, now having a 180-degree crankshaft, twin carburettors and 9.5:1 compression. The cycle parts were different too, with telescopic forks and a tubular frame heralding the start of Honda's departure from lumpy, angular styling. It was joined in 1962 by a trail bike derivative, the CL72. With knobbly tyres, bashplate and high-level exhaust it looked the part, though its weight and close-fitting mudguards prevented serious off-road use. What it did do was to introduce a new generation of American riders to non-competitive trail riding, thus opening up a whole new market sector.

Meanwhile, the sporting 305s got the same telescopic forks, 180-degree crank and tubular frame as the CB72 in 1963, numbered as CB77 and CP77. Power was

ABOVE and BELOW: The 1965 CB450 Dream led Honda into direct competition with the British

quoted as 28.5bhp at 9,500rpm for a top speed of 153km/h (95mph). The following year, the 125 went the same route and changed its name to CB93. The 150cc (9cu in) twins were bored out to 50mm for 161cc (10cu in), and the CB160 was the result with 16.5bhp at 10,000rpm. It could top 129km/h (80mph) and cruise at 70mph, and this at a time when a 150cc BSA Bantam would have had trouble touching 60mph flat-out. Standards were changing.

Honda could thank its growing race experience for this ability to produce high-revving, high-performing four-stroke twins that were reliable. From 1953, it had raced at home with some (though not complete) success, but it was the 1959 TT that marked Honda's first overseas event. It went about it seriously, with a comprehensive team for the 125 race of five riders, nine machines, and many mechanics. Unfortunately, the 125cc twins just weren't as fast as the NSUs and were well off the pace. They returned the following year, with a four-cylinder 250 as well as the 125, and were rewarded with fourth in the 250cc TT and second in the Ulster GP. But in 1961, with MV Agusta not competing in the smaller classes, Honda's bikes fully developed and with riders like Jim Redman back in the fold, they dominated both 125 and 250 classes through the year. The same thing happened in 1962 when Redman also took the new 350-4 to a championship win. Other talented riders (Mike Hailwood to name but one) rode for Honda in the sixties, and evocative machines like the five-cylinder 125 and 250-6 thrilled enthusiasts across the world, as much by the noise they made as their performance. In 1967 the exemplary talent of Hailwood won Honda the 250 and 350 crowns and narrowly lost the 500 to Agostini on the MV. After 136 GP wins, Honda decided to withdraw from Grand Prix racing for a while.

Just as Honda kept creeping into higher capacity classes for racing, so it did for the road, with the launch of the CB450 Dream in 1965. Although it had much in common with the smaller twins, the new engine had twin overhead camshafts and torsion bar valve-springs. Well over-square, the 445cc (27cu in) twin revved happily to 8,500rpm for its 43bhp. It used a conventional cradle frame where Honda's earlier tubular frames had hung the engine from a spine. Twin carburettors, of course, and (later) a five-speed gearbox, and the Black Bomber, as it was nicknamed, could easily make 161km/h (100mph). In short, it was as fast as a 650cc

ABOVE: *The CB350/4, the smallest in-line (road) four*

BELOW: *The 1973 CB500/4, the smaller version of the 750*

(40cu in) British twin, but was just as reliable and easy-going as any other Honda. The CB450's real significance lay in being the first Japanese machine to challenge the British and European manufacturers head-on, and it was followed by performance bikes from Suzuki, Yamaha and Kawasaki. If the Western manufacturers had cause for complacency before, they certainly needed to think twice now.

But Honda wasn't forgetting that its roots were in commuters and in 1967 announced the CD175 twin, a kind of super commuter where a 125 was too small. A single carburettor and four-speed gearbox confirmed its workhorse intentions. But the rest of Honda's twins were continuing the sporting theme – the CB160 was enlarged to a 175, while the 250s were replaced by a new, more highly tuned CB250, with 30bhp at 10,500rpm (though as ever, there was a touring CD and off-road CL version), while the new CB350 had 36bhp at the same revs. All received front disc brakes in 1970, and all now had the more rounded styling they were to retain until the Superdream appeared in 1977. They looked a little portly towards the end, which the final CJ250/360T did something to rectify. Meanwhile, the Black Bomber had its major update in 1974, as the CB500T, though the emphasis had changed, with a lower compression and longer stroke. However, it was soon overshadowed by the smaller fours, and did not last long.

Notable among the small singles were the SS50 sports mopeds, which in pre-restricted form produced 6bhp at 11,000rpm. Or the ST70 DAX. This was more of a cross between a Monkey Bike and a conventional machine – certainly midway in size – with 50 and 90cc (3 and 5.5cu in) versions following. There was no weather protection, so Honda's description of 'fun bikes' was probably about right. The PC50 was a new moped in 1969, with the familiar ohc engine but a more basic layout than the step-thru. The early twins had pioneered the trail bike class, and Honda now followed them up with more suitable singles, the SL and XL series, which came in 125 and 250cc (7.6 and 15cu in) sizes, and later a 185 and 500cc (11 and 30.5cu in) as well. This brief list of Honda's smaller bikes of the late sixties and early seventies includes highlights only, but the CG125 single must not be left out. With a reversion to pushrod-operated valves, it was simple and reliable in the extreme, not to mention economical on fuel, and is still made to this day in Brazil.

ABOVE: A rare automatic-transmission CB750

BELOW: CBX1000, a café racer version

The First Superbike

Two Hondas had a profound impact on the fortunes of the company, and on motorcycling in general – the step-thru C100, and the CB750. It is hard to imagine now, 30 years after the event, just what an impact the CB750 had. There had, of course, been four-cylinder bikes before, but never mass-produced with luxury features and available at local dealers at a keen price. True, the Kawasaki two-stroke and BSA/Triumph triples were potentially as fast in a straight line, and the British bike certainly handled better. But the CB750 came with all the usual features that people had now come to expect from Honda. It was reliable, clean and civilized, as well as docile at low speed. Far from being over-tuned, it was actually quite mild, and its 67bhp at 8,000rpm was well within the new four's limits.

Although there were cries of over-complexity from diehards at the time, the new engine was relatively simple and based on well proven features that Honda had been using for over a decade. Just two valves per cylinder, and the single overhead cam was driven by a central chain. True, there were four carburettors, but they did not appear over-ready to drop out of tune. The frame was an utterly conventional tubular cradle, with sensibly gaitered telescopic forks. Five-speed gearbox, electric start and a front disc brake completed the specification. The flexible engine and big comfortable seat made it practical for touring, yet this was a 200km/h (125mph) motorcycle which did not need constant attention. Not surprisingly, just like Honda's other milestone bike, the CB750 immediately sold well, and the opposition had good cause for anxiety. Kawasaki, which had its own 750 four under development, returned to the drawing board to produce the dohc 900cc (55cu in) Z1. In fact, so successful was Honda's concept of a big, affordable in-line four, that all the Japanese manufacturers were to build one. It got to the point where the format acquired the faintly derogatory term UJM – 'Universal Japanese Motorcycle'.

Faced with this success, Honda not surprisingly followed it up with smaller fours, the CB500 in 1971 (similar in layout, though with a wet sump engine of 50bhp at 9,000rpm), and the jewel-like CB350 the following year; the 350 was upsized into the classic 400/4 in 1974. It was a favourite

ABOVE: *A late seventies Superdream*

in Europe (not to mention the home market, where 400cc/24cu inches was a big licence barrier), and the 400's small size and attractive looks, largely due to the sensuous four-into-one exhaust, made it a big seller. Meanwhile, the 500 was bored out to 544cc (33cu in) as the CB550. Less predictable was an automatic transmission version of the 750cc (46cu in), detuned to 47bhp at 7,500rpm and with a torque converter replacing the clutch. Like the similarly-equipped 400cc twin Hondamatic, it only sold in small numbers. By the late 1970s, the original single-cam 750 was outclassed by the opposition, so Honda brought in a dohc four-valves-per-cylinder replacement; the new CB750 was certainly more powerful (77bhp was claimed) but also weighed a massive 245kg (540lb). If that wasn't enough, a 95 horsepower CB900 was launched alongside it. It could top 217km/h (135mph) when new in 1979, though at the time Japanese chassis were only just beginning to catch up with their engines. Perhaps more trustworthy at speed was the CB1100R into which it developed, with a half-fairing and attention paid to handling as well as power.

One might have thought that a bike like the original CB750 would have been the perfect flagship for anyone. Not a bit of it. Honda knew that its rivals would bring out something to top the 750 soon enough; the question was whether it would respond with the ultimate sportster, tourer, or a little of both. In the event, the Gold Wing was

BELOW: *The CB125 Twin*

BELOW: *The 1975 Gold Wing was a new concept motorcycle*

An early CB750, made to police specification

very much the tourer, with more power, capacity (Harleys excepted) and sophistication than anything else then on the market. The 1000cc (61cu in) flat four was water-cooled and, despite four carburettors, in a very soft state of tune which still allowed it 80bhp at 7,000rpm. With radiator, oil and water, the engine alone weighed 103kg (226lb), and the complete bike 295kg (650lb). Its saving grace was that much of that weight was carried low down, thanks to the flat engine and the underseat fuel tank. (What looked like the tank was actually a dummy and could hinge apart to reveal the electrics.) So the Gold Wing could handle surprisingly well, as well as cruise effortlessly at any speed you liked up to 161km/h (100mph). It was ultra-comfortable and low-maintenance (shaft-driven of course) and set new standards for touring bikes.

By degrees, the engine got bigger, to 1085cc (66cu in) in 1980 and 1182cc (72cu in) in 1984. The end of the eighties saw the ultimate Gold Wing in the form of the six-cylinder GL1500, a silky-smooth 100bhp monster that came with fairing, stereo and all the usual touring gee-gaws as standard. It also had a reverse gear (in case you parked it in an awkward spot)! As this is written, there is a rumour that Honda is considering an eight-cylinder two-litre Gold Wing for the next millennium, possibly diesel-powered. Now could anyone top that?

Back in the 1970s, excess certainly seemed to be the rule rather than the exception, and if Kawasaki's Z1 was bigger and more powerful than the CB750, then Honda would just have to bring out something even bigger! It was the CBX

ABOVE: Honda still does well providing police bikes. This is a 1997 ST1100

which, as it happens, wasn't the first six-cylinder road bike of modern times when it was unveiled in 1978. That honour went to the Benelli Sei, which beat it to market by a year; ironically, the Italian six owed much to early single-cam Honda fours. In any case, the CBX had no trouble commanding centre stage with six cylinders, 24 valves, 105bhp and (if you were brave or foolhardy enough) 217km/h (135mph). The CBX did not sell in large numbers, but perhaps by this time this was no longer the point of the exercise. In 1981, Honda turned the bike into a sports tourer by fitting a half-fairing and detuning it slightly. It lasted until 1984.

Vee Power

Throughout the sixties and seventies, Honda had based its reputation on a succession of in-line twins and fours. But by the late seventies, everyone had got in on the act, and it was time for a change. For Honda, the eighties was the decade of the Vee engine, whether it be V-twin or V4, air- or liquid-cooled. In-line engines were still in the range: the CB250/400 Superdreams, with three valves per cylinder and the same 'Eurostyling' as other Hondas of the time, were good sellers, and developed into the CB450 of 1989. In the mid-range, there was the four-cylinder CBX550, with four valves per cylinder and a curious enclosed front disc brake. Singles also were well-established; the four-stroke trail bikes were perennial favourites, and there were two attempts to sell a 500cc road-going single, notably the FT500 (odd-looking, and a flop) and the attractive XBR500. More successful (at least in Britain) was the RS250 from 1980, a light and slim road bike using the 248cc (15cu in) single for 145km/h (90mph) with good economy.

But all these were sidelines to Honda's new strategy centred on Vee engines. First off was what appeared to be an extreme oddity at the time. The CX500 of 1978 soon acquired the unkind nickname of 'Plastic Maggot', due to its rounded, bulbous styling. The CX was certainly different, with a liquid-cooled transverse V-twin of 499cc (30cu in) giving 50bhp. It had four valves per cylinder but (unusually for Honda) pushrod operation. Despite some early problems with wear in the camchain tensioner, the shaft-driven CX evolved into a thoroughly reliable machine, and became a favourite with despatch riders – the ultimate compliment to its high mileage and reliability. A CX650 followed in 1984, but more interesting was the Turbo, which boosted the original power to 82bhp. Unfortunately, weight and complexity blunted its advantage, and turbocharged bikes failed to take off.

While the CX was clearly intended as a middleweight tourer, Honda followed it with a series of more sporting longitudinal Vees with chain-drive. The first was the liquid-cooled VF750 of 1983 which handled well and promised to be a good all-rounder. Four hundred and 500cc (24 and 30.5cu in) versions in the same format soon followed, and it looked as if Honda was to undergo a Vee revolution, there being the liquid-cooled V-twin VT250 and VT500 from 1984 as well. There was something of a setback when the VF750 was discovered to have valvegear problems, which caused Honda to think again. It replaced the VF with the

BELOW: Honda's new V4 adopted cruiser guise for the U.S.A.

ABOVE: A late seventies CB750F

RIGHT and OPPOSITE PAGE: Sales brochures for the retro CB750 (above) and VT250F (below)

VFR750 in 1986, and with gear-driven camshafts this overcame the earlier bike's shortcomings. In fact, it turned out to be one of Honda's great success stories, since the VFR750, and the fuel-injected VFR800 which replaced it in 1998, proved to be a great all-rounder. It was fast enough, with 100bhp, for the vast majority of riders, yet comfortable enough to tour on, as well as reliable and undemanding to ride. More exciting was the RC30 race replica of 1988, closely related to the RVF racer. Although road-legal, most of these, and the RC45 which replaced them, were destined for race tracks. Perhaps the most eagerly awaited of the V4s was the NR750, Honda's road-going oval-pistoned bike, echoing the technology used in the NR500 with which it had challenged the two-strokes in 1979, and failed. Sadly, there seemed little point to the NR750, except as a work of art, despite its eight valves per cylinder, 125bhp at 14,000rpm and more exotic alloys than you'd find on a spacecraft. It weighed too much, and was no faster than conventional 750s. At the other end of the scale were ultra-sensible V-twins, like the trail-styled 583cc (35.6cu in) Transalp (an early

Refined simplicity: the air-cooled 747 cc engine

The Seven Fifty's heart is its handsome DOHC four-cylinder powerplant, which produces impressively smooth power over a broad rpm range. An up-to-date version of the engine that powered the popular CB750 introduced in 1984, the Seven Fifty unit features the same 16-valve cylinder head configuration, allowing excellent combustion efficiency for optimum performance.

Honda's proven engineering plus a large, high-efficiency oil-cooler ensure the Seven Fifty backs up its timeless appeal with long-lasting reliability. Four 34 mm CV carburettors provide flexible delivery and crisp throttle response, while the deeply-chromed 4-into-2 exhaust system adds power and elegance while emitting a quiet yet pleasing tone.

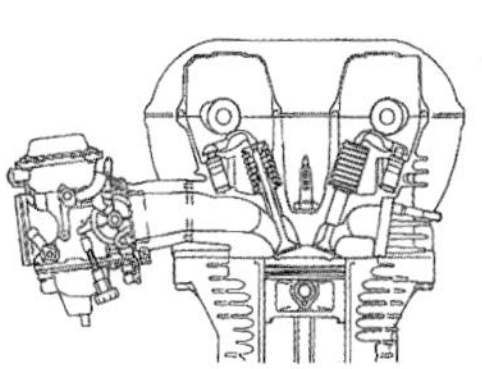

A remarkably low maintenance requirement is an important advantage of the Seven Fifty motor. Its hydraulic valve lifters and automatic camchain tensioner are maintenance-free, as are the battery and the accurate transistorised ignition system. The convenient spin-on oil filter is yet another Seven Fifty feature designed to give the minimum amount of fuss – for maximum riding pleasure.

Technology plus tradition: the Seven Fifty chassis

Honda's all-rounder for the nineties combines high-tech chassis components with a basic layout that allows a dry weight of just 215 kg. Its double-cradle frame features a large-diameter backbone, giving impressive rigidity that is increased still further by solid engine mounts and a stiff, rectangular-section swing arm. The low centre of gravity and long-wheelbase geometry allow agility allied to impeccable stability.

Sophisticated supsension gives a smooth ride, while retaining a taut, controlled feel for sports riding. The front fork is a rigid, 41mm R-Taper Free Valve unit similar to that used by the class-leading CBR600F. This configuration ensures the valve remains centred in the oil passages at all times for more stable oil flow and optimum roadholding capability. The twin-shock rear system features high-performance SPV dampers with remote, gas-charged reservoirs for improved temperature control and reduced aeration.

Attractive 17-inch diameter wheels with long-lasting radial tyres provide cornering performance that riders of the original CB750 could only dream about. The Seven Fifty's potent triple disc-brake system is equally impressive. At the front, large 296 mm diameter twin discs are gripped by dual-piston calipers using sintered-metal pads, while a single 240 mm disc with single-pot caliper adds extra security at the rear.

V-TWIN PERFORMANCE

THE BE ALL AND END ALL OF SPORTS LIGHTWEIGHTS

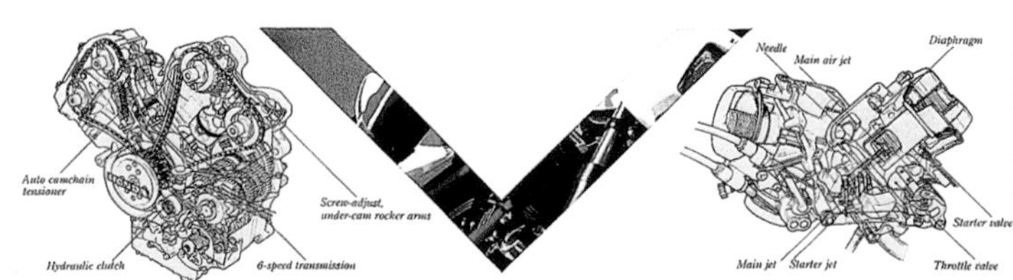

The heart of the VT250F is a totally new 90° liquid cooled quarter liter V-twin engine with perfect primary balance for zero primary vibration. It pumps out a whopping 140PS/liter from a DOHC, 8-valve layout and sports a no-maintenance, ever smooth hydraulic clutch (the first ever on a production 250), precise 6-speed transmission with a compact planetary gearshift mechanism and a long-life 'O'-ring lubrication sealed drive-chain. A thermostatically controlled, electric fan equipped liquid cooling system handles cooling, increasing engine life and reducing mechanical noise. The left hand downtube is employed to move coolant from the radiator to the engine while maintenance is reduced with a pair of auto camchain tensioners and a hot, transistorized pointless ignition with an electronic advance.

To answer the complex intake demands of the V-twin engine, new dual draft constant vacuum VD type carburetors were developed. These small, compact units fit neatly between the cylinders and give instant throttle response and phenomenal all-range power output. To streamline the intake tract for added power, a bi-starter system replaces the conventional choke. To permit use of a higher compression ratio without inducing detonation, a new combustion chamber and squish area design is employed. Compression ratio is 11 : 1 on unleaded gas for a big overall power increase.

adventure tourer) and the shaft-drive NTV650 (with its chain-driven brothers the 400 and 650) which proved very reliable. Latest in this line of twins is the Deauville launched in 1998 as a fully-equipped mid-range tourer with fairing, panniers and shaft-drive as standard, and it answered those who considered motorcycling to be a horsepower race to nowhere. There is one other major chapter in the Honda Vee story: the ST1100 Pan-European. As the Gold Wing got ever bigger and fatter, it appeared less suited to European conditions. The ST1100 was specifically designed for the more tortuous roads of Europe, and if the VFR was a 50/50 sports/tourer, the ST was more like 25/75. Launched in 1990, it proved to be a long-running success: its 100bhp V4 was enough for 201km/h (125mph), and the rider could cruise for hours at speed behind the efficient fairing. The Pan-European also became a favourite with emergency services.

Return to Roots

Although some of Honda's V4s had turned out all right in the end, they evidently hadn't been the thoroughgoing takeovers that some had been expecting. Perhaps it was as a reaction to this that in 1987 Honda launched a bike that was just as good an all-rounder as the VFR, but powered by an in-line four – the CBR600. There was nothing new or innovative about the CBR; its 599cc (36.6cu in) liquid-cooled four produced a respectable 85bhp, hiding behind smooth (even bland) bodywork. But it was massively popular and over 100,000 were sold in its first eight years, making it the best-selling motorcycle worldwide, and for the same reasons as the VFR. The new bike struck the right balance for most riders between speed, comfort and practicality, with enough performance boosts over the years (to 100bhp and 241km/h/150mph by 1995) to retain a sporting edge. The 1999 version claimed 108bhp and around 257km/h (160mph), though Yamaha's new super-sporting R6 looked even faster.

There was also (launched alongside the 600 in 1987) a similar-looking CBR1000, with a 130bhp 998cc (61cu in) four. Much heavier than the 600, it made more sense as a trans-continental sports tourer, but also confirmed that in the 1990s Honda was determined to hedge its bets on engine layouts by offering both in-lines and V4s.

ABOVE: CX500 Turbo

BELOW: VF400 was the smallest V4

Much more of a milestone, however, was the CBR900RR FireBlade of 1992. The sports market had come on in leaps and bounds since the VF750F had first appeared, let alone the CB750. In the 1990s, sportsbikes were expected to provide exceptional handling as well as scintillating performance, and the FireBlade managed to do both. Its secret was low weight, for at 185kg (407lb) it weighed no more than the average 600 middleweight, yet its 893cc (54.5cu in) in-line four produced 123bhp, enough for a top speed of 266km/h (165mph). An aluminium beam frame helped (sportsbikes had long since abandoned tubular steel), as did attention to detail. Unlike the CBR600 and VFR, the FireBlade was much more of a single-minded sportsbike and, as the sales figures showed, that was what many riders wanted. It did have a few of its rough edges smoothed off over the years, but remained true to its sole purpose – going fast. Only

The new-generation Gold Wing for the nineties, with six cylinders, 1500cc (91cu in) and every conceivable extra

in 1998, when Yamaha's R1 set new standards for sportsbikes did the FireBlade look seriously threatened. At the time of writing, everyone is waiting to see what Honda will do next.

In fact, the horsepower race is as strong as it ever was. When Honda launched its sports touring CBR1100 Blackbird in 1997, it could rightly claim to be the fastest production bike on sale, at 285km/h (177mph). Then late the following year, Suzuki announced its 1300cc (79cu in) Hayabusa, which claimed 303km/h (188mph)! Happily, the nineties motorcycle market was concerned with more than sheer power – it was fragmenting into niches which allowed Honda to produce a naked cruiser version of the GL1500 Gold Wing – the Valkyrie. Then there was the Ducati-challenging VTR1000 Firestorm, a 996cc (61cu in) V-twin sportster with Honda reliability. Or, with perhaps an eye on a congested, more restricted future, the 250cc (15cu in) Foresight 'super scooter' – quick enough to keep up with motorway traffic yet with scooter convenience. Far from the UJM jibes which followed the CB750 and its rivals, there is more motorcycling variety now than there ever was before. Were he still alive, Soichiro Honda would be having a field day.

ABOVE: Pan-European ST1100

BELOW: Jim Redman is reunited with the 250/6 racer

BELOW: 1997 SLR650

The 1999 Valkyrie uses a Gold Wing six-cylinder engine for the ultimate in smooth cruisers

ABOVE: The Shadow, a retro scooter

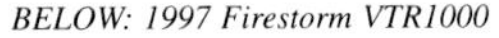

BELOW: 1997 Firestorm VTR1000

ABOVE: The shaft-driven Revere V-twin was a 'sensible' buy

BELOW: The VFR400R revved like a miniature racer

The 1998 FireBlade. The original offered 1000cc performance in a 750-sized package

ABOVE: Hongdu HD125

HONGDU *China 1965–*
A licence-built Yamaha YG1. Still builds Yamaha-based lightweights.

HOOCK *Germany 1926–28*
The German Villiers importer also fitted the 342cc (21cu in) unit to some of its own frames.

HOREX *Germany 1923–60*
Diversification for a glassware manufacturer. The first bikes used Oberursel engines of 250–600cc (15–37cu in) but were not a huge success, so Horex began to build Sturmey-Archer engines under licence, and went on to design its own power units, all sold under the Colombus name. There were a great variety on offer, the most famous being the large, technically advanced ohc vertical twins of 1932, which grew up to 980cc

RIGHT and OPPOSITE: A 1951 Horex 400cc (24cu in) with Steib sidecar

(60cu in) and saw competition success. Production restarted in 1948 with a 350 single, though 250 singles and a 500 twin were soon added, plus a scooter and a 98cc (6cu in) lightweight. Production ceased in 1960, though there was an attempt at a relaunch in 1980 with Sachs-engined mopeds which was short-lived.

HORSY *France 1952–53*
An 83cc (5cu in) two-stroke scooter.

HOSK *Japan 1953–57*
A complete range, from 123cc (7.5cu in) two-strokes to 498cc (30cu in) four-strokes (similar to Horex) twins.

HOSKINSON *England 1919–22*
Step-through frames and choice of three engines (Villiers, Union, Blackburne) of similar sizes.

49
T.T
1975
HOREX

HOWARD *England 1905–07*
A pioneering attempt at fuel injection with a 2.5hp single.

H&R *Germany 1921–25*
Forerunner of Heros, with its own 155–249cc (9.5–15cu in) sv engines.

H&R (R&H) *England 1922–25*
147cc (9cu in) Villiers-engined two-strokes. The H&R stood for Hailstone and Ravenhall, which sometimes (blood on the boardroom carpet?) became Ravenhall and Hailstone.

HRD *England 1927–55*
See Vincent-HRD.

HT *England 1920–22*
Another attempt at a car-like motorcycle, with enclosed engines and leaf-sprung rear-end. First produced machines with 292cc (18cu in) Union two-strokes, then 346cc (21cu in) Barr & Strouds.

HUC *Germany 1924–25*
Used 145/172cc (9/10.5cu in) DKW engines.

HUFFER *Germany 1923–25*
Used a variety of engines for these up-to-198cc (12cu in) lightweights.

HULBERT-BRAMLEY *England 1903–06*
Built lightweights and the Binks-designed 385cc (23.5cu in) four-cylinder machines.

HULLA *Germany 1925–32*
Mainly DKW-powered two-strokes of 173–298cc (11–18cu in) in its own frames.

HULSMANN *The Netherlands 1939–55*
Used exclusively Villiers engines of 123–225cc (7.5–14cu in).

HUMBER *England 1896–1930*
Humber's involvement in motorcycles was a relatively sporadic one, even though it was spread over 34 years. Thomas Humber had begun making bicycles in the 1870s, but exhibited a number of solo and tandem motorized cycles at the International Horseless Carriage Exhibition in May 1896. It wasn't until 1902 that Humber Ltd. began selling motorcycles, and then it was a 2hp machine built under licence from Phelon & Moore (*see* Panther). Variations on the theme followed, but after three years the range was dropped.

Humber's next was a 3.5hp machine of its own design, announced in 1909, with the advanced feature of sprung front forks. It was joined in 1910 by a smaller 2hp single, a year which also saw a works team entered for the TT and P.J. Evans winning the Junior for Humber. A Tourist Trophy model joined the catalogue soon after, proving that there is nothing new about the race replicas. Meanwhile, bikes were getting bigger, and Humber responded with a decidedly odd three-cylinder 6hp designed for sidecar work. The three cylinders were horizontally opposed, with one large one (78mm x 78mm) facing forwards, and a smaller twin (55mm x 78mm) to the rear. Few were made.

A seed of an idea must have taken root, however, as flat twins soon became a staple part of the Humber range, with both air- and water-cooled 6hp versions offered until civilian production ceased during World War I. Production restarted in 1919, and the

ABOVE: Humber 341cc (21cu in)

following year saw an updated 600cc 4.5hp version of the air-cooled twin, now with chain-drive and a three-speed gearbox. A 349cc (21cu in) single joined the range in 1923, which did well in the Six Days Trial that year, and when the twin was phased out became Humber's sole motorcycle offering. It acquired an overhead-valve engine in 1927, and in 1928 a bevel-drive overhead-cam version appeared. Like Velocette, the Humbers were quality machines which cost more than a BSA or Ariel, for example, but unlike Velocette, Humber no longer had the racing success to back it up. The Rootes company was taking increasing control of Humber, and motorcycles did not feature in its plans. The Humber 350s were dropped in 1930.

HÜMMEL Germany 1951–54
Best known for the 120–149cc (7–9cu in) Sitta scooters, but produced lightweights as well. All were Ilo-powered.

HUNWICK HALLAM *Australia 1999–*
Australia is known for many things, but until recently motorcycling wasn't one of them, hence the surprise worldwide when the Hunwick Hallam V-twin was revealed in October 1996. It was the result of a partnership between Australia's largest bike dealer, Rod Hunwick, and the race-bike tuner Paul Hallam. They proposed an all-new, all-Australian range of 90-degree one-litre V-twins, which would include the X1R, a new contender for World Superbike racing.

Much was made of the X1R at the original launch, as much for its proposed use of pneumatic valves as anything else, and the partners confirmed it to be part of a range which would include a 1350cc (82cu in) muscle bike named the Power Cruiser, and a 1150cc (70cu in) version, the Rage sports roadster. By early 1999 the X1R had already raced successfully (ridden by Honda rider Mal Campbell) and the Rage was undergoing final homologation tests, on target for production in the following June. What with Hunwick Hallam, Voxan, Excelsior-Henderson and Victory, 1999 seems a good year for all-new motorcycle marques.

HURIKAN *Czechoslovakia 1947–49*
An advanced 247cc (15cu in) ohc single sportster, though few were made.

HURTU *France 1906–58*
Intermittent production, but produced mostly 49cc (3cu in) mopeds after 1945.

HUSAR *Germany 1923–25*
269cc (16cu in) sv singles with leaf-sprung rear suspension on all models.

HUSQVARNA *Sweden 1903–*
Began using Moto-Rêve, NSU and FN engines, and in fact didn't produce its own engine (a 550cc/34cu inch sv V-twin) until 1920. Continued to buy in singles, however, notably from Sturmey-Archer and JAP, while the V-twin grew to a 992cc (60cu in) version with 22hp. But Husqvarna's most famous inter-war model was a racer, the new ohv V-twin of 1932. Designed by Folke Mannerstedt and Calle Heimdahl, the 498cc (30cu in) twin was a new challenge to racing dominated by single-cylinder machines. Development pushed the power up to 36hp, while weight was cut to 125kg (276lb) and a 348cc (21cu in) version was developed as well. It managed three successive victories in the Swedish GP, and

ABOVE: Husqvarna 250cc (15cu in) motocrosser

BELOW: Husqvarna 250cc road bike

Stanley Woods broke the lap record on one during the 1934 TT. Husqvarna built its first two-stroke (a basic 98cc/6cu inch two-speeder) in 1935, and after the war was to concentrate most of its attention on two-strokes. It also focused increasingly on off-road competition, and was rewarded with great success with ten World Motocross titles between 1960 and 1970. Four-stroke off-roaders were reintroduced in the 1980s, and in 1986 the company was taken over by the rapidly growing Cagiva group. Production was transferred to Italy the following year, where the Husqvarna range has continued to develop, an example being the 577cc (35cu in) TC610 of 1992, with a 50bhp water-cooled four-valve dohc single, six-speed gearbox and high quality suspension. In 1998, with the market for supermotos in full swing, Husqvarna announced a return to the road market with the TE610, a slightly more civilized TC with road tyres and electric start.

HUY *Germany 1923–26*
198cc (12cu in) sv singles, followed by 347cc (21cu in) MAG-engined machines.

I

IBIS *Italy 1925–28*
Piazza 173cc (11cu in) engine in a step-through frame.

IDEAL *Germany 1924–25*
Used own 173cc (11cu in) three-port two-stroke engine.

IDEAL-JAWA *India 1960–80*
A Jawa-based 250cc (15cu in) two-stroke single, still in production under the Monarch and Road King names.

IDRA *Italy 1923–25*
A 123cc (7.5cu in) ohv single, available as a clip-on or as a complete lightweight bike.

IDROFLEX *Italy 1949–54*
A 105cc (6cu in) two-stroke engine was mounted on the swinging arm.

IFA *East Germany 1945–60*
See MZ.

ILO *Germany 1923–25*
Built two-stroke singles of 117–170cc (7–10cu in), and supplied countless small German assemblers with ready-made power units. Ilo built its own machines for a couple of years, but demand for its engines soon put a stop to that.

IMHOLZ *Switzerland 1924–27*
Own 123/173cc (7.5/11cu in) two-strokes, and a Moser-powered ohv 173cc.

IMME *Germany 1948–51*
An unusual 148cc (9cu in) two-stroke whose power unit swung with rear-wheel movement. The exhaust pipe formed part of the frame and there was a single-sided front fork.

IMN *Italy 1950–58*
The Naples-based firm first built 49–248cc (3–15cu in) two-strokes, but lost its way with an underdeveloped 198cc (12cu in) flat twin which was enough to bring down the company.

IMPERIA *Germany 1923–25*
Assembled 346 and 496cc (21 and 30cu in) JAP engines in step-through frames.

The Imperial, a very early American V-twin

IMPERIA *Germany 1924–35*
No connection with the above, it started off using mainly MAG power units, most of which were V-twins. Collapsed after a couple of years, but was bought by the Schrödter family in 1926. At first, the new owners continued the buy-in philosophy, from MAG, JAP and Python, but new boss Rolf Schrödter designed an unorthodox double-pistoned supercharged single and a flat-twin two-stroke. It was all too ambitious for Imperia's limited resources and the company closed.

IMPERIAL *England 1901–04*
Used 3.5hp Coronet engines, with atmospheric inlet valves.

IMPERIAL *U.S.A. 1903–c.1910*
A 444cc (27cu in) single-cylinder machine.

INDIAN *U.S.A. 1901–53*
Only one manufacturer seriously challenged Harley-Davidson's bid for domination of the American motorcycle market – Indian. In fact, the Wigwam, as it was known, was a couple of years ahead of Harley's offering right from the start, and in Indian's peak year of 1913 (when it built nearly 32,000 bikes) could claim to be the largest manufacturer in the world. But within a couple of decades it was well and truly the runner-up, and only survived another few years after World War II. It all came down to ownership: in that same record year of 1913, control of Indian passed from the two enthusiasts who established it, to shareholders whose main priority was neither design, nor the long-term health of the company, but profits. Harley-Davidson, on the other hand, was owned and controlled by the same two families right up until the late 1960s. Continuity of leadership counts for a lot, as Indian was to find to its cost.

All this was in the future when George Hendee and Oscar Hedström met at a cycle race in 1900. It was to be the perfect combination: Hendee was the businessman, Hedström the slightly younger engineer, and both these keen cyclists wished to get into the motorized

1915 was the year Indian offered an electric-start option. However, there were few takers

bicycle business. But they had a different approach to Bill Harley and the Davidsons who had proceeded with rather more caution and sold their early machines by word of mouth. Instead, the two signed a contract to produce 'a motor-driven bicycle that could be produced in volume' and Hedström built the first 213cc (13cu in) prototype in less than five months. It was then demonstrated in front of public, press and potential investors and there was a national advertising campaign. From the start, Indian appeared to be a serious business proposition.

It had a good basis in Oscar Hedström's first prototype, for the Swedish-born engineer incorporated such advanced features as chain-drive (when everyone else relied on the likely to slip belt-drive) and his motor proved tractable and reliable. Money was duly raised and production began in Hendee's bicycle factory in Springfield, Massachusetts. Production soared: from 143 bikes in 1902, to 376 the following year, then to nearly 600, then to approaching 1,200 by 1905 in comparison to Harley who built just 16 machines that year. The Indian single soon became a familiar sight in hillclimbs, endurance runs and beach racing, either ridden by Hedström himself or a gifted young rider named Jacob DeRosier.

Nor was the design laying stagnant: a twist-grip throttle was added in 1905 (actually pioneered by Glenn Curtiss), a spring fork featured on the road bikes and in 1907 Indian unveiled its first road-going V-twin. It was rated at 4 horsepower and was of 640cc (39cu in), with a side exhaust valve and overhead atmospheric inlet valve. Its 42-degree cylinder angle (like Harley's 45) was to become an Indian trademark. It was at about this time that Indian began to build its engine in-house, where it had previously been contracted out to Aurora.

A 1906 Indian. At this time, the company had a headstart on Harley-Davidson

In 1908 (with production now at over 3,000) the single and V-twin racers received mechanical inlet valves, which appeared on the road bikes the following year. Loop frames were another new feature, signifying a final break with the bicycle-style diamond frame. It was in fact a period of innovation, particularly for American manufacturers, and 1910 saw the leaf-sprung front fork and a two-speed transmission, plus a clutch for the single-speed direct-drive single. The following year, four valves per cylinder arrived, with the 8-valve V-twin racer which won a whole string of speed records and was usually ridden by Jacob DeRosier. This was also the year of Indian's historic 1-2-3 placing in the Isle of Man TT. Indian's star rider actually finished 12th that time, being unused to inferior European roads, but

A 1912 V-twin, produced when Indian was at its peak

made up for it the following week at Brooklands by beating Charlie Collier of Matchless.

End of an Era

Meanwhile, with demand and production ever increasing (nearly 20,000 machines were built in 1911, which produced profits of half a million dollars), Hendee was initiating ambitious plans for growth, with new plant and machinery, and the only way to do this was to offer more shares to the public. Alarmed by the high cost of the racing and expansion programme, the new army of shareholders began to pressurize Hendee into cutting costs and increasing profits. It was all too much for Oscar Hedström, and when his friend and protégé Jacob DeRosier died of injuries sustained in an earlier race accident, he resigned from Indian. What was in many ways Indian's golden era had passed.

One of Hedström's last jobs had been to develop an electric start for the V-twin (another Indian innovation). He had been sceptical, but the far-sighted George Hendee had insisted that this was the route to expanding the motorcycle market, and the Hendee Special of 1914 boasted electric lights as well as starting. However, it was possibly too far ahead of its time and only lasted a year. Better news that year was

Erwin G. Baker's record-breaking run across America when he rode from San Diego to New York in 11½ days, the first of many such records. Although electric starting had failed to find favour with the buyers, electric lighting did, and remained an option in 1915. But then George Hendee resigned from Indian and the last link with the golden era was over. Moreover, for the second year running, production and profits were down and Indian was beginning to feel the pinch of competition from Harley-Davidson and Henry Ford's Model T. Neither did Indian do well out of the war when it neglected the home market in favour of army contracts which failed to be very lucrative in any case: Harley-Davidson, however, was not slow in leaping in to fill that breach.

The year 1916 saw a replacement for the pioneering V-twin in the form of the Powerplus, a sidevalve twin that was slightly more powerful and easier to maintain. It was the work of Charles Gustafson, who had replaced Oscar Hedström, and laid the foundation for Indian's big V-twins for the future. Less successful was the little two-stroke Model K and the 257cc (16cu in) Model O, a flat twin aimed at non-enthusiasts. Both were soon dropped. It was not a happy time, and in 1919 Indian's board of directors decided to sell to a group of investors headed by a banker named Henry Skinner. Fortunately, general manager Frank Weschler was a long-term employee and remained committed to the firm, Oscar Hedström was tempted back for a short time to try to solve racing and production problems, while an Irishman named Charlie Franklin (he had been the third-placed rider in that 1911 TT) took over the engineering side.

Matters began to improve, notably with Franklin's 600cc (37cu in) Scout V-twin of 1923, which was basically a smaller version of the Powerplus. He was quick to realize that in the new leisure motorcycle market there would be an unfulfilled demand for a middleweight bike similar to those in Europe. He was right, and the Scout was strong, fast and durable, and turned out to be a real success, the Springfield factory finding it necessary to add a second shift to cope with demand. This, in turn, made the Powerplus look a little old-fashioned, and it wasn't long before the factory responded with an enlarged Scout, the 1000cc (61cu in) Chief, a name that was to remain with Indian right to the end. It was soon followed by the 1200cc (73cu in) Big Chief, in direct response to the Harley Seventy-Four. At the time, the two bitter rivals were becoming obsessed with the idea of wresting market leadership from one another, a battle that endured for nearly 20 years.

Singles & Fours

Despite its earlier experiences with small bikes, Indian seemed determined to sell one, and in 1926 came up with the Franklin-designed Prince, a 350cc (21cu in) sidevalve single that owed much to British practice. Small, light, economical and easy to ride, the Prince had much to recommend it and sold fairly well in America, though the hoped-for exports to Britain were to be dashed by new tariff barriers. Franklin also designed an ohv version for racing (Indian was at last winning races again despite the Harley-Davidson onslaught), and even a few overhead-cam prototypes were built. In

A 1924 Indian Chief. Sidevalve V-twins were to see Indian through to the end

A 1924 Indian Chief. It was a nice bike, but Harley-Davidson was fast catching up

The 1938 1265cc (77cu in) Indian 438. Note the beautiful detailing (right)

1927, Indian bought the remains of the Ace Motorcycle Company, which had built the four-cylinder Henderson. Meanwhile, the Scout was enlarged to 750cc (45.8cu in) in response to Excelsior's very fast Super X. The Scout 45, or 101, was the result, and backed up the Excelsior in forming a new class with almost the same performance as the big twins, but in a smaller, lighter package. It had great success in oval track racing and, like its predecessor, sold well. The four-cylinder Ace had been revived as well, and by 1929 had a new in-house chassis as the Indian Four. In fact, there were several changes to the original Ace; capacity increased, there was a five-bearing crankshaft and new cylinder head. It gave Indian a big range of bikes, from the 350cc Prince to 1265cc Four, while the 101 Scout was the best-selling bike on the market.

Despite all of this, the American motorcycle market as a whole continued to decline, which encouraged Indian's owners to spend what little profits there were on attempts at diversification by using an increasingly underused factory for other projects. Outboard motors, aeroplanes, a small car – all came to nothing and left the company very short of capital. It was hardly surprising then, that in the aftermath of the Wall Street Crash, Indian changed hands three times in the space of a year. A saviour arrived in the form of wealthy industrialist E. Paul duPont, who assumed a majority shareholding with the idea of using Springfield to produce aero-engines. With the Depression continuing to bite, the plan came to nothing but duPont, unlike the fly-by-night investors, hung on and succeeded in turning Indian round. Hard times were to come before this was achieved, and in 1933 Indian built a mere 1,667 bikes.

Costs were cut by standardizing the same basic frame for Scout, Chief and Four, while the Prince frame was used for the 500cc (30.5cu in) Scout Pony and

ABOVE: Ed Kretz on his Indian racer

750cc Motoplane. But one of duPont's finest legacies came in the form of paint. Part of his industrial empire encompassed the manufacture of paint, and consequently Indians became available in an unheard-of range of 24 different colours where the previous choice had been the traditional Indian red, or nothing. It transformed the appeal of the bikes, and Harley-Davidson had no choice but to follow suit. There was also a move towards streamlined art deco-like styling, with deep, graceful mudguards and rounded flowing tanks (the former not until 1940).

BELOW: Another Ed Kretz race bike

Motorcycling was discovering a new elegance, but there were mechanical changes too; the Sport Scout was the latest in the middleweight line and in 1935, along with the Chief, received the Y engine, which signified aluminium cylinder heads and barrels. And there was a three-wheeled Dispatch Tow, to compete with Harley-Davidson's similar Servi-car.

The Four kept going right through the Depression, with just a hiccup in 1936 when the engine was changed to a side inlet/overhead exhaust-valve layout. It may or may not have worked better, but ruined the looks of the motor. By popular demand, it reverted to ioe after a couple of years, and then survived up to 1941, increasingly out on a limb and serving a tiny sector of the market. There was still a small following for this smooth, quiet, civilized motorcycle, but not enough to resume production of it after the war. In the late 1930s, the recovery continued, but although Indian finally matched Harley's output in 1939, it would never again reach the production heights of its early days. Nor was there any sign of an ohv twin to meet Harley-Davidson's successful Knucklehead. Perhaps, by this time, Indian had finally settled for second place.

Still, the war provided fresh impetus, particularly when France ordered 5,000 Chief sidecar outfits. However, the final batch of 2,000 never made it, though whether they ended up at the bottom of the Atlantic or not was never finally confirmed. But the factory was too rundown after years of underuse to capture the lion's share of military contracts. There was a militarized Chief and the M1, a lightweight 221cc (13cu in) sidevalve designed to be dropped into battle zones by parachute. The 841 was different again: impressed by Rommel's BMWs in North Africa, the army was insisting on shaft-drive, and Indian's transverse 90-degree V-twin was the result. It was a sidevalve 750, with four-speed gearbox and that shaft-drive, and over 10,000 were built. Less exotic was the 640B, basically a detuned Sport Scout in military guise.

1946, and Indian returns to its pre-war V-twins

A 1943 militarized Indian. The transverse 841 V-twin was very different, and was designed from scratch

LEFT: A 1949 Indian Chief

ABOVE: A 1969 Indian Velo 500

Last Gasps ... then Revival?

Shortly after the war ended, E. Paul duPont sold Indian to the industrialist Ralph Rogers. Although duPont had apparently lost interest by this time, the company owed as much to him as it did to Hendee and Hedström, for he had kept it going right through the Depression when many would have given up. Ralph Rogers had great hopes for Indian, believing he could revive it with a combination of the traditional Chief and new European-style lightweights. In the short term, the 1941 Chief went back into production, with the addition of the 841's girder fork. For the future, Ralph Rogers bought the Torque Manufacturing Company which had single- and vertical-twin lightweights under development and the whole enterprise was moved to Springfield. Rogers was a shrewd man and after researching the market predicted that smaller, lighter singles and twins would be the next growth area in the United States.

Sadly, when the long-awaited 220cc (13cu in) Arrow and 440cc (27cu in) Scout finally appeared in mid-1948, they simply weren't a match for the BSAs, Triumphs and Nortons. They actually looked spot-on, with telescopic forks, hand clutch and foot gearchange, just like the imports. But they lost out in engine capacity against the 250/500 opposition, were rushed into final production, and were poorly made to boot. Oil leaks, difficulty in starting and ignition problems ensued. The real tragedy was that the small bikes had absorbed a huge

ABOVE and BELOW: Indian persevered with four cylinders

amount of money ($6.5 million was mentioned) which could have been spent updating the Chief. The faithful V-twin was still selling in reasonable numbers (having been Indian's sole product until the tiddlers came along) and prototypes had been built with telescopic forks and foot change; now, however, there were just not sufficient funds to put them into production. In the face of all this, Ralph Rogers was forced to resign, and manufacture passed to the Titeflex Corporation (part of the Atlas group which had helped finance Rogers' venture). There were some useful improvements in that the Scout twin gained power and reliability as the 500cc (30.5cu in) Warrior, while the Chief returned with an enlarged 1340cc (82cu in) motor and telescopic forks. Meanwhile, the British-built Brockhouse Brave, a sidevalve 250, was imported to replace the home-built singles. None of this was enough, however, and the Warrior was dropped in 1952, while the Big Chief finally rolled over and died the following year. Harley-Davidson had finally won the contest.

However, this wasn't the end of the Indian name, even though some uses for it in the next 20 years would cause palpitations in the hearts of diehard enthusiasts. After the Brockhouse Brave fell by the wayside, there was an arrangement with Royal Enfield to badge its 250/350/500cc singles as Indians for the American market, which lasted until 1959. The model names were suitably Americanized as well, so the Meteor 700 became the Trailblazer or Apache, the 250 single Hounds Arrow, and so on. There was even an Enfield badged as the Indian Chief – sacrilege!

Then the name lapsed for a few years before an ex-Indian dealer revived it in 1967 with a mini-scooter, the Papoose, which was imported first from Britain, then from Italy. This was followed by the 50cc (3cu in) Bambino (a size similar to the Honda Monkey Bike) and in the early seventies by the off-road Junior Cross, which used a Jawa/CZ 50cc engine, and 100, 125 and 175 versions followed. Floyd Clymer (a publisher and ex-racing driver, who had undertaken to breathe new life into the company) was nothing if not eclectic, and his 1969 Indian Velo 500 used a combination of Italian cycle parts with some of the last Velocette 500cc singles. Sadly, Clymer died in 1970, but the Indian baton passed to a Los Angeles lawyer named Alan Newman. His venture was truly international, with Indian minibikes using

Indian
Roadmaster

OPPOSITE: The 1953 Chief was the last of the 'true' Indians

ABOVE: The Indian Woodsman, a rebadged Royal Enfield

Italian engines in a Taiwanese chassis. After three years, however, he had had enough and sold the name to a bank, which in turn allowed its use by the American Moped Company, its project being a Taiwanese four-stroke moped, the Indian 'Four'. All was quiet for a while until the mid-1980s when American entrepreneurs claimed rights to the name, both having plans for a new modern Chief. Neither succeeded. Then in 1994 the name was bought by Australian businessman Marits Hayim-Langridge. He commissioned the late John Britten (builder of a successful V-twin race bike) to develop a new range of V-twins to be produced in America in 1998. Like all recent plans, this came to nothing, but the good news was that in February 1999 the name had been bought by a Canadian firm for $17 million. The latest owners promise a new Indian Chief for later in the year, first with an S&S V-twin, and with the company's own engine the following year. Could this mean the long awaited rebirth of Indian? If recent experience is any guide, don't hold your breath!

Sales brochure for the 1999 Indian Chief – reborn at last?

Or should we stick to the memories?

INDUS *Germany 1924–27*
Had front and rear leaf-sprung suspension, with bought-in single-cylinder engines from Kühne, Küchen and JAP.

INTRAMOTOR *Italy 1971–81*
Produced Minarelli-engined mopeds and a selection of 122cc (7cu in) off-road machines.

INVICTA *England 1902–06*
An assembler who utilized Minerva and Kelecom engines.

INVICTA *England 1913–23*
Used 269cc (16cu in) Villiers, 499cc (30cu inch) sv Abingdon and 346/678cc (21/41cu inch) sv JAP engines, the bikes having been built in the Francis-Barnett factory.

INVICTA *Italy 1951–54*
74–123cc (4.5–7.5cu in) two-strokes.

IRESA *Spain 1956–59*
Used Spanish licence-built Villiers units up to 198cc (12cu in).

IRIS England 1902–06
A 5hp water-cooled V-twin, with hand starter and friction clutch, which is unusual.

IRIS *Italy 1952–53*
Utilized 123cc (7.5cu in) Ilo two-stroke power.

IRUNA *Spain 1953–59*
Built scooters with in-house 123cc (7.5cu in) two-strokes.

ISLO *Mexico 1958–*
Began with a 175cc (11cu in) scooter-style bike assembled from Italian parts. Later used 48–248cc (3–15cu in) two-strokes, built under licence from Sachs. Also sold in the U.S.A. under the Cooper badge.

ISOMOTO *Italy 1949–64*
Used its own double-pistoned two-stroke engines of up to 248cc (15cu in), plus 123cc and 173cc (7.5 and 11cu in) ohv engines.

ITALA *Italy 1933–39*
Was an importer of French Train engines, so used the Train 98cc (6cu in) two-stroke first, then progressed to bigger Chaise and Python engines.

ITALEMMEZETA *Italy 1958–66*
Used MZ engines of 98–248cc (6–15cu in) in Italian cycle parts.

ITALJET *Italy 1966–*
Established by Leopoldo Tartarini, who used CZ, Velocette and Triumph engines in his own frames, as well as Minarelli, MZ and Yamaha units later on. Also built Floyd Clymer's Indian Velocette in 1970 and concentrated on sub-125cc trials and motocross bikes after that, including children's off-road machines. There was also a road-going two-stroke twin, the 124cc (8cu in) Buccaneer. By the mid-1990s, and still owned by the Tartarini family, Italjet was now making scooters and doing very well out of a growing market, planning to double production to 40,000 bikes in 1996 to make it second only to Piaggio in Italian scooter production. The company has sought to differentiate its scooters from the competition with the sports-style hub-centre-steered Formula 50 and 125, the retro-style Velocifero and radical Dragster.

ITAR *Czechoslovakia 1921–29*
Its mainstay was a 746cc (45.5cu in) sv flat twin, built for the Czechoslovak army as well as for civilians. A 346cc (21cu in) single failed to reach production, but JAP-engined singles did.

ABOVE and ABOVE RIGHT: A 150, with its twin-pistoned two-stroke

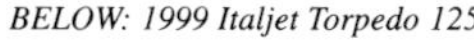

BELOW: 1999 Italjet Torpedo 125

BELOW: 1999 Italjet Dragster D50LC Race Replica

ITOM *Italy 1945–68*
Started with a 48cc (3cu in) clip-on and progressed to mopeds and 65cc (4cu in) sports lightweights.

IVEL *England 1901–05*
Utilized De Dion and MMC engines.

IVER-JOHNSON *U.S.A. 1907–15*
Produced singles and V-twins up to 1090cc (66.5cu in).

IVO LOLA RIBAR *Yugoslavia 1956*
Made Vespa scooters under licence.

IVY *England 1908–32*
First used Precision and JAP engines, then its own two-strokes. Later resumed production, once again with two-stroke and JAP options.

IXION *England 1901–03*
Used De Dion and MMC engines.

IXION *England 1910–23*
Used various bought-in engines from Abingdon, Precision and Peco.

IZH *Former U.S.S.R. 1933–*
One of the oldest Soviet motorcycle factories is at Izhevsk, and is home to a number of marques. Earliest bikes were 746 and 1200cc (45.5 and 73cu in) V-twins, followed by 198cc (12cu in) two-strokes and 498cc (30cu in) ohc singles. From 1938 there was the DKW-based 348cc two-stroke single (the Ish), with 18bhp. It was reintroduced in 1946 as the Planeta, and in 1961 was joined by a 350cc (21cu in) twin, the Jupiter, with 25bhp at 4,600rpm.

J

JAC *Czechoslovakia 1929–32*
An interesting 498cc (30cu in) single-cylinder sleeve-valved unit-designed machine with shaft-drive and a welded frame of pressed steel. Designed by J. A. Cvach, the machines had a leaf-sprung fork, a low saddle position and a triangular fuel tank between saddle and gearbox.

JACK SPORT *France 1927–31*
349/498cc (21/30cu in) four-strokes.

JAK *Germany 1922–25*
Used 119–173cc (7–11cu in) bought-in two-strokes from DKW and Bekamo.

JALE Germany 1923–25
Air- and water-cooled 170cc (10cu in) two-strokes.

JAMATHI *The Netherlands 1969–71*
Sporting 49cc (3cu in) two-strokes.

JAMES *England 1902–66*
Harry James set up on his own quite late in life when already well-established as works manager of a Birmingham engineering works, at an age when most contemporaries would be looking forward to a comfortable retirement. His James Cycle Company was successful, and in 1902 he did what so many cycle manufacturers were doing and tentatively ventured into the motorization market.

The James version was entirely conventional, with a bought-in Minerva engine clipped to the front downtube, and was belt-driven. But 1908 saw something very avant-garde indeed. A man named P.L. Renouf designed for James a motorcycle

OPPOSITE and ABOVE: A 1928 James 350SS

ABOVE: Early James machines seemed modern by the standards of their times

that thoroughly bristled with innovation. Both wheels were carried on stub axles, and there was hub-centre-steering: the 600cc (37cu in) single had concentric inlet and exhaust valves, and internally expanding brakes, probably the first bike to be so fitted. With the exception of the brakes, few of these features lasted long but one became a James trademark, i.e. the cylinder cooling fins were staggered in a 'pineapple' arrangement.

James followed this in 1911 with an up-to-the-minute all-chain transmission with two-speed gearbox and multi-plate clutch, followed by a whole array of models in the next few years. There was a small two-stroke in 1913, a 500cc (30.5cu in) sidevalve V-twin in 1914, a little autocycle after the war, and eventually an ohv version of the 500 twin. Perhaps it was the expense of building this wide range of engines that persuaded James to stop and do what many small British manufacturers did – buy in from Villiers. In fact, the decision dictated the subsequent James policy of building up to 250cc (15cu in) only, and the firm's motorized bicycle of 1938 was a result of Villiers' launch of a 98cc (6cu in) autocycle engine of which 6,000 were made for essential private transport during World War II. The company also sold a little 125 to the army, the ML (Military Lightweight).

In fact, when civilian production resumed in 1946, it was merely with these two models – the fuel-sipping Autocycle (ideal for petrol-rationed Britain) and a civilianized version of the ML in maroon and grey. As Villiers' post-war engine range expanded, so did James' motorcycles, though in 1951 the company was taken over

BELOW: A 1949 James utility – leisurely transport with a sidecar

A 1935 Jawa 350cc (21cu in)

by Associated Motor Cycles. As part of the group, James was obliged to use the corporate two-stroke engine in its Cadet, Cavalier and Commodore, all of which used partly pressed steel frames. There was also a belated attempt to capture a slice of the growing scooter market, but although the 150cc (9cu in) James offering had its good points (notably a low centre of gravity and generous luggage space) it had much in common with other British scooters in being too heavy, too clumsy and too late.

Still, until the advent of Bultaco, there was competition success for the trials Commando and scrambler Cotswold, and the road range was topped by the good-looking Sports Captain and 250cc Superswift twin. However, this was no match for the new Japanese lightweights streaming onto the market. Even if James hadn't been sucked under by the AMC collapse of 1966, it is unlikely that it could have survived on its own.

JAP *England 1904–08*
One of the most prolific engine manufacturers of all, with capacities ranging from 123–1098cc (7.5–67cu in). The demand was such that JAP stopped building complete bikes in 1908, but the engine factory was taken over by Villiers after World War II.

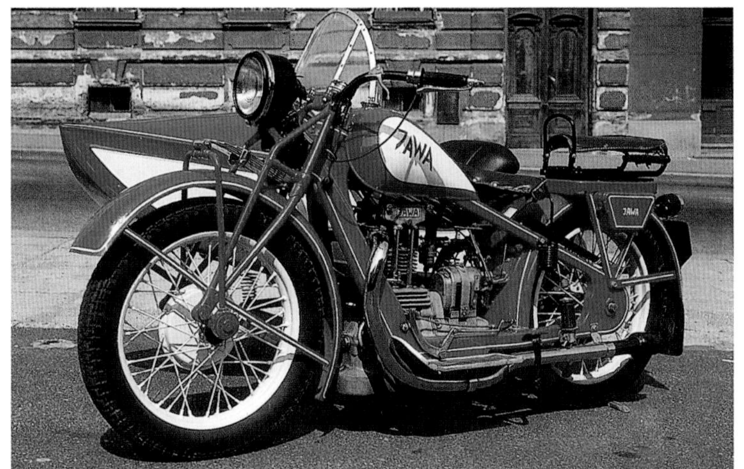

ABOVE and ABOVE RIGHT: 1929 Jawa 500cc (30.5cu in)

BELOW: This makeshift three-wheeler (photographed in Romania by Roger Fogg) is a CZ, produced when it later merged with Jawa

JAVON *Germany 1929–32*
Used 198cc and 498cc (12 and 30cu in) JAP singles.

JAWA *Czechoslovakia 1929–*
The name Jawa derives from JAnacek-WAnderer. Arms industrialist F. Janacek wished to get into the motorcycle market and bought the rights to the German Wanderer, a 498cc (30cu in) ohv single with shaft-drive and pressed steel frame. It was underdeveloped, and various teething troubles prevented its commercial success. However, the fledgling Jawa concern was saved by the arrival of English designer George Patchett, who set about creating a successful racer, and by the introduction of a 173cc (11cu in) Villiers-powered machine in 1932. Patchett also designed 346cc (21cu in) sv and ohv road bikes for Jawa,

250/350 two-stroke twins were Jawa's main product from the 1960s on

ABOVE: A CZ 175 Sports

BELOW: A later CZ 175 trail bike

Czech designer Jozif produced a 98cc (6cu in) two-stroke. After the war, Jawa was nationalized and 250 two-stroke singles and 350 twins were introduced which have formed the backbone of Jawa's output since. There were still sophisticated dohc racers (some supercharged), and an ohc 500cc (30.5cu in) twin in the mid-1950s. Jawa enjoyed much success in six-day trials, motocross and speedway after the war, but its mainstay bikes were the 250/350 two-strokes, plus a 49cc (3cu in) moped.

JB-LOUVET *France 1926–30*
Made Aubier-Dunne-powered 173/246cc (11/15cu in) two-strokes and 348/498cc (21/30cu in) JAP engines were also used.

JD *England 1920–26*
Made by Bowden, the JD was a 116cc (7cu in) clip-on. It was also supplied with a strengthened bicycle frame.

JEAN THOMANN *France 1920–30*
98–248cc (6–15cu in) two-strokes and a 499cc (30cu in) ohv single with external flywheel.

JE-BE *Germany late 1950s–late-1960s*
98/123cc (6/7.5cu in) Sachs-powered two-strokes for the U.S. market, the name inspired by its importer, Joe Berliner.

JEECY-VEA *Belgium 1923–27*
Specialized in flat twins of up to 746cc (45.5cu in), all bought-ins. King Albert of the Belgians rode one.

JEFFERSON *U.S.A. 1911–14*
Front and rear suspension appeared on this development of the PEM.

BELOW and RIGHT: A rare 1955 500cc (30.5cu in) Jawa overhead-camshaft twin

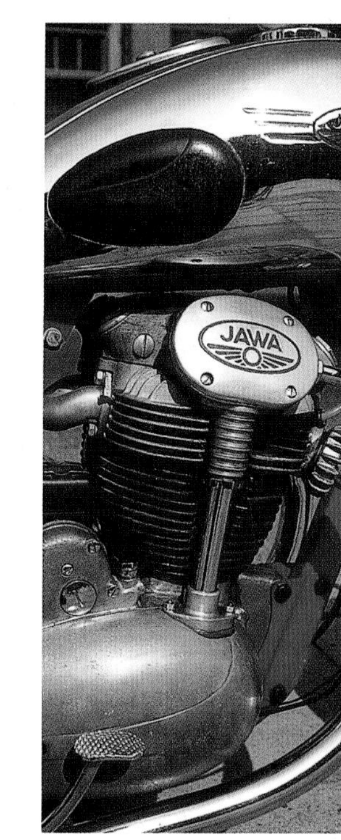

JEHU *England 1901–c.1910*
Used Minerva and MMC engines as well as its own 2.25–3hp units.

JELINEK *Czechoslovakia 1904–07*
Utilized Minerva, Orion or Fafnir power.

JES *England 1910–24*
Before 1914, there was early use of ohv engines, then came two-strokes and bigger Blackburne singles before takeover by Connaught.

JESMOND *England 1899–1907*
A choice of De Dion, MMC and Sarolea power was on offer.

JFK *Czechoslovakia 1923–26*
An advanced ohc 348cc (21cu in) single, designed by J.F. Koch.

JH *England 1913–15*
Utilized JAP, Villiers and MAG engines.

JHC *Germany 1922–24*
Used own 183cc (11cu in) three-port two-stroke.

JNU *England 1920–22*
Utilized a 312cc (19cu in) two-stroke Dalm engine but production of the motorcycles was limited.

JNZ *New Zealand 1960–63*
Jawas and CZs assembled in New Zealand; also known as N-ZETA.

JOERNS *U.S.A. 1910–15*
The 996cc (61cu in) Cyclone was probably the first ohc V-twin built in reasonable numbers.

JONGHI *France 1931–56*
Produced 348cc (21cu in) sv singles first, then ohc singles of 173–348cc (11–21cu in).

JOOS *Germany 1900–07*
Built flat-twin motors at first, later complete bikes powered by Fafnir singles and V-twins.

JOUCLARD *France 1903–07*
1.5/2.25hp singles.

JOYBIKE *England 1959–60*
Scooter-like lightweight with 49cc (3cu in) Trojan or 70cc (4cu in) JAP engines.

JSL *Germany 1923–25*
Choice of own 132/180cc (8/11cu in) two-strokes or DKW's 206cc (12.6cu in) unit.

JUCKES *England 1910–26*
Built all its own gearboxes and engines, from 269–399cc (16–24cu in) two-strokes and a 348cc (21cu in) ohv single.

JUERGENSEN *Denmark 1904–14*
Built Humber machines under licence.

JUÉRY *France 1931–39*
Built its own engines, but also offered Chaise 346/498cc (21/30cu in) sv and ohv units.

JUHÖ *Germany 1922–24*
Produced in-house 148cc (9cu in) sv or 195cc (12cu in) two-strokes.

JULES *Czechoslovakia 1929–34*
A 120cc (7cu in) two-stroke clip-on was made, together with Praga bicycles.

JUNAK *Poland 1956–64*
In-house 247/347cc (15/21cu in) four-stroke singles.

JUNCKER *The Netherlands 1932–35*
Used 98–198cc (6–12cu in) Ilo or Villiers engines.

JUNCKER *France 1935–37*
Stainless and Aubier-Dunne-powered two-strokes of 98–147cc (6–9cu in).

JUNIOR *Italy 1924–35*
Began with own two-strokes of up to 346cc (21cu in), later buying in JAP and Blackburne four-strokes.

JUNO *England 1911–23*
Engines were from Villiers, Precision and JAP (770cc/47cu inch V-twin), with frames from Sun.

JUPP England 1921–24
A step-through frame, rear suspension and 269cc (16cu in) Liberty two-stroke made this a cross between a scooter and a motorcycle.

K

KADI *Germany 1924–30*
Used own 198cc (12cu in) sv and the Küchen three-valve ohc 498cc (30cu in) single.

KAHENA *Mexico 1992–*
VW Beetle-engined, like the Amazonas, but a more modern, compact design with single-sided swinging arm and twin-spar frame.

KANTO *Japan 1957–60*
Just one model, a 124cc (8cu in) two-stroke.

KAPTEIN *The Netherlands 1938–51*
Fitted four-stroke engines and other parts from Motobécane.

KARÜ *Germany 1922–24*
A 398cc (24cu in) Bosch-Douglas flat twin.

KATAKURA *Japan 1958–c.1962*
120–200cc (7–12cu in) two-stroke singles and twins.

KATHO *Germany 1923–25*
Used 198cc (12cu in) sv Alba engines.

KAUBA *Austria 1953–55*
Sachs-engined scooters to 124cc (8cu in).

KAWASAKI *Japan 1960–*
This, the fourth of the Japanese Big Four manufacturers, came late to motorcycles and didn't built its first complete bike until 1960, even though it could trace its roots back in the 19th century. But although, in Europe at least, Kawasaki has sometimes been overshadowed and outsold by its three well known competitors, the motorcycles bearing this badge are the product of a giant Japanese corporation – a classic *zaibatsu* – that makes everything from helicopters to gas turbines to recycling machines. Even the English Channel Tunnel boring machine was built by the 'Big K', not to mention the famous Japanese Shinkensen Bullet train.

Shozo Kawasaki founded a shipyard at Tsukiji, Tokyo in 1878, and another at Hyogo just three years later. He was an

The Kawasaki 900 ZI was designed to outshine Honda's CB750, and it did

early player in Japan's rapid transition towards modernization which was beginning to gather pace around this time. Kawasaki Dockyard both contributed to and benefited from this process, able to diversify into railway equipment in 1906, then into steam turbines, then (just 15 years after the Wright brothers' first flight) aircraft. Already, the foundations were being laid for Kawasaki's enduring success, which was diversification into all branches of engineering.

Perhaps it was this versatility that allowed Kawasaki to recover so quickly after 1945. Never a one-product company, it was able to benefit from the general striving for reconstruction as a Japan, devastated by war, sought to rebuild itself. As Soichiro Honda was to discover, one of the first demands of early post-war Japan, once the basics of life had been met, was for some form of motorized transport. The country was still a generation away from mass car use, but powered two-wheelers (as long as they were cheap and reliable) were just the thing.

Kawasaki refrained from plunging straight into this market, but began by supplying engines to other manufacturers, the first being a 148cc (9cu in) ohv four-stroke, complete with four-speed gearbox. It was such a success that different capacities soon followed, and within a few years a new Kawasaki subsidiary was busy building engines for a large range of customers. Among them was Meguro, which was selling (among other things) a licence-built version of the BSA A7/A10. Meguro proved to be the Big K's route into motorcycle manufacture, being absorbed by the giant in 1960/61. At the same time, an all-new assembly plant was being built in Akashi, dedicated to building bikes, and in 1962 produced its first product with a Kawasaki badge, the B8. There was nothing unusual about it. It was a straightforward, sensible 125cc (8cu in) two-stroke and was, like almost every other Japanese motorcycle made at the time, a utility product. However, an early attempt to export the B8 to the U.S. met with disappointing sales. What the Americans wanted was something to rival the British bikes and Harley-Davidson – something large.

Up a Blind Alley – Then Success

Unlikely as it may seem, Kawasaki had (or thought it had) something suitable right away. It had inherited Meguro's BSA-based parallel twin, which offered a quick route into the big bike market. No matter that even BSA had recently dropped the pre-unit twin as outdated (it had first seen the light of day in 1946), Kawasaki launched a 624cc (38cu in) version named the W1 in 1966. With 50bhp at 6,500rpm it was at least able to compete with younger British twins, and it looked and rode much like a pre-unit BSA. Kawasaki persevered with the W1, and it actually survived for five years in one guise or another, notably in the W1SS and street scrambler-style W2TT Commander.

ABOVE: A KH-series bike, the later two-stroke triple

BELOW: KM90, a 90cc (5.5cu in) single-cylinder two-stroke midibike with a 5-speed gear box

However, with the best will in the world, the Meguro/BSA was never going to form the basis of Kawasaki's success. That came from something launched the same year as the W1. It was a small, highly tuned two-stroke that set new standards for small bike performance – the A1 Samurai. The A1 couldn't have been more different from the W1, but it was to be the first of a long line of high-performance two-strokes that would put Kawasaki firmly on the motorcycle map. It was unusual in that the 247cc (15cu in) twin used a disc-valve, which of necessity meant a side-mounted carburettor; but Kawasaki avoided excessive width by mounting the alternator behind the crankshaft rather than on one end. Together with a 338cc (21cu in) version (the Avenger) the Samurai sold well in the U.S., and Kawasaki learnt an important lesson regarding the 1960s motorcycle market – that performance sold.

Kawasaki responded in no uncertain terms with the three-cylinder H1, the Mach III. The year of the Mach III's launch, 1968, was particularly memorable for the birth of what soon became known as the superbike; but it also saw three very different interpretations of that concept. From BSA/Triumph came the three-cylinder, four-stroke Rocket Three/Trident, while Honda's CB750 added a new level of sophistication with more power than the British bike, and disc brake, electric start and overhead cam as well. But Kawasaki's offering was different again. Despite being a 'mere' 500cc (30.5cu in), it equalled the 740cc (45cu in) Triumph in power and was lighter. Not surprisingly, it had stunning

ABOVE: *The Estrella 250 (1991) was a real retro bike*

acceleration, though it also gained a reputation for less than stable handling: not for the first time in motorcycling, the Mach III was a bike with an engine ahead of its chassis!

Perhaps the Mach III was a bit too fierce for its own good, and it certainly mellowed a little over the years, being gradually detuned from its original 60bhp to 52bhp by 1976. What it did do, of course, was to bring Kawasaki to everyone's attention, and it was successful enough to spawn a whole family of two-stroke triples: the S1 250cc (15cu in), S2 350cc (21cu in) and 399cc (24cu in) S3. Plus, of course, the amazing H2 or Mach IV, an enlarged Mach III powered by a 748cc (46cu in) version of the triple, which produced 74bhp at 6,800rpm and had an alleged top speed of 209km/h (130mph). It was a fitting climax to the two-stroke era of raw performance and horrendous fuel consumption. But even as the Mach IV went on sale, Kawasaki was already close to launching its real flagship for the next decade, the Z1.

A New Era

Exciting though its manic two-strokes were, Kawasaki had no intention of abandoning four-stroke engines. By the late 1960s, the W1 650 was sadly outdated, and work began on a successor. It couldn't have been more different for the company had decided that its new flagship would not merely be a competitive bike but one that would be bigger and faster than anything comparable. So when the Honda CB750 appeared in late 1968, the prototype Kawasaki was rapidly upgraded to 900cc

BELOW: *Sales material for the Kawasaki Z650C*

ABOVE: Sales material for the original Z1-R

BELOW: The 1999 Drifter (800 or 1500cc) aped the Indian look

(55cu in). The Honda had a single overhead camshaft, so the secret Kawasaki had two. The Honda produced 67bhp, the Z1 had 82.

Here was something with the performance of the fearsome Mach IV, but which was also easy to ride, happy at low speeds and relatively simple to service. Intensive testing of prototypes (mainly in America, which was after all the biggest market for this type of bike) ensured it was free of teething troubles as well. In fact, the Z1's air-cooled 903cc dohc engine became something of a design classic, forming the basis, not only of a long line of big road bikes, but also of much success in endurance and drag racing as well.

While all this was going on, Kawasaki had not forgotten its roots in smaller, utility bikes. The original B8 had hung on until 1966, but the year before that came the

ABOVE: A KH100 EX commuter

ABOVE: The Z750 four was overshadowed by the big Z1000s

BELOW: KZ1000 ST

85cc (5cu in) J1, first of a long line of disc-valved two-stroke singles. It was soon replaced with a 90cc version, which in turn led to the long-running KC90 and KC100 commuter bikes. At complete odds with the glamorous, high performance bikes at the top of the range, these simple two-strokes were reliable and well-priced and, of course, able to bask in the reflected glory of their less utilitarian brothers. A little more exciting were the two-stroke trail bikes which Kawasaki, like its competitors, designed in response to (or perhaps as encouragement to) the new American craze for off-roading, for leisure as much as for sport. This market demanded something very different from the big, heavy four-stroke 'street scramblers' of the time, which even if they did venture off-road were too much of a handful for all but the brave.

Instead, the new lightweights allowed novice off-roaders to have a bit of fun on the dirt without fear of over-stretching themselves. Kawasaki's contribution came in 1969, with two 100cc (6cu in) trail bikes, two 250s, and a 346cc (21cu in) single known as 'Bighorn'. With 33bhp, the Bighorn was one of the most powerful 'trailies' you could buy, and was on sale until the mid-1970s.

A plethora of trail bikes followed as the market continued to grow, notably the 175 Bushwhacker and 250 Bison (which later became the less flamboyantly named KE175 and KE250 respectively). These were all two-strokes, of course, but in 1978 Kawasaki departed from tradition and unveiled two small four-stroke singles. The KL250 was the trail bike and was to survive until replaced by the dohc KLR in 1984.

ABOVE: *An early 650 twin on the production line*

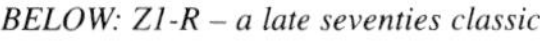

BELOW: *Z1-R – a late seventies classic*

A GPZ1100 of the 1980s

Meanwhile, the Z200 was a mildly-tuned four-stroke single that was quite a luxury commuter, with electric start and a balancer shaft to reduce vibration. Still, the two-stroke AR50, 80 and 125 of a few years later underlined Kawasaki's commitment to the two-stroke engine. They had sharp styling and were well specified, with Kawasaki's own Uni-Trak (monoshock) rear suspension system, a front disc brake and 21bhp from the full-powered liquid-cooled 125. A KMX125 was the trail bike version, which arrived in 1986.

Four-Stroke Expansion

The Z1, then the Z900, had been great successes; but they left a big gap in Kawasaki's range with the advent of the KH500, which was serving an increasingly specialist market (the days of the big two-stroke would soon be over). The logical thing to do was to follow the competition and come up with medium-sized four-stroke fours to capitalize on the Z bike's success, which is exactly what Kawasaki did.

First along was the 652cc (40cu in) Z650 in 1976, which was notable for virtually resurrecting a near-forgotten capacity class (650s were part of the folk-memory of old British twins), but now there was a torquey, easy to ride all-rounder, without the weight and intimidation of the bigger four-cylinder bikes, but still with reasonable performance. The 500 class had never gone away, and Kawasaki duly came up with a Z500 in 1979, plus a smaller Z400 version as well. Logically, a four-cylinder Z750 followed on in 1980, with 79bhp at 9,500rpm. It wasn't actually the first 750-4 sold by Kawasaki – that honour went to a Japanese market version of the original Z1.

In fact, Kawasaki seemed to be approaching the mainstream, producing bikes ever closer to those of the other three Japanese manufacturers. There was good reason for this, with the two-stroke triples losing favour, but the company still decided to hedge its bets and carry on offering the KH250/400/500 (as they now were)

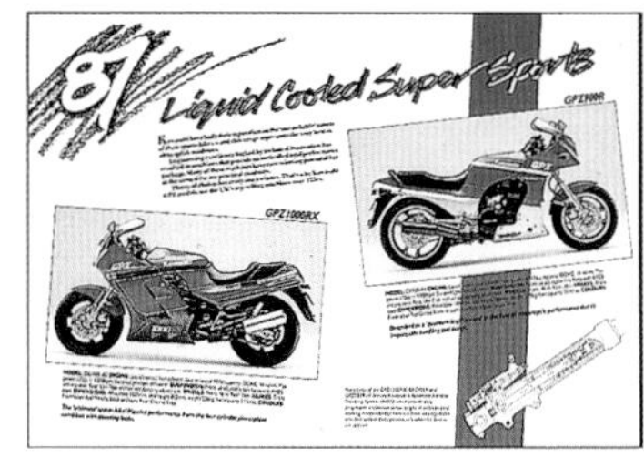

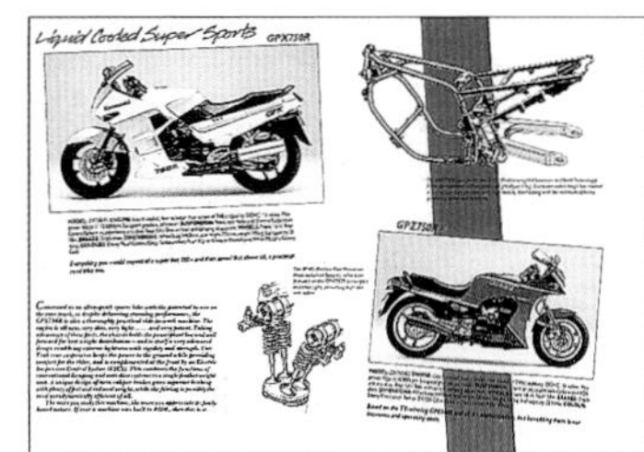

ABOVE and RIGHT: A sales brochure for the Kawasaki 1987 range of motorcycles

alongside the new-for-1974 Z400. Perhaps it was being in parallel with the more sporting KH series that dictated the Z400's role as a sound all-rounder. Its sohc 398cc (24cu in) twin produced sufficient power for a near-100mph top speed, but hardly added up to exciting motorcycling. Still, it was reliable and reasonably economical, with all the usual mod cons now expected of a budget bike, with electric start, disc brake and twin helmet locks. It also had balancer shafts to help quell the parallel twin's vibration. Its only major change came in 1980 when it was bored out to 443cc (27cu in). More interesting, from an historical point of view, was the 745cc (45cu in) Z750 twin of 1977; interesting, because no other Japanese rival was building a 750 twin for the road. Yamaha's XS650 had sold quite well as a more modern equivalent of the traditional British twin, and logically a 750 should have done so too. However, the public now seemed to prefer four cylinders for an engine this large, and the Z750 was not a success.

At the other end of the scale, Kawasaki's smallest road-going four-stroke twin certainly was. The Z250 Scorpion faced very similar competition from Honda,

BELOW: The Z1300 with six cylinders and 1300cc (79cu in)

Yamaha and Suzuki, but was a full 10kg (22lb) lighter than Honda's Superdream, and with a claimed maximum of 60km/h (97mph) was faster. It did well in Britain where, at the time, learners could ride a 250cc bike with no power limit. The Z250 later grew into the oddly-sized GPZ305, which was also distinguishable from the ordinary by virtue of its toothed belt-drive. Two steps up from the 305 was the GPZ500S, which first appeared in 1987. Following the lead of the new big Kawasakis, the new twin used a liquid-cooled engine with four valves per cylinder and twin overhead camshafts; the similarity was hardly surprising as the 500S was no more nor less than half of a GPZ1000 RX four-cylinder engine. With 60bhp at 9,800rpm and relatively light weight (169kg/373lb), it offered something approaching four-cylinder performance in a slimmer, handier package. It also boasted Uni-Trak rear suspension, which was patented by Kawasaki as one of the first 'monoshock' systems, and used a single spring/damper unit to control the swinging arm rather than the usual two. The top of the damper was attached to the frame, the bottom to the swinging arm via a compound linkage. First used on KR250 racers in 1976, it went on to appear on most of the Big K's bigger road bikes. Today, monoshock rear systems of one sort or another are almost universal.

Something else very common in today's market is the cruiser or custom bike, straight out of the factory. Harley-Davidson has been customizing for years, but Kawasaki was the first of the Japanese Big Four to wake up to this potentially lucrative market. The trend had been started by

The 1984 GPZ900R set new standards in its class

Kawasaki's U.S. importer, which took it on itself to sell a few Z900s with custom parts ready fitted. The factory soon responded with 'custom' versions of the Z750 (both four and twin), Z250C, 440 and Z1000. In each case, the formula was the same – higher bars, extra chrome, a stepped seat and different paintwork; but Kawasaki went on to produce factory customs which were models in their own right, notably the EN450 (the engine unique to that model) and the Z900-powered ZL900 Eliminator. In the eighties, the trend began for customs (or cruisers, as they were increasingly called) to be designed from the ground up, with little in common with the sports road bikes. So came purpose-designed V-twins like the VN750 (later 800) and VN1500. The *raison d'être* for these bikes was to get as close as possible to the Harley style, albeit with added reliability and ease of riding. In that, they succeeded.

BELOW: The KLE500, a twin-cylinder trail bike

ABOVE: The nineties Cyclone looked to the past

BELOW: The 1997 ER-5 was deservedly popular

Racers

Remember Meguro? Kawasaki's early partner in the bike business had successfully competed in Japanese dirt-track racing in the 1950s, with a 500cc (30.5cu in) single. The effect wasn't lost on Kawasaki, which won the Japanese 125cc motocross championship as early as 1963. Track success took longer, and it wasn't until 1969 that it finally won a GP championship. Ironically, this was due to Englishman Dave Simmonds who had been taken on in 1967 to ride the 125cc (8cu in) two-stroke twin and, having sat out 1968 due to a serious accident, was loaned his old 125 for the 1969 season, together with a box of spares. Competing on a shoestring, he won eight of the GP rounds that year and clinched the championship.

It was the 500cc two-stroke triple that gave Kawasaki its first Production Racing successes in both the U.S. and Europe. The factory was even inspired to produce its own track version of the road bike, the H1-R, which managed 70bhp at 9,000rpm due to various tweaks here and there. Several successes followed until the 750cc triple took over as the H2-R, almost sweeping the board in America during the 1973 season. Better was to come as the new Z900 proved a natural for endurance racing. Frenchmen Georges Godier and Alain Genoud won the Endurance Championship in 1975, heralding a whole string of successes for big Kawasaki four-strokes in long-distance racing. Meanwhile, the 750 two-stroke had been liquid-cooled and was doing well in shorter races and Mick Grant won the Senior TT on one that year.

But Kawasaki still hadn't cracked the intermediate class until it came up with a tandem (cylinders fore-and-aft rather than side-by-side) two-stroke, which scored its first GP victory in the 1977 Dutch TT. The following year, Kork Ballington took both 250 and 350 GP titles on Kawasaki tandem twins. More 250/350 championships followed and a 500cc four (the KR500) for the top GP class. But the KR500 never achieved the same success, and Kawasaki pulled out of GP racing in 1982. In the 1990s, World Superbike racing has tended to overshadow the Grand Prix, and Kawasaki was an early competitor in this form of racing, which only achieved true

ABOVE: ZXR750 was an uncompromising race replica

BELOW: The ZZR series was a more civilized breed of sports tourers

world status in 1988. The four-cylinder ZXR750-R was a racing version of the road-going ZXR, and won various smaller Superbike championships before securing a WSB title in 1993. It was replaced by the ZX-7RR in 1996.

Of course, off-road competition had long been the source of success for Kawasaki, often under the Team Green label. There were motocross wins in the 250 and 400 classes in the early 1970s, and Jim Weinert won the American AMA championship in 1974. Although the company also competed in trials, it was motocross and enduro that remained the most successful arenas, with first air-cooled, then liquid-cooled, KDX 250s, 420s and others having sold well to private riders.

The Big Fours

We left the biggest Kawasaki as a 900cc (55cu in) air-cooled four, but within a few years it was bored out to 1015cc (62cu in) to create the Z1000. The company seemed determined to offer its latest flagship in every conceivable form: the Z-1R was the café racer of the range, with the obligatory cockpit fairing. The Z1000H had no fairing but was the first production Kawasaki with fuel injection; it was electronically controlled, the precursor of the GPZ1100's digital fuel injection. Then there was the Z1000ST tourer, complete with shaft-drive, the price-leading Z1000J and the Z1000R, a road-going version of the bikes ridden by Eddie Lawson and others in the U.S. But the horsepower race continued, and Kawasaki responded on two fronts. The 750 Turbo was the standard Z750 four with the addition of a turbocharger (112bhp), while the 120bhp GPZ1100 used yet another enlargement of the air-cooled four, plus a Uni-Trak rear-end and anti-dive front forks. It was fast (over 209km/h/130mph) but, at 224kg (494lb), very heavy.

ABOVE: The ZXR750 gave way to the ZX7-R

Just as the Z1 heralded a new era for Kawasaki in the early seventies, so did the GPZ900R ten years later. The big shift here was from air- to liquid-cooling. This might have been expected to add more weight to an already bulky bike, but in fact the new engine was physically smaller than the old one, as well as 5kg (11lb) lighter (though the GPZ900 actually weighed slightly more than the 1100). It produced 114bhp, only slightly less than the air-cooled 1100, though it was interesting that the company stuck with carburettors for its new sportster (fuel injection didn't yet offer sufficient advantages in the cost/benefit balance). No matter, the new GPZ could top 254km/h (158mph), whatever its fuel system, and was the first departure from the big one-

BELOW: The 1998 ZX9-R still sells well

BELOW: The 1986 GPZ1000 RX

DREAM MACHINE

A MAGIC CARPET RIDE

Lean, light, and packing a two-fisted punch of proven Kawasaki power, the all-new GPZ500S is ready to carry you wherever your imagination runs.

It's tractable and easy-to-handle. So whether you're letting the good times roll down city streets, highways, or twisting mountain roads, the GPZ's easy-going nature inspires new levels of confidence.

Then there's its high-tech engine. Sporty suspension systems. And aerodynamics slippery enough to deceive the wind.

So you get a performance package that's exciting for any rider to open up.

OUR SECRET FORMULA

We knew that to develop a 500cc powerplant with the kind of performance that Kawasaki is famous for, we would need to look beyond conventional means.

Inspiration came from the GPZ1000RX—the world's fastest production motorcycle.

By cutting the big Four in half, we got exactly what we wanted—a high-flying Twin with all the right stuff:

Efficient liquid cooling. Eight quick-breathing valves. High-revving dual overhead cams. Exclusive semi-flat-slide carbs.

Technology that translates into proven reliability, a strong dose of easy-riding torque, and lots of high-performance fun.

THE ROAD IS YOURS

Weighing in at just 169kg the GPZ500S is lean enough to make every pony count.

Sophisticated Uni-Trak rear suspension keeps the wide tyre tracking smoothly over the pavement, while a box-section high-tensile steel frame provides the strength for spirited cornering and braking.

The front disc brake is the best in the business. Featuring Kawasaki's exclusive Balanced Actuation Caliper (BAC), this new system delivers stronger stops with more precise feel.

And the super-nimble 16-inch wheels help you maneuver through the esses with the greatest of ease.

In short, the new GPZ500S offers you everything you'd expect in a high-tech sport bike.

And that's a dream come true.

All-new fairing-mounted instrument console is compact and easy-to-read.

With a smaller leading piston, the exclusive BAC caliper outperforms conventional dual-piston setups.

Uni-Trak rear suspension adjusts for optimum performance.

ABOVE and RIGHT: Sales material for the GPZ500S

BELOW: The GPX750R

litre plus sportsbikes to something more wieldy. When the last GPZ900Rs were sold in the mid-1990s, the world of hypersports motorcycles had moved on a long way, but Kawasaki's first liquid-cooled four played a big part in bringing that class about.

Not content with that, the 592cc (36cu in) GPZ600R arrived the following year, 1984. This was another first, though this time the new class was for supersports liquid-cooled 600s. This has since became the standard format for all-round sportsbikes that combine good performance (this GPZ produced 75bhp and could better 209km/h/130mph) with reasonable running costs. Honda soon responded with its highly competent CBR600, which has dominated this class ever since. But Kawasaki was there first. Its answer was the more powerful, lighter GPX600, and the physically bigger ZZR600 which, at the time of writing, is still selling in reasonable numbers.

While the company was concentrating on getting its sportsbikes right, the monstrous Z1300 was still selling to a limited market. Launched in 1978, this 294kg (648lb) machine was one of three sixes at the time, the other two being the Honda CBX and Benelli Sei. It came at a time when the horsepower race was in full swing, when cubic capacity and sheer size seemed to be a priority over handling and rideability. It is tempting now to see the

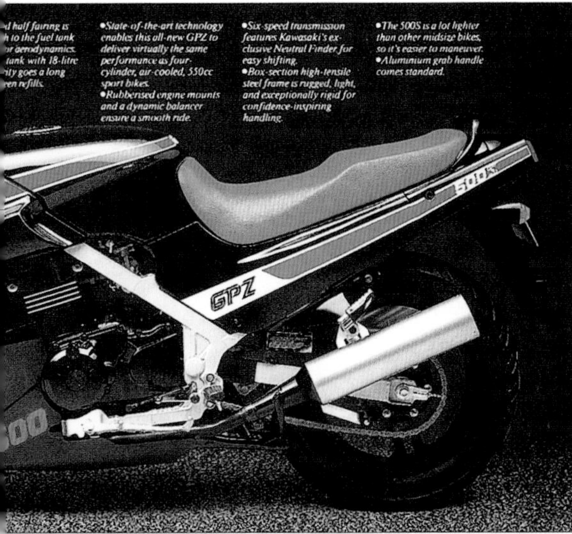

BELOW: A 1998 VL1500 in the cruiser mould

ABOVE: The KR-1S, a highly tuned 250cc two-stroke for the road

Z1300 as a dinosaur; smooth and sophisticated it may have been, but in the opinion of some, the description 'dinosaur' is probably right.

If the Z1300 was a model of conspicuous excess, the GTR of 1986 was something very different. It was Kawasaki's attempt at a purpose-built tourer, with shaft-drive, standard fairing and panniers, big comfortable seat and a huge six-gallon fuel tank for those cross-Europe jaunts. Although it looked all-new, the GTR was really an intelligent mix of existing components with its frame based on that of the GPZ900 (with, of course, a Uni-Trak rear-end) and the engine a detuned version of the 997cc (61cu in) liquid-cooled four from the GPZ1000RX. In GTR guise, the engine produced 108bhp, though it was restricted to 100bhp for some markets. Twelve years on, the GTR was still in production and had acquired a loyal following; Kawasaki's bid for a slice of the BMW market had worked well.

But the company had never forgotten its love affair with the ultimate big bike market which had begun with the Z1. The liquid-cooled GPZ1000RX had replaced the old air-cooled 1100, and was in turn dropped in favour of the faster ZX-10. Both of these led to something rather longer-lived and which made a much bigger impact – the ZZR1100. When it was launched in 1990, the ZZR1100 was simply the fastest

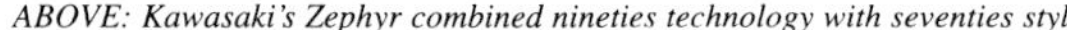

ABOVE: Kawasaki's Zephyr combined nineties technology with seventies style

OPPOSITE: The ZZR1100, the user-friendly GPZ305 and KLR250 and the two-stroke KR-1S

production bike on sale (283km/h/176mph), a sports-tourer that handled very well indeed and really blurred the edges between the pure sports and sports-touring markets. Although it was developed from the ZX-10, the ZZR was also substantially new, with major changes to the engine with a new frame, bodywork and suspension. The bike's sheer zest and long legs which, for several years, made it the fastest one could buy, also made the ZZR1100 (always the ZX-11 in the U.S.) something of a cult motorcycle. Only in the late 1990s has it been overtaken in speed and power, but for some it is still the ultimate Japanese machine. In Britain, to members of the ZZR Owners Club, its slogan still holds good: 'Nowhere's far on a ZZR!'

Fast the ZZR most certainly was, but it still weighed 233kg (514lb). For the pure sports market, Kawasaki needed a nimbler answer to Honda's all-conquering FireBlade, and unveiled it in 1994 as the ZX-9R, the first of the Ninja family. It was developed from the existing ZXR750, itself a more sporting development of the GPX750. Although it looked the part, and gave near-ZZR levels of performance, the original ZX was just too heavy and softly suspended to really challenge the FireBlade. Steady development and an almost complete redesign for 1998 brought it much closer to the top. The 599cc (36.5cu in) ZX6 was closer to the mark straight away, with its own very compact and all-new power unit (98bhp at 12,600rpm) and aluminium frame. It certainly equalled the CBR600 on performance, though perhaps wasn't such an accomplished all-rounder. In 1996 the family was completed with the ZX7, which replaced the ZXR. This (like the ZXR had become) was as much a means of providing a competitive basis for 750cc Superbike racing as a road bike, something true of most 750 sportsters in the late 1990s.

But while the horsepower race continues, there was also a move in the nineties towards retro bikes. Whether it was part of a general nostalgia for past times, or that most riders were now aged 40 or over and yearning for the bikes of their youth, the 1970s look was back. Kawasaki's contribution was the Zephyr, with air-cooled engine, no fairing, and distinctly 1970s styling. In 500, 550, 750 and 1100 forms, the Zephyr was quite a success. And if the roly-poly Zephyr was too laid-back, the ZRX1100 for 1997 echoed the café racer Z1-R, albeit with a detuned ZZR1100 engine. Or if one couldn't remember the seventies, Kawasaki's answer was the new GPZ1100 of 1995 which had a distinct family resemblance to the GPZ500 twin, but again used detuned ZZR1100 power. The Big K had come a long way from the B8 125.

CUSTOM CLASSIC
If you had the time and means to build the bike of your dreams, one that encompassed every idea you had, chances are you'd be disappointed if you built it. Why? Because Kawasaki has already done it for you.
Introducing the all-new 1991 Kawasaki Zephyr.
Created by the builders of the legendary Z-1 and GPz series, the Zephyr was conceived to fulfill the dreams of motorcyclists whose idea of the perfect machine is embodied in the clean, classic lines of bikes like the Z-1, but with the advantages of today's modern technology.
To start, we designed a double-cradle, high-tensile steel frame to create a low, lean chassis—one that's as nimble around town as it is on the bends.
Then we added a fork with rigid 39mm diameter stanchions and a pair of nitrogen-charged adjustable piggy-back-reservoir shocks that deliver riding characteristics that will keep you satisfied for years to come.
For plenty of legendary Kawasaki performance, we bolted in a GPz-descended powerplant that's been specially updated to give a better power feeling in the low and middle ranges.
Semi-floating discs and dual-piston pin-slide calipers up front, and a strong disc brake on the back bring you to a stop with great "feel" and fade resistance.
Wide tyres grip the road for confidence-inspiring feel, while cast aluminium five-spoke wheels add to overall rigidity.
And from the luxurious chrome to the immaculate fit and finish, it's obvious Kawasaki paid attention to the small details that enthusiasts notice.
So take a ride on a Kawasaki Zephyr.
It's one classic that won't take long to appreciate.
•Proven 550cc In-Line Four packs plenty of reliable Kawasaki firepower.
•Digital electronic ignition provides the right spark at any rpm.
•From headers to muffler, the four-into-one exhaust system glistens in high-quality chrome.
•Six-speed gearbox features Kawasaki's convenient Positive Neutral Finder.
•Adjustable dual rear nitrogen-charged shocks feature piggy-back reservoirs for consistent damping action and less fade.
•Aluminium swingarm features eccentric chain adjusters that turn a chore into a piece of cake.
•Semi-floating front discs and dual-piston calipers bring the Zephyr to strong, sure stops.
•Adjustable handlevers and retractable bungee-cord hooks are just some of the Zephyr's rider-friendly extras.
•One-piece saddle is roomy enough to keep you and a friend comfortable on long rides.
•Instrumentation is clean, simple, and tells you what you need to know at a glance.

1992
RANGE
Kawasaki
THE GREAT ESCAPE

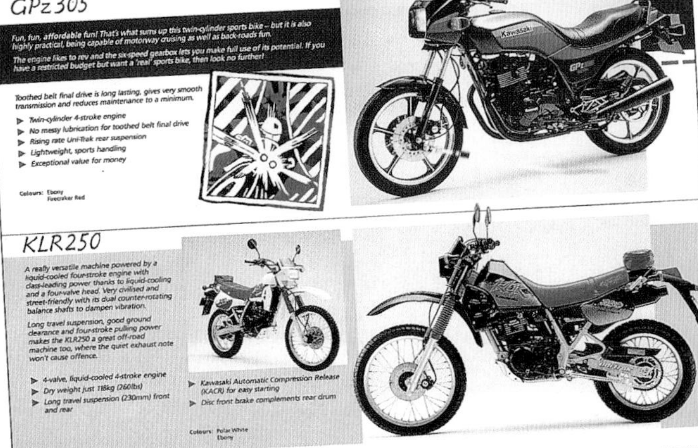
GPz305
Fun, fun, affordable fun! That's what sums up this twin-cylinder sports bike – but it is also highly practical, being capable of motorway cruising as well as back-roads fun.
The engine likes to rev and the six-speed gearbox lets you make full use of its potential. If you have a restricted budget but want a 'real' sports bike, then look no further!
Toothed belt final drive is long lasting, gives very smooth transmission and reduces maintenance to a minimum.
Twin-cylinder 4-stroke engine
No messy lubrication for toothed belt final drive
Rising rate Uni-Trak rear suspension
Lightweight, sports handling
Exceptional value for money
Colours: Ebony
Firecraker Red
KLR250
A really versatile machine powered by a liquid-cooled four-stroke engine with class-leading power thanks to liquid-cooling and a four-valve head. Very civilised and street-friendly with its dual counter-rotating balance shafts to dampen vibration.
Long travel suspension, good ground clearance and four-stroke pulling power makes the KLR250 a great off-road machine too, where the quiet exhaust note won't cause offence.
4-valve, liquid-cooled 4-stroke engine
Dry weight just 118kg (260lbs)
Long travel suspension (230mm) front and rear
Kawasaki Automatic Compression Release (KACR) for easy starting
Disc front brake complements rear drum
Colours: Polar White
Ebony

KR-1S
If the KR-1S looks like it has strayed from the race tracks, then that is hardly surprising – for it has excelled in Production and Supersport 400 events.
In the heat of competition, the light, rigid chassis has proved its worth in providing superb handling, allowing rapid changes of direction in safety and liberating the (considerable) potential of the liquid-cooled twin-cylinder two-stroke engine.
But the KR-1S was designed first and foremost as a road machine, so it remains civilised, despite its obvious sporting potential. The electronically-operated Kawasaki Integrated Power-valve System (KIPS) significantly broadens the power band, while balance shafts effectively dampen vibration.
Double box section alloy frame and strong swing arm give superb handling
Super-rigid 41mm dia. front fork stanchions
Remote reservoir rear shock absorber has adjustable preload and damping
Twin semi-floating front disc brakes with 4-piston calipers
Wide, low profile, radial ply tyres
Colours: Firecracker Red/Pearl Gentry Grey
Lime Green/Blue 24/Pearl Alpine White

GPZ1100 used a detuned ZZR engine in a cheaper package

KELLER *Switzerland 1930–32*
An ultimately unsuccessful 347cc (21cu in) sv single.

KEMPTON *England 1921–22*
Used an ABC 124cc (8cu in) ohv engine to power both lightweights and scooters.

KENI *Germany 1921–23*
145/158cc (9/10cu in) three-port two-strokes.

KENILWORTH *England 1919–24*
An advanced scooter with front and rear suspension and Norman, Villiers or JAP power.

KENZLER-WAVERLEY *U.S.A. 1910–14*
Produced own ohv singles and V-twins.

KERRY *England 1902–66*
Originally only lasted until 1914, using Kelecom, FN and finally Abingdon engines. The name was used again from 1960 to sell Italian mopeds.

KESTREL *England 1903*
Used 211cc (13cu in) Minerva and MMC engines.

KG *Germany 1919–32*
An advanced shaft-driven single, using first an ioe 503cc (31cu in), then an ohv 499cc. There were several owners: the Krieger brothers, Cito, Allright and Paul Henkel, but was in any case outdated by the late 1920s.

KIEFT *England 1955–57*
Rebadged Hercules scooters and lightweights for the British market.

KILEAR *Czechoslovakia 1924–26*
Own 247cc (15cu in) three-port two-stroke machines.

KINETIC *India 1972–*
A licence-built Vespa Ciao moped (sold as the Luna), later producing its own Minarelli/Morini-inspired two-strokes, and a licence-built 100cc (6cu in) Honda scooter from 1986.

KING *England 1901–07*
Used a wide variety of power units, among them De Dion, Minerva, MMC, Daw, Antoine and Sarolea.

KING-JAP *Germany 1928–31*
Built from mostly English parts, including the sv and ohv singles.

KINGSBURY *England 1919–23*
A brief dalliance with scooters and lightweights, with its own 261cc (16cu in) engine.

KINGSWAY *England 1921–23*
Motorcycles of simple design with 293cc (18cu in) sv JAP engines.

K&K *Germany 1924–25*
Built its own 170 and 289cc (10 and 18cu in) three-port two-strokes.

KLOTZ Germany 1923–26
Another in-house two-stroke of 246cc (15cu in).

KM *Germany 1924–26*
Limited production 142 and 159cc (9 and 10cu in) two-stroke machines.

KMB *Germany 1923–26*
4.2–6hp machines of its own design and manufacture.

KMS *Germany 1922–24*
Used own 196cc (12cu in) ohv single, and a bought-in Grade two-stroke.

KÖBO *Germany 1921–26*
A 276cc (17cu in) two-stroke from a maker of chains.

KOCH *Czechoslovakia 1934–35*
Advanced unit-construction 348cc (21cu in) ohc single from ex-Praga designer J.F. Koch.

KOEHLER-ESCOFFIER *France 1912–57*
Produced mostly ohc engines, including the only 996cc (61cu in) ohc V-twin of the 1920s. Also used ohc singles, both in-house and bought-in. After 1945, concentrated on Villiers-powered lightweights.

KOFA *Germany 1923–25*
Used bought-in 283cc (17cu in) two-strokes.

KOHOUT *Czechoslovakia 1904–06*
Used 2.5/2.75hp Minerva and Fafnir engines.

KOLIBRI *Germany 1923–30*
A 110cc (7cu in) clip-on.

KOMAR *Poland c.1958–68*
Brand-name for ZZR mopeds.

KOMET *Germany 1902–05*
One of the first makers of two-strokes in Germany, with licence-built Ixions.

KONDOR *Germany 1924–25*
Machines with Simplex two-strokes or an Ideal sv unit was offered.

KOSTER (KS) *Germany 1923–25*
Used a pressed steel frame, disc wheels, and enclosed belt/chain-drive. Bekamo or Cockerell-powered.

KOVROV *Former U.S.S.R. 1946–*
Like many others, it built a copy of the DKW RT125, soon increasing capacity to 175cc (11cu in). Also built the Voskhod from 1966 and a few 250cc (15cu in) motocrossers.

KR *Germany 1924–25*
Used the 492cc (30cu in) sv flat-twin BMW engine, or a 998cc (61cu in) MAG V-twin was available.

KR *Germany 1930–1933*
No connection with the above and using bought-in JAP singles.

KRAMMER *Austria 1926–29*
Used 172cc (10.5cu in) Villiers, 496cc (30cu in) ohv Anzani or MAG, or 996cc (61cu in) Anzani 8-valve V-twins.

KRASNY-OCTOBER *Former U.S.S.R. 1930–34*
First mass-produced bike from Soviet Russia, similar to the equivalent DKW.

KRAUSER *Germany 1976–*
As well as running the Kreidler racing team in later years, BMW dealer Mike Krauser built a limited run of tubular frames to take BMW engines, which were sold as kits or complete bikes.

KREIDLER *Germany 1951–82*
At one time the biggest manufacturer in Germany, despite concentrating solely on 49cc (3cu in) machines. The sporting Florett, with 6.25bhp, could top 85km/h (53mph) and was also very successful in 50cc racing, gaining several World Championships. Closed in 1982 due to falling sales.

KRIEGER *Germany 1925–26*
Used 347cc (21cu in) Blackburne engines, and the Krieger brothers' own 499cc (30cu in) shaft-driven singles (then owned by Allright). Also sold frames to other manufacturers.

Krauser reframed BMW twins to good effect

From the 1970s, KTM was increasingly dominated by the off-road market

KRS *Germany 1921–26*
Used Paqué four-stroke singles and the SWM-built Bosch-Douglas flat twin.

KRUPP *Germany 1919–21*
Scooter, with 185 or 198cc (11 or 12cu in) engine fitted outside the front wheel.

KSB *Germany 1924–29*
Fitted a variety of engines from DKW, Kühne, Blackburne and JAP.

KTM *Austria 1953–*
The most successful Austrian manufacturer began with 98cc (6cu in) Rotax-powered machines and went on to produce mopeds, scooters and lightweights with Puch, Sachs as well as Rotax engines, all two-strokes. KTM went through phases, concentrating solely on mopeds in 1960–65, and from 1967 began to develop motocross bikes which came to dominate its production. Won the 1977 250cc Motocross Championship, and experience gained from the competition bikes trickled down to the production machines, resulting in water-cooling and rising-rate rear suspension. After near-bankruptcy in 1991, KTM made a rapid recovery, and now produces a large range of off-road machines from a 125cc (8cu in) two-stroke trail bike to more serious Enduros (two-strokes of 193, 297 and 368cc/12, 18 and 22cu inches, and four-strokes of 398, 539 and 625cc/24, 33 and 38cu inches). Some of these are road-legal and have electric start. Another recent development has been a return to the pure road market with the LC4 Supermoto (basically the Enduro, but with road tyres and other minor changes) and the 625cc Duke, the magazine testers' favourite for wheelies and stoppies! Although there were

KTM four-stroke Pro-Lever 500 GS

rumours of a merger and takeover in 1998 (notably by Harley-Davidson) KTM remains independent in early 1999, is profitable, and is now developing its own V-twin.

KULI *Germany 1922–24*
145cc and 198cc (9 and 12cu in) two-strokes.

KUMFURT *England 1914–16*
Utilized 269cc or 496cc (16 or 30cu in) Precision V-twins.

KURIER *Germany 1921–24*
Used own 147cc (9cu in) two-strokes and also sold to other manufacturers.

KURRAS *Germany 1925–27*
Utilized 173cc (11cu in) water-cooled Bekamo two-strokes in its own triangular frames. Not many were made.

KV *Germany 1924–27*
Produced 197cc and 246cc (12 and 15cu in) sv singles.

KYMCO *Taiwan 1962–*
A recent entry to the huge Taiwanese industry, at the time of writing, Kymco (short for Kwang Yang Motor Co.) is one of the largest scooter manufacturers in the world, and has achieved great success in Europe. Began with Japanese-derived 50cc (3cu in) scooters, but in the late 1990s offers a complete range of 50, 100 and 250cc scooters, both two- and four-strokes, plus a 125 (8cu in) cruiser-style motorcycle.

The Kymco Zing 125 cruiser

KYNOCH *England 1912–13*
Mainly used its own 488cc (30cu in) single and 770cc (47cu in) V-twin.

KZ *Germany 1924–25*
Utilized 198cc (12cu in) Alba engines, and ohv 348cc (21cu in) singles made by Kühne.

L

L-300 *Former U.S.S.R. 1932–*
Produced DKW-like 294/346cc (18/21cu in) two-strokes, built in large numbers for the military.

LABOR *France 1908–60*
Part of the Alcyon group, with 98–248cc (6–15cu in) two-strokes and 174–498cc (11–30cu in) four-strokes.

LADETTO *Italy 1923–32*
Produced 123/173cc (7.5/11cu in) two-strokes at first. The Ladetto brothers were later joined by Angelo Blatto, and built four-strokes.

Kymco Top Boy off-road-style scooter

LADIES PACER *England 1914*
Probably the only motorcycle ever built on the island of Guernsey, it had a step-through frame with a JES 110cc (7cu in) two-stroke.

LADY *Belgium 1925–38*
Used a variety of engines up to 498cc (30cu in), which included units from Villiers, MAG, Blackburne *et al.*

LAFOUR & NOUGIER *France 1927–36*
Aubier-Dunne, Chaise, Stainless, Train, Villiers and JAP supplied the power.

LAG *Austria 1921–29*
Produced 118/148cc (7/9cu in) clip-ons at first, later fitted JAP engines and designed its own 246cc (15cu in) two-stroke.

LA GALBAI *Italy 1921–25*
Own two-strokes from 276cc to 492cc (17 to 30cu in), the biggest of which was a V-twin.

LAGONDA *England 1902–05*
Mostly used De Dion, MMC or Minerva engines.

L'ALBA *Italy 1924–26*
Produced 198cc (12cu in) Alba sv machines, assembled in Milan.

LA LORRAINE *France 1922–25*
Built own two-stroke engines up to 248cc (15cu in).

LAMAUDIÈRE *France 1901–07*
Surely the biggest single ever made at 942cc (57cu in).

LAMBRETTA *Italy 1947–1971*
It can be no coincidence that the world's two most popular scooters both originated in post-war Italy within a year of one another. That Vespa and Lambretta turned out to be so similar – and for a time equally successful – was no accident of history. Italy in the late 1940s desperately needed cheap, basic personal transport, but so did the rest of Europe. Germany had its own post-war scooter boom, but it was in Italy that scooters became part of the cultural scenery with the sound of buzzing two-strokes filling the streets of every town and city. Whether it was climate, or Italian flair, or even those crowded cities with narrow streets, scooters seemed to suit Italy. So where scooter manufacturers in Germany, Britain or France went back to motorcycles, or gave up altogether, the Vespa and Lambretta went on to achieve huge worldwide success, being built under licence all over the globe. If one includes three-wheelers, 24 million Lambrettas have been built over the years.

Side and front views of the Lambretta A Model – simple, basic transport, and ideal for late 1940s Italy

Ferdinando Innocenti had no ambition to build scooters, but he was a talented engineer and possessed of great energy and drive. He opened his own small workshop at the age of 18 and began experimenting with the application of steel tubes. He moved to Rome, then Milan, where in 1931 he set up a plant to mass-produce his steel tubes. It was a great success and grew into a huge factory until Allied bombing heavily damaged it in World War II. Undaunted, he set about the task of reconstruction and typically succeeded before the end of the war.

History does not record what gave him the idea for a scooter, but the Lambretta (named after the Lambrate area of Milan) was an ideal way to diversify. It was a simple thing with a pressed steel main-frame and a rear sub-frame to carry the engine made of (you've guessed it) steel tubes. The engine itself was a 123cc two-stroke, coupled to a three-speed gearbox and with foot change, though the famous twistgrip change was to come the following year. With 4.1hp at 4,500rpm, it could push the A Model along at 64–71km/h (40–44mph), and at a 48km/h (30mph) cruise sipped fuel at around 39km per litre (110mpg). There was no rear suspension on this first Lambretta, but luckily the tiny (7-inch) tyres were like

The Lambretta Model B gained rear suspension and longer wheels, though it was still not the ideal sidecar machine!

The Lambretta 50cc (3cu in) J Model, whose familiar style was by now well-established

LD150LC introduced full bodywork

ABOVE: The TV175 was the biggest yet

BELOW: The Series III 150, four-speed with 10-inch wheels

low-pressure balloons that no doubt softened the ride. Available in several colours, plus a dash of chrome, the Lambretta A was a great success, and over 9,000 were sold in the first year.

However, Innocenti soon learned from this experience, and the B Model of late 1948 had rear suspension, slightly larger 8-inch wheels and the twistgrip gearchange. And the cables now ran outside the handlebars, which didn't look as neat but were a lot easier to manipulate. It cost more than the A, but Innocenti was obviously moving in the right direction as 35,000 were sold in just 13 months. But things were moving fast, and February 1950 saw the C model, whose main innovation was the large single-tube frame which has formed the basis of every Lambretta since. It was described as a 'sports model' (presumably because it did without leg guards, though in reality was no faster than the earlier bikes).

Full Enclosure

But none of these Lambrettas resembled the classic Italian scooter that we all recognize. That came in April 1950 with the 125LC. Mechanically, there was little change, with the same mildly tuned 123cc single. What was new was the full bodywork with leg guards right up to the handlebars, full enclosure for the engine, and proper footboards for both rider and passenger. (From the start, all Lambrettas had room for two, for what self-respecting young Italian could be expected to ride solo?) This didn't mean the end of the basic open Lambretta, though, and these were produced right up to 1956. But the future of the scooter lay in full weather protection and a 150cc (9.2cu in) version of both soon appeared, now with fan cooling thanks to blades on the flywheel. With 6hp, the Lambretta could top 80km/h (50mph) on a good day, and came in both open and enclosed versions.

The LD was now the mainstream Lambretta, with a 125 or 150cc engine and leading link front suspension. One innovation, which appeared in February 1954, was an electric start version which utilized a 6-volt battery hidden behind the left-hand panel, though it was soon uprated to 12 volts. At the time, however, it seems to have been less popular than the simpler, cheaper kickstart model. But the basic Lambrettas were selling better than ever and the Series III 150LD sold over 100,000 in 18 months which was partly due to rapidly expanding exports. In 1948, just 96 Lambrettas had been sold outside Italy: ten years on, the figure was 109,000. For many developing countries, the Lambretta was ideal transport, but too expensive to import fully-built. The best solution was to build it under licence, thereby creating jobs and skills at home. Factories were set up in India (where Lambrettas are still made) and in various parts of South America, Indonesia and Pakistan, among other locations.

Meanwhile, Europeans had the updated LI range with shaft-drive, larger 10-inch wheels and four-speed twistgrip. Engine power was slightly up, though the basic unit was still a 123c two-stroke. But the new top of the range scooter had already appeared, the 170cc (10.4cu in) TV175. With 8.6hp, it promised 103km/h (64mph) and a mere 31km per litre (88mpg) and it even had a front disc brake! Unfortunately, engine problems led to its replacement by a Series II in 1959, which was slower but more reliable. But export markets (notably British) wanted still more power, and Lambretta's response was the TV200 of 1963. It had the same basic underpinnings as every other Lambretta (apart from that front disc brake), albeit with a 10.75hp 198cc (12cu in) engine. Top speed was 97km/h (60mph). By 1966, it had become the SX200, with 11hp and a claimed 106km/h (66mph), yet according to Innocenti could still manage 33km per litre (93mpg). Inevitably, the British importer coined the advertising slogan 'SX Appeal'.

ABOVE: GP125 was the final update

BELOW: The Vega 50/75 had a period look

In the late sixties, Lambretta also attempted to branch out from its traditional scooters into various mopeds; these were boosted by Italian legislation which treated 50s as bicycles. There were very basic big-wheel mopeds in the 1950s, but the Vega (in 50 and 75cc/3 and 4.6cu inch forms) looked like a miniaturized, space-age Lambretta scooter, and was in production from 1968–70. 50cc versions of the scooters appeared from 1964 on, as the three-speed J50, which lasted right up to the end of production in 1971.

The more basic Lambrettas had another update in January 1969 with the Grand Prix (GP), which featured styling by the famous Bertone design house, though it was very obviously still a Lambretta. Rather than attempt anything too radical, Bertone had simply updated the basic lines, which was probably wise. Still, the period racing stripe was distinctive and the GP125, 150 and 200 carried on until April 1971. For the Italian factory this was the end, as sales were well past their peak and Innocenti had other projects to pursue. But as we have seen, Lambretta lives on all over the world.

SX200 was Lambretta's top-range scooter in 1966 and could top 106km/h (66mph)

LA MONDIALE *Belgium 1924–33*
No connection with the Italian Mondial, 308/349cc (19/21cu in) two-strokes or bigger ohc Chaise engines were used in pressed steel frames. There were also Villers and JAP options.

LAMPO *Italy 1925–27*
123–247cc (7.5–15cu in) two-stroke lightweights, also offered with the 173cc (10.5) ohv Piazza unit.

LANCER *Japan 1957–early 1960s*
Two-strokes up to 248cc (15cu in) and a 248cc V-twin like the more famous Lilac.

LANCO *Austria 1922–26*
Used MAG engines at first before utilizing its own 496cc (30cu in) singles.

LANDI *Italy 1923–26*
Produced 122/172cc (7.4/10.5cu in) three-port two-strokes.

LA PANTHERRE *France 1928–32*
Utilized 346/490cc (21/30cu in) JAP singles.

LAPIZE *France 1930–37*
Used Aubier-Dunne, LMP, JAP and other bought-in units.

LATSCHA *France 1948–53*
Only used Aubier-Dunne two-strokes.

LAURIN & KLEMENT *Austria 1899–1908*
One of the leading pioneer motorcycle factories in the early years, Laurin & Klement produced singles, V-twins and even four-cylinder in-line four machines. There were some innovations, notably water-cooling and, on the CC V-twin, front suspension. Concentrated on cars from 1908, and was later taken over by Skoda.

L'AVENIR *Belgium 1959*
Used HMW and Sachs 49cc (3cu in) engines.

LAVERDA *Italy 1949–*
Pietro Laverda never built motorcycles, but then his business lay in agricultural machinery. He set up a factory to build ploughs and harrows in Breganze in north-eastern Italy in 1873 and it grew into an industrial group, still owned by the Laverda family. But it wasn't until 1948, two generations later, that Francesco Laverda built his first bike, a 75cc (4.6cu in) four-stroke. It was really for his own amusement, but so many friends asked him to build replicas that he set up Moto Laverda the following year and went into production. He had a distinct advantage in that he had a background of engineering resources and plenty of capital, and the little 75cc ohv single was made by the fledgling company itself, hanging the bike from a pressed steel frame. Despite the small capacity, this was no utility bike but a true miniaturized sportster, a fact which was underlined in 1953 when an example won its class in the 1,127-km (700-mile) Milan–Taranto road race. Other long-distance races like the Giro d'Italia were contested, encouraging Laverda to design a larger bike.

A 100cc (6cu in) racer followed, and there were more basic bikes as well, such as a moped (albeit with a front disc brake) and a four-stroke scooter. In fact, at this time Laverda was as much concerned with utility bikes as anything else, which belied its later association with powerful road-burners. Take the 200cc (12cu in) Gemini, announced in 1960. This still used a pressed steel frame to house its 11bhp twin-cylinder four-stroke engine. It was high geared for quiet cruising, had a large comfortable dual seat, enclosed chain and a useful luggage rack. Leg guards were among the options, and when the American magazine *Cycle World* tested one in 1967, it found that the top speed was an underwhelming 84km/h (52mph). If Laverda had gone on building bikes like this in the face of nippier Japanese lightweights, it surely would not have lasted far into the 1970s.

A Big Leap
Fortunately, the company had something radically different up its sleeve. Radically different, that is, compared to what it had built before. Not so radical by Honda standards, for Laverda's new 650cc (40cu in) twin, announced in late 1966, had much in common (in both looks and general layout) with Honda's CB450. As unveiled, there was something of a Honda about the whole bike. Still, none of that seemed to matter because wherever the inspiration had come from, Laverda had evidently done a good job. The sohc twin, with 360-degree crankshaft and five-speed gearbox, produced 52bhp at 6,500rpm for a claimed top speed of 190km/h (118mph). Just as important, Laverda claimed that it was designed to run at least 60,000 miles before major overhaul, the crankshaft being supported by massive ball and roller bearings. Here was a thoroughly modern

ABOVE and OPPOSITE: The Laverda 1000 triple was the first of a generation

update of the vertical twin, with competitive power, long-distance stamina and such niceties as electric start. This surely was what the British industry should have been building at the time and it was instructive that contemporary British twins of the same capacity should be plagued with vibration, while Laverda was not, neither was it over-tuned.

At the behest of the importers, the 650 quickly became a 750 for the bike's U.S. launch, and in this guise the 744cc (45cu in) American Eagle, as it was known, pushed out 60bhp at 6,500rpm, still on a very modest compression ratio of 7.0:1 and with mild tuning for a tractable, torquey engine. Tests praised the performance, quality and handling, only finding it a little heavy in town (it weighed well over 227kg/500lb). In the space of a couple of years, Laverda had transformed itself from an obscure maker of decidedly Italianate lightweights to mainstream sportsbikes in the up and coming 750 class.

LAVERDA
1000
1000 LAVERDA

T. Parker riding a 750cc (46cu in) Laverda SFC at Brands Hatch

Inevitably, with such a mildly tuned standard machine, a sportster (the SF) soon appeared, with a higher 8.9:1 compression and other changes for 65bhp at 7,500rpm, and a top speed of near 193km/h (120mph). The softer original continued as the GT, but that wasn't all as the SFC ('Super Freni Competiziono') from 1971 again had higher tune, with bigger valves and fiercer profile cams. Bottom-end components were polished, and the pistons were balanced in matched pairs. Power was up to 70bhp, later 75bhp. It was really designed for Production Racing, though was fully road-legal with lights and silencers. It certainly fulfilled its promise, taking the top three places in the Barcelona 24-hour Endurance race in 1971, not to mention wins at Vallelunga, Modena and Zeltweg the following year, and the Zandvoort 6-hour in 1973.

But in those days, Moto Laverda was not a company to rest on its laurels, particularly with brothers Massimo and Pietro Laverda on the Board. Both were keen riders and realized that good though the twin was, it would soon be outclassed by ever bigger and faster fours from Japan. The three-cylinder 1000 was their response. When first revealed to the press in 1970, it looked very much like a three-cylinder version of the twin, but the production engine of 1972 was neater, more compact, with twin overhead camshafts and a claimed 80bhp. Apart from Triumph, no one was making a four-stroke triple at the time, so it showed courage on Laverda's part. There was still much of the twin about it, with a strong bottom-end and an initial tune aiming at mid-range rather than top-end power, yet top speed was over 209km/h (130mph) and it completed the standard quarter-mile in less than 14 seconds. Perhaps most surprising, after the somewhat heavy 750, was the fact that road testers found the big bike lighter and easy to handle and at 214kg (471lb), it actually *was* lighter. On the other hand, the stiff suspension, high first gear and heavy clutch ('requires a fine, manly grip', said *Cycle*) made it clear that this was a bike intended for the open road.

The triple may have been a great success, and turned out to be Laverda's most enduring model, but there were some failures, notably the Zündapp-powered two-stroke road bikes of 125 and 175cc (8 and 11cu in). The later 125/250 Enduros, this time using Husqvarna units, were similarly unsuccessful, though Laverda had earlier designed its own 250/400cc (15/24cu in) two-stroke Enduro. The company evidently had ambitions to build smaller bikes again, for 1977 saw the launch of the Alpino 500, a slim and lightweight vertical twin whose looks (engine-wise) reminded one of the first 650, except this one had twin overhead cams and four valves per cylinder. Power was 44bhp at 8,000rpm. Although more expensive than the Japanese opposition, it certainly handled well, and was just as fast

The Laverda 500cc (30.5cu in) Alpino was an attempt to meet the Japanese head-on

at 167km/h (104mph). The Alpino lasted until 1981, by which time it was supplemented by the 52bhp café racer-style Montjuic. In its final form, as the 500T/S from 1982–84, it had a balance shaft and was a little more sophisticated. In the final analysis, though, none of Laverda's 500s were sufficiently different to the opposition, not in the way that the bigger bikes were.

The Jota

Meanwhile, Laverda's most famous bike of all time had been launched in 1976. The U.K. importer, Roger Slater, just like Laverda's U.S. importer a decade earlier, had persuaded the factory to produce something faster. The result was the Jota. It was the basic triple, with high-compression pistons, sharper cams and freer-breathing exhausts to produce 90bhp or so, and a top speed of 225km/h/140mph (some said 150mph). There were now twin disc brakes at the front too, which was probably just as well. Despite the higher state of tune, in the Laverda tradition it remained strong on torque and mid-range power. It was one of the fastest things on the road at the time, and the low-set bars emphasized the fact that this was the sports version. It also served to take over where the SFC left off, and Production Racing success once more fell to Laverda.

As was the way with legends, it became diluted over the years, notably after Laverda made it smoother with a 120-degree crankshaft (this was in pre-balance-shaft days) and a little easier to ride. It was supplanted by the 1115cc (68cu in) Mirage in 1980, which had even more mid-range power but was otherwise little advanced on the original 981cc (60cu in) triple. In 1982 came the more civilized RGS, with a half-fairing, hydraulic clutch and the 120-degree engine, though it only lasted a couple of years, as did the tuned 241km/h (150mph) Corsa version, and the naked RGA. But Laverda knew that the air-cooled triple was coming to the end of its useful life, and in 1983 work was progressing on a water-cooled four to replace it. This was not a clean-sheet design, but owed much to the abortive V6 Endurance racer of the late seventies. The V6 was a real departure for Laverda: it not only had a water-cooled engine, but four valves per cylinder, shaft-drive and electronic ignition. Only six months after work began, an engine was running and producing 118bhp at the rear wheel, well on the way to the 140bhp target. Designed solely with Endurance racing in mind, the bike enjoyed a wide spread of power but was heavy. It had just one outing, at the 1978 Bol d'Or, where it retired after eight and a half hours, due to a broken driveshaft joint. Despite stunning speed (at 282km/h/175mph on the Mistral straight, it was 18mph faster than the works Hondas) it never raced again.

The V6 had also cost a great deal of money to develop, and work on other

Laverda's softly-tuned GTL750, seen here in Basano, was popular with the Italian police

ABOVE: Laverda Mirage 1200

BELOW: Laverda 750 SF

ABOVE: The Laverda 750S of 1997 served a specialized sports market

projects in the early 1980s also swallowed capital, notably a 600/750cc (37/45cu in) triple that was based on half the V6, and a V3 two-stroke 350 that reached prototype form but ran into pollution and fuel consumption problems. Instead, the new owner (Prinefi, a Milan-based investment house) authorized work on an eight-valve V-twin, though this too came to nothing. Meanwhile, a 125cc two-stroke and 600cc twin-cylinder trail bike carried on. It wasn't until 1992 that the bike that would finally get Laverda properly up and running again appeared. It was an oil-cooled 668cc (41cu in) vertical twin, with Weber/Marelli fuel injection and around 70bhp at around 8,900rpm. Although not as powerful as the Japanese supersport 600s, the 650 did push Laverda back into the performance market. It was replaced by the 668 in 1996, basically the same bike, but with a broader spread of power, and joined by the naked Ghost. The following year came the substantially new water-cooled 750 twin, with 78bhp or 92bhp, and this machine takes Laverda through to the year 2000.

The man behind this new impetus was textile tycoon Francesco Tognon, who had taken over the company and injected fresh capital in 1994. There was talk of a successor to the original triple (water-cooled this time) for launch in September 1998. However, Laverda was no stranger to the company politics which had long been a part of the Italian bike industry. In early 1998, Tognon sold a part-share in the company to the Spezzapria brothers before later in the year departing to pursue other interests. All this delayed the new Jota, as it was known, but the company was confident of a September 1999 launch. In the meantime, a long-stroke version of the 750 twin, the 800TTS, was displayed at the October 1998 Munich Show, and is promised for production by the middle of 1999. All this was thrown into doubt in January 1999, when Francesco Tognon left to take over Bimota. Now in majority control, the Spezzapria brothers have revealed a prototype of the 899cc 135bhp water-cooled triple to attract new investment from outside. If that investment materializes, the reborn Laverda will be building on quite a legacy.

LAZZATI *Italy 1899–1904*
One of Italy's first manufacturers, it used De Dion engines.

L&C *England c.1904*
Fitted De Dion, Minerva and Antoine engines.

LDR *Germany 1922–25*
Produced its own 548cc (33cu in) sv single, with external flywheel.

The V6 racer with Massimo Laverda (left) – heavy but powerful

LEFT and ABOVE: The water-cooled Laverda V6 was designed for Endurance racing

LEA FRANCIS *England 1911–26*
Used JAP or MAG engines, usually V-twins. The famous writer and dramatist George Bernard Shaw rode one.

LECCE Italy 1930–32
Used 173cc (11cu in) ohv Moser engines, but with a modified valve layout.

LE FRANÇAIS-DIAMANT *France 1912–59*
Alcyon-owned, it built 98–498cc (6–30cu in) machines and, after 1945, small two-strokes only.

LEGNANO *Italy 1932–68*
First built under the Wolsit name and after the war made Garelli, Sachs or Mosquito-engined mopeds.

LE GRIMPEUR *France c.1900–32*
Produced a variety of machines from 98cc (6cu in) two-strokes to big V-twins with engines by MAG, JAP, Aubier-Dunne, Stainless, Chaise, etc.

LELIOR *France 1922–24*
A 174cc (11cu in) flat twin and 246cc (15cu in) single, both two-strokes.

LEM *Italy 1974*
Used Minarelli and Franco-Morini engines in mopeds and children's bikes.

LEONARD *England 1903–06*
Used Minerva, MMC and Fafnir engines.

LEONARDO FRERA *Italy 1930–34*
Used 173–346cc (11–21cu in) sv and ohv singles from JAP.

LEOPARD *Germany 1921–26*
Built own engines, both 248/346cc (15/21cu in) two-strokes and ohc singles.

LEPROTTO *Italy 1951–54*
Produced its own ohv singles of 123–198cc (7.5–12cu in) capacity.

LETHBRIDGE *England 1922–23*
Utilized 247 or 269cc (15 or 16cu in) Villiers power.

LETO *Germany 1926–28*
The pressed steel frame incorporated the fuel tank, with Rinne two-stroke engines.

LE VACK *England 1923*
A 346cc (21cu in) JAP-engined machine, built by famous rider Herbert (Bert) Le Vack.

LEVIS *England 1911–40*
A leading producer of two-strokes, conventional 211/245cc (13/15cu in) singles, as well as a six-port version and prototype flat twin. Produced ohv and ohc four-stroke singles as well.

LFG *Germany 1921–25*
The 163cc (10cu in) four-stroke powered wheel could be fitted to any bicycle. Odder was the 305cc (19cu in) two-stroke motorcycle with airship-like body.

LGC *England 1926–32*
A Villiers- or JAP-engined sportster.

ABOVE: A 1932 350 Levis

BELOW: Lilac produced upmarket lightweights

LIAUDOIS *France 1923–27*
Used Train two-strokes of 98–173cc (6–11cu in).

LIBERATOR *France 1902–c.1929*
Used mainly Antoine, Sarolea and JAP engines.

LIBERIA France 1920–65
98–248cc (6–15cu in) Aubier-Dunne-powered two-strokes.

LILAC *Japan 1949–67*
One of the longer-lived Japanese marques, Lilac began with a simple 148cc (9cu in) four-stroke, but soon went upmarket with a successful shaft-driven 90cc (5.5cu in) single, following it with a 339cc (21cu in) flat twin in 1954 and a 247cc (15cu in) V-twin in 1959, all shaft-driven. There was a 493cc (30cu in) flat twin from 1964.

LILIPUT Germany 1923–26
Used Namapo, DKW, Baumi, Gruhn and other bought-in engines.

LILLIPUT *Italy 1899–c.1906*
Produced one horsepower (285cc/17cu in) engines.

LILY England *1906–14*
Used Minerva, Villiers or T.D. Cross units to 499cc (30cu in).

LINCOLN-ELK *England 1902–24*
Used own sv singles designed by James Kirby, with a V-twin after World War I.

LINER *Japan 1955–56*
Another upmarket shaft-driven Japanese bike of up to 246cc (15cu in). Like Lilac

and Honda, the company learned to concentrate on the bikes that made most money for the company.

LINSER *Austria 1904–10*
Produced its own 492cc (30cu in) singles and 618cc (38cu in) V-twins. Also known under the Zeus name.

LINSNER *Germany 1922–24*
All flat twins, with Bosch-Douglas or early BMW power.

LINX *Italy 1929–1941*
Used 173–598cc (11–36cu in) singles from Blackburne, Piazza, JAP and there was also a four-valve Python.

LION-RAPIDE *Belgium 1936–53*
Used Villiers, Ilo and FN singles up to 347cc (21cu in).

LITTLE GIANT *England 1913–15*
225cc (14cu in) two-strokes and 199cc (12cu in) sv singles.

LLOYD *England 1903–23*
Heavy sidevalves, with own 499cc (30cu in) singles and 842cc (51cu in) V-twins.

LLOYD *Germany 1922–26*
Its sole model was a 144cc (9cu in) two-stroke.

LLOYD *Germany 1923–26*
A 137cc (8cu in) clip-on, then JAP-engined mid-size bikes using many English parts.

LLOYD *The Netherlands 1930–31*
Bought in both its engines (DKW) and most of the pressed steel frame (Hulla).

LMP *France 1921–31*
Produced two- and four-strokes of up to 497cc (30cu in).

LMS *Germany 1923*
Another ex-airship builder which, like its compatriot LFG, attempted to apply airship-shaped bodies to motorcycles. Not many were made.

LOCOMOTIEF *The Netherlands 1952–66*
Pluvier and Sachs-powered mopeds.

LOHNER *Austria 1950–58*
Made scooters with Sachs or Ilo two-stroke power.

LOMOS *Germany 1922–24*
Early scooter with a pressed steel frame made by DKW and later by Eichler. Used a DKW two-stroke engine of 142cc (9cu in).

LONDON *England c.1903*
De Dion, Minerva and MMC engine power.

LORD *Germany 1929–31*
Used a 198cc (12cu in) JAP sv engine.

LORENZ *Germany 1921–1922*
A short-lived early scooter of 211cc (13cu in).

LORENZ *Germany 1921–25*
Perhaps the only twin-cylinder clip-on, a 126cc (8cu in) flat twin on in-house frame.

LOT *Poland 1937*
Advanced 346cc (21cu in) two-stroke with unit-construction and shaft-drive.

LOUIS CLÉMENT *France 1920–32*
Produced its own 598/996cc (36/61cu in) ohc V-twins, but a 98cc (6cu in) two-stroke only from 1928.

LOUIS JANIOR *France 1921–24*
A 499cc (30cu in) sv flat twin.

LUBE *Spain 1949–65*
Used NSU two- and four-strokes up to 249cc (15cu in), then its own two-strokes when NSU closed.

LUCAS *Germany 1923–24*
First utilized a Bekamo two-stroke, then its own 148cc (9cu in) ohv single.

LUCER *France 1953–56*
Used a 173cc (11cu in) AMC ohv, or Aubier-Dunne two-strokes.

LUCIFER *France 1928–56*
Bought-in engines from Train, MAG and Chaise.

LUDOLPH *Germany 1924–26*
Designed its own two-strokes of up to 299cc (18cu in).

LUGTON *England 1912–14*
Used 498cc (30cu in) Precision or JAP engines.

LUJAN *Argentina 1946*
Used various brand names for its sub-125cc (8cu in) lightweights, some licence-built from Malaguti.

LUPUS *Germany 1923–26*
Its sole model was its own 148cc (9cu in) two-stroke.

LUTÈCE *France 1921–26*
Some of the few French big bikes, they were large vertical twins of 997 and 1016cc (61 and 62cu in), with shaft-drive.

LUTRAU *Germany 1924–33*
Built its own two-strokes of 198–346cc (12–21cu in), and also a 497cc (30cu in) sv single.

LUTZ *Germany 1949–54*
Mostly produced 49cc (3cu in) scooters and mopeds, though there was also a 173cc (11cu in) scooter.

LUWE *Germany 1924–28*
Bought-in engines from Paqué, JAP, MAG and Blackburne.

LWD *Germany 1923–26*
In-house 197/247cc (12/15cu in) sv singles.

M

MABECO *Germany 1923–27*
Actually a copy of the Indian Scout, with engines supplied by Max Bernhardt & Co. of Berlin (596cc and 749cc/36 and 46cu inch sv V-twins). From 1925 there was a 728cc (44cu in) ohv version.

MABON *England c.1905*
Used MMC, Fafnir and its own engines.

MABRET Germany *1927–28*
Used only Kühne engines, both 346cc and 496cc (21 and 30cu in).

MACKLUM *England 1920–22*
2.5hp Peco two-strokes were used in this scooter-like machine.

MACO *Germany 1921–26*
Used own engines as well as DKWs.

MACQUET *France 1951–54*
Produced a 125cc (8cu in) clip-on.

MAFA *Germany 1923–27*
Used 119–246cc (7–15cu in) DKW and 348/496cc (21/30cu in) Kühne units.

MAFALDA *Italy 1923–28*
Built own three-port two-strokes to 173cc (11cu in).

MAFFEIS *Italy 1903–35*
First used a 2.25hp Sarolea, then designed its own singles and V-twins before finally using Blackburne engines. The Maffeis brothers raced their own bikes.

MAGATY *France 1931–37*
98cc (6cu in) two-strokes, powered by Train and Stainless units.

MAGDA *France 1933–36*
98/123cc (6/7.5cu in) two-strokes.

MAGNAT-DEBON *France 1906–58*
Started with Moser and Moto-Rêve singles and V-twins before designing its own engines after World War I. It was taken over by Terrot in 1924, and thereafter was used as a badge only. The Magnat-Moser subsidiary at Genoble used a V-twin Moser only.

MAGNEET *The Netherlands 1950s–early 1970s*
Moped maker, mainly using Sachs power.

MAGNET *Germany 1901–24*
Built own ioe and sv engines, including a 4.5hp V-twin.

ABOVE: An early post-war Maico

BELOW: A 420cc (26cu in) motocrosser

MAGNI *Italy 1928–30*
An ohc 348cc (21cu in) twin and 498cc (30cu in) single.

MAICO *Germany 1926–83*
Began with mopeds and lightweights fitted with 98/123cc (6/7.5cu in) Sachs and Ilo engines. Switched to making aircraft parts in the 1930s, and resumed motorcycle production in 1948 with its own 123cc two-stroke. Was soon offering a full range of small/mid-sized bikes including the fully-faired Maico-Mobil and Maicoletta touring scooter. From the late 1950s concentrated increasingly on off-road competition, which underpinned its fortunes right to the end. It built two-stroke motocross and enduro bikes

OPPOSITE: Maicos won World Motocross Championships

75

ABOVE: A Maico two-stroke scrambler

and won the Manufacturers World Championship, though continued to build road bikes (both singles and twins) right through to the early 1980s. The motocrossers developed bigger engines (including a 48bhp 501cc) with water-cooling, disc-valves and trailing link forks. Maico went bankrupt in 1983 which spelt the end of all production, though another company bought the name.

MAINO *Italy 1902–56*
Intermittent production, but used 2.25hp Souverain engines and Sachs and NSU power after 1945.

MAJESTIC *France 1927–34*
Used Train, Chaise and JAP engines and was notable for a 498cc (30cu in) four-cylinder bike with full bodywork, car-like chassis and rear suspension.

MAJESTIC *Belgium 1928–31*
Made from English components, this machine was fitted with 346cc and 490cc (21 and 30cu in) single-cylinder sv and ohv JAP engines, with Burman gearboxes and other proprietary parts.

MAJESTIC *England 1931–35*
When the London-based Collier brothers of Matchless fame bought AJS, the parts department was bought by Ernie Humphries, boss of OK-Supreme of Birmingham. He built slightly modified AJS bikes and called them Majestics, most versions having 348cc and 498cc (21 and 30cu in) ohv engines.

MAJOR *Italy 1947–48*
Own 347cc (21cu in) engine, fully enclosed with shaft-drive.

MALAGUTI *Italy 1945–*
First mopeds used 38cc (2.3cu in) Garelli Mosquito engines, then units from Sachs and Franco-Morini. It still concentrates on mopeds and scooters, now up to 100cc (6cu in), both air- and water-cooled, notably the retro-styled Yesterday.

MALANCA *Italy 1956–86*
124/149cc (8/9cu in) two-stroke twins, as well as mopeds.

MAMMUT *Germany 1925–33*
Built Coventry-Eagle pressed steel frames under licence, with own two-strokes, and also used Villiers, Baumi and Blackburne engines.

MAMMUT *Germany 1953–56*
No connection to the above. Used Sachs and Ilo engines of 49–198cc (3–12cu in).

MAMOF *Germany 1922–24*
DKW and Grade-powered two-strokes, plus own 155cc (9.5cu in) sv single.

MANET *Czechoslovakia 1948–67*
Produced an 89cc (5.4cu in) double-pistoned two-stroke single, later 123cc (7.5cu in) scooters.

MANON *France 1903–c.1906*
Own 1.5hp engines.

MANTOVANI *Italy 1902–10*
1.5–4hp machines, some of which were in-house and water-cooled.

MANUFRANCE *France 1951–55*
Lightweights and scooters with 124/174cc (8/11cu in) engines.

MANURHIN *France 1955–62*
Took over production of the Hobby scooter after DKW dropped it.

MARC *France 1926–51*
Unremarkable bikes with Staub-JAP and LMP engines.

MARCK *Belgium 1904–08*
499cc (30cu in) ioe singles.

MARIANI *Italy 1930–34*
Made a 486cc (30cu in) single in two-valve form for the road, or with three valves if one chose to run it on naptha.

MARINI *Italy 1924–28*
124cc (8cu in) two-strokes.

MARLOE *England 1920–22*
Step-through frames with Precision or Blackburne engines.

MARLOW *England 1920–22*
346cc and 409cc (21 and 25cu in) JAP-engined machines, built to order.

MARMONNIER *France 1947–51*
Usually came supplied with Aubier-Dunne engines.

MARS (MA) *Germany 1903–57*
Built Fafnir and Zedel-engined bikes before World War I, but was most famous for the 986cc (60cu in) white Mars of 1920. The big flat-twin engine was supplied by Maybach and there was a two-speed gearbox and leg guards. German inflation killed it, but Mars was revived as MA with a variety of bought-in engines, concentrating in the 1930s on Sachs-powered mopeds and clip-ons. It used Sachs engines of up to 198cc/12cu inches up to the end for its well-made lightweights and mopeds.

MARS *England 1905–08*
Fitted Fafnir engines (as did the German Mars company) as well as the 211cc (13cu in) Minerva unit.

MARS *England 1923–26*
Used a variety of engines such as Bradshaws, Barr & Strouds and the inevitable Villiers.

MARSH *U.S.A. 1901–06*
Built its own singles and V-twins and was later known as MM.

MARSEEL England 1920–21
A 232cc (14cu in) scooter.

MARTIN *England 1911–22*
Fitted Precision and JAP engines to 498cc (30cu in).

MARTIN *Japan 1956–61*
Used bought-in two-strokes of 124–246cc (8–15cu in).

MARTINA *Italy 1924–57*
Built own 173cc (11cu in) two-strokes.

MARTINSHAW *England 1923–24*
Limited production using the Bradshaw 346cc (21cu in) single.

MARTINSYDE *England 1919–25*
Had its own range of ioe singles and V-twins of 346cc to 676cc (21 to 41cu in). When it closed, BAT bought what was left.

MARUSHO *Japan 1964–67*
A rebadged Lilac 493cc (30cu in) flat twin for the U.S. market. It had poor sales.

MARVEL *U.S.A. 1910–13*
Used Curtiss single-cylinder and V-twin engines.

MAS *Italy 1920–56*
Designed and built its own engines until the last few years, starting with small four-strokes which grew to 498cc (30cu in) during the 1930s. A modern 492cc vertical twin was added, as well as the Lupatta, MAS's first two-stroke. After the war, the 122cc (7.4cu in) Stella Alpina and ohc vertical twin were unsuccessful, though the company did better with the 173cc (11cu in) ohv Zenith and a Sachs-powered mini-scooter.

MAS *Germany 1923–24*
A 183cc (11cu in) two-stroke.

MASCOTTE *France 1923–24*
A 174cc (11cu in) sv lightweight.

MASERATI *Italy 1953–61*
Maserati's bikes never achieved the fame of its cars but a 123cc (7.5cu in) two-stroke and an ohc 248cc (15cu in) vertical twin were produced.

MASON & BROWN *England 1904–c.1908*
Used De Dion, Antoine, but mainly the 2hp Minerva engine.

MASSEY *England 1920–31*
Lightweights up to 490cc (30cu in). E.J. Massey also designed the first HRDs.

MAT *Czechoslovakia 1929–30*
Produced the 498cc (30cu in) Votroubek, similar to the Ariel Square Four but sv, with shaft-drive.

MATADOR *Germany 1922–27*
Blackburne or Bradshaw engines for this Bert Houlding-designed bike.

MATADOR *Germany 1925–26*
Own 369cc (22.5cu in) two-strokes.

MATCHLESS *England 1899–1966*
Matchless was unusual in the British motorcycle industry in that it operated outside the West Midlands, being established instead in Plumstead, South London. It was also one of the first marques in the business, H.H. Collier having been a maker of bicycles until joined in 1899 by his two eldest sons, Charlie and Harry, when he built his first motorized version. Matchless motorcycles would rarely show much innovation (with one or two notable exceptions) but built on commercial success by taking over no less than five rivals over the years, only for the whole construction to come to an undignified collapse in the mid-1960s. This was the first tangible sign that the British industry was heading for oblivion.

All this was in the future when the

ABOVE: Martinsyde built its own engines and survived for nearly seven years

BELOW: A 1939 Matchless 350cc (21cu in) G3

Colliers added a V-twin to their range in 1905, and which was to feature right up to 1939. It was powered by a bought-in engine, and indeed Matchless would not start making its own engines on a large scale until the 1920s. That first V-twin was quite advanced for its time, with leading-link forks and a type of swinging-arm rear supension. Both Charlie and Harry were keen racers, and enjoyed some success riding it. Charlie actually won the first-ever Isle of Man TT race in 1907, his single-cylinder JAP-engined machine averaging 61.5km/h (38.22mph), not to mention fuel consumption of over 32km per litre (90mpg). Sibling rivalry was satisfied in 1909 when Harry won the TT, though Charlie snatched it back the following year. The two were also successful at Brooklands, riding Matchless bikes, of course.

Meanwhile, the road bikes were developing, with a three-speed hub gear added in 1912, which sadly meant dropping the innovative spring frame. Given the company's involvement in racing, there was also an adjustable engine pulley available to give two ranges and in theory six speeds, and belt tension was maintained by moving the rear wheel backwards. Also that year came the Colliers' first in-house engine, a four-stroke single of almost square 85.5mm x 85mm dimensions, though it lasted only a couple of years. Perhaps more successful were V-twins like the 8B, which now used an ioe V-twin built by MAG of Switzerland, and up-to-the-minute three-speed gearbox and enclosed chain-drive.

During World War I, Matchless did not supply motorcycles to the army, but went over to making munitions and aircraft parts. Still, it did patriotically rename its V-twin the 'Victorious' in 1918. The civilian twins went back into production, now updated with electric lights and a return of the spring frame; but it wasn't until 1923 that a single rejoined the range. Once again, the engine came from outside, a 348cc (21cu in) sidevalve Blackburne, though the company's own 591cc (36cu in) single went into production the following year. It had been a while since there had been a sporting Matchless, and the 347cc overhead-camshaft single looked like it. Unfortunately, it only developed 13bhp, and although it remained in production for a short time, it was soon overshadowed by sharper ohc bikes from Velocette and others.

Undaunted, Matchless designed its own V-twin in 1925, a 990cc (60cu in) sidevalve that owed much to the 591cc single. Perhaps it was on more familiar ground here, for it was more of a success and stayed in production right up to 1939. It was followed by the company's smallest bike yet, a 250 sidevalve, the model R. At around this time H.H. Collier died, and shortly afterwards the family relinquished its control and Matchless went public. For 1927, the whole range was given a new look, with white-panelled fuel tanks in the new-style saddles, and meanwhile the range had grown to include 347 and 495cc (21 and 30cu in) ohv singles, followed by a 250cc (15cu in) ohv (the R3) in 1929.

All of these, however, were highly conventional bikes, though it has to be said that it was probably this full range of uncomplicated good-value machines that saw Matchless through the Depression. But the Silver Arrow of 1930 was

A 1958 Matchless 650cc (40cu in) G12

ABOVE and BELOW: The 650cc (40cu in) G12 was Matchless' answer to BSA's A10 and Triumph's Thunderbird, but in comparison was not a success

ABOVE: Ernie Dorsett's diesel-powered G80

anything but conventional. Quiet, well-mannered and with clean lines, the Silver Arrow was a narrow-angled V-twin of 398cc (24cu in). It continued Matchless' love of sprung rear frames but, as ever, the conservative public could not take to it. The same was true of the Silver Hawk which followed it a year later, a V4 along similar lines, with overhead camshaft and 593cc. Like the Arrow, it was much discussed, generating a good deal of interest but few sales.

So perhaps it was with a cynical eye on the fickle yet conservative public that Matchless turned its attention to sprucing up the singles in the latest style (sloping cylinders) and probably sold more bikes as a result. The company certainly hadn't suffered too much from the Arrow/Hawk failures, and was able to take over AJS in 1931. In 1935 it introduced the famous G range of singles (first named Clubman), with either ohv or sidevalve engines, which grew into a range of 250, 350 and 500cc by 1938, the year Matchless also swallowed Sunbeam (only to sell it on to BSA a few years later). And it was the 350cc (21.4cu in) Matchless G3 that became the staple transport of the British Army from 1939. Two years later, in the midst of war, Matchless was to exhibit another one of its rare moments of innovation, with the Teledraulic telescopic fork. It wasn't a wholly new idea, but the Matchless version, with oil damping, was sufficiently new to be patented. (After the war, as all other manufactures rushed to build their own telescopics, it was clear that this time Matchless had got there first.)

Forks or not, Matchless' first post-war bikes were civilianized G singles, though the new G9 500cc (30.5cu in) twin appeared in 1948, complete with swinging-arm rear suspension with the company's own 'jampot' suspension units. A racing version, the G45, won the Senior Manx Grand Prix in 1952. That was the year Matchless (now Associated Motor Cycles, or AMC) bought up Norton and James. (Francis-Barnett had had already joined in 1947 and Brockhouse Engineering in 1959.) This combination of famous names, all of which would be concentrated at Plumstead, became renowned for badge engineering; in other words, whether you bought an AJS or Matchless made no difference as only the badge (and maybe the colour) could tell them apart.

In the spirit of the times, the twins grew in size and sporting aspirations with the 592cc (36cu in) G11, 646cc (39cu in) G12 and the tuned G12 CSR. There was also a new 250cc single, the G2, while the G45 racer was dropped to make way for the G50 ohc single (really an enlarged AJS 7R). The 650 twins were supplemented by 750s in the early 1960s, but in keeping with strategy, the engines came from Norton. This sharing of parts actually made economic sense, and perhaps in different circumstances might have helped save AMC. As it was, the finances were in such a mess that a receiver was called in in 1966. Manganese Bronze Holdings stepped in to form the new Norton-Villiers Ltd., and for a couple of years produced Matchless-badged bikes that were really Nortons. Its real hopes, however, lay with the new Norton Commando, and with that Matchless finally died.

BELOW and RIGHT: Matchless G80 500cc singles

The 592cc (36cu in) G11 was not a sporting bike, but it was a flexible tourer

MATRA *Hungary 1938–47*
98 or 198cc (6 or 12cu in) Sachs and Ardie two-strokes.

MAURER *Germany 1922–26*
Built its own two-strokes, including a 1.5hp clip-on, 247cc (15cu in) vertical twin, and 494cc (30cu in) water-cooled flat twin.

MAUSER *Germany 1924–32*
The most car-like bike ever, the Einspurauto used a car-type body and chassis, with two retractable outrigger wheels to keep it upright when stationary. At 289kg (638lb) it was rather heavy for its 10bhp, 510cc (31cu in) sv single. Mauser didn't sell many, though French firm Monotrace made them under licence.

MAVISA *Spain 1957–60*
Upmarket two-stroke twin with shaft-drive.

MAWI *Germany 1923–30*
Used bought-in two-stroke DKW and four-stroke JAP engines to 546cc (33cu in).

MAX *Germany 1924–25*
Produced a 180cc (11cu in) two-stroke and 446cc (27cu in) sv single, both in-house.

MAX *France 1927–30*
Used a variety of bought-in engines to 496cc (30cu in).

MAXIM *England 1919–21*
Fitted 318cc (19.4cu in) Dalm single-cylinder two-strokes.

MAXIMA *Italy 1920–25*
Built its own big flat twins of 690/747cc (42/46cu in).

MAZZUCHELLI *Italy 1925–28*
Imported the 198cc (12cu in) Alba engine to power its simple machine.

MB *Czechoslovakia 1927–28*
A rotary-valve 498cc (30cu in) single, in which the valve controlled both inlet and exhaust.

MB *U.S.A. 1916–20*
Advanced for its time, it was a 746cc (45.5cu in) vertical-twin with shaft-drive.

MBM *Italy 1974–81*
Minarelli-engined mopeds.

MCB *Sweden 1960–75*
The Monark Crescent Bolagen group, the result of Monark's takeover of other Swedish makes.

MCC *England 1903–c.1910*
Used De Dion, Minerva and other engines, and built its own under licence from Minerva.

McEVOY *England 1926–29*
Started with a Villiers-engined lightweight, then used Blackburne and JAP engines plus Anzani big V-twins. Designer George Patchett (ex-Brough-Superior, pre-Jawa) produced a prototype 346cc (21cu in) three-valve ohc single and 498cc (30cu in) in-line four.

McKECHNIE *England 1922*
688cc (42cu in) Coventry-Victor flat twin, with rear suspension.

McKENZIE *England 1921–25*
196cc (12cu in) two-strokes in conventional or step-through frames.

MDS *Italy 1955–60*
Modern unit-construction four-stroke singles of 65–80cc (4–5cu in).

MEAD *England 1911–16*
Wide range of machines, with engines from Precision, JAP and Premier.

MEGOLA *Germany 1921–25*
Perhaps the oddest motorcycle ever to reach production, the Megola mounted a five-cylinder radial engine (640cc/39cu in) within the front wheel. No clutch, no gears, and the only way to alter the direct-drive ratio was to purchase a different sized wheel. There was no room in the front wheel for a brake, so the maker fitted two to the rear. It could top 113km/h (70mph) on the road (racers managed 137km/h/85mph) and some had rear suspension. The low centre of gravity gave good handling, and Megola actually sold nearly 200 of them.

MEGURO *Japan 1937–64*
Mainly English-influenced singles up to 498cc (30cu in) and a copy of the BSA A10 twin from 1961. Taken over by Kawasaki late in its life.

MEIHATSU *Japan 1953–61*
Kawasaki subsidiary, with two-strokes up to 248cc (15cu in).

MEISTER *Germany 1951–56*
All two-stroke lightweights and mopeds of 49–198cc (3–12cu in).

MEMINI *Italy 1946–47*
Own 173cc (11cu in) two-stroke.

MENON *Italy 1930–32*
Small tourers, with 174 and 198cc (11 and 12cu in) sv singles.

MENOS *Germany 1922–23*
Almost identical to the Aristos, with the same water-cooled 614cc (37.5cu in) flat twin.

MERAY *Hungary 1921–44*
A wide variety of bought-in engines were used by this leading Hungarian company, with its own singles from 1936.

MERCIER *France 1950–62*
Used engines from Lafalette, Villiers and Ydral.

MERCO *Germany 1922–24*
Own 148cc (9cu in) three-port two-strokes.

MERCURY England 1956–58
Lightweights and scooters up to 98cc (6cu in).

MERKEL *U.S.A. 1901–22*
Built own singles and V-twins up to 986cc (60cu in) before takeover by Indian.

MERLI *Italy 1929–31*
Used 173cc (11cu in) Train two-strokes.

MERLONGHI *Italy 1927–30*
132cc (8cu in) two-stroke, two-speed machines.

METEOR *Czechoslovakia 1909–26*
211cc (13cu in) clip-ons, then utility two-stroke lightweights.

METEOR *Germany 1924–26*
Used a 172cc (10.5cu in) two-stroke, possibly imported from Thumann of France.

METEORA *Italy 1953–66*
Used various bought-in engines for these lightweights, which included a motocross bike.

METRO *England 1912–19*
269cc (16cu in) two-stroke with two- or three-speed gearbox.

Sales brochure for the Meguro range

MEYBEIN *Germany 1922–26*
Bike with low-slung frame and 119/142cc (7/9cu in) DKW power.

MEYBRA *Germany 1923–25*
Used own 168cc (10cu in) two-stroke.

MEZO *Austria 1923–26*
Used imported Villiers and JAP engines for a limited production run.

MF *Germany 1922–25*
First used BMW's early flat twin, later Blackburne singles to 497cc (30cu in).

MFB *Germany 1923–24*
Wooden frames distinguished MFB from the rest, with 198cc (12cu in) Nabob or 293cc (18cu in) JAP units.

MGC *France 1927–29*
Had a light alloy frame which incoporated the fuel tank and was JAP or Chaise-powered.

MGF *Italy 1921–25*
Used bought-in Bekamo engines, but also made its own and sold them to others.

MG/TAURUS *Italy 1926–50*
Founded by Vittorio Guerzoni, who first used 173cc (11cu in) Train engines before building his own 248/496cc (15/30cu in) ohv, and later ohc singles. From 1933 also sold under the Taurus name, and when taken over by the Bergamini brothers after the war they sold the 250/500cc (15/30.5cu in) machines under the Centaurus name.

MIAMI *U.S.A. 1905–23*
Connected with Merkel, it also built its own 298cc (18cu in) sv singles.

MICHAELSON *U.S.A. 1910–15*
Advanced singles and V-twins with ohv, leaf-sprung forks and chain-drive.

MIDGET-BICAR *U.S.A. 1908–1909*
A welded and riveted steel frame was powered by a big V-twin – not a success.

MIELE *Germany 1933–62*
Began fitting Sachs engines to its bicycles, and after 1945 remained loyal to Sachs to power its mopeds and lightweights.

MIGNON *Italy 1923–32*
123cc (7.5cu in) clip-ons led to a 246cc (15cu in) sv twin, then a 498cc (30cu in) single with either ohv or ohc.

MILANI *Italy 1970–81*
Built mopeds and off-road bikes, Minarelli-powered. Many were exported to the U.S.A.

MILITAIRE *U.S.A. 1911–17*
One of the American in-line fours, though at 1306cc (80cu in) it was one of the biggest. It had a one-piece frame, three-speed plus reverse gearbox and leaf-sprung rear-end. The Militaire was built by no less than eight companies in its short history.

MILLER *U.S.A. c.1903*
Over the years there were numerous small motorcycle companies which quickly came and went during the industry's formative years. This is one of them and there is little evidence of its existence beyond yellowing advertisements in old cycling magazines.

MILLER-BALSAMO *Italy 1921–59*
First used 123cc (7.5cu in) two-strokes, but was soon building four-valve Python singles under licence. Later there was a 98cc (6cu in) Sachs-engined lightweight and fully-enclosed 198cc (12cu in) bike. Concentrated on two-strokes after 1945, apart from slightly updated pre-war singles and an ohc 169cc (10cu in) single.

ABOVE and RIGHT: The Miller was an American pioneer

MILLIONMOBILE *England c.1902*
1.5hp engine in a cycle frame.

MIMOA *Germany 1924*
Used the Julius Löwy-designed two-stroke that would run on crude oil.

MINERVA *Belgium 1900–09*
Prolific engine maker which sold its power units (and the licences to make them) all over the world, but also made complete bikes up to 1909. There was a motorized cycle in 1900, culminating in a 580cc (35cu in) V-twin by 1909.

MINETTI *Italy 1924–1927*
124cc (8cu in) three-port two-stroke.

MINEUR *Belgium 1924–28*
Paul Mineur built his own 348/496cc (21/30cu in) sv singles, as well as using JAP, Bradshaw, MAG and Sarolea units.

MINISCOOT *France 1960–62*
A folding 74cc (4.5cu in) two-stroke mini-scooter.

MINNEAPOLIS *U.S.A. 1908–15*
Used various V-twins as well as its own unit-construction sv single. It had early chain-drive and (according to one source) telescopic forks.

MINSK *Russia 1954–*
Another version of the much-copied DKW 125, this one updated over the years. Five million have been sold.

MIRANDA *Germany 1951–54*
Scooter with 173cc (11cu in) Sachs or 198cc (12cu in) Küchen power.

MISTRAL *France 1902–early 1960s*
Started with a 1.75hp bike, and remained with lightweights up to 247cc (15cu in) after World War II. Also supplied moped engines to others.

MITCHELL *U.S.A. 1901–c.1906*
345cc (21cu in) single with rearward-facing cylinder.

MI-VAL *Italy 1950–66*
123cc (7.5cu in) two-stroke followed by four-strokes up to 199cc (12cu in).

MIYATA *Japan 1909–64*
One of the few pre-war Japanese makes offering 123cc (7.5cu in) two-stroke, mid-sized four-stroke singles, and 496cc (30cu in) vertical twins.

MJ *Germany 1924–25*
Its own 249cc (15cu in) two-stroke never reached full production, but MJ supplied flat twins to other manufacturers.

MJS *Germany 1924–25*
Built its own 245cc (15cu in) three-port two-strokes.

MM *U.S.A. 1905–c.1914*
Used a variety of bought-in engines from Thomas, Marsh, Royal, Holley and Pope.

MM *Italy 1924–64*
Concentrated on racers until producing its first road bikes in the 1930s. They were ohv and sv singles up to 498cc (30cu in), but were still heavily biased towards racing. One of the founders was Alfonso Morini who left in 1937 to set up his own firm. After 1945, MM based its 350 and 500cc (21 and 30.5cu in) singles on pre-war designs, though there was also a new ohc 250. Also made a 125cc (8cu in) two-stroke in its final years.

M&M *England 1914*
Step-through frame with 169cc (10cu in) Villiers engine.

MMM *Germany 1925–27*
148cc (9cu in) two-stroke machines.

MOCHET *France 1950–55*
149cc (9cu in) Ydral-powered lightweights.

MOFA *Germany 1920–25*
Clip-ons of 70 and 148cc (4.3 and 9cu in).

MOHAWK *England 1903–25*
Pioneered with 2.5/3hp engines, then withdrew until the 1920s to have another attempt at using a wide range of bought-in engines, including a 346cc (21cu in) JAP.

MOLARONI *Italy 1921–27*
Built its own 269cc (16cu in) two-stroke and 596cc (36cu in) flat twin (which had automatic lubrication). On one model, also used the Blackburne 348cc (21cu in) single.

MOLTENI *Italy 1925–27*
Forward-thinking use of aluminium alloy for the frame, fork and chain cases and with Bradshaw or MAG power. Not a success.

MONACO-BAUDO *Italy 1926–28*
Own unit-construction single of 496cc (30cu in), though later used bought-in JAP and Blackburne engines.

MONARCH *U.S.A. 1912–25*
Another North American factory which produced 496cc (30cu in) singles and 990cc (60cu in) V-twins with its own ioe engines in sprung frames.

MONARCH *England 1919–21*
A cheaper version of the Excelsior, Villiers-powered.

MONARCH *Japan 1955–62*
Ohv singles of 346/496cc (21/30cu in), with Norton influence.

MONARK *Sweden 1927–75*
Actually built its first bike in 1913, but the Monark name was not used until 1927 on a range of Blackburne-engined singles to 600cc (37cu in). Built a 98cc (6cu in) Ilo-powered lightweight from 1936, and Albin 500cc four-strokes for the Swedish army during World War II. Concentrated largely on Ilo-engined lightweights of 50–250cc

The Montesa was an important marque for Spain

(3–15cu in) and some 500cc machines with British parts after the war until production ceased in 1975.

MONFORT *Spain 1957–59*
123/197cc (7.5/12cu in) Hispano-Villiers two-strokes.

MONOPOLE *England 1911–28*
Used Abingdon, JAP or Villiers engines to 680cc (41.5cu in).

MONOTRACE *France 1926–28*
Licence-built version of the German Mauser car-like bike.

MONTEROSA *Italy 1954–58*
Made 49cc (3cu in) mopeds only.

MONTESA *Spain 1945–*
Spain's first major marque, the company was founded by Francesco Bulto and Pedro Permanyer and has always built its own two-strokes. Started with a 98cc (6cu in) lightweight, which was soon followed by a 125cc (8cu in). Montesa also found its niche in off-road competition, and was a dominant force there for many years. Bulto left in 1958 to set up Bultaco, but 1962 saw the unveiling of the Impala, with an all-new 175cc (11cu in) engine. A 250cc (15cu in) and racing versions followed. Alongside all of this, Montesa continued to make road-going two-strokes of up to 349cc (21cu in). Sales collapsed at the end of the 1970s, but even the successful relaunch of the Impala in 1981 couldn't prevent a Honda takeover. Montesa still makes its own Cota trials bike, and assembles small Hondas.

MONTGOMERY *England 1902–39*
Always used bought-in engines, from Villiers to Anzani, though from the mid-1930s only mid-sized JAP singles were used, notably in the sporting Greyhound model. Also built frames for Brough-Superior and P&P.

MONTLHÉRY *Austria 1926–28*
A 346cc (21cu in) JAP-powered machine.

MONVISO *Italy 1951–56*
All bikes utilized Sachs engines of 98–173cc (6–11cu in).

MOONBEAM *England 1920–21*
Romantic name for a 296cc (18cu in) Villiers-powered utility.

MORETTI *Italy 1934–52*
Limited production, but with engines from Ladetto, DKW and JAP as well as ohc units after 1945.

MORRIS *England 1902–05*
Lord Nuffield (William Morris) built motorcycles before achieving a fortune and knighthood from producing cars. Used 2.75hp De Dion or MMC engines.

MORRIS *England 1913–22*
Made 247cc (15cu in) three-port two-strokes. No connection with the above.

MORRIS-WARNE *England 1922*
A 248cc (15cu in) two-stroke, oddly offered with a vertical or horizontal cylinder.

MORS (SPEED) *France 1951–56*
Scooters from 60cc to 124cc (4 to 8cu in), produced in part of the original Mors car factory.

MORSE-BEAUREGARD *U.S.A. 1912–17*
Advanced unit-construction in-line twin, with shaft-drive.

MORTON-ADAM *England 1923–24*
Built 292cc (18cu in) two-strokes, and 248/348cc (15/21cu in) ohc singles designed by Harry Sidney.

MOSER *Switzerland 1905–35*
Built a complete range of bikes from 123–598cc (7.5–36.5cu in), and supplied ready-made power units to many rival factories. Most of these were ohv singles, especially the 123/173cc (7.5/11cu in) units.

MOSER *Austria 1953–54*
Used a 98cc (6cu in) Rotax engine, and was the forerunner of KTM.

MOTAG *Germany 1923–24*
An interesting machine, its frame was made of electron and there was the option of air- or water-cooling for its vertical twins of 514, 642 and 804cc (31.4, 39 and 49cu in).

MOTA-WIESEL *Germany 1948–52*
Small-wheeled scooter of 74–98cc (4.5-6cu in).

MOTOBÉCANE (MBK) *France 1923–*
Long-lived French factory, which changed its name to MBK in 1984 and has recently been taken over by Yamaha. Began with low-cost 172cc (10.5cu in) belt-driven two-strokes which were soon joined by one of 308cc (19cu in). Also introduced 'Moto Confort', under which name Motobécanes were also sold. It made four-stroke singles of 172–498cc (10.5–30cu in) in the twenties and thirties, and in-line ohc fours (biggest was 749cc/46cu in) with shaft-drive. Smaller ohv singles remained in production until 1960. Most popular post-war product was the 49cc (3cu in) Mobylette, though motorcycle production ceased in 1964 only to restart five years later. There was a 125 two-stroke and 350 triple in the 1970s, but the company has really concentrated on mopeds. The Yamaha takeover means that MBK will make Yamaha mopeds for Europe bearing either badge.

MOTOBI *Italy 1950–80*
Giovanni Benelli left the family firm to set up MotoBi, whose trademark was the horizontal-cylinder, egg-shaped power unit. Began with 98cc (6cu in) two-strokes, progressing to 248cc (15cu in) and from 1956 produced 123/172cc (7.5/10.5cu in) four-strokes. MotoBi was re-absorbed by Benelli in 1962 when Giuseppe Benelli died, and after a while the bikes became rebadged Benellis, the MotoBi tradename being used up to 1980.

MOTOBIC *Spain 1949–65*
Produced mopeds and a 122cc (7.5cu in) lightweight and later made the Agrati Capri scooter under licence.

MOTOBIMM *Italy 1969–71*
Limited production of Minarelli-powered 49cc (3cu in) motocross and trials bikes.

MOTOBLOC *France 1948–54*
Produced mopeds, the 65cc (4cu in) Sulky scooter and lightweight motorcycles up to 248cc (15cu in), the latter with two-stroke or AMC four-stroke singles.

The 1949 Motoleggera: Moto Guzzi later had to abandon its enthusiast machines for a while

Moto Guzzi Falcone

MOTO-BORGO *Italy 1906–26*
Built big singles in the early days up to 827cc (50.5cu in), but developed a 990cc (60cu in) V-twin during World War I. Later produced a unit-construction 477cc (29cu in) V-twin, which could be had with four-valve heads. The Borgo brothers stopped making motorcyles in 1926 to concentrate on piston-making.

MOTOCLETTE *Switzerland 1904–15*
Fitted with Zedel and Moser engines.

MOTO GELIS *Argentina c.1955–62*
Licence-built 125cc (8cu in) Sachs engines, with other parts from Italy.

MOTO GUZZI *Italy 1921–*
Soichiro Honda, Michio Suzuki, Bill Harley and the Davidson brothers – many motorcycle companies still bear the names of their original founders, and Moto Guzzi is no exception. As World War I came to its final stages, Carlo Guzzi had played his part in Italy's new Air Corps, but his real love was motorcycles. He was an instinctive designer and given to producing innovative ideas. However, there was one small flaw in the Guzzi dream of a new career in motorcycling – he came from a poor Milanese family and there was no money.

It is at this point that the origins of Moto Guzzi begin to sound like a fairy tale. Among Carlo's friends were two well-heeled young flying officers, Giorgio Parodi and Giovanni Ravelli, both of whom shared his fascination with bikes. Between them it was agreed that Guzzi should design a new world beater, Parodi would find the money to build it, and Ravelli would ride the bike to victory on the race tracks. Sadly, Ravelli was killed in a flying accident only days after the war ended, and it is said that Moto Guzzi's flying eagle badge was a tribute to a potential champion. Undaunted, the other two pressed on, Parodi hoping to persuade his father to fund the building of the first prototype. Parodi Snr. was suitably impressed, and he did.

Completed in 1920, that first bike bristled with innovative features: unit-construction, oversquare bore/stroke, four valves per cylinder (with ohc) and gear primary-drive. It also established an engine layout which was to remain with Moto Guzzi for many years, in which the single 498cc (30cu in) cylinder was laid horizontally, with an external flywheel. That flywheel (the 'bacon slicer') was eventually enclosed, but the basic layout of an air-cooled, horizontal four-stroke single, in unit with the gearbox, would still be in production in the mid-1970s. The rest of the machine was more conventional, with a three-speed hand-change gearbox, girder front forks and rear brake only. As a matter of fact, when the realities of production and sales made themselves felt, Guzzi's advanced prototype had to be somewhat diluted and the four-valve overhead-cam layout was abandoned for an overhead inlet/side-exhaust system (common at the time) with just two valves.

But although Guzzi had to compromise on his original vision, the racing success did come, and with it the means to build more exotic machinery. In only its second event, the new 'Moto Guzzi' (it was Parodi, incidentally, who suggested the name) won the Targa Florio race, ridden by Gino Finzi. Over the next couple of years, more race wins in Italy encouraged Guzzi to resurrect his four-valve design, which rewarded him by winning the German Grand Prix in 1924. A smaller 249cc (15cu in) version followed, which was only denied a debut second place at the Isle of Man TT by disqualification, allegedly because the wrong make of spark plug had been used. Still, Moto Guzzi had its revenge and went on to win both Junior and Senior TTs in the same year, both of them ridden by Stanley Woods.

Falcone Flies

During the war, of course, Moto Guzzi carried on building its horizontal singles for the military, though only 8,000 were delivered in four years. But in the late

1940s, Italy needed cheap, basic transport rather than machines for enthusiasts like the big singles. So Moto Guzzi, like just about every other Italian manufacturer at the time, turned its attention to small two-strokes. The 65 Guzzino (Little Guzzi) was the result, a 64cc (3.9cu in) single in a mild state of tune (just 2bhp at 5,000rpm), which meant a top speed of little more than 48km/h (30mph), but up to 71km per litre (200mpg)! It was a great success, with 200,000 sold before the Guzzino was replaced by the Cardellino in 1954. Telescopic forks and a larger 73cc (4.5cu in) version followed, as well as the 98cc (6cu in) Zigolo, with its pressed steel frame and 19-inch wheels. But unusually, Guzzi made small four-strokes as well. The 160cc (9.8cu in) Galletto was unveiled in 1950, and was a large-wheeled scooter which sold very well, benefiting from capacity increases to 174 and 192cc (10.6 and 11.7cu in) over the years: it survived until 1966. A more exotic lightweight was the 175cc overhead-cam Lodolo (launched 1956), of which there were later 235 and 250 versions, not to mention the works ISDT bikes. The Stornello, meanwhile, was a cheaper ohv roadster, which started off in 1960 as a 125, growing to 160cc in 1967.

The post-1950 Falcone was an update of the pre-war single

But Moto Guzzi had not forgotten its roots, and continued to offer big 'flat' singles after the war. Most famous was the Falcone of 1950, which was actually no more nor less than a mild update of the pre-war big single. The frame was new and the electrics were uprated, but the Falcone was substantially the same as the 1938 GTW. Far from being outdated, however, it was still fast enough (tuned Falcones could exceed 161km/h/100mph) to excel in long-distance road racing. In Grand Prix too, the 350cc (21cu in) racer (thanks in part to Scotsman Fergus Anderson) retained the World Championship right up to 1957. And the customers loved the traditional Guzzi big single, so much so that the company simply updated it in 1963 and 1969, and it went on selling to private buyers as well as to the usual police and military markets. But back in the 1950s, Moto Guzzi realized that the single could not go on dominating world-class racing forever, and its answer was the astonishing V8 of 1956. Just like that very first prototype, the 500cc (30.5cu in) V8 racer was advanced for its day, with liquid-cooling, twin overhead camshafts and a rev limit of 12,000rpm. It had tremendous speed and great promise, but Guzzi pulled out of racing in 1957. So that was that.

The V-twin is Born

Apart from all the racing success (and even after the withdrawal from track racing, ISDT medals and speed records came Moto Guzzi's way), much of the company's business which earned it its living came

ABOVE: *Moto Guzzi 350cc (21cu in)*

from selling flat singles to the Italian police and army. But by the early 1960s, even these uniformed customers were looking for more power and the answer was to come from an unusual quarter. In the late 1950s, the army itself had outlined the need for a type of mini-tractor, and Moto Guzzi had duly come up with a 90-degree overhead-valve V-twin. Of 754cc (46cu in), it was suitably tractor-like. However, it was also to be the basis of Guzzi's fortunes for the next three decades.

History does not record who it was at Moto Guzzi who suggested adapting the tractor engine for a tough, utilitarian motorcycle, but that's what was done. Capacity was reduced to 703cc (43cu in), and the engine was mated to a car-type dry clutch, four-speed gearbox and shaft-drive. Just like the original flat single, this basic layout was to stay with Moto Guzzi for a long time (and at the time of writing, still does). The V7, submitted for governmental approval in early 1965, looked what it was – big, heavy and solid rather than stylish. Despite its lumpy looks, the V7 got an enthusiastic reception when unveiled at the Milan Show at the end of the year. Here was a 161km/h (100mph) tourer that promised simple maintenance and long life, and there was nothing else quite like it. Apart from Harley-Davidsons, V-twins had virtually disappeared, and at the time no one else (BMW excepted) offered shaft-drive.

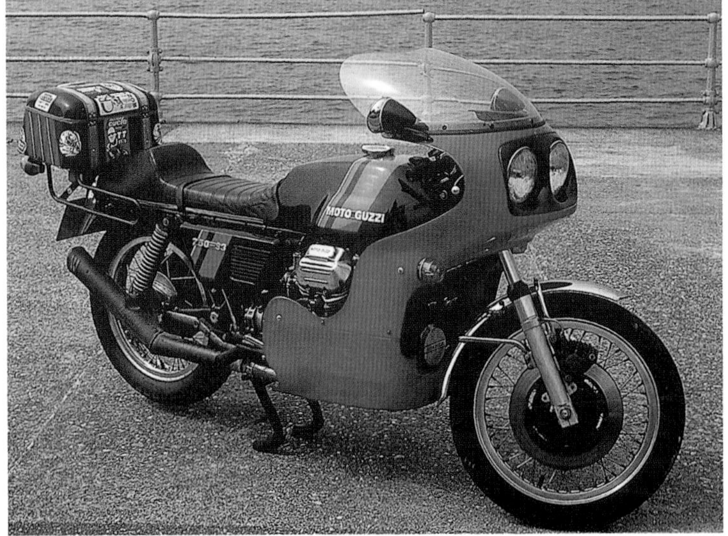

BELOW: *The S3 was precursor to Le Mans*

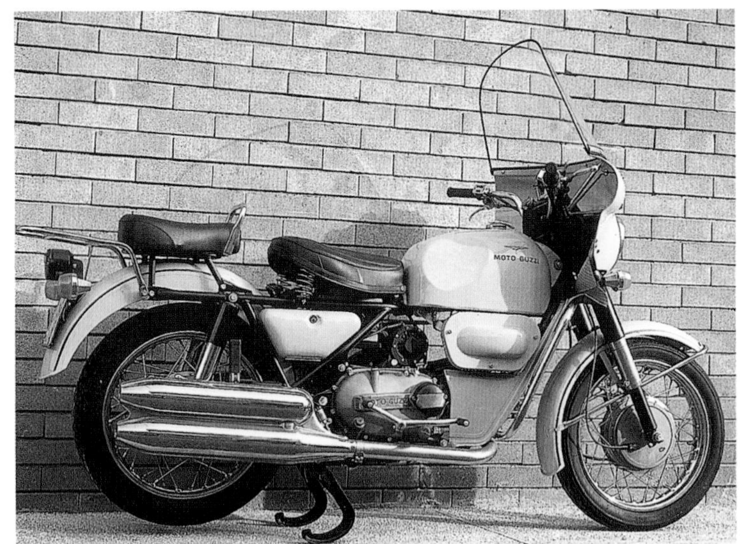

BELOW: *The 1974 Moto Guzzi Sahara, the last of the 500 singles*

The V50, seen here in traffic-police form, was a new series of smaller V-twins

ABOVE and BELOW: Sales brochure for the Moto Guzzi V50 Monza. The 'small' V-twin eventually grew to 750cc

Although the first civilian V7s did not reach customers until 1967, development for the civilian market continued rapidly thereafter. A V7 Special (now 757cc, and with power up to 45bhp) sold in America in 1969 as the Ambassador, while in 1971 came variations on a theme that sparked off three distinct models: another capacity increase produced the 850GT (844cc/51.5cu in) which took care of the touring market; the GT California was in the American mould (screen, panniers, high and wide bars), and a California has featured in the Guzzi range ever since. The V7 Sport was the first in a long line of sporting Guzzi V-twins and while the first two were close developments of the original V7, the Sport was one step further

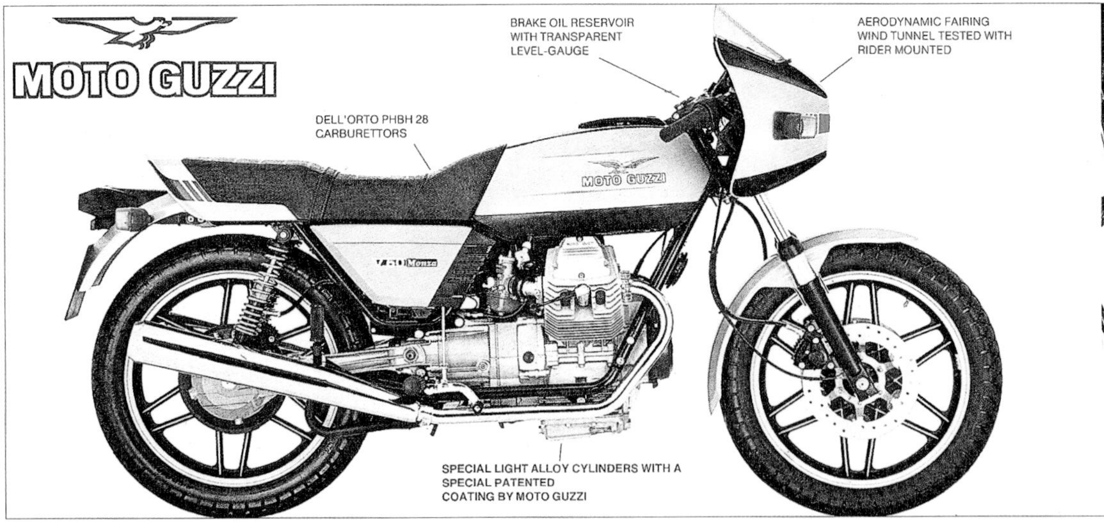

ABOVE and BELOW: The V7 Sport was the first development of the touring V7

on. New design head, Lino Tonti, transformed the chassis by lowering it (the trick was replacing the high-mounted dynamo with an alternator on the end of the crank), which changed the whole character of the machine. Higher compression, bigger carburettors and more sporting cam profiles added up to 52bhp at 6,300rpm, while Tonti made sure to keep the Sport's capacity below 750cc (actually 749cc) to keep it eligible for 750 racing. This new style of Guzzi V-twin went on sale in 1972.

The V7 Sport became a 750S in 1974, but a real leap forward came the following year with the Le Mans. As well as a new name, it used a tuned version of the 844cc touring twin, now with 10.2:1 compression, bigger than ever 36mm Dell'Orto carburettors, larger valves and 71bhp, enough for a top speed of 200km/h (124mph). A factory race kit liberated still more power, and the Le Mans went on to several racing victories. It was heartening that with the same gearing as the tourers, the Le Mans would lope along at high speeds in a very relaxed manner, providing a true alternative to the Japanese four-cylinder sportsbikes. Unfortunately, it also became famous for poor finish, a recurring Moto Guzzi problem. There were no fundamental changes to the Le Mans in the next few years, though it did get a little softer as tougher noise regulations came into force. A 948cc (58cu in) Le Mans arrived in 1984, which produced 86bhp and a claimed 225km/h (140mph), as well as Moto Guzzi's infamous experimentation with 16-inch front wheels. The latter was an attempt to ape Japanese sportsbikes, but were fundamentally unsuited to the heavier, long-wheelbased Guzzi. They were quickly dropped, and the Le Mans continued with an 18-inch wheel up to 1991

Variations on a Theme

Meanwhile, the 850GT and California had acquired the lower, alternator-equipped engine, and were joined by the automatic transmission V1000 Convert. The latter had a clutch, but this was only needed for swapping ratios in the two-speed gearbox and a Sachs torque converter took care of stopping and starting. It was an interesting idea, but not a commercial success. Honda

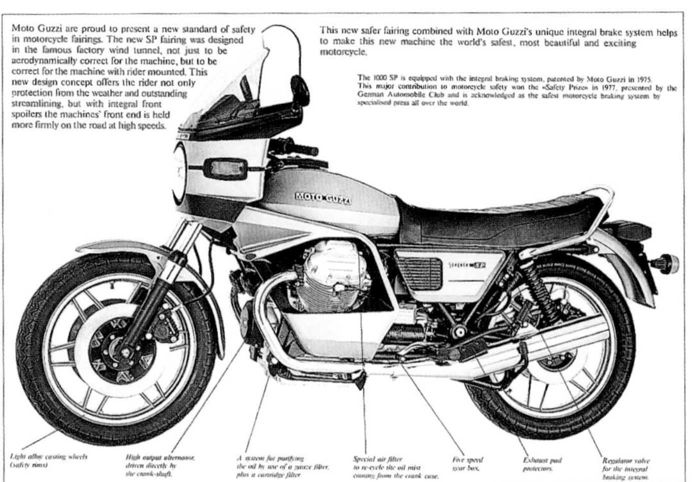

ABOVE: The 1000SP – Moto Guzzi's tilt at the BMW market

found the same thing when attempting to sell its 400cc (24cu in) twin and 750cc (46cu in) Hondamatics at about the same time. More promising was the SP, or Spada, unveiled in 1977, which used the 949cc twin with a conventional five-speed gearbox and designed-in fairing. The fairing was a two-piece affair, with the top half handlebar-mounted, and the whole was allegedly designed in Moto Guzzi's own wind tunnel at the Mandello del Lario factory. With decent weather protection, it certainly made the most of the Guzzi V-twin's long-legged nature, and cost less than a BMW; but again, the finish was below par and the SP failed to take a big chunk out of BMW's market. An SPIII (from 1984) used a conventional one-piece, frame-mounted fairing.

The 1980s was also the decade when retro bikes first appeared, with no fairing and vaguely 1970s styling with modern underpinnings. Moto Guzzi's first offering was the 1000S, with the latest version of the 948cc V-twin, but with styling which echoed that of the 750S. Similarly, the Mille GT of 1989 reintroduced the basic roadster Guzzi, albeit with the biggest engine. Another variant on the big V-twin theme was the Quota, which with its vaguely off-road styling was part of the 'adventure-tourer' sector, made popular with bikes like the Cagiva Elefant and Honda Africa Twin. The Quota followed a familiar formula, using a roadster engine (the 949cc twin) with its own chassis, longer travel suspension and dual-purpose tyres. Like most bikes of its type, though,

BELOW: The Galletto scooter had a single-sided swinging arm

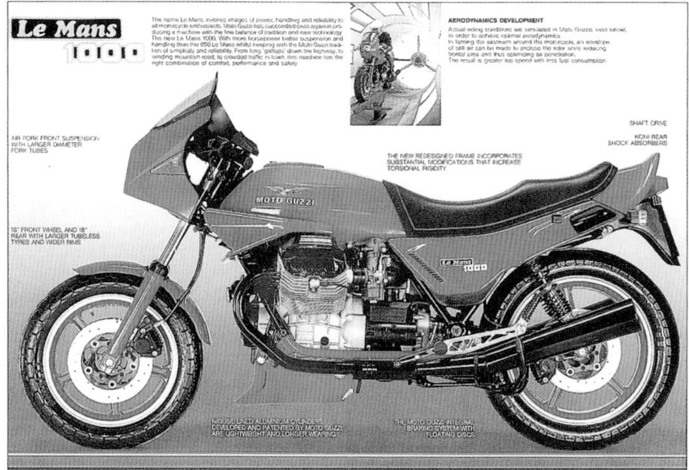

the heavy Quota (it weighed 269kg/593lb) could tackle little more off-road than a dry-surfaced track.

Moto Guzzi's smaller trail bikes were better liked, however, especially the V35 TT, which was lighter and handier but still had enough torque for riding off-road. Together with the similar-looking V65 TT, it was restyled as the NTX in 1987, and had another makeover in the early nineties. Incidentally, those smaller V-twins had been part of the Moto Guzzi range for some time. Their origins lay in the early 1970s when Argentinian-born industrialist Alejandro de Tomaso took over Moto Guzzi (not to mention Benelli) and determined to raise production, cut costs and build the Italian industry back up again. Early attempts to attach Moto Guzzi badges to the small two- and four-stroke Benellis met with

BELOW: The V10 Centauro Sport filled the gap between California and the four-valved sports Guzzis

ABOVE: The late-edition Le Mans was replaced by the four-valved Daytona (BELOW)

limited success, so De Tomaso decided to do it properly, authorizing chief designer Lino Tonti to build a smaller version of the classic big V-twin.

Tonti succeeded in no uncertain terms, as the V35 (346cc/21cu in) and V50 (490cc/30cu in), unveiled in September 1976, were real big Guzzis in miniature. They had the same transverse air-cooled pushrod V-twin layout, with shaft-drive and Guzzi's linked braking system. The V50 in particular won a lot of friends; compared with the rival Honda CX500, it was lighter and handled very well with about the same performance, and it was even cheaper! Sadly, the small twins suffered from quality problems which weren't really addressed until the much-improved V50III of 1980. There was still a gap in the Guzzi range, filled first by V65, then V75 developments of the small twin. And as well as the trail bikes, there were cruisers with various engine sizes. Four-valve versions of the roadsters followed in 1984, but these suffered from the now familiar teething troubles. Overall though, the De Tomaso-inspired mini-Guzzis did much to bolster the company's fortunes, and developments remain in the line-up to this day.

Dr. John's Magic

But perhaps more significant for Moto Guzzi in the 1990s has been the arrival of the overhead-camshaft V-twin – the Daytona. It came about largely thanks to one John Wittner, an American who had had great success in endurance racing with his own Guzzi-powered racer. So successful was he that Alejandro De Tomaso gave the former dentist from Philadelphia a prototype eight-valve ohc twin that had been designed at the factory. In fairy-tale fashion, the resultant race bike was third in its debut race (the 1988 Daytona Twins) and more podium positions followed that year. As a result, Wittner (or 'Dr. John' as he became known, in deference to his medical background) was invited to Italy to develop a road-going version of the Daytona.

This he did, and the new Daytona made its debut for customers at the 1991 Milan Show. It was a success. The new engine, with its belt-driven overhead cams and Weber-Marelli fuel injection, produced 100bhp (more than any previous road-going Moto Guzzi). Better still for the enthusiasts, its well-finned, air-cooled cylinders on proud display below the half-fairing could not be mistaken for anything else – this was not a Guzzi made bland by the modern world. So well received was the Daytona that the company soon came up with a cheaper alternative in the 1100 Sport (all the big twins had since grown to 1100cc/67cu in) which married Daytona styling with the older pushrod V-twin. At the time, the motorcycle market was beginning to fragment into niches, and it made sense to produce a number of variations on the same theme. The Centauro was one result of this, using the Daytona's fuel-injected twin in a decidedly retro motorcycle whose styling owed little to previous Moto Guzzis, or indeed anything else. Still a big, heavy motorcycle with shaft-drive, but now with a lot of power that was arguably best used in a straight line, journalist Alan Cathcart described the Centauro as 'a two-wheeled AC Cobra', which was about right.

But the world was moving on, and Moto Guzzi knew that ever-tighter noise and emission regulations meant it couldn't remain with an air-cooled engine for ever. Its answer was an all-new 75-degree V-twin whose basic layout (though not a running engine) was shown to the press in the summer of 1998. Financial backing from the American Tamarix Investment Bank had given the project a further boost, and Moto Guzzi announced that the liquid-cooled eight-valve dohc V-twin – its first all-new engine for 20 years – would power a complete range of bikes, in sizes ranging from 850cc to 1200cc (52 to 73cu in). The 998cc (61cu in) prototype was projected to produce 170bhp at the rear wheel in race form (an assault on World Superbike racing was part of the plan) with 135bhp at 11,000rpm for the road. And it would retain that unique Moto Guzzi feature, being mounted transversely in the frame, which would make it more compact than the Ducati-inspired rivals.

However, as time went on it became clear that all was not well. Moto Guzzi's recently-appointed chief executive, Oscar Cecchinato, had ambitious plans to triple production and take Moto Guzzi back into mass-production and this, in turn, dictated a move from the lakeside Mandello del Lario factory (historic, evocative, but cramped). A new factory was lined up but, at what seemed like the eleventh hour, there was a revolt. Faced with a four-hour commute to the new factory, the workforce voted against moving, while upper management threatened mass resignation if the now unpopular Cecchinato refused to leave. He was duly dismissed, and at the time of writing, Moto Guzzi was set to stay at Mandello; mass-production plans had been pruned but development of the all-new V-twin would continue. Life was never dull at Moto Guzzi.

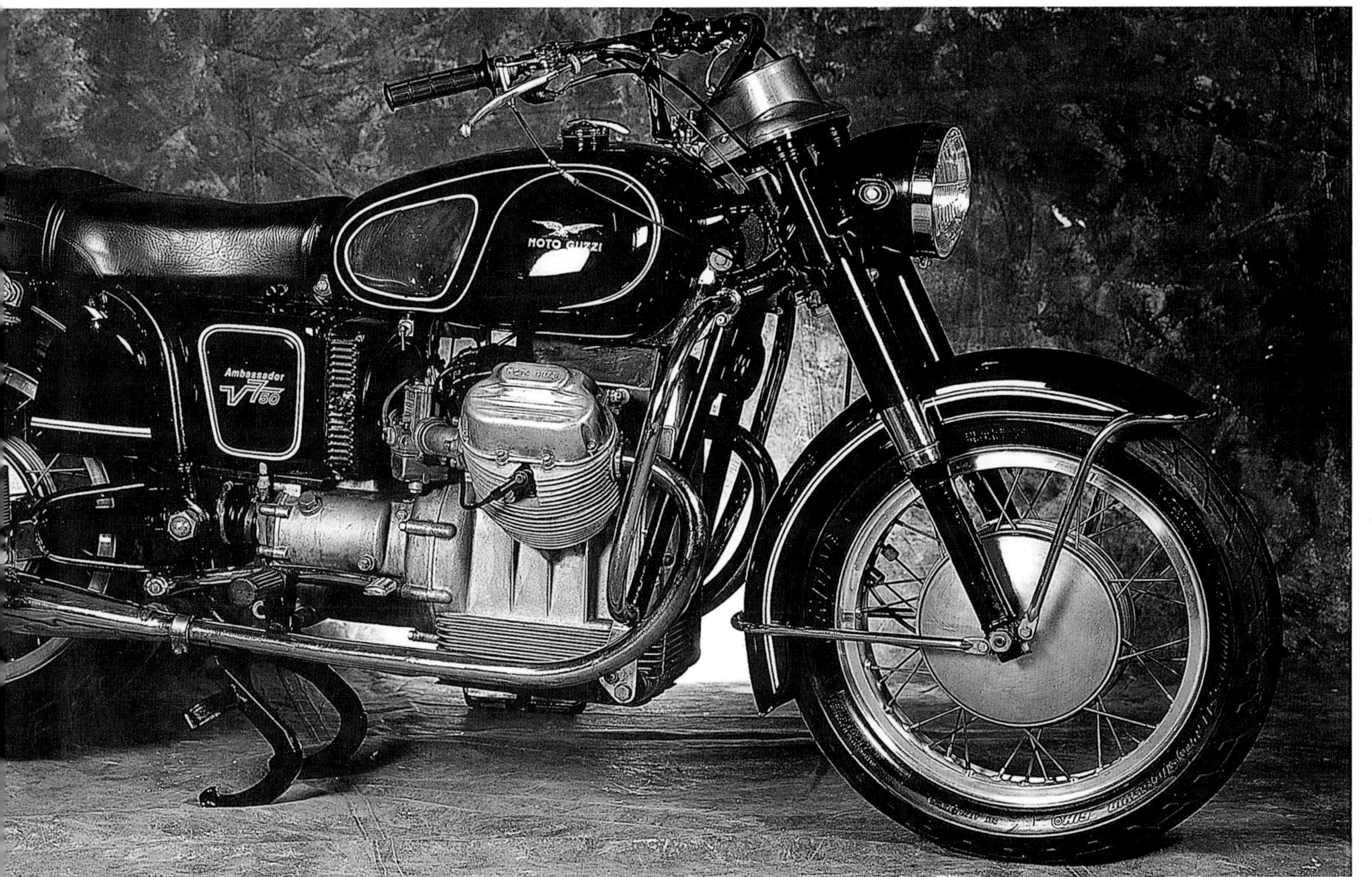

The Ambassador V7, Moto Guzzi's first V-twin, used an engine derived from a military mini-tractor

MOTO GUZZI
DAYTONA 1000
FUEL INJECTION
GUZZI

MOTOM *Italy 1947–71*
Produced various lightweights, most with four-stroke engines and nearly all with pressed steel frames. A 48cc (3cu in) clip-on was followed by the 147cc (9cu in) Delfino and a fully-enclosed 98cc (6cu in) unit. The company bought in a two-stroke 48cc Peugeot engine in 1964, also a Zündapp.

MOTO MONTE *France 1927–38*
Produced 175–250cc (11–15cu in) two-strokes.

MOTO MORINI *Italy 1946–*
Alfonso Morini had already had a long motorcycling career when he set up the firm which bore his name. He had helped establish MM in 1924, and successfully raced its products until 1937. His first bike appeared in 1946, a copy of the ubiquitous DKW RT125 (also copied by BSA and Harley-Davidson, among others), which he followed up with a 246cc (15cu in) two-stroke single in 1949. Racing was important to Morini in the company's early years, and the ohc Rebello was successful in both 123 and 174cc (7.5 and 11cu in) versions, and was often ridden by Tarquino Provini.

A range of road-going ohv singles followed from 1952, starting with a 175 and developed in both directions to 50 and 250cc. These were very successful and led to the Settebello sportsbike as well as mirroring continuing competitiveness on the track; Morini only narrowly lost the 250 World Championship to Honda in 1963.

OPPOSITE and BELOW: The Moto Guzzi Daytona 1000, part-developed by American Dr. John Wittner

Alfonso Morini died in 1969 and, with the company in a parlous state, it was left to his daughter Gabriella to take over. She succeeded in no uncertain terms, overseeing the launch in 1972 of Morini's most famous bike of all, the 3½. This 72-degree pushrod V-twin was quite unique at a time when the Japanese big four seemed to be developing towards two-strokes or ohc twins and fours. But the new engine was remarkably efficient with its Heron cylinder heads, in which the combustion chamber was formed by the piston crown, and it was housed in some well-designed cycle parts that won Morini a well-deserved reputation for excellent handling. Light in weight and relatively simple and economical, the Morini V-twin developed into Strada and Sport versions, as well as later 239cc and 479cc (15 and 29cu in) versions and ensured Morini's survival into the 1980s.

There were other variations as the years went by: the Kangaroo 350 and Camel 500 were trail bikes, and there was even a turbocharged prototype in 1981. Neat 125 and 250cc singles, using many of the V-twin parts, were also produced. The only substantial update came in 1991; the Dart 350 sat the V-twin in a new alloy frame covered in all-enveloping bodywork. But 20 years after its first appearance, the V-twin was beginning to look dated. The company had been taken over by Cagiva in 1987, which in the 1990s continued to use the name on a limited scale for custom and trail bikes. At the time of writing, the Morini name is dormant but owned by Ducati and, given that company's new-found prosperity, who is to say that there won't be a lightweight sporting Morini in years to come?

ABOVE: A K2 350, one of the later V-twins

BELOW: The Moto Morini 3½ was a design classic

BELOW: Moto Morini had its beginnings in singles

Moto Morini 350cc (21cu in) V-twin. The pushrod 72-degree twin had a long lifespan, and kept the company going for many years

MOTOPEDALE *France 1933–39*
Used 98/123cc (6/7.5cu in) Aubier-Dunne engines and bigger four-strokes from JAP and Python.

MOTOPIANA *Italy 1923–31*
Used Villiers and JAP engines in its own frames, but unveiled its own 248cc (15cu in) sv in 1927.

MOTO RÊVE *Switzerland 1904–25*
Built V-twins of up to 497cc (30cu in) and an early vertical twin in 1909 to power its own machines and for sale to other manufacturers.

MOTOSACOCHE (MAG) *Switzerland 1899–1956*
Motosacoche was the leading Swiss manufacturer, the name translating as 'motor in a bag', describing the firm's first clip-on engine. It went on, as MAG, to be one of the biggest engine suppliers in Europe, alongside JAP and Villiers. The Defaux brothers began with that 215cc (13cu in) clip-on in 1905, having experimented with engines for several years. It was followed in 1908 by a 438cc (27cu in) V-twin, then a 750, and by the outbreak of World War I was producing a complete range of engines from 350–1000cc (21–61cu in). The French company NEW-MAP started making MAG units under licence from 1923. Motosacoche resumed business in 1945 with an ohc 250, ending motorcycle production in 1956.

MOTOTRANS *Spain 1957–82*
Built Ducati singles under licence, as well as mopeds. Introduced its own ohc 410cc (25cu in) trial bike in 1978, and later built Zündapp-powered two-strokes under the MTV badge

MOUNTAINEER *England 1902–26*
Used Minerva, Fafnir and MMC engines before World War I, but produced only one model, a 269cc (16cu in) two-stroke afterwards.

MOVEO *England c.1907*
3.5/5hp V-twin JAP engines were used by this assembler.

MOVESA *Spain 1952–62*
Used Peugeot 172cc (10.5cu in) two-strokes.

BELOW and ABOVE LEFT: 1918 Motosacoche 1000cc (61cu in) V-twin

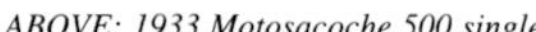
ABOVE: 1933 Motosacoche 500 single

A 1932 Motosacoche 1000cc (61cu in) V-twin. However, the company was better known for its MAG engines

MÖWE *Germany 1903–08*
3.5hp singles and 5hp V-twin Fafnir units.

MOY *Poland 1937–40*
Built its own 172cc (10.5cu in) two-stroke.

M&P *France late 1920s–late 1930s*
Used 98/123cc (6/7.5cu in) Aubier-Dunne engines.

MP *Italy 1934–35*
Combined a pressed steel frame with Sturmey-Archer engines of 347 or 497cc (21 or 30cu in).

MPH *England 1920–24*
A 269cc (16cu in) Wall-powered two-stroke with two-speed gearbox.

MR *France 1924–26*
Equipped with various Train engines. There was also an Italian version.

MR *France 1926*
Aubier-Dunne, Ydral and Sachs engines were used by this company (different from the above).

MT *Italy 1949–53*
Advanced ohc vertical twins of 248cc (15cu in), but there were few takers.

MT Austria 1925–37
Count Matthias Thun imported Villiers engines into Austria, and his MT machines were strongly English-influenced. JAP and Blackburne engines, as well as Villiers, were used.

MÜCO *Germany 1921–24*
A 118cc (7.2cu in) clip-on.

MUFI (IMPERATOR) *Germany 1925–26*
A 348cc (21cu in) two-stroke.

MÜLLER *Austria 1924–26*
A 138cc (8.4cu in) unit-construction engine in a strengthened bicycle frame.

MÜLLER *Italy 1950–79*
First made an NSU-engined 98cc (6cu in) lightweight then, after a gap in production, built off-roaders with Zündapp, Hiro, Sachs and Franco-Morini engines.

MÜNCH-4 *Germany 1966–early 1980s*
Ex-Horex engineer Friedl Münch is best known for the bike that bears his name. Originally known as the Mammut, it used a 996cc (61cu in) NSU four-cylinder car engine, offering unheard-of performance in a heavy, bulky package, and was highly priced. The Mammut grew to 1177cc (72cu in) with 88bhp, acquired fuel injection (100bhp) and in final 1278cc (78cu in) form produced 104bhp at 7,500rpm. It had a top speed of around 201km/h (125mph) and was something of a cult bike. Friedl Münch carried on making bikes to order into the early 1980s after splitting with his business partner.

MUSTANG *U.S.A. 1946–64*
A 314cc (19cu in) sv single intended for short trips.

MV AGUSTA *Italy 1946–1980*
MV Agusta – fast, exclusive and always expensive. This, one of the most evocative names in motorcycling, is now making a comeback 20 years after the last bikes

ABOVE: The Münch-4's engine came from an NSU car

BELOW: The distinctive, bulky Münch TTS

Mustang, a basic lightweight in the Cushmann mould, it stood no chance when pitted against Japanese machines

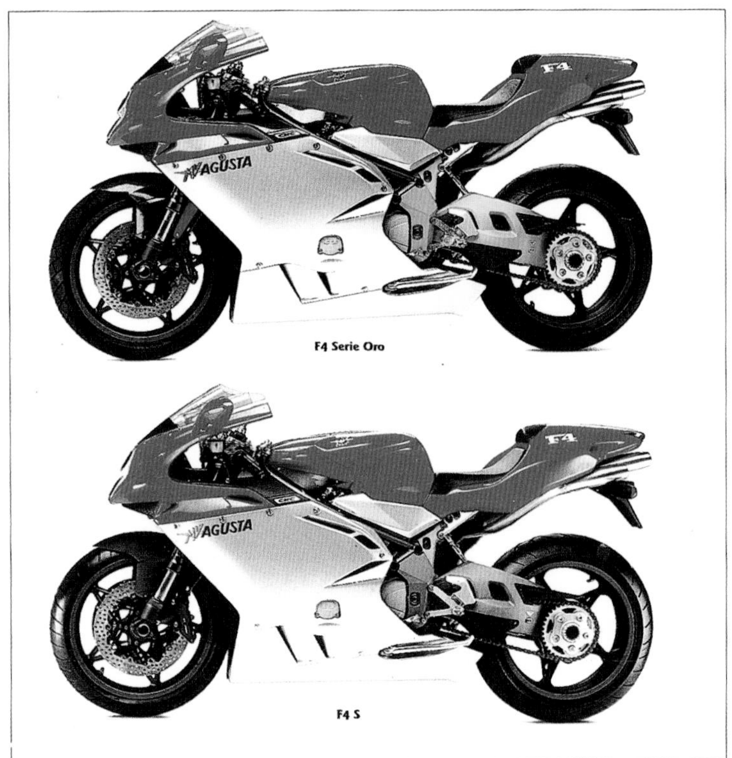

Concentration unmatched anywhere else in the world.

The art of subtracting volume and adding performance. A record wheelbase in a dismountable front and rear trellis frame. A drastic reduction of the overall dimensions of the engine in both the head and the gearbox, to concentrate the zone of the tank and underlying area to levels never before realized in a four-cylinder. An ergonomic design in which the rider closes the mass of the vehicle to perfection. The F4 is energy at its maximum concentration.

The all-new MV Agusta F4 heralded the rebirth of an old name

bearing its name were built. Motorcycles were something of a hobby with Count Domenico Agusta, who had inherited his father's aviation business in 1927. He built it into a successful enterprise, later diversifying into helicopters, but his ambition was always to build racing motorcycles. And he succeeded. MV's domination of the tracks in the fifties and sixties with 270 Grand Prix wins and no less than 75 rider or manufacturer world championships justify the magic behind the MV name.

But despite its association with exotic dohc fours, MV Agusta's first two-wheeler was, appropriately enough for Italy in 1946, a little 98cc (6cu in) two-stroke. A 123cc (7.5cu in) version soon followed, as did small four-stroke singles. But the Count's true ambitions for Meccanica Verghera (hence MV) were made plain in 1950 when designer Pietro Remor was persuaded to join the strength. With an ex-Gilera man at the drawing board, what else could MV do but make a racing four?

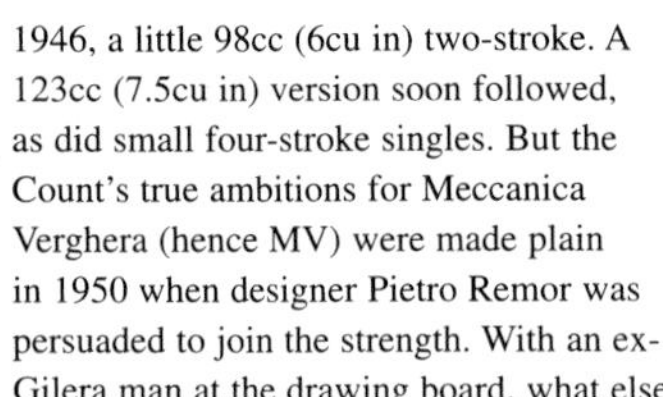

It naturally owed much to the Gilera, with its four cylinders, 500cc (30.5cu in), twin carburettors, 50bhp at 9,500rpm and a top speed of around 209km/h (130mph). Success didn't come immediately to MV's first big racer, but the talent of rider Les Graham gave the bike its first wins in the

The original 750S was the MV everyone was waiting for. Expensive, a little heavy, but very desirable

Italian and Spanish GPs of 1951. In fact, MV always seemed able to attract the best riding talent available: Lomas, Ubbiali, Amm, Surtees, Hailwood, Agostini – the list is a long one. While the 500 was honing its GP dominance, MV's smaller machines were doing the same in their classes. Ubbiali became the man to beat on the 125cc (8cu in) dohc single, which was followed by a 203cc (12cu in) single and 250cc (15cu in) twin. At the time, the little two- and four-strokes were MV's only offerings for the road. But on the tracks, MV was entering its own golden age. A 350cc (21cu in) four joined the 500, and after its main racing rivals pulled out, the company swept the GP board, winning the 125, 250, 350 and 500 classes in 1958, '59 and '60. It couldn't last, and Honda's arrival in the early sixties put paid to MV's domination of the lightweight classes, though it hung on to the 500 title. Honda's withdrawal from racing in 1968 allowed the new three-cylinder MVs to reclaim both 350 and 500 classes for another few years until the Japanese two-strokes finally outran them.

The 750 America, an update on the original 750S

A Slow Start

With all this racing success, it is surprising that MV failed to produce a road-going four until 1965, and even then it was an ugly, overweight thing that few people seemed to like. One theory is that Count Agusta wished to avoid producing a sporty four in case some privateer took it racing and beat the factory team! For whatever reason, the 600 was detuned to 50bhp, was laden with chrome and weighed over 227kg (500lb). Naturally, some people saw the 600's potential, and stripped it down to produce a real sportster. Among them was a heating engineer named Massimo Tamburini, who went on to help found Bimota and design the milestone Ducati 916. He was also to apply his talents to another MV, but we'll come to that in a moment.

Meanwhile (things seemed to move slowly at MV), the company eventually replaced the 600 with the bike it should have been in the first place – the 750 Sport. The air-cooled dohc four was enlarged to 743cc (45cu in) for 69bhp at 7,900rpm. Out went the black and chrome, in came red, white and blue; the wide touring handlebars were replaced with clip-ons, there was a big Grimeca four-leading-shoe front brake (just like the racer's) and top speed was around 193km/h (120mph). It was still a little heavy (due in part to the shaft-drive that all the fours shared) but the road-burning MV four had (belatedly) been born. It was updated in the early 1970s with disc brakes, more power and a fairing, while the 750S America of 1975 featured more angular styling and a capacity boost to 789cc (48cu in) and 75bhp.

But like the bike it replaced, the 750S was hugely expensive to make and despite a price tag double that of mass-produced 750s, was still losing money and MV was now an unprofitable part of the Agusta aviation company. By 1977 the Agusta family had lost control, and the new owners had little enthusiasm for loss-making motorcycles. Production ended soon afterwards, though MV did not actually close until 1980.

The name was bought by the resurgent Cagiva in 1991, it being well known at the time that Cagiva was working on a 750cc four, developed in conjunction with Ferrari, work for which had actually begun in 1988. But it wasn't until 1995 that the new engine was revealed, with four radial valves per cylinder (a Ferrari touch), Weber/Marelli fuel injection and a projected 155bhp in race form. It was an ultra-short-stroke, high-revving engine, with peak power at 14,000rpm. But Cagiva's financial problems caused the engine to be put on hold until an American-based buy-out of Ducati (then also Cagiva-owned) in 1997 allowed the company to clear its debts and start afresh. There was talk by now of a 900cc (55cu in) version, but interest in the project rocketed in late 1997 when it became known that Cagiva would use the MV Agusta name on its new F4. Such was the interest that by early the following year the company claimed to have received an incredible 7,000 orders for the bike. Cagiva announced it would make a limited run of 200 F4s, then a much less expensive, rather more mass-produced version. When it was finally unveiled to the public at the Milan Motorcycle Show in September 1997, no one was disappointed; the 125bhp road-going F4 was a worthy recipient of the MV name.

BELOW and RIGHT: The 1971 750S gained disc brakes

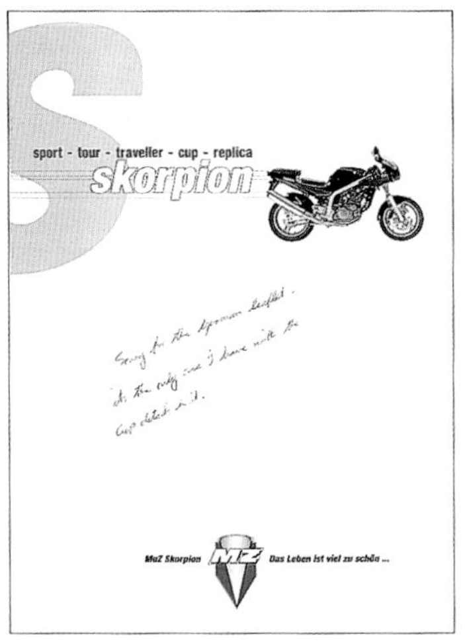

ABOVE: *The Yamaha-powered MuZ Skorpion had nothing in common with previous MZs*

MVB *Italy 1954–56*
Produced 49cc (3cu in) mopeds and lightweights up to 147cc (9cu in).

MW *Germany 1923–26*
An unusual frame of light alloy and pressed steel utilized a 249cc (15cu in) single, and later a 144cc (9cu in) two-stroke twin. Designer Paul Paffrath moved to West Germany after World War II and built a clip-on called the Eilenriede.

MYMSA *Spain 1953–62*
Produced 75–175cc (4.6–11cu in) two-strokes.

MZ/MUZ *Germany 1945–*
If there had never been an Iron Curtain MZ would not have existed at all. It arose from the ashes of DKW, whose extensive plant at Zschopau had been nationalized and was now part of the state-owned IFA. DKW itself, meanwhile, resumed production at Ingolstadt, in the Western sector, in 1949.

It wasn't until May 1950 that Zschopau was once again churning out motorcycles, and it was perhaps predictable that its first bike should be the DKW RT125, which had been launched in 1939 and was built in large numbers during the war. Powered by a unit-construction 122cc (7.4cu in) two-stroke, this simple little bike can probably claim to be the most copied of all time. As well as the IFA version, it was built by BSA as the Bantam, by Harley-Davidson as the Hummer, by Morini, Moska (a Soviet make) and even Yamaha!

However, IFA (which was soon to begin marketing the bikes under the MZ name) came up with its own design in

BELOW: *The MZ S51 Simson*

ABOVE: The MZ Trophy was distinctive and practical, while the ETZ 250 (BELOW) was an update on the same theme

1952, the BK350. This was actually quite contemporary in design being a two-stroke flat twin with telescopic forks, plunger rear suspension and shaft-drive. MZ built it for seven years. Meanwhile, the RT125 was updated as the 125/3, with more power (now 6.5bhp at 5,200rpm), a four-speed gearbox, telescopic forks, rear plunger and (something that was to become an MZ trademark for the next 30 years) a chain fully enclosed in rubber gaiters. In some ways it was in advance of the other DKW clones being built across the world, and at least as well made as any of them. The next big update came in 1955 with the ES models, which filled the gap in the range with 172 and 249cc (10.5 and 15cu in) two-stroke singles. With 11 and 14bhp respectively, they were quite lively performers, and the 250 could manage 113km/h (70mph). Both had Earles-type forks (this other MZ trademark lasted into the 1970s) and swinging-arm rear suspension, while the 250 was also offered with sidecar attached.

At this point MZ was clearly keeping pace with the technical tide of small machines of the time, but it was well ahead in some areas, experimenting with the Wankel rotary engine. Well before Hercules, Suzuki and Norton even approached bringing such bikes into production, MZ had a running rotary-engined machine, the KKM175W, in 1963. Water-cooled, it was the work of Herbert Friedrich, the company's chief engineer. Based on ES250 cycle parts, the prototype also had shaft-drive, and was followed up by an air-cooled version two years later, which produced 24bhp at 6,750rpm and allowed a 129km/h (80mph) top speed. Sadly, the project was dropped.

But this wasn't the only way in which MZ developed a technical lead. For a time, it actually led the world in the design of performance two-strokes. Walter Kaaden was an engineer who had worked on the V1 and V2 rockets during the war, and in the late 1940s occupied himself with the more peaceful task of tuning DKW/MZ racers. So successful was he that IFA offered him a job in 1953, and Kaaden was able to begin the work that almost made MZ world champion. In 1951, a tuner named Daniel Zimmerman had already modified his own racing MZ with a disc valve, and two of his bikes finished fourth and fifth in the German GP of that year. Kaaden built on this, and in his first year with MZ boosted the 125 racer's power by 25 per cent. He was developing great expertise in port design, and realized the importance of expansion chamber exhaust design to high-output two-strokes, as well as multiple transfer ports, a squish-type combustion chamber and disc-valve induction.

Equipped thus, his 125cc MZs failed to have immediate success (fifth and sixth in the 1955 German GP) and if anything held them back, it was the company's tiny racing budget compared to Western teams. By 1958 Kaaden and his team had squeezed an impressive 160bhp/litre out of the two-strokes (20bhp for the 125, and 36bhp from the newer 250 twin) which

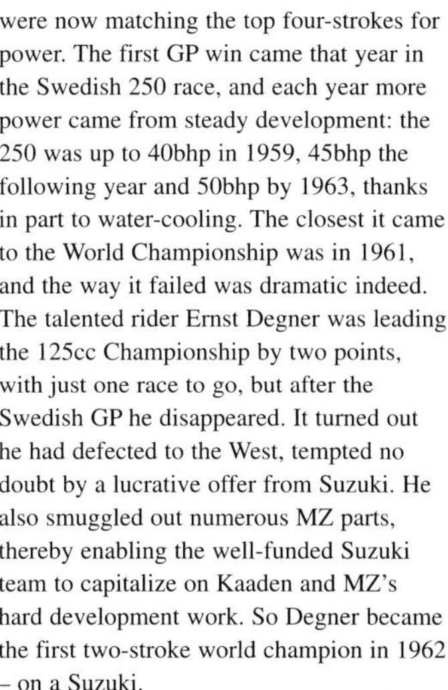

were now matching the top four-strokes for power. The first GP win came that year in the Swedish 250 race, and each year more power came from steady development: the 250 was up to 40bhp in 1959, 45bhp the following year and 50bhp by 1963, thanks in part to water-cooling. The closest it came to the World Championship was in 1961, and the way it failed was dramatic indeed. The talented rider Ernst Degner was leading the 125cc Championship by two points, with just one race to go, but after the Swedish GP he disappeared. It turned out he had defected to the West, tempted no doubt by a lucrative offer from Suzuki. He also smuggled out numerous MZ parts, thereby enabling the well-funded Suzuki team to capitalize on Kaaden and MZ's hard development work. So Degner became the first two-stroke world champion in 1962 – on a Suzuki.

But if MZ was robbed of ultimate road-racing success, things were different off-road, where it secured a whole string of international victories. Under Walter Winkler, a succession of 125, 175, 250 and 300cc off-road bikes were developed, and the MZ-mounted GDR team won the ISDT in 1963 and the following three years, not to mention in 1968 as well. When the ISDT became the ISDE in 1981, it signalled another line of MZ victories, in 1982, '84, '85 and '87.

Export Developments

While MZ was having its first run of trials successes, the road bikes were beginning to lose their heavy unconventional look with the telescopic-forked ETS250 in 1969; it lacked the Trophy model's ultra-large tank and mudguards, though was still very much

The 1996 MuZ Baghira was Yamaha-powered like the Skorpion, but with a new flamboyance

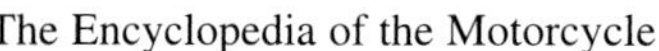

The addition of a fairing and panniers produced the Skorpion Traveller

an MZ. The TS125/150 of 1972 continued the same trend, by which time MZ had built over one million bikes. The following year a TS250 followed, but with a rubber-mounted engine that did much to eliminate vibration. In fact, although MZs were now looking a little more conventional, they were making something of a comeback with riders who eschewed more highly strung Japanese bikes of the time. The softly tuned, highly geared two-stroke 250 could lope along quietly at 97–113km/h (60–70mph) all day, with softish long-travel suspension for a comfortable ride. And because of the Eastern bloc's lower costs and drive for exports, it was much cheaper than anything built in the West.

It was perhaps with an eye on exports that MZ periodically updated the bike (though in some ways it was now falling behind), notably with a five-speed gearbox in 1977 and with the ETZ250 in 1982. The ETZ boasted slimmer styling, 12-volt electrics, more power, oil-pump lubrication and even a Brembo-like front disc brake. (The oil pump was Japanese!) ETZ versions of the smaller bikes followed a couple of years later, and an ETZ301 with 23bhp soon after. At this time, MZs were still being made in relatively large numbers (around 80,000 a year), with exports still strong due to their reliability and low price. What changed everything was the fall of the Berlin Wall.

Now part of the larger Germany, MZ's price advantage almost disappeared. Sales collapsed and the company went into liquidation in December 1991 with 3,000 workers losing their jobs. However, it was resurrected as MuZ the following year, though on a much smaller scale. The new management had ambitious plans to move MuZ upmarket and away from the traditional two-strokes (now being made in Turkey under licence). Rotax 500cc (30.5cu in) four-stroke singles were bought in to fit the existing chassis, followed by Yamaha's 660cc (40cu in) five-valve single to power the new generation Skorpion. Styled by the Seymour-Powell consultancy in Britain, the Skorpion made quite an impact when announced. There was a whole range built in a new factory (not far from the Zschopau original), from the naked Tour to the race Skorpion Replica, plus a prototype Kobra (a big roadster using Yamaha's TDM850 twin-cylinder engine). But it wasn't enough for independent survival, and in 1996 MuZ was taken over by the Malaysian motorcycle manufacturer, Hong Leong. The new owners announced plans for a new range of four-strokes, so perhaps MuZ at last had the finance it needed. Meanwhile, in Turkey, the Kanuni corporation went on building 250 and 300cc two-stroke MZs.

N

NAMAPO *Germany 1921–24*
Built its own 147/197cc (9/12cu in) sv singles, the smaller of which was also sold as a clip-on.

NARCISSE *France 1950–53*
Used 48/98cc (3/6cu in) Aubier-Dunne and Sachs engines.

NARCLA *Spain 1955–67*
Produced 123cc (7.5cu in) two-strokes.

NASSETTI *Italy 1951–57*
Combined a 49cc (3cu in) friction-drive engine with a modern frame and telescopic forks.

NASSOVIA *Germany 1925*
Used a 2.75hp Anzani engine.

NAZZARO *Italy 1926–28*
Limited production of a 173cc (11cu in) single.

NEALL England 1904–14
Used 2.5/3hp Precision units.

NEANDER *Germany 1924–29*
An unusual machine, with a cadmium-coated duralumin frame, leaf-sprung forks and bucket seat. Opel made it under licence, but Neander offered a vast range of other engines up to a 996cc (61cu in) V-twin.

NECCHI *Italy 1951–53*
98/123cc (6/7.5cu in) Villiers two-strokes.

NECO *Czechoslovakia 1923–27*
Used JAP 346/490cc (21/30cu in) singles.

NEGAS & RAY *Italy 1925–28*
Own-design unit-construction 348cc (21cu in) engine.

NEMALETTE *Germany 1924–25*
Had a car-like body with 173cc (11cu in) DKW power.

NERA *Germany 1949–50*
One of Germany's first post-war scooters with 120 or 149cc (7.3 or 9cu in) bought-in engines.

NERACAR *U.S.A. 1921–26*
Comfortable, low-slung two-wheeler with a car-like chassis frame. Used 283cc (17cu in) two-strokes with friction-drive, though also built under licence in England with bigger four-stroke engines and chain-drive.

NERGINI *Italy 1954–*
After building 123cc (7.5cu in) two-strokes, it later concentrated on mopeds.

NERVOR *France 1947–58*
Built by Radior, using a mix of its own and NSU or AMC power units.

NESTOR *England 1913–24*
Utilized 269cc (16cu in) Villiers or 296/347cc (18/21cu in) Precision engines.

NESTORIA *Germany 1923–31*
Produced own two-strokes of up to 346cc (21cu in), but later used various bought-in four-strokes up to 596cc (36cu in).

NETTUNIA *Italy 1950–53*
Had a four-speed gearbox and 123 or 158cc (7.5 or 9.6cu in) two-stroke engines.

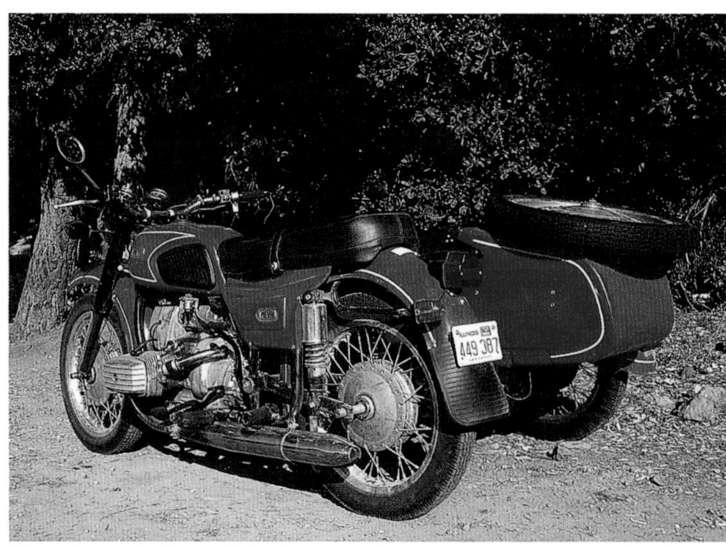

ABOVE: Neval was a BMW-derived design

NEVA *France 1926–27*
Used the 347cc (21cu in) Anzani ohv single.

NEVAL *Former U.S.S.R. c.1945–*
Post-war, the policy of the U.S.S.R. was to seize valuable plant from occupied Germany and take it back to the Motherland. This was the case with BMW, and many Soviet factories built BMW-derived motorcycles which included the Neval, which along with the Kiev, Irbit, Cossack and Dnieper were all basically the same machine. (See Ural.)

NEVE-ILO *Germany 1924–26*
One of the first to buy the new Ilo two-stroke proprietary engine.

BELOW: New Hudson's 211cc (13cu in) baby

ABOVE: 1929 New Hudson 496cc (30cu in) ohv

NEW COMET *England 1905–32*
Used various bought-in engines until production ceased in 1924. Attempted a revival in 1931 with a 198cc (12cu in) Villiers.

NEW COULSON *England 1922–24*
Had leaf-sprung suspension at both ends, with various engine options including a 496cc (30cu in) JAP for racing.

NEW-ERA *U.S.A. c.1908–13*
Step-through frame, with 546cc (33cu in) sv single mounted under the seat.

BELOW: A handsome New Imperial of the 1930s

NEW ERA *England 1920–22*
Mostly used the 311cc (19cu in) Dalm two-stroke engine, plus some Precision and JAP units.

NEW GERRARD *Scotland 1922–40*
Edinburgh-based, New Gerrard was run by the racer Jock Porter who won TT and Grand Prix races on these bikes. Blackburne engines were used up to the 1930s, followed by JAPs.

NEW HENLEY *England 1920–29*
Very similar to the Henley.

NEW HUDSON *England 1909–57*
Had the knowledge of leading designer/riders Fred Hutton and Bert Le Vack behind it and produced mostly mid-sized four-stroke singles, though also big V-twins and a 211cc (13cu in) two-stroke. Also experimented with engine enclosure. Production ceased in 1933, but BSA revived the name after 1945 for a 98cc (6cu in) autocycle.

NEW IMPERIAL *England 1903–39*
Until 1926, depended on Precision and JAP for its engines when New Imperial's own four-stroke singles began to appear in various sizes up to 498cc (30cu in). Acquired rear suspension early in 1938, but by then was in financial trouble. Was taken over by Ariel and the name was dropped.

NEW KNIGHT *England 1923–27*
Used 147cc to 344cc (9 to 21cu in) Villiers two-strokes and a 293cc (18cu in) JAP.

NEW-MAP *France 1920–58*
Bought engines from many sources ranging from 98–998cc (6–61cu in). After the war, concentrated on sub-250 scooters and motorcycles, some of which were fully enclosed, with Ydral, AMC and Sachs engines.

A New Imperial JAP Special

NEW MOTORCYCLE *France 1925–30*
A pressed steel frame housed a 250cc (15cu in) Train or 350/500 (21/30.5cu in) ohc Chaise units.

NEWMOUNT *England 1929–33*
Heavily Zündapp-based, though with its own tubular frames.

NEW PARAGON *England 1919–23*
Own two-stroke singles of 235–478cc (14.3–29cu in).

NEW RAPID *The Netherlands 1933–36*
Used Villiers two-strokes of up to 346cc (21cu in) and JAP or Python four-strokes to 498cc (30cu in).

NEW RYDER *England 1913–22*
Used Precision engines at first, but later switched to Villiers.

NEW SCALE *England 1909–25*
Offered a variety of engines in this two-speed chain/belt-driven machine. It was taken over by Dot in 1925.

NEWTON *England 1921–22*
Low-priced machines with 269cc (16cu in) Villiers power.

NFK *Germany 1924–5*
A licence-built 123cc (7.5cu in) Bekamo.

NICHOLAS *England pre–World War I*
1.5hp engines, probably from MMC.

NICKSON *England 1920–24*
Assembled a variety of models with engines from Villiers, Bradshaw and Blackburne.

The Danish Nimbus was always a shaft-driven four, but was only built in small numbers

NIESNER *Austria 1905–11*
One of the first Austrian manufacturers to use 3–5hp Minerva and Fafnir engines.

NIMBUS *Denmark 1920–57*
Denmark's leading maker concentrated on just one model, a 746cc (45.5cu in) in-line four in a pressed steel frame with shaft-drive. Was later updated with ohv and unit-construction. Few were sold.

NINON *France 1931–35*
499cc (30cu in) JAP-engined.

NIS *Germany 1925–26*
Produced small two- and four-strokes in own frames.

NISSAN *Japan 1951–56*
For a short while, built 60cc (3.7cu in) ohv machines.

NLG *England 1905–12*
Famous for its 2.9-litre JAP racer, though road machines were a more modest 499 or 770cc (30 or 47cu in).

NMC *Japan early 1950s–early 1960s*
123/173cc (7.5/11cu in) two-strokes.

NOBLE *England 1901–c.1906*
Used 2.25 to 4.5hp units from De Dion,

ABOVE: A 1938 unit-construction Nimbus

ABOVE: A 1936 Nimbus: note the fuel tank inside the frame rails

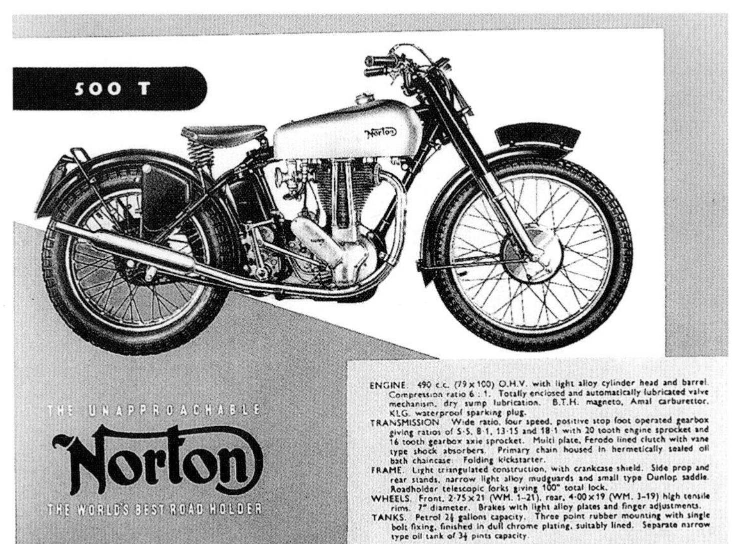

BELOW: The 'Unapproachable' Norton

Minerva, MMC and Coronet, as well as its own engines.

NORBRECK *England 1921–24*
Normally used Villiers or Arden two-strokes but larger machines with Blackburne units were made to order.

NORDSTERN *Germany 1922–24*
Built its own 2.5hp two-strokes.

NORICUM *Austria 1903–06*
2.75–5hp V-twins.

NORMAN *England 1937–61*
Started out with 98cc (6cu in) autocycles, later progressing to lightweights, all Villiers-powered. Was taken over by Raleigh in 1961.

NORTON *England 1902–*
One of the best known names in the British industry and perhaps, for a time, the best known in the world. The company had an impressive string of competition successes (Norton dominated international racing in the twenties and thirties) and a deserved reputation for building the finest-handling bikes of the fifties and sixties. Sadly, it also illustrated all that was wrong with the British industry, at least post-war. There was little forward planning or long-term investment, plant and machinery was out-dated, and it was possibly over-relying on past successes in order to safeguard its future.

James Landsdowne Norton had a remarkable life. Born in Birmingham in 1869, his was a strict religious upbringing, and early photographs of him as a young man show him, his handsome moustache freshly waxed, resplendent in his Salvation Army uniform. But James' main interests (and certainly his talents) lay in engineering. At the age of 12 he had built a model steam engine which he would place

ABOVE: An overhead-camshaft International Norton of 1936

OPPOSITE: An ohv ES2 single

in his front window, attracting such crowds that the police asked him to remove it. Inevitably, he became apprenticed to a toolmaker, but fell ill with rheumatic fever at the age of 19. He was to suffer ill health for the rest of his life, and appeared to age prematurely (hence the nickname 'Pa' which he acquired early on), none of which prevented him from leading a full and active life.

In 1898 he set up on his own with the Norton Manufacturing Company, initially to make chains, but within four years was advertising the first Norton motorcycle. In the manner of the time, it wasn't so much a motorcycle as a bicycle with a proprietory motor bolted on, in this case a French Clément. The 160cc (9.8cu in) engine was able to push the Norton Energette along at 32km/h (20mph) and it is not known how many were made, though Norton also chose to sell parts to other manufacturers. The demand was for bigger bikes, so Norton began to offer these as well, though at this stage still with bought-in engines. In 1906, seven models were listed, from a 200cc (12cu in) single to a 985cc (60cu in) V-twin and, apart from the Clément-engined 200, all were Peugeot-powered. And all, of course, were belt-driven, single-speed machines with neither clutch nor gearbox.

Until 1907, Norton's competition success had been limited to a few local hillclimbs, but that was the year Pa Norton persuaded Rem Fowler to ride a Norton in the TT, though neither had competed in a road race before. In fairy-tale fashion, the almost unknown bike and rider led from the start and, despite a puncture and numerous mechanical problems, won the race. This raised Norton's profile considerably, and back at home he got on with designing the first all-Norton engine. Although units were still being bought in (from Moto Rêve and Motosacoche as well as Peugeot) Pa was pinning his hopes on his own $3\frac{1}{2}$hp (475cc) sidevalve single (it had the 90mm stroke which was to become a Norton favourite). He also oversaw a return to the TT in 1908 with two bikes, but both failed to finish. Despite this, competition was beginning to dominate Norton's efforts, with actual production taking second place, a state of affairs that was to recur 40 years later. He actually rode in the TT himself in 1909 (now aged 40 and grey-bearded) on one of his own singles, but retired late in the race.

However, fortunately for the company, there was some work on road bikes. The famous Big Four, actually a sidevalve single of 660cc (40cu in), went on sale in 1910. With its massive 125mm stroke and low-speed lugging character, the Big Four was designed from the outset as a sidecar machine and was to be Norton's mainstay for many years. There was a JAP-powered 'ladies model' as well, and a two-stroke, a little 154cc (9.4cu in) lightweight designed by Pa himself. The 'Nortonette' weighed only 29.5kg (65lb) and offered a top speed of 56km/h (35mph), though at £33 it was little cheaper than the bigger four-strokes. And in 1911 a new 490cc (30cu in) single was announced, with the 79mm x 100mm cylinder dimensions that were to remain part of the range until 1963. There were no Peugeot engines now, and Norton was becoming known as a maker of big singles; the JAPs and two-strokes were soon dropped.

Recovery & War

Despite the pruned-back range, Norton was in financial trouble (Pa was more interested in bikes and racing than in finance), and was only saved from collapse by a businessman named R.T. Shelley, who bought the company but kept Pa on as joint managing director. The big singles continued as the company's mainstay, but competition success was becoming more elusive. A sign of the times was when Indians took the first three places in the 1911 TT. They had proper clutches and three-speed gearboxes and easily outpaced the belt-driven single-speed bikes. In 1915, Norton finally fitted chain-drive, clutch and gearbox to the Big Four and 490cc singles. The gearbox was a three-speed Sturmey-Archer, with a two-plate clutch and hand gearchange. If you insisted, you could still have an outmoded belt-drive on the 490. This was also the year that the famous Norton logo, with its curly 'N', made an appearance. It was designed by Pa Norton and his daughter Ethel, and must surely be one of the most enduring of all time.

Norton was to do well during World War I, due mainly to the fact that the War Office failed to approve its bikes for military use, thereby allowing the company to concentrate on the civilian market. As far as it was concerned, the main problem was the non-availability of German magnetos! In 1916, another long-running Norton first saw the light of day, the 16H. It was in fact not new, merely the existing 490cc TT model with the addition of a Sturmey three-speed gearbox and enclosed primary chain. In various guises, the 16H was to form a central part of the range until 1954. In fact, Norton was obviously on the road to recovery, able to transfer to a bigger factory that year, a site it was to occupy, in enlarged form along the famous Bracebridge Street, until the 1960s.

After the war, the Norton range had been reduced to just two models, the Big Four and 490, though there were variations on each theme. Pa Norton's health wasn't improving; he was a chronic neuritis sufferer and he actually had a nervous breakdown in 1919, though returned to work fairly swiftly. He was rewarded with a second place in the 1920 TT, though the following year only three Nortons out of 15 entered managed to even finish, the best taking sixth place, broken valves being blamed for the retirements. In fact, it was time for a rethink. Although Norton's sidevalve singles held many speed records at Brooklands, they were in danger of being eclipsed by newer overhead-valve rivals. Fortunately, Pa had the matter in hand, and came up with an ohv version of the 490cc single which went on sale in late 1922, the most expensive model in the range. It had already proved its speed when Rex Judd set a fresh round of Brooklands records earlier in the year, while Graham Walker used one to win the sidecar TT in 1923.

Shortly before that competition debut Pa, now aged 52, undertook an astonishing three-month tour of South Africa on a Big Four and sidecar. Most of the journey was on dirt roads which turned into quagmires in the inclement winter weather. Many rivers had to be forded and Pa was travelling alone, apart from a native boy named Jim. At times they were forced to wrap a bicycle chain around the rear tyre in order to get sufficient grip, and at one point Pa had to ride 50 miles in first gear. In the event, he covered the 3,000 miles from Durban to Cape Town and probably enjoyed himself in the process, while Norton the company received valuable publicity from the trip, the Big Four having happily remained trouble-free. Unfortunately, it was to be Pa's last big trip and though he was now suffering from cancer, he managed to keep on working throughout 1923 and early '24 and even patented an ohc design with desmodromic valve control in April 1924. Happily, he also lived to see a Norton win the TT that year – the first time since Rem Fowler's 1907 victory. He died the following spring.

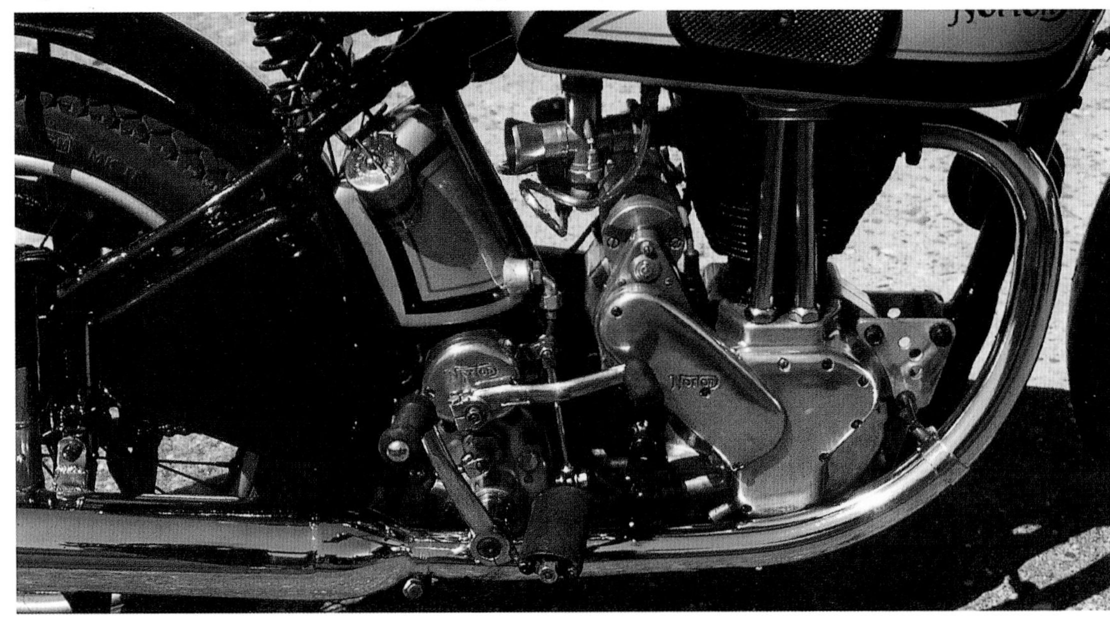

A 1919 Norton 500. The first bikes were Peugeot-engined

ABOVE: Did Norton build the first race replicas?

OPPOSITE: 1928 Norton CS1 490cc (30cu in)

Race Replicas

Meanwhile, the post-war boom had ended and, along with most manufacturers, Norton had to cut its prices in order to compete. The Big Four, costing £135 in 1920 was now in 1923 on offer at £76, though the ohv Model 18 was only slightly down at £89. For the first time, electric lighting was an option (an extra £13) though no new bikes were announced; the ohv, still in its first full year, was new enough. A 588cc (36cu in) version joined the range in 1926, equipped with a new four-speed gearbox (now also fitted to the Big Four). Stanley Woods won the TT for Norton that year, and the Irish rider was to dominate road racing right up to 1939. He played a major part in Norton's history and the company naturally capitalized on this, reminding its customers that what was basically the same bike (the 490cc Model 18) could very well be theirs. It was also one of the fastest bikes of its day.

The following year was a significant one, featuring the competition debut of the first overhead-camshaft Norton. It had been designed by Walter Moore and, just like the ohv, was based on the familiar 79mm x 100mm bottom-end, albeit with the addition of a bevel-drive overhead cam. It was a success and Alec Bennett won the TT on one in 1927. It was a good year, with the new machine winning all but one of the international races. A road-going replica of that bike, the CS1 was announced and *Motorcycling* magazine tested it and was most impressed with its low-speed docility, describing it as 'like a lamb in traffic or like a lion on the open road'.

For a long time, Norton had made nothing smaller than a 500, but 1929 saw a 350 version of the CS1, the Norton Junior or CJ (which had had an unsuccessful debut at the 1928 TT), and an ohv version, the JE, both with the same 71mm x 88mm dimensions. In fact, there were signs of a new emphasis on road bikes. The factory now had its own chrome plating plant, and added two twin-port machines for 1930, though electric lighting was still an extra. At the last minute, at the same Olympia Show in London, a redesigned ohc engine with new crankcase was displayed on the Norton stand. It was to underpin Norton's racers for the next 35 years.

The road bikes were beginning to look rather outdated, a foretaste of the Norton tendency to concentrate too hard on racing and leave the bikes that earned them a living to take care of themselves. Sure enough, the 1930s saw little really new for the road bikes, and perhaps the biggest change came in 1931 when both sidevalve and ohv bikes adopted dry sump lubrication with a geared pump and the magneto moved to the back of the engine. Still, there was more racing success from the redesigned ohc engine, and dedicated road-burners continued to choose the Norton International – a real race replica of its day. Meanwhile, the twin-port ohv JE models were dropped. There were some updates in the years that followed, notably a tank-top instrument panel option in 1933 and (far more useful) the four-speed footchange gearbox was made standard across the

Norton
35
DC-8159
3.00-19
AVON SPEEDMASTER MK II

range in 1935. As ever, though, the race-based Internationals were ahead in the technology stakes, with an optional aluminium-bronze head and aluminium barrel, not to mention plunger rear suspension from 1938. Also that year, but not catalogued, was the combination of the 597cc (36cu in) with bevel-drive overhead cam, intended for sidecar use in road racing and the ISDT. All of which had to be abandoned the following year, along with the planned 1940 range which would have included engine and frame changes to many of the bikes. Instead, the outbreak of war meant a dedication to 16H production for the army. Just like Harley's sidevalve WLA, Norton's 500 now assumed a new importance, and this most basic of Nortons was built by the thousands for the war effort.

The 1939 500cc (31.5cu in) Norton ES2, faster than the sidevalve 16H, less exotic than the ohc International

Back into Profit

After the war it was very much business as usual, for the first couple of years at least. The civilian 16H went straight back into production, based closely on the 1939 version, while an overhead-valve 500 single returned as the Model 18. The two bikes shared much, notably the engine bottom-end, the frame, clutch and four-speed gearbox. Still no telescopic forks or rear suspension, but in late 1945 most of the British factories returned directly to pre-war designs. The ohc Nortons returned the following year as the 350 and 500 Manx Nortons, with the basic engine format largely unchanged from the 1930 original, though they did have Roadholder telescopic forks and plunger rear suspension. Meanwhile, the faithful Big Four returned for 1947, as did the 40 and 30 Internationals, with cast-iron versions of the racing ohc engine. There were also 350 and 500 Trials models (the wartime 16H frame with ohv engines). The latter didn't last long, being replaced in 1949 by the 500T, a well-regarded trials machine with an all-alloy ohv single, a shorter frame and lower weight. It was popular with private competitors and lasted for five years.

But the big news for 1949 (and of far more relevance to Norton's post-war history) was the new Model 7 Dominator, Norton's first vertical twin. It was the work of Bert Hopwood, late of BSA and Triumph, who arrived at the Norton works in April 1947. Coming straight from the dynamic atmosphere of Meriden, Hopwood was appalled by what he found at Norton, which he related in his book *Whatever Happened to the British Motorcycle Industry?* Not only was it a cramped and crowded factory ('a noisy, dirty conglomeration'), but a competition-orientated policy had caused most of the funds to be set aside for development of race bikes. Hopwood later discovered the reason for this; race chief Joe Craig was paid by results. The awe with which racing in general and Craig in particular was held by Norton was quite something. It was said that if managing director Gilbert Smith knocked on Craig's office door and received no 'Come in', he would just quietly walk away!

The range of road singles was decidedly elderly – certainly no match for rival twins – and Hopwood's first job was to design a Norton twin. The Dominator was the result, a 497cc (30cu in) vertical twin which looked superficially similar to rivals though Hopwood, drawing on his Triumph experience, placed all four pushrods behind the cylinder barrel and splayed valve-gear, all to improve cooling (the Norton had an iron head and barrel so this was more critical). As ever, Norton was strapped for cash, which forced some compromises: Hopwood couldn't have the one-piece crankshaft he wanted, while the new engine was housed in ES2 cycle parts. But the Dominator was well-received though, by the time it went on sale, Hopwood was not there to take the credit, Joe Craig having insisted on a last-minute hold-up to boost the power. At this point, Hopwood (on the point of resigning in disgust) was dismissed. However, as far as Norton was concerned, he had done his job in providing the new twin which it desperately needed, and one which was to form the backbone of its range for the next 30 years.

Another idea which had had its source outside the company and which did Norton a lot of good was the famous Featherbed frame. It was the brainchild of Ulsterman Rex McCandless, who had been working on it for eight years. It looked simple, but provided unrivalled standards of handling and roadholding that put Norton ahead of everyone else (and was coveted by café racer builders as the best frame of its time). According to McCandless, there was initial resistance to the frame from Norton until it became clear that the racers' new-found success in the early fifties wasn't just down to the riding skills of a young Geoff Duke. The factory relented, and Manx Nortons had the Featherbed frame which was eventually adopted throughout the whole range.

Despite the advent of the Dominator, and Featherbed-inspired race successes, Norton simply wasn't able to survive on its own and in 1953 was taken over by Associated Motor Cycles (AMC, the AJS/Matchless concern). For Norton lovers, AMC tends to have the same associations as AMF does for Harley-Davidson. The parent company appeared to have little sympathy with its new acquisition, and as its own financial situation worsened, began to siphon off the profits that were at last coming Norton's way. It refused to sell Norton through its own U.S. export channel, and even prevented Norton from moving out of the cramped Bracebridge Street factory.

Much of the reason for Norton's improving fortunes in the late fifties was down to Bert Hopwood, who had returned as managing director in 1955. From previous experience he knew where the problems lay and set about solving them: when an export deal finally got Nortons selling in America, releasing previously untapped potential, and though his plan to

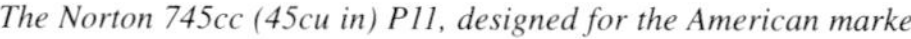
The Norton 745cc (45cu in) P11, designed for the American market

Norton's first vertical twin, the Dominator

The 1948 International. The ohc Norton returned after the war, to be developed into the Featherbed-framed Manx

move out of Bracebridge was thwarted, he did manage to instil some team spirit into the plant. The already respected Dominator was given a capacity boost to 596cc (36cu in) as the Dominator 99 and he was able to start work on a new Norton 250.

This was the Jubilee (to celebrate 60 years since Pa Norton had set up on his own), and it was actually quite modern with unit-construction and a short stroke of 44mm that made it high-revving (up to 8,500rpm) though it was a little buzzy compared to equivalent singles. But it handled well and was easy to ride, and its arrival in 1959 was just in time to take advantage of the new 250cc learner laws. Unfortunately, it soon gained a reputation for unreliability when crankshafts broke on the early bikes (apparently someone in the drawing office sent out the wrong specification) and the Francis-Barnett electrics were poor. This was unfortunate,

ABOVE: A 1956 500cc (31.5cu in) Norton International

BELOW: A 1975 850 MK3 Norton Commando roadster

BELOW: A late-1955 ES2

ABOVE and RIGHT: The Dominator grew into the 650cc (40cu in) 99

ABOVE: An interesting 1974 prototype, a BSA single in a Norton Isolastic frame

The McCandless brothers' Featherbed frame soon found its way into such mainstay bikes as Norton's ES2

as the Jubilee had some very good points, and many of the criticisms were overcome by the 1961 350cc (21cu in) Navigator version and the 1963 Electra 400, complete with electric start and indicators. Due to the parent company's problems, all three were dropped in the mid-sixties.

Meanwhile, the big twin had become Norton's only other product, with the singles, whether sidevalve, ohv or ohc, gradually dropped (though in 1965 the Norton badge was stuck on AMC's own 350 and 500 singles). The 600 Dominator had become the U.S. market 650 Manxman in 1961, then the 650SS for Britain, though the 500 was still offered as well. Some regarded the SS as one of the finest British twins. With its twin carburettors, 49bhp at 6,800rpm, and in traditional Norton silver, the SS looked and performed the part, and thanks to its Featherbed frame handled better than the Triumph and BSA equivalents. Dealer Syd Lawton had great success with one in production endurance racing.

But just like BSA and Triumph, Norton was under pressure from its American customers for yet more power, so the SS was joined in early 1964 by the 750cc (46cu in) Atlas. They had actually asked for something that would accelerate from 20 to 100mph in top gear, and Doug Hele obliged by boring out the 650, while keeping a modest rate of tune. With its 7.6:1 compression ratio, the Atlas was an untemperamental, torquey engine; it was only when the 750 was over-tuned in later years that serious problems with reliability arose. There was also an Atlas Scrambler, which was suited to the engine's characteristics and, thanks to demand in the States, these nominal off-roaders were to remain part of the Norton range for the rest of the decade.

In 1966, AMC instructed its bank to appoint a receiver – it had run out of money. Norton, however, was now very much the healthier partner and a buyer was soon found, though the other AMC marques (AJS, Matchless, James and Francis-Barnett) soon disappeared. Manganese Bronze was the new owner, headed by Dennis Poore.

The Commando Era

The advent of Poore appeared to bode well for the future of the new Norton-Villiers company, and one of his first actions was to call a meeting to decide on a replacement for the Atlas. A five-year-old prototype, an 800cc (49cu in) dohc unit-construction twin, was resurrected and named the P10. Unfortunately, P10 had problems with its immensely long cam-chain as well as bad vibration, and with three months to go before its intended launch, was dropped.

Designer Bernard Hooper suggested an alternative, namely that of rubber-mounting the proven Atlas engine to eradicate the twin's vibration once and for all. They worked fast, and soon had a prototype that gave a vibration-free ride above 1,800rpm. To emphasize the new concept, the 750 twin was inclined in the frame and design house Wolf Ohlins was consulted on styling. The result was the Norton Commando, which made a huge impact when launched at the 1967 Motorcycle Show. Launched ahead of the BSA/Triumph triples and the Honda CB750, it could claim to be the first superbike. It certainly looked good, and combined light weight (195kg/430lb) with the grunty Atlas engine, which still had to be kick-started but, when rubber-mounted, represented the acceptable face of big British twins. It seemed as if the old bugbear of vibration had been cured at last, though the Commando's Isolastic chassis failed to handle as well as a Featherbed, and if the vital shim adjustment of the Isolastic mountings was neglected could be positively dangerous. For the moment, though, the Commando was certainly the bike to have.

This was just as well, as Norton was having to move again. Under AMC, it had already had to leave Bracebridge Street for Plumstead, south London. Now that factory was due for demolition, and Norton-Villiers decreed that Commandos should be made near Andover in Hampshire, despite the fact that the engines were already being built in

The overhead-cam Norton single came in 350 and 500 sizes

Wolverhampton, over 100 miles away. Still, the Commando was proving a competitive racer as well as road bike, so much so that Norton announced the Production Racer, with tuned engine, front disc brake and half-fairing. There were other variations on the theme, notably the 750S, with high-level exhausts and high, wide bars (a hangover from the street scrambler look), the custom style Hi Rider of 1971 and the police-specified Interpol. The latter was the brainchild of Neale Shilton, an ebullient supersalesman who travelled everywhere by bike. He had had the Interpol accepted by many forces, and it was all useful business for Norton.

What wasn't so useful were the problems of reliability that were beginning to emerge. Main bearings and pistons could sometimes give trouble, but the real nasties were exposed when highly-tuned versions such as the 65bhp, 10:1 compression 'Combat' engine was introduced. It was too much for what was now an elderly design. Norton realized it had gone too far and detuned the 750, adding an 828cc (50.5cu in) version in 1973 to make up for any performance shortfall. In reality, the Commando 850 was no faster than the early ones, but it was more reliable. Many of the Commando's weak points were addressed with this bike, but it couldn't hide the fact that the venerable Norton twin was simply outdated when compared with the Japanese and German opposition. The JPN race replica of 1974, with its twin headlight fairing, looked good, and the Commando even gained an electric start the year after; but it was all too little, too late, and Commando production (this was Norton's sole model, remember) ended in 1975, with a final batch built in 1977. (Norton had returned to racing in 1971, with a team sponsored by John Player, which culminated in Peter Williams winning the Formula 750 race during TT week.)

However, this was far from being the end of the Norton story. Whether it was the beginning of the end, or the end of the beginning is still in doubt a quarter of a century later. The background is complicated. In 1972, the British Government had agreed to save the motorcycle industry with an injection of cash, but only on condition that BSA/Triumph and Norton-Villiers merged. It also required Dennis Poore to head the new company, since he appeared to have made a success of Norton. Norton-Villiers-Triumph (NVT) was the result. Ever since, arguments have been bandied back and forth as to whether this was a good or bad

A 1957 348cc (21cu in) Norton Manx Model 40M

The final electric-start version of the Commando 850

thing for the industry. Norton certainly had a successful product, and was profitable. On the other hand, although BSA/Triumph was losing money, it did have a forward product plan well under way, whereas Poore's plans were uncertain and unambitious. Two NVT projects were in progress, one of which was the liquid-cooled racing engine designed by Cosworth. This eight-valve 750cc twin was modern, but a long way from being ready for the road. It was also heavy and on the few occasions it raced, failed to distinguish itself.

In the meantime, NVT was in the process of immediate and severe contraction. An announcement that Meriden was to close led to sit-ins (*see section on* Triumph) and similar actions at Wolverhampton and Andover. This in itself was a serious financial drain, but there was also a downturn in the vital U.S. motorcycle market in 1975 (as important to the British industry as ever) and NVT went into liquidation in August that year. The outcome of this period of complications was NVT Engineering Ltd. in late 1976, set up with the remainder of Government money which had already been promised. This was a much smaller operation than any of its predecessors and carried on to produce a moped (the Easy Rider) and a 125cc (7.6cu in) trail bike, the Rambler. These machines were built up from mostly imported parts; the moped was Morini-

ABOVE and BELOW: First (497cc/30cu in) and final (828cc/50cu in) versions of the Norton vertical twin

OPPOSITE: A 1959 Model 88

The race-styled John Player Norton was designed to capitalize on the race programme

powered, while the Rambler's engine came from Yamaha. The presumption was that they would be an eventual route back to in-house designs, and while the Rambler later sold reasonably well as the BSA Tracker, this never happened, though the company did manage to sell its expertise in setting up plants in the Third World.

But NVT's great hope for the future was really none of these and it turned instead to the rotary engine project, which had been inherited from BSA. Now trading as Norton Motors, based at Shenstone, the idea was to productionize the rotary for an all-new range of Nortons. Running prototypes had actually been on the road since the early 1970s, and were now acceptably reliable. In fact, the bike showed a great deal of promise: it weighed a reasonable 204kg (450lb) and claimed over 80bhp from its nominal 588cc (36cu in), with a top speed of 209km/h (130mph). Norton could not afford to go into full production, but from 1981 began to first loan, then sell, limited numbers of Interpol IIs to various British police forces. A 90bhp liquid-cooled version was also under development.

But by 1985 there was no sign of the necessary finance to begin full production, and the parent company, Manganese Bronze, decided the time had come to sell. Matters came to a head when Dennis Poore, after a difficult ten years, fell terminally ill. He died in February 1987. But beforehand, he had negotiated the sale of Norton to Philippe Le Roux, a South African-born financier who was to inject new life into the company by financing the building of a limited-edition rotary for the civilian market, the Norton Classic. All 100 Classics sold quickly. He also gave the go-ahead for a return to racing, which led to a very successful few years for the rotary on track, masterminded by Brian Chrighton and with sponsorship from first Duckhams, then John Player. Meanwhile, the Norton Commander with the liquid-cooled engine had been launched. Basically a civilianized version of the police machine, with fairing and panniers, it filled a niche and was good to ride, if a little expensive. There was also a road-going version of the racer, the F1. But sadly, in the early 1990s, everything fell apart again. Le Roux came under investigation by the Department of Trade and Industry, and resigned.

The Norton F1, a highly priced rotary sportster

LEFT and ABOVE: Norton's outrageous Nemesis V8 was unveiled to a sceptical press in 1998. 235bhp, 362km/h (225mph) and imminent production was promised

Yet it still wasn't the end of Norton; the Midland Bank was still owed £7 million, and stood more chance of getting it back by keeping Norton afloat. It replaced Le Roux with David McDonald, who sold the company to Canadian entrepreneur Nelson Skalbania in 1993. Skalbania was unable to repay the money he had borrowed to buy Norton, so ownership reverted to the company which had backed him, the Aquilini Investment Group. By now, a skeleton staff at Shenstone was making spares and servicing bikes, which was all they could afford to do. Aquilini had acquired Norton by default, and was therefore keen to sell.

In 1998 it happened. Norton's latest owner was a group of American financiers who in 1995 had bought March, the British racing-car manufacturer. Since then, it had commissioned engine designer Al Melling (based in the north of England) to draw up a four-cylinder 750cc (46cu in) superbike engine. The chance to buy Norton offered the opportunity to build bikes with a well respected name, which counts for a great deal. And so Norton Motors International was born. The shock came in April 1998 when it was announced that the new Norton company would soon be making, not only the 750 but also a 1497cc (91cu in) V8 (two 750s spliced together), and a range of 600cc (37cu in) singles as well. The V8 would power a hyper sportsbike, the Norton Nemesis, with a projected 235bhp and a top speed of well over 322km/h (200mph). There were doubters, of course, especially when Al Melling confidently predicted that the V8 would be in production that autumn. It wasn't, which was hardly surprising given such a wildly ambitious scheme. Still, by January 1999, there were reports that the V8 was now running on the test bench, so perhaps this latest chapter in Norton's long and varied history could still become reality. By the time this book is published, we may very well know the answer.

NORVED *Germany 1924–25*
Small production of Kühne-powered singles.

NOVA *Hungary 1925–28*
Assembled sporting bikes from mainly English parts, including engines from JAP and Blackburne.

NOVY *Belgium c.1935–1960s*
Produced Villiers-powered lightweights before the war, adding a 250cc (15cu in) Ilo in 1954. Date of closure of the company is uncertain.

NSH *Germany 1923–28*
Used Villiers and JAP engines of 173–490cc (11–30cu in).

NSU *Germany 1900–63*
In the 1930s, NSU was one of the largest motorcycle manufacturers in the world, yet it pulled out of the market voluntarily to concentrate on cars. It first fitted a 1.5hp Zedel to one of its bicycles, and within a couple of years was building its own 329cc 2.5hp engine, and an 804cc (49cu in) V-twin the year after that. It offered a wide variety of singles and V-twins over the next 30 years, notably a unit-construction 498cc (30cu in) single and two ohc racing singles designed by Walter Moore, fresh from Norton. There were also 98–200cc (6–12cu in) two-strokes. Big V-twins were still in evidence, but after 1945 NSU concentrated on sub-250 machines. The first new one, in 1949, was the ohv 98cc Fox, a lightweight machine with pressed steel frame, leading link forks and cantilever rear suspension and, being well made and reliable, set the seal on NSU's post-war success. This was underlined by the Quickly moped in 1953 (over a million were sold in ten years) and the new Prima scooter in 1956 which replaced a licence-built Lambretta. Meanwhile, the pre-war ohv singles had continued to 1952, to be replaced by the ohc Max, which continued the NSU trademarks of pressed steel frame and leading link forks with a modern, powerful engine. In 250 Supermax form it could top 121km/h (75mph) and was a good seller and competitive racer, though there were also dohc pure racers as well. Unfortunately, quality didn't come cheap, and sales began to decline to the point where NSU ceased production of motorcycles in 1963, and of mopeds two years later.

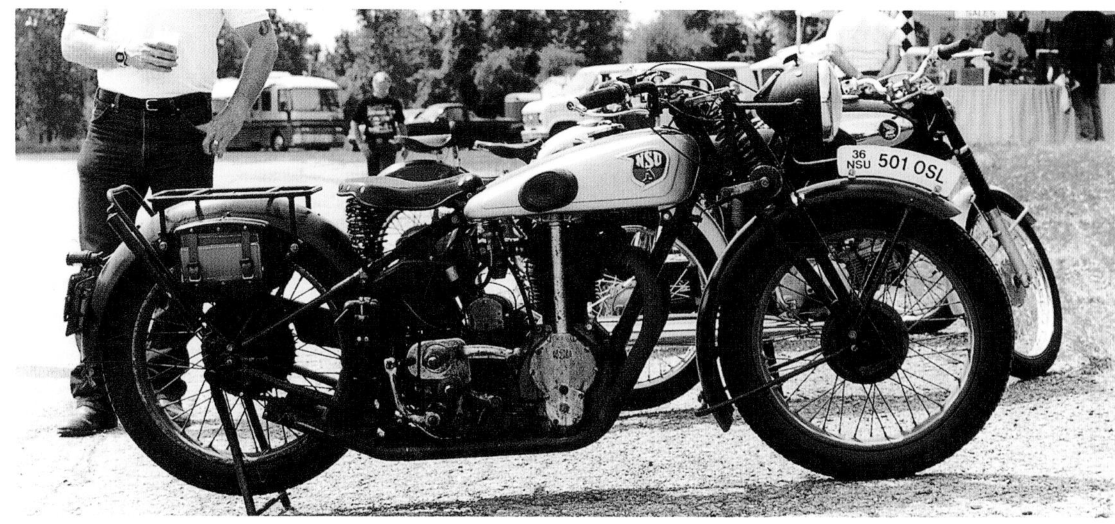

ABOVE and BELOW: NSU built a long line of overhead-camshaft singles

ABOVE: Actress Jill Curzon tries out the NSU Quickly LF

ABOVE: The NSU Delphin III record-breaker

BELOW: A 1954 250cc (15cu in) NSU

BELOW: The Max made a successful racer

NUT England *1912–33*
Newcastle-based, it won the TT in its second year, and built its own V-twins and singles as well as using JAP units. Financial weakness often interrupted production in the 1920s, and NUT failed to survive the world slump.

NUX *Germany 1924–25*
Produced 170cc (10.4cu in) three-port two-strokes.

NV *Sweden 1926–60*
Best known, until 1932, for a fast 246cc (15cu in) ohv single, but from then on concentrated on small two-strokes, apart from a 1000cc (61cu in) V-twin for the military, and made the Royal Enfield Bullet under licence.

ABOVE and BELOW: A 1927 700cc (43cu in) NUT V-twin

O

OASA *Italy 1930–32*
Used a 173cc (11cu in) Ladetto engine, also 246/346cc (15/21cu in) JAP ohv singles.

OB *Austria 1904–07*
Built own 2hp single/3.5hp V-twins, with shaft-drive.

OBERLE *Germany 1927–29*
147/172cc (9/10.5cu in) Villiers-powered two-strokes.

OCMA *Italy 1953–57*
A rebadged Devil, otherwise identical.

OCRA *Germany 1923–25*
Clip-ons of 137cc (8cu in), plus 293/346cc (18/21cu in) sv and ohv machines.

OD *Germany 1927–35*
Mostly used MAG engines of 347–996cc (21–31cu in), though there were also alloy-framed lightweights with Bark two-stroke engines.

ODA Germany 1925–26
Produced 293cc (18cu in) JAP-powered motorcycles.

OEC *England 1901–54*
Frederick Osborn built some Minerva and MMC-powered bikes, and his son John resumed production in 1920 with Blackburne engines which included 348/547cc (21/33cu in) singles and 998cc (61cu in) V-twins. There was also an ohc 350 racer and record-breaking V-twins, not to mention other engines from Anzani, Atlantis, Villiers and JAP. The company was famous at this time for the duplex steering frame. Production restarted in 1949 with Villiers engines.

OFRAN *Germany 1923–25*
Its sole model was its own 425cc (26cu in) three-port two-stroke.

OGAR *Czechoslovakia 1934–50*
Concentrated on one model, its 246cc (15cu in) two-stroke, though water-cooled versions were made for racing.

OGE *Germany 1921–24*
A 118cc (7cu in) clip-on.

OGSTON *England 1911–13*
Wilkinson-TMC adopted this name for a while.

OHB *Germany 1927–1928*
A JAP-powered 490cc (30 cu in) sv single.

OEC

OLYMPIQUE *France 1922–58*
Zurcher and JAP two- and four-strokes, to which small AMC four-strokes were added after the war.

OLYMPUS-KING *Japan 1956–60*
An English-influenced 123cc (7.5cu in) two-stroke and 346cc (21cu in) ohv single.

OM *Germany 1923–25*
Used JAP engines of 173–490cc (11–30cu in).

OMA *Italy 1952–55*
Built 173cc (11cu in) unit-designed ohv and ohc singles with three-speed gearboxes.

OMB *Italy 1933–34*
174cc (11cu in) ohv singles, designed by Angelo Blatto.

OMC *Italy 1933–35*
Another 174cc single, this one was Ladetto-designed.

OMEA *Italy 1950–53*
A 124cc (8cu in) two-stroke in a cast alloy frame with swinging-arm rear suspension and leading link fork.

OMEGA *England 1909*
Had a 1.5hp horizontally-mounted engine.

OMEGA *England 1919–27*
Bought in a range of 269–678cc (16–41cu in) Villiers and JAP units to supplement its own two-strokes.

OMEGA *Japan 1960s*
Rebadged Kawasakis for the U.S. market.

OK (OK-SUPREME) England 1899–1939
The first bikes used De Dion, Minerva, Precision and Green engines, but OK developed its own 292cc (18cu in) two-stroke after World War I and also used Blackburne sv and ohc singles and oil-cooled Bradshaws. Final offerings were powered by the JAP high-camshaft singles of 248–498cc (15–30cu in).

OLIVA *Italy 1920–25*
A 120cc (7cu in) clip-on, followed by a 173cc (11cu in) lightweight (Train-powered two-stroke).

OLIVERIO *Italy 1929–32*
Sturmey-Archer ohv singles of 346/496cc (21/30cu in).

OLIVOS *England 1920–21*
Used a 496cc (30cu in) Blackburne in its own sprung frame.

OLLEARO *Italy 1932–52*
Advanced unit-construction singles of 173–499cc (11–30cu in) with four-speed gearboxes and shaft-drive which remained in production after World War II, alongside a 45cc (3cu in) clip-on.

OLMO *Italy 1951–61*
Used a 38cc (2.3cu in) Mosquito and 48cc (3cu in) two-strokes of various makes.

OLYMPIC *England 1903–23*
Used MMC engines first, then Verus and Orbit two-strokes after eventual relaunch in 1919. Also sold as the cheaper New Courier brand.

Ogar

OMER *Italy 1968–81*
Minarelli- and Morini-engined mopeds.

OMN *Italy 1924–25*
Produced 147/172cc (9/10.5cu in) Villiers-engined lightweights.

OMNIA *Italy 1949–53*
Rebadged MTs with 248cc (15cu in) ohc vertical twins.

ONAWAY *England 1904–08*
Had a low-slung frame and Kelecom 5hp V-twin.

OPEL *Germany 1901–30*
Until 1930, car manufacturer Opel dabbled in motorcycles, from a 1.75hp pioneer to a four-stroke clip-on (1918). In 1922–25 came 148/498cc (9/30cu in) complete bikes then, for a couple of years, a takeover of the pressed steel Neander, the Motoclub. Fritz von Opel tested one of the latter with six rockets strapped to it to assist progress, but it never went beyond the experimental stage.

OR *Italy 1928–31*
Produced own clip-ons and 173cc (11cu in) lightweights.

ORBIT *England 1913–24*
Utilized its own 261cc (16cu in) two-stroke and a variety of larger bought-in four-strokes.

OREOL *France 1903–14*
Used a 333cc (20cu in) single and bought-in V-twins from Zedel, Moto Rêve *et al.*

ORI *Germany 1923–25*
Produced 145cc (9cu in) two-strokes.

ORIAL *France 1919–26*
Fitted only MAG singles and twins, due to close connections with the factory.

ORIAL *Germany 1929–31*
When the English and German arms of Triumph separated, Orial replaced Triumph of Nuremberg, with MAG engines replacing the Coventry-sourced parts.

ORIENT *U.S.A. 1900–c.1906*
Used 2.25/2.5hp engines in strengthened cycle frames.

ORIGAN *France 1929–50*
Produced 98–174cc (6–11cu in) lightweights, mainly with Aubier-Dunne engines.

ORIGINAL-KRIEGER *Germany 1925–26*
Made a 498cc (30cu in), then 346cc (21cu in) Blackburne-engined bike, related to the KG.

ORION *Czechoslovakia 1902–33*
Produced own singles and V-twins, including a 594cc (36cu in) double-pistoned two-stroke.

ORIONE *Italy 1923–28*
Sporting two-strokes of 123 and 173cc (7.5 and 11cu in).

ORIONETTE *Germany 1921–25*
All two-strokes of 129–346cc (8–21cu in), mostly unit-constructed, but also an interesting combined two/four-stroke with a valve in the crankcase.

ORIX *Italy 1949–54*
Made 123/183cc (7.5/11.2cu in) scooters and 173cc (11cu in) Ilo-powered lightweights.

ORMONDE *England 1900–c.1906*
Used 2.25/2.75hp Kelecom and 3.5hp Antoine engines.

ORTLOFF *Germany 1924–26*
Used 185 and 198cc (11.3 and 12cu in) Gruhn sidevalves.

ORTONA *England 1904–06*
Its sole model was a 3.5hp single.

ORUK *Germany 1922–24*
A 198cc (12cu in) sv single was mounted outside the rear wheel, with direct-drive.

OSA *Poland 1958–*
123/173cc (7.5/11cu in) two-stroke scooters with trailing-link forks.

OSA-LIBERTY *France 1920–32*
Used licence-built JAPs as well as its own 173 and 246cc (11 and 15cu in) two-strokes.

OSCAR *England 1953–55*
A Villiers-powered scooter, a brainchild of Dennis Poore.

OSCAR *Italy 1965–82*
Various mopeds, with the usual Minarelli or Franco-Morini power.

OSCHA *Germany 1924–25*
An unusual 496cc (30 cu in) flat twin with water-cooling.

OSMOND *England 1911–24*
Used own 102/110cc (6/7cu in) two-strokes after 1918 (built for Osmond by Simplex) and a 485cc (30cu in) Precision single.

OSSA *Spain 1951–84*
Made a few four-strokes, otherwise its road and motocross bikes used air-cooled two-strokes. A 124cc (8cu in) single from 1949 was replaced by a 159cc (9.7cu in) in 1962 which grew to 230cc (14cu in) and formed the mainstay of Ossa production. There was also a 250cc (15cu in) twin racer from 1967 and a 461cc (28cu in) road twin from 1972. However, new 244 and 302cc (15 and 18cu in) engines in the late 1970s couldn't prevent Ossa's collapse in the following harsher decade.

OTTO *Germany 1921–37*
Rebadged Flottweg bikes, using 198 and 293cc (12 and 18cu in) JAP engines.

OTTOLENGHI *Italy 1928–32*
Produced mostly 174cc (11cu in) ohv sportsters with a choice of engine makes, also 246/346cc (15/21cu in) JAPs.

OVERDALE *England 1921–22*
Used a 169cc (10cu in) Villiers and was offered by a Glasgow firm though made in the English Midlands.

OVERSEAS England 1909–15
An 842cc (51cu in) V-twin, designed exclusively for export to what were then referred to as 'The Colonies'.

P

PA *Belgium 1921–29*
An English-type design equipped with 174–247cc (11–15cu in) sv and ohv Blackburne engines. From 1925 onwards, PA built its own 245cc two-stroke and 345cc (21cu in) ohv engines and after 1927 also fitted 348cc and 490cc (30cu in) JAP and MAG sv and ohv engines.

PACER *England 1914*
A 116cc (7cu in) single from JES.

PAFFRATH *Germany 1923–26*
Very similar to the MW, with cast alloy/pressed steel frame.

PAGLIANTI *Italy 1958–60*
Two-stroke mini-scooters.

PALLION *England 1905–14*
Used Minerva, Fafnir, JAP and Villiers engines.

PALOMA *France 1954–64*
Gillet and Lafalette engines powered a 70cc (4.3cu in) scooter, among others.

PAMAG *Germany 1952–53*
Ilo-engined two-strokes of 123–197cc (7.5–12cu in).

PAN *Germany 1924–25*
Used 346cc (21cu in) ohv Kühne power units.

PANDRA *Japan 1958–60*
A 147cc (9cu in) scooter with period styling.

PANNI *Hungary 1959–62*
A 48cc (3cu in) mini-scooter.

PANNONIA *Hungary 1951–65*
This 247cc (15cu in) two-stroke was built with a choice of one or two cylinders.

PANTHER *Germany 1903–07*
Used Fafnir engines in cycle frames.

PANTHER *England 1904–1966*
Actually, the company was not Panther at all, but Phelon & Moore Limited, but it was so

ABOVE: The 461cc twin was Ossa's largest bike

BELOW: Ossa built a range of road bikes, but is best remembered for its trials bikes

BELOW: Ossa trial motorcycle

LEFT and ABOVE: A 1934 250cc (15cu in) Panther

closely identified with the Panther model that the two names became interchangeable. From start to finish, the Panther was a big four-stroke 'sloping' single, which made up in slogging ability for what it lacked in agility and no other manufacturer has remained so true to one concept for so long.

In 1901, Jonah Phelon was experimenting with motorized bicycles when he hit upon the idea of using the engine as a stressed member of the frame, sloping the single cylinder forward to replace the downtube. It was more rigid than the conventional arrangement, and very common today, but Phelon was one of the first to think of it. First produced under licence by Humber, the 500cc (30.5cu in) bikes were built from 1904 by Phelon and his new partner, Richard Moore, who had designed a novel two-speed gear, and this was incorporated.

The P&Ms soon acquired a deserved reputation for reliability, and were so much in demand by the military that the factory in Cleckheaton, Yorkshire was put on 24-hour working during World War I. After the war, when Jonah Phelon had retired, the new sporting 555cc (34cu in) 'Panther' was unveiled, with (unusually at the time) a four-speed gearbox. Two years later, the firm's first overhead-valve engine was

ABOVE and RIGHT: Most Panther 'Slopers' were used to pull sidecars, a task to which they were well suited

designed by Granville Bradshaw, a 500cc single in the now-familiar Panther format, albeit with a large wet sump. Within a few years, P & M's engineer, Frank Leach, had evolved this Panther into the classic one, bored and stroked to 598cc, with a deeply-finned two-port cylinder head and two downpipes emerging from the single cylinder.

P&M did try to diversify with the little Pantherette, a 250cc transverse V-twin with pressed steel frame. The engine was a failure, but once the frame had been quickly adapted to take proven Villiers engines, sold reasonably well. Also helpful were 250 and 350cc (15 and 21cu in) versions of the big Panther, using a conventional frame. The basic 250cc Red Panther sold for the incredibly low price of £29 17s 6d, with all costs pared to the bone. The little factory sold 3,000 a year for a while, and it undoubtedly helped keep P&M afloat through the Depression years.

During World War II, P&M suspended motorcycle production to concentrate on war work, but it was business as usual from 1945, with the 600cc (37cu in) Model 100, 250 and 350 singles all back in production. However, the latter were not successful and were replaced by Villiers-engined commuters in 197, 250 or 324cc (12, 15 or 20cu in) versions. Like many other British manufacturers, P&M was keen to capture a slice of the late fifties scooter boom, and despite burning its fingers by importing the lacklustre Scooterrot from France, went ahead with designing its own scooter anyway. Like other British attempts, the Panther Princess was too heavy, too expensive and launched too late.

Meanwhile, the big 'proper' Panther had had a couple of updates, notably swinging-arm rear suspension and (more questionably) a capacity boost to 645cc (39cu in). The Model 120, as it was called, now produced 27bhp, still laughably low when measured against a comparable 650 twin. Sales of this now outdated motorcycle were falling fast, and P&M called in the receiver in 1962. However, so many parts were left in stock that it made more sense to carry on production until they were used up. Even so, venerable items like the Lucas magneto and Burman non-unit gearbox were no longer in production, and P&M had to fit reconditioned parts to keep going. The last Model 120 left the Cleckheaton works in 1966.

Peco

PANTHER *Germany 1933–c.1975*
Used Ilo-engined lightweights in the 1930s, joined by Sachs engines afterwards. Motorcycle production ceased in 1959 but mopeds were made into the mid-1970s.

PAQUÉ *Germany 1921–25*
Produced a 140cc (8.5cu in) clip-on and 147/197cc (9/12cu in) lightweights, the latter being sold to other manufacturers.

PARAGON *England 1919–23*
Produced a 348cc (21cu in) three-port deflector-type model only.

PARAMOUNT-DUO *England 1926–27*
Used 490cc and 990cc (30 and 60cu in) sv and JAP or Blackburne units.

PARILLA *Italy 1947–67*
Started with 247cc (15cu in) ohc racers, then a range of small two-strokes by 1950 which were joined by a 174cc (11cu in) single and 348cc (21cu in) ohc twin in 1952, plus the part-enclosed Slughi (two- or four-stroke) in 1956.

PASCO *Australia 1919–22*
American-influenced, though it used a JAP single or V-twin

PASQUET *France 1932–c.1939*
Used Aubier-Dunne 98cc and 123cc (6 and 7.5cu in) engines. Limited numbers were produced.

PASSONI *Italy 1902–04*
A pioneer of the motorcycle trade, it used its own 2hp engines in strengthened bicycle frames.

PATRIA *Germany 1925–50*
The first models had the 248c/348cc (15/21cu in) Roconova single-cylinder Rossig, but from 1927 to 1949 only.

PATRIARCA *Italy 1925–33*
Produced 124, 174cc and eventually 248cc singles (8, 11 and 15cu in). Most were of unit-construction with ohv.

PAUVERT *France 1932–c.1939*
98 to 198cc (6 to 12cu in) two-strokes.

PAWA *Germany 1922–23*
Produced a 226cc (14cu in) two-stroke with inlet valve which was underdeveloped.

PAWI *Germany 1922–24*
Another user of BMW's early flat twin.

PAX *England 1920–22*
Used 348/499cc (21/30cu in) Blackburne sv singles.

PDC *England 1903–06*
Used Coronet 2–3.5hp engines.

PE *Germany 1923–24*
Built own 132cc (8cu in) three-port two-strokes.

PEARSON *England 1903–04*
Used 3hp Aster engines.

PEARSON & SOPWITH *England 1919–21*
Offered a choice of a 318cc (19.4cu in) Dalm, a 293cc (18cu in) JAP or a 497cc (30cu in) Blackburne.

PEBOK *England 1903–09*
Bikes with in-house engines up to 3.5hp.

PECO *England 1913–15*
Produced a 349cc (21cu in) two-stroke, also sold as a proprietory engine.

PEERLESS *England 1902–c.1908*
2–2.5hp engines.

PEERLESS *England 1913–14*
An interesting design, with early use of the telescopic fork and shaft-drive with ioe engines up to an 8hp V-twin.

PEGASO *Italy 1956–64*
48cc (3cu in) ohv lightweights.

PEM *U.S.A. 1910–25*
Built its own 4hp ohv single.

PENTA *Czech Republic 1992–94*
A water-cooled 125cc (8cu in) trail bike which had limited production.

PER *Germany 1924–26*
Designed for comfort, with full enclosure and bucket seats. The 308 or 342cc (19 or 21cu in) two-stroke could allegedly run on crude oil.

PERFECTA *Switzerland 1946–50*
Used 123–173cc (7.5–11cu in) French AMC ohv singles.

PERKS & BIRCH *England 1899–1901*
A 222cc (13.5cu in) sv single was built into the driving wheel.

PERLEX *Germany 1924–26*
197cc (12cu in) sv Gruhn engines.

PERMO *Germany 1952–54*
Used 32cc (2cu in) Victoria two-strokes to power its mopeds.

PERNOD *France c.1900*
A 1hp-powered wheel that could be attached to bicycles. Eighty years later, the same name was applied to a 250cc (15cu in) GP racer representing the Pernod drinks company.

PERPEDES *Austria 1922–26*
A 110cc (7cu in) clip-on

PERSCH *Austria 1922–25*
Another two-stroke clip-on, with frames to suit from Krammer of Vienna.

PERUGINA *Italy 1953–62*
Built 158 and 173cc (9.6 and 11cu in) two- and four-stroke machines.

PERUN *Czechoslovakia 1904–24*
Fafnir-powered singles and V-twins.

PETA *Czechoslovakia 1921–1924*
170cc (10cu in) two-stroke scooters and lightweights.

PETERS *Germany 1924*
Used a 143cc (9cu in) DKW two-stroke.

PEUGEOT *France 1899–*
The Peugeot brothers were true pioneers of motorized two-wheelers. In business since 1810 (they started out making watch springs), they built bicycles from the mid-1880s and a motorized one in 1899. It was a success, and Peugeot replaced that bought-in engine with its own atmospheric inlet valve single in 1903. Bigger machines soon

followed, notably a 726cc (44cu in) V-twin in 1906, and other V-twins of all sizes were added. Peugeot began making cars in 1907 but, unlike some, continued to build motorcycles alongside. Notable was the 494cc (30cu in) racer, an advanced ohc vertical twin from 1913, which achieved much success. After World War I, the company concentrated on singles, including a new two-stroke and from 1926 a unit-constructed 346cc (21cu in) ohv single. In fact, unit-construction became a feature of the entire range, which encompassed singles up to 496cc. After wartime interruption, production resumed in 1949 with a range of two-strokes up to 346cc, and a 125cc (8cu in) scooter, the S55, from 1953; the latter was somehow unmistakably French, with its flat load platform over the front wheel. Motorcycle production ceased in 1959, but Peugeot went on making mopeds, and added an 80cc (5cu in) lightweight in 1980. Great success came with the company's new generation of 50/100cc (3/6cu in) scooters, particularly the sharp-looking Speedfight, which dominated Britain's scooter market in the late 1990s.

PG *Italy 1927–31*
Variations on a 173cc (11cu in) ohv single.

PGO *Taiwan 1964–*
Produced lightweights first, then licence-built Vespas from 1972, later having links with Peugeot. Still makes lightweights and scooters.

PHÄNOMEN *Germany 1903–40*
Used Fafnir engines for the first few years, then there was a gap until 1930 when small lightweights and clip-ons carried the name.

ABOVE: A Peugeot in military guise

BELOW: A 1600cc (98cu in) PGO V-twin prototype

PHÄNOMEN *Germany 1950–56*
Rebadged Meisters and Mammuts.

PHANTOM *Germany 1921–28*
Used 98–197cc (6–12cu in) Sachs and Ilo engines.

PHASAR *England early 1980s*
Designed by Malcolm Newell, like the earlier Reliant-engined Quasar, the Phasar was a simpler design without a roof, and aimed to use a range of motorcycle engines, including the Moto Guzzi V-twin. One was built with the Kawasaki Z1300 six-cylinder unit.

PHILLIPS *England 1954–64*
Made 48cc (3cu in) mopeds.

PHOENIX *England 1900–08*
211 and 345cc (13 and 21cu in) Minerva units were used.

Peugeot Speedake, part of the 1990s scooter boom

PHOENIX *England 1955–64*
A Villiers-powered scooter of 147–323cc (9–20cu in).

PIAGGIO *Italy 1946–*
Few marques are better known than Vespa. However, it is not the name of a manufacturer at all, but a model, as Vespas have always been made by the long-established Italian company of Piaggio. In 1884, Rinaldo Piaggio, then aged only 20, had set up his own general engineering concern, which went on to encompass shipping, railways and aeronautics, and seaplanes and bombers were built between the wars. In between times, Piaggio also founded Italy's first airline and became a member of the Italian Senate. He also initiated his sons Armando and Enrico into the business which they continued after his death in 1938.

By 1945, however, this thriving company was laid low and the huge plant at Pontedera was destroyed by both Allied bombing and sabotage by the retreating Germans. Just like Ferdinando Innocenti, Enrico Piaggio was casting around for something that could be put into production quickly. And, in a transport-starved Italy (as Innocenti had also realized) the answer was obvious – a small powered two-wheeler. The difference was that Piaggio got there first and he handed the project over to aeronautical engineer Corradino d'Ascanio. Despite his background, d'Ascanio was actually the ideal man for the job. Not only did he come up with a prototype in just three months, but it turned out to be a design classic.

D'Ascanio was not a motorcycle enthusiast, actually disliking their dirty chain-drives and non-interchangeable wheels. So his prototype MP6 was nothing like one. There was no frame, but a spot-welded steel chassis with full, all-enclosing bodywork (four years before Innocenti's Lambretta); the 98cc (6cu in) two-stroke engine drove the rear wheel through an enclosed gear drive; a single-sided swinging-arm and stub-axle front suspension allowed easy wheel changes, and the gearchange was a handlebar twistgrip – all the key points of the Vespa were there from the start. The name, incidentally, was Piaggio's idea when he noticed that the narrow-waisted bike rather resembled a wasp, so Vespa (Wasp) it was.

ABOVE: 1954 vintage publicity photograph for the Piaggio

BELOW: The top-selling Peugeot Speedfight scooter

1977 Piaggio Vespa Ciao moped which was light and easy to handle

Vespa in a familiar street café setting

ABOVE: The Vespa ET2 50cc two-stroke, a 'retro' scooter

BELOW: Piaggio Liberty

ABOVE: The Vespa T5 updated the original concept

BELOW: Sfera was the first of a new generation

Work proceeded fast. The prototype was fully tested by the end of 1945, and the Vespa went into production in April 1946. While most motorcycle factories were busy producing warmed-over pre-war designs, Piaggio was already making something genuinely new. Just 2,484 were sold in that first year, but it was soon clear that the new Vespa was a runaway success. Over 10,000 were sold in 1947, then 20,000. In 1956, just ten years after the first scooters went on sale, the millionth left the line, the two millionth in 1960 and the four millionth in 1970. With production still continuing all over the world, current production is at 15 million and still counting. In fact, from very early on, licenced production played a large part in the Vespa's success: they were being built in Germany in 1950, and the following year the Douglas concern in Bristol, England began production. There was also a French Vespa, from ACMA.

A 125cc (8cu in) version soon followed the original 98cc, and there were three-wheeled commercial variants as well, all powered by the same two-stroke single, with 4bhp at 4,500rpm, and a four-speed gearbox. A major change came in 1953 with the G model, which replaced the rod-controlled gearchange with a cable enclosed in a rubber casing which was neater than the old arrangement and made operation easier. But customers wanted more power, and the 150GS was launched in 1955, complete with larger 10-inch wheels, four-speed gearbox and new handlebar layout (with the speedometer in its now familiar position), not to mention smoother styling. The GS in particular appeared to attract odd stunts, particularly in Britain: a dealer named André Baldet (actually a Frenchman living in England) rode one to Paris for the weekend (for £10, all in), while another dealer beat the London–Paris express train on a GS. And inevitably, someone crossed the English Channel on one.

Bigger & Faster

Model changes were evolutionary rather than radical in the early sixties, a 160cc (9.8cu in) GS arriving in 1962, followed by a 90cc (5.5cu in) Standard a couple of years later. The latter had an 88.5cc rotary-valve two-stroke engine that produced 4.5bhp at 4,500rpm but in all cases the basic Vespa format remained unchanged. This was the time of the sporting scooter, and even the 90 spawned a 'Super Sport' version, complete with centrally positioned spare wheel and tool box for an ostensibly motorcycle look but which, in reality, only served to spoil the advantage of the Vespa's step-through design. There was more power still from the 180SS of 1965 when the upmarket Vespas also acquired squared-off headlamps. Perhaps more significant was the new Automatic Fuelmix system, which gave (as it suggested) automatic fuel/oil mixing according to throttle position and precluded tiresome pre-mixing at the pump.

By 1972, the top model was the 200 Rally Electronic, which boasted 12.3bhp at 5,700rpm, though Piaggio also took advantage of the growing moped class with the 50cc (3cu in) VSA (9-inch wheels, three-speed gearbox). The company has made 50s in the Vespa style ever since, though it began making conventional mopeds in the sixties. The year 1978 saw a comprehensive restyle (the New Line) though remained still recognizably Vespa (the PX125 and 200 became the PK Series in 1983) and there was also a PK80 with electric start. A further update was the T5 of 1986.

However, the T5 was still an update on the same Vespa theme, and it wasn't until the early 1990s that Piaggio began to introduce a range of truly new, modern scooters. The Sfera of 1991 was the first, winning the Compasso d'Oro design prize. There was still something of the Vespa about it, but it was very different at the same time and a 125cc (8cu in) four-stroke version (Piaggio's first four-stroke scooter) followed. There were also cheaper 50s as well, the Zip and Free, plus the racy-looking Typhoon of 1993. The latter pointed the way to a new breed of aggressively styled scooters, of which Peugeot's Speedfight is another prime example.

Popular though the Typhoon and its ilk are, the Zip is perhaps a more likely example of what we will be riding through cities in the 21st century. With a choice of 50cc two-stroke or electric motor, its time may come if internal combustion engines are banned from city centres. More conventional was the 125cc Skipper of 1995, the first fully automatic 125 scooter. Or the Hexagon, a big, luxury scooter with lots of space, comfort and luggage capacity. With 125 and 180cc (8 and 11cu in) two-strokes, and the Honda-sourced 250cc four-stroke option, it typified the new late nineties breed of 'super scooter'. But the end of the century has also seen the popularity of the retro bike, and Piaggio's answer was the ET2 of 1996, which used fuel injection to produce a cleaner-running two-stroke, there being fears at the time that the conventional two-stroke might be outlawed by anti-pollution laws. (Piaggio hedged its bets with a four-stroke ET4 later.) The 'retro' part came in the styling, as this 50th anniversary Vespa echoed the looks of the first one, albeit in softer, rounder 1990s form. With electronic direct injection planned for the year 2000, Piaggio looks set to meet the competition head-on, be it European or Japanese.

A prototype luxury scooter, which was later offered for sale as the Piaggio Hexagon

PIANA *Italy 1923–31*
Used Villiers and JAP engines, joined in 1927 by Piana's own 248cc (15cu in) ohv single.

PIATTI *Belgium, England 1955–58*
A 123cc (7.5cu in) scooter, made under licence in England and Belgium.

PIAZZA *Italy 1924–34*
Produced own 173cc (11cu in) ohv single (sold to others) with JAPs and two-strokes as well.

PIERCE-ARROW *U.S.A. 1909–13*
A shaft-driven single and FN-inspired in-line four, the tubular frame incorporating fuel and oil tanks.

PIERTON *France 1922–25*
Used Aubier-Dunne, Train, Villiers and Blackburne engines of 98–498cc (6–30cu in).

PILOT *England 1903–15*
Used 174–598cc (11–36cu in) Precisions and JAPs and a 318cc (19cu in) two-stroke.

PIMPH *Germany 1924–26*
Assembler using JAP singles and MAG V-twins.

PIOLA *Italy 1919–21*
A 620cc (38cu in) sv flat twin.

PIRATE *U.S.A. 1911–15*
Ioe singles and V-twins of 3–8hp.

PIROTTA *Italy 1949–55*
Lightweights of up to 158cc (10cu in).

PITTY *East Germany 1954–64*
An MZ-powered scooter of 147cc (9cu in).

PLANET *England 1919–20*
Step-through frames with Villiers, Union and Blackburne power units.

PLASSON *France 1921–24*
Two-strokes and own 197cc (12cu in) sv single.

PMC *England 1908–15*
Used JAP engines of up to 996cc (61cu in).

PMZ *Russia 1921–c.1939*
Fitted BMW-like sv flat twins and 996cc (61cu in) V-twins.

PO *Italy 1921–23*
A 346cc (21cu in) two-stroke single.

POINARD *France 1951–56*
Used 123–248cc (7.5–15cu in) Aubier-Dunne, Ydral and four-stroke AMC engines.

POINTER *Japan 1946–62*
Built own two-strokes to 247cc (15cu in).

POLENGHI *Italy 1950–55*
48cc (3cu in) mopeds.

POLET *Italy 1923–24*
A 481cc (29cu in) single with own ioe engine.

PONNY *Germany 1924–26*
Mainly 142/172cc (9/10.5cu in) DKW two-strokes.

PONY *Germany 1924–26*
Not to be confused with the above, it produced 185cc (11.3cu in) sv singles.

PONY *Spain 1952–54*
Hispano-Villiers-powered 123cc (7.5cu in) singles.

PONY-MONARCH *Japan 1951–55*
Built by Monarch with 142cc (9cu in) ohv Meguro engines.

POPE *U.S.A. 1911–18*
Produced 499cc (30cu in) singles and 998cc (61cu in) V-twins, with early plunger rear suspension.

POPET *Japan 1957–early 1960s*
A 47cc (3cu in) mini-scooter.

POPMANLEE *Japan 1953–61*
49/79cc (3/5cu in) scooters and 124/174cc (8/11cu in) lightweights.

PORTLAND *England 1910–11*
JAP or Peugeot-powered.

POSDAM *Italy 1926–29*
123–173cc (7.5–11cu in) ioe singles.

POSTLER *Germany 1920–24*
Produced its own 246cc and 252cc (15cu in) ioe singles.

POTTHOFF *Germany 1924–26*
A 158cc (9.6cu in) ohv engine was used.

POUNCY *England 1930–38*
Villiers-engined lightweights and 147–346cc (9–21cu in) singles. OEC rear suspension was optional.

POUSTKA *Czechoslovakia 1924–1934*
Used 147–346cc (9–21cu in) Villiers power.

POWELL *England 1921–26*
Built its own two-strokes of 168–245cc (10–15cu in).

POWERFUL *England 1903–06*
Used Buchet and MMC power units.

P&P *England 1922–30*
Utilized an enclosed and well silenced Barr & Stroud, or JAP engines to 996cc (61cu in).

PRAGA *Czechoslovakia 1929–35*
Took over production of the 499cc (30cu in) ohc BD in a pressed steel frame with shaft-drive.

PRECISION *England 1902–06*
Mainly used 211cc (13cu in) Minerva engines.

PRECISION *England 1912–19*
Built a wide range of proprietory engines, later becoming Beardmore-Precision.

The Pope, a short-lived rival for Indian and Harley-Davidson

PREMIER *England 1908–20*
First built big V-twins, then mid-sized singles, and later a 322cc (20cu in) two-stroke twin.

PREMIER *Germany 1910–13*
Nuremberg branch of the English Premier, producing a 346cc (21cu in) sv single.

PREMIER *Czechoslovakia 1913–33*
The German Premier moved to Czechoslovakia and used JAP units as well as its own engines of various sizes.

PREMO *England 1908–15*
A rebadged English Premier.

PREMOLI *Italy 1935–37*
Used 498cc (30cu in) Python or OMB singles, and produced its own 174cc (11cu in) singles.

PRESTER *France 1930–55*
A 98–498cc (6–30cu in) machine with various bought-in engines.

PRESTO *Germany 1901–40*
Used a variety of proprietory engines, from the 74cc (4.5cu in) Sachs upwards.

PRIDE & CLARKE *England 1938–40*
A 63cc (4cu in) two-stroke sold by the famous London dealer.

PRIM *England 1906–07*
A Sarolea-powered 5hp V-twin, the frame containing the fuel tank.

PRINA *Italy 1949–54*
Badged as Orix, it produced scooters and lightweights to 173cc (11cu in).

Premier

PRINCEPS *England 1903–07*
Built own singles and V-twins.

PRINETTI & STUCCHI *Italy 1898–1911*
Began with its own 2hp engines.

PRIOR *Germany 1904*
A rebadged Hercules for the English market.

PRIORY *England 1919–26*
Used Arden, Union and Villiers motors, all two-strokes.

PROGRESS *Germany 1901–14*
Fafnir and Zedel-powered at first, later produced its own engines to 698cc (43cu in).

PROGRESS *England 1902–08*
Fitted MMC, Antoine and Minerva engines.

PROGRESS *Germany 1951–57*
A Sachs-powered scooter of 98–198cc (6–12cu in).

PROMOT *Poland c.1968–73*
Produced 123cc (7.5cu in) Puch-engined trials and motocross bikes.

PROPUL *France 1923–26*
Racing machines with Blackburne, MAG and JAP units to 498cc (30cu in).

ABOVE: A Puch moped at the Frankfurt Motor Show of 1962

BELOW: Puch Ranger

P&S *England 1919–21*
A rebadged Pearson.

PSW *Germany 1924–29*
Produced own 247cc (15cu in) two-stroke, with inlet and exhaust ports in front of the cylinder.

PUCH *Austria 1903–87*
Austria's leading, most prolific and enduring firm was a real two-stroke specialist which adopted the split-single (two pistons sharing a common combustion chamber) and stuck with it for nearly 50 years. Johann Puch built his first bike in 1903, a 244cc (15cu in) single, as well as tricycles and cars. The company always used its own engines (singles and V-twins at first, plus a flat twin during World War I), apart from a JAP-engined bike in the late 1920s. Puch's only other four-stroke after 1923 was an 800cc (49cu in) flat four, mainly for military use. The first split singles were introduced in 1923, designed by Giovanni Marcellino, and appeared in 122–486cc (7.4–30cu in) form. The biggest were four-pistoned split twins from 1931 which were smooth runners. The company merged with Steyr and Daimler in 1934 and produced a 60cc (3.7cu in) clip-on, the Styriette from 1938, and there were also fast racers between the wars. After 1945, it added conventional 49–125cc (6–8cu in) two-strokes and exported split-singles to the U.S. under the Sears and Allstate names. There was a very successful 49cc Maxi from 1968 and motocross wins in the mid-1970s. Puch concentrated on mopeds from the late seventies, and was taken over by Piaggio, who closed the factory in 1987.

PV *England 1910–25*
Offered the usual range of bought-in engines from JAP, Villiers *et al.*

PZI *Poland 1936–37*
Built its own 598cc (36cu in) single and a 1196cc (73cu in) V-twin.

Puch Grand Prix Supreme

Puch Maxi N Moped

Q

QUADRANT *England 1901–29*
Began by using Minerva 211cc (13cu in) units, but these W.L. Lloyd-designed bikes were soon powered by a whole range of in-house engines with 374cc (23cu in) two-strokes, singles from 498–780cc (30–48cu in) and 498 ohv, 654 ioe or 1130cc (30, 40 or 69cu in) sv V-twins.

QUAGLIOTTI *Italy 1902–07*
Leading Italian pioneer, with 2–3hp singles and 5hp V-twins.

QUASAR *England 1977–82*
A motorcycle with a roof, the limited-production Quasar was of the 'feet-forward' type, sitting the rider in a car-type seat with his legs out in front. In theory, seating the rider thus gives better

Quasar, pictured outside Buckingham Palace with Phil Read, after receiving his OBE

aerodynamics and weather protection. Designed by Malcolm Newell, the Quasar used a 750cc/46cu inch (later 850cc) four-cylinder Reliant engine and four-speed gearbox. Although heavy, it was very aerodynamic, offering the potential of a comfortable cruiser capable of high average speeds over distance. Feet-forward machines like the Quasar failed to turn motorcycle design upside down, but in the early 1990s, the Japanese manufacturers did begin to use the concept (albeit without roofs) for 250cc (15cu in) scooters.

R

RABBIT *Japan 1946–68*
A 90–199cc (5.5–12cu in) two-stroke scooter.

RABENEICK *Germany 1933–63*
Produced mopeds in the 1930s, and after 1945 progressed to a full range of lightweights up to 247cc (15cu in) with Sachs or Ilo power. Was eventually taken over by the former.

RACER *France 1953–56*
Produced its own 49/74cc (3/4.5cu in) two-strokes as clip-ons and lightweights.

RADCO *England 1913–32*
Apart from a 247cc (15cu in) ohv single, it bought in all its engines, from a 145cc (9cu in) Villiers to a 490cc (30cu in) JAP.

RADEX *Germany 1951–late 1950s*
Rebadged Express machines.

RADIOLA *France 1933–39*
98cc (6cu in) clip-ons.

ABOVE: Quasars with designer Malcolm Newell

RADIOR *France 1904–60*
Pre-1939 used a mixture of its own two-strokes and bought-in four-strokes. After World War II, engines came from Nervor, AMC and NSU.

RADMILL *England 1912–14*
Mainly used a 269cc (16cu in) Villiers or 346cc (21cu in) Precision engine.

RADVAN *Czechoslovakia 1924–26*
Produced 145/174cc (9/11cu in) DKW-powered lightweights.

RAGLAN *England 1909–13*
Offered own engines as well as machines with air- or water-cooled Precision units to 496cc (30cu in).

RAJDOOT *India 1962–*
First built 175cc (11cu in) two-strokes with help from WFM of Poland, followed by variations on the same engine through the 1960s/70s. Licence-built the Yamaha RD350 from 1983 and the RXS100 from 1985.

RALEIGH *England 1899–1933*
Built complete machines up to 1906 and after 1919. Its greatest contribution to the industry was probably through its Sturmey-Archer subsidiary, which supplied proprietary engines to many different companies.

RAMBLER *U.S.A. 1903–14*
A 4hp single and 6hp V-twin.

RAMBLER *England c.1951–61*
A rebadged Norman produced for export.

BELOW: A 1924 7hp Raleigh

RANZANI *Italy 1923–31*
Utilized 170–175cc (10–11cu in) in-house engines, as well as units from Heros and Norman.

RAS *Italy 1932–36*
Sold under the Fusi name using mainly JAP singles, apart from its own 248cc (15cu in) ohc single in 1935.

RASSER *France 1922–23*
A 98cc (6cu in) two-stroke with pressed steel frame.

RATIER *France 1955–62*
An ex-car producer which made BMW-like bikes based on parts left by the departing German army. Later 494 and 597cc (30 and 36cu in) bikes were all French.

RATINGIA *Germany 1923–25*
170/195cc (10/12cu in) sv singles.

BELOW: A Raleigh, with period three-wheel conversion

RAVAT *France 1922–54*
Built its own 175–350cc (11–21cu in) two-strokes, and used a vast range of bought-in four-strokes over the years.

RAY *England 1919–20*
Used own 331cc (20cu in) two-stroke.

RAY *England 1922–25*
Produced what was literally, a lightweight (59kg/130lb) 193cc (12cu in) sv single, and another 172cc (10cu in) model with a Villiers engine.

RAYNAL *England 1914–53*
Used 269cc (16cu in) Villiers power up to the mid-1930s, thereafter the 98cc (6cu in) unit.

READING-STANDARD *U.S.A. 1903–22*
A popular marque in America's pioneer years, with its own 499cc (30cu in) singles and 990/1170cc (60/71cu in) V-twins.

READY *England 1920–22*
Used 293/346cc (18/21cu in) JAPs, and later a 147cc (9cu in) Villiers.

READY *Belgium 1924–39*
Imported all power units from England, apart from some Swiss MAG engines.

REBRO *England 1922–28*
A simple, cheap (£37) Villiers-powered lightweight.

RECORD *Germany 1922–24*
Used own 147cc (9cu in) two-stroke.

REDDIS *Spain 1957–60*
Hispano-Villiers power was used for this short-lived Spaniard.

BELOW: A 499cc (30cu in) Reading-Standard single

REDRUP *England 1919–22*
A rarity, a 304cc (18.6cu in) three-cylinder radial, few of which were made. Also produced a doubled-up six-cylinder prototype.

RED STAR *Belgium 1902*
Fitted with a 211cc (13cu in) Minerva.

REFORM *Austria 1903–05*
Used 2.25hp sv engines from Excelsior.

REGAL *England 1909–15*
Mainly offered four-stroke 346–620cc (21–38cu in) air- or water-cooled Precision units, plus a 349cc two-stroke.

REGENT *England 1920–21*
Fitted the 688cc (42cu in) Coventry-Victor flat twin into heavy frames of its own design and manufacture.

REGINA *England 1903–15*
Used Fafnir, Minerva and MMC power until 1907, resuming production a few years later with its own 292cc (18cu in) two-stroke.

REGINA *France 1905–10*
Used Zurcher, Buchet, or Peugeot engines.

REH *Germany 1948–53*
Used only Ilo two-strokes of 173–248cc (11–15cu in).

REITER *Italy 1927–29*
Imported mostly English components, including Blackburne or Bradshaw singles.

RELIANCE *U.S.A. 1912–15*
Built 4.5hp ioe singles.

RENÉ GILLET *France 1898–1957*
Favoured by the French military, often with big (up to 996cc/61cu in) V-twins and sidecars. Also a 346cc (21cu in) sv single. After 1945 built its own 98–250cc (6–15cu in) two-strokes.

RENNER-ORIGINAL *Germany 1924–32*
Used JAP, Kühne and Küchen V-twin power units up to 678cc (41cu in).

RENNSTEIG *Germany 1925–30*
Took over the KG design, and fitted Blackburne engines.

REPUBLIC *Czechoslovakia 1899–1908*
Rebadged Laurin & Klement machines.

REVERE *England 1915–22*
Used a 269cc (16cu in) two-stroke by Villiers, with frame by Sparkbrook.

REVOLUTION *England 1904–06*
NRCC supplied the 2.75hp single.

REX *England 1900–33*
A real pioneer, but despite merger with Acme in 1922 (to form Rex-Acme) and success in the 1920s, failed to survive much longer. Designed its own singles and V-twins at first, including a 372cc (23cu in) single and 896cc (55cu in) twin, with Roc gear-hub. There was a 349cc (21cu in) two-stroke just before World War I and a 550cc (34cu in) sv single just after, which were dropped in favour of sv and ohv Blackburne engines, though it also offered the Barr & Stroud sleeve-valve single and later added JAPs up to a 746cc (45.5cu in) V-twin, plus MAG and Sturmey-Archer units. It was taken over by sidecar maker Mills-Fulford in 1932, which closed it down the following year.

REX *Sweden 1908–57*
Used Motosacoche engines at first, but full production didn't begin until 1923. Later used Villiers, Sachs, Sturmey-Archer two-strokes, and JAP singles to 500cc (31cu in). Built a battery-powered bike during World War II.

REX *Germany 1923–25*
A 283cc (17cu in) two-stroke.

REX *Germany 1948–64*
Produced various clip-ons of up to 40cc (2.4cu in), and later 48cc (6cu in) mopeds.

REX-JAP *England 1908–15*
Built by Premier of Coventry with JAP engines of 293–996cc (18–61cu in).

REYNOLDS-RUNABOUT *England 1919–22*
Step-through scooter-like bike with a 269cc (16cu in) Liberty or 346cc (21cu in) JAP unit.

REYNOLDS-SPECIAL *England 1930–33*
Improved Scotts, built by Albert Reynolds.

R&F *Germany 1924–26*
Used own 348cc (21cu in) ohv single.

RHONSON *France 1952–58*
A 49cc (3cu in) moped and 123cc (7.5cu in) lightweight.

RHONY-X *France 1924–32*
Produced 98–246cc (6–15cu in) two-strokes and JAP or Chaise singles up to 498cc (30cu in).

RIBI *Germany 1923–25*
Built own 196/248cc (12/15cu in) singles.

RICHARD *France 1901–04*
Used bought-in engines from Peugeot and others.

RIEJU *Spain 1952–*
Produces scooters and lightweights up to 174cc (11cu in). Now makes 49–74cc (3–4.5cu in) machines.

RIGAT *Italy 1912–14*
A 487cc (30cu in) Fafnir-powered machine.

RIKUO *Japan 1935–62*
Imported Harley-Davidsons in 1920 and began building them under licence from 1935, as well as 750–1200cc (46–73cu in) V-twins which were in production right up to 1962. Also produced BMW-inspired shaft-driven singles to 348cc (21cu in).

RILEY *England 1901–c.1908*
Used engines from De Dion, Minerva and MMC before building its own.

RINNE *Germany 1924–32*
Produced 124–248cc (8–15cu in) two-strokes

RIP *England 1905–08*
Used bought-in engines (from Peugeot, Stevens and White & Poppe) in sprung frames.

RIVIERRE *France c.1903*
This interesting two-stroke radial was built into the rear wheel and was of 1.75–20hp.

RIWINA *Germany 1924–25*
Used a DKW 142cc (9cu in) two-stroke, among others.

RIXE *Germany 1934–1970s*
Made Sachs-powered mopeds pre-1939, extending up to 248cc (15cu in) after 1945.

RIZZATO *Italy 1972–*
Franco-Morini and Minarelli-powered two-strokes to 123cc (7.5cu in). Bought Atala in 1977.

R&K *Czechoslovakia 1924–26*
Used 147/172cc (9/10.5cu in) Villiers power units.

RMW *Germany 1925–55*
Used a wide range of bought-in units as well as its own two-strokes. Added bought-in four strokes later on, but made very few bikes after 1945.

ROA *Spain 1952–63*
Used 197–325cc (12–20cu in) Hispano-Villiers engines.

ROBAKO *Germany 1924–26*
Fitted 192cc (12cu in) Bekamo engines.

ROC *England 1903–15*
One of the first manufacturers to replace traditional cycle frames with longer, lower motorcycle frames. Utilized Precision and in-house engines.

ROCHESTER *France 1923–29*
Built lightweights up to 174cc (11cu in).

ROCHET *France 1902–c.1908*
Built its own 1.75hp ioe single.

ROCKET *Italy 1953–58*
A 198cc (12cu in) ohv flat twin.

ROCKSON *England 1930–32*
Offered 296cc (16cu in) Villiers and 346cc (21cu in) Blackburne engines.

ROCO *Germany 1922–25*
Produced 110–147cc (7–9cu in) two-stroke lightweights.

ROCONOVO *Germany 1924–26*
Made 248/348cc (15/21cu in) ohc singles.

ROÉS *France 1932–24*
Lightweights with 98/123cc (6/7.5cu in) two-strokes.

ROESSLER & JAUERNIGG
Czechoslovakia 1902–07
Produced 2–4 hp singles, some with sprung frames.

RÖHR *Germany 1952–58*
Made scooters with 197cc (12cu in) Ilo power.

ROKON *U.S.A. 1959–*
Possibly the only two-wheel-drive solo motorcycle to reach production, the Rokon was designed as a working bike for foresters and had big, low-pressure tyres and a 134cc (8cu in) Chrysler two-stroke. Variations on the theme have been intermittently produced ever since, with a Sachs-engined automatic-transmission competition bike from 1973.

ROLAND *Germany 1904–07*
Produced 2.25hp singles and 5hp V-twins with Truffault swinging-arm forks as an option.

ROLAND *Germany 1923–24*
Bekamo or DKW two-strokes to 145cc (9cu in).

ROLFE *England 1911–14*
Utilized JAP singles (498cc/30cu in) or Precision V-twins (770cc/47cu in).

ROMEO *Italy 1969–75*
Used 49cc (3cu in) Minarelli two-strokes in mopeds and minibikes.

ROMP *1913–14*
A Precision-powered sv single of 499cc (30cu in).

RONDINE *Italy 1923–28*
No connection with the famous Gilera Rondine racer, these used 98cc (6cu in) Train two-strokes.

RONDINE *Italy 1952–57*
124/147cc (8/9cu in) Sachs-powered two-strokes.

ROSELLI *1899–1910*
A 1.75 and 2.5 hp 'ladies' model.

Rover built motorcycles before progressing to cars

ROSENGART *France 1922–23*
Used a 98cc (6cu in) Train two-stroke.

ROSSI *Italy 1950–55*
123cc (7.5cu in) Sachs-engined lightweights.

ROSSI *Italy 1929*
A 480cc (29cu in) V-twin, unusual by virtue of its aluminium frame.

ROTARY *Japan early 1950s–61*
124cc (8cu in) two-strokes.

ROTER TEUFEL *Germany 1923–25*
170cc (10cu in) sv singles – rare four-strokes in 1920s Berlin.

ROULETTE *England 1918–19*
Used 269cc (16cu in) three-port two-stroke Villiers engines.

ROUSSEY *France 1948–56*
Produced lightweights, including 48cc (3cu in) clip-ons as well as motorcycles and scooters with 123cc and 174cc (7.5 and 11cu in) power units.

ROVA-KENT *Australia 1913–14*
Interesting, advanced 496cc (30cu in) four-valve unit-construction single.

ROVER *England 1902–25*
Used JAP engines up to a 676cc (41cu in) V-twin, but final bikes had in-house 248/348cc (15/21cu in) ohv singles.

ROVETTA *Italy 1900–06*
Early use of water-cooling in its own 2.5hp unit of 1904.

ROVIN *France 1920–34*
Built own two-strokes of 98–175cc (6–11cu in), plus 499cc (30cu in) JAP singles.

ROVLANTE *France. 1929–35*
98/124cc (6/8cu in) two-strokes.

ROYAL *Switzerland 1900–08*
1.5–3hp Zedel singles and V-twins were used.

ROYAL *U.S.A. 1901–10*
Built the 2.75hp prototype in 1901 which took six years to reach production.

ROYAL *Italy 1923–28*
The Santagostino brothers offered their own 132cc (8cu in) two-stroke or 490cc (30cu in) JAP.

ROYAL-AJAX *England 1901–c.1908*
2.5hp and belt-driven, a typical pioneer machine.

ROYAL-EAGLE *England 1901–10*
Rebadged Coventry-Eagle.

ROYAL ENFIELD *England 1901–70*
'Made Like a Gun' was Royal Enfield's slogan, and in a way it was true. Like BSA (Birmingham Small Arms company), Enfield grew directly from the armaments industry (who else would call one of its bikes a 'Bullet'?) Although, by the 1960s, Royal Enfield was just another of the British manufacturers making outdated singles and twins, its bequest was a good track record in innovation. But it was small (at one point just 6,600 bikes were built over four years), and motorcycles were something of a sideline for a company that had other, more profitable lines to follow.

Royal Enfield made its first powered vehicles (De Dion-engined trikes and four-wheelers) in 1899, with the ubiquitous motorized bicycle following in 1901. But it wasn't until 1912 that continuous production began, with the Model 180, a

ABOVE, BELOW and OPPOSITE: A Royal Enfield V-twin of 1921, which used the company's own engine. JAP units were used earlier on

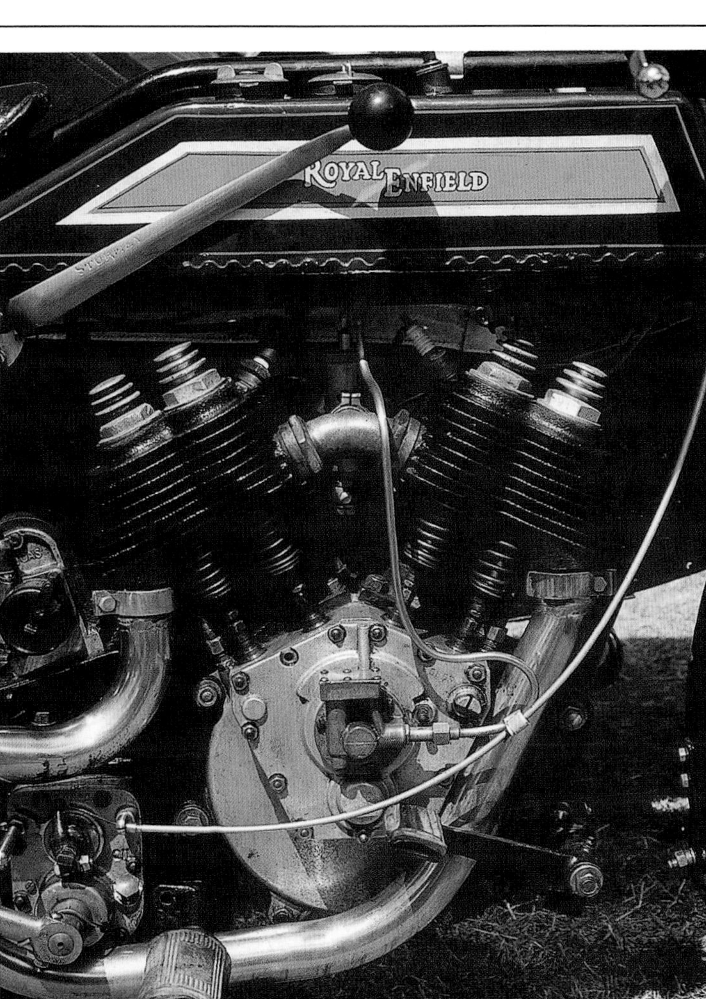

complete sidecar outfit powered by a 770cc (47cu in) sidevalve JAP V-twin. Its chain-drive and two-speed gearbox were bang up-to-date, but what really set the 180 apart was its rubber cush hub. The first of many Enfield innovations, this was a rubber shock absorber built into the rear hub to reduce chain snatch. It was followed the year after by a much smaller V-twin, an ioe of 425cc (26cu in) producing 4hp, which had an automatic oil pump when most motorcyclists were resigned to giving the manual pump a squirt every now and then. A 350cc (21cu in) version followed, and Enfield soon added a 225cc (14cu in) two-stroke as well.

The company's primary contribution to the Allied effort in World War I were bicycles (still the main line of business) though some sidecar outfits were supplied for use as machine-gun carriers or mini-ambulances. These were still JAP-powered, but in the 1920s Enfield began to design its own engines, notably a 350cc sidevalve single in 1924, and a 500 in 1927, which shared bore, stroke and piston with the company's own V-twin.

Although a small company, Enfield showed remarkable stability right through the Depression years: continuity of both ownership and management had much to do with this, the company having been run by Robert Smith since the very early days and one of his sons, Major Frank Smith, was to lead Enfield right into the sixties. All three Smith brothers were keen trials riders, which had a bearing on the firm's later success off-road. And there were two talented designers in the persons of E.O. Pardoe (the man behind the Bullet) and Tony Wilson-Jones, who became head of development in 1925. The latter (another trials buff) was more of a forward thinker than a gritty-fingernailed production man, but his drive and energy kept the flow of Enfield innovations coming.

The famous Bullet line first saw the light of day in 1930, as 350 and 500cc (21 and 31cu in) singles, with the cylinder inclined forward in the frame, and was joined by a 250 in 1933. The 500 gained a four-valve head in 1934, then was tried with three valves before reverting to four as the 1936 Model JF (now with the cylinder vertical). Twin-port heads were tried as well. During the war, Royal Enfield supplied 55,000 bikes to the Allies, which sounds a lot but is put into perspective by BSA's 130,000. Most were 350s in the form of the sidevalve WD/C or ohv WD/CO. Sidevalve 570cc (35cu in) machines went to the Navy, and many recruits learnt to ride on an Enfield 250 (sidevalve again). A less typical wartime product was the Flying Flea, a 125cc (8cu in) two-stroke tiddler that folded into a canister for dropping by parachute into the battle zone. The idea was that airborne troops, having safely parachuted in, could kick their Flying Fleas into action while they swiftly regrouped. The Flea had quite an interesting history: the design was based on a German DKW whose Dutch importers were refused further bikes unless all Jewish employees were expelled. The importers refused, went to Royal Enfield instead, who was persuaded to build the little bike, which it did from 1939.

Out of the Cave

Enfield's first act once peace was restored was to buy back many of its WD bikes and sell them on, suitably refurbished, to members of the public who, it was said, would buy anything with two wheels and an engine in those early post-war days. The other wartime legacy was an underground factory in Wiltshire where the company had undertaken secret war work. Nicknamed 'the cave', it was where Enfields were produced right up to the end.

Meanwhile, the company lost no time in producing a 500cc vertical twin to compete with Triumph. Designed by Ted Pardoe, it actually owed much to the pre-war 248cc (15cu in) single, remembering that Enfield had ensured commonality of parts with some of its 1920s engines, a sensible policy to which it remained true. Engine-wise, there was nothing particularly remarkable about the 500 Twin, though it had separate cylinder barrels (a mixed blessing) and produced a mild 25bhp. But its real innovation, along with other Royal Enfields of the time, was in the area of suspension. Announced in November 1948, the Twin had two-way damped telescopic forks (bigger rivals had these as well, but for them full damping was still some years away) and a swinging-arm rear suspension. The latter was Royal Enfield's trump card, and at a time when contemporaries had either crude, short-travel plunger rear-suspension, or a rigid frame, this was sophistication indeed.

In fact, the swinging arm was behind the company's enviable record in trials. The Twin did very well in the 1951 and '53 ISDTs, while the 350 Bullet, particularly after the gifted rider Johnny Britain showed what it could do, became the bike to beat in trials right up to the early sixties. Even without competition success, the

ABOVE: Royal Enfield Crusader Sports
ABOVE RIGHT: Royal Enfield 150cc Villiers

BELOW: The Indian-built Enfield Robin of 1993, a diesel conversion

Bullet was one of Enfield's better sellers. The 350 was joined by a 500 in 1953 but, for many, the original size was the best one; as a 350, the Bullet was fast enough (around 121km/h/75mph), responsive to tuning yet torquey as well. Reflecting Enfield's size, only 9,000 were built in 13 years, but its reputation spread further abroad.

At a time when bigger rivals were producing 600–650cc (37–40cu in) twins, Enfield decided to go one better with the 692cc (42cu in) Meteor 700 in 1953. It so happened, of course, that this capacity was equivalent to joining two 350 Bullets together. Still, once the Vincent had passed away, the Meteor was the biggest bike on

LEFT: A 1954 500cc (31.5cu in) Royal Enfield

BELOW: Airflow fairing was a Royal Enfield first

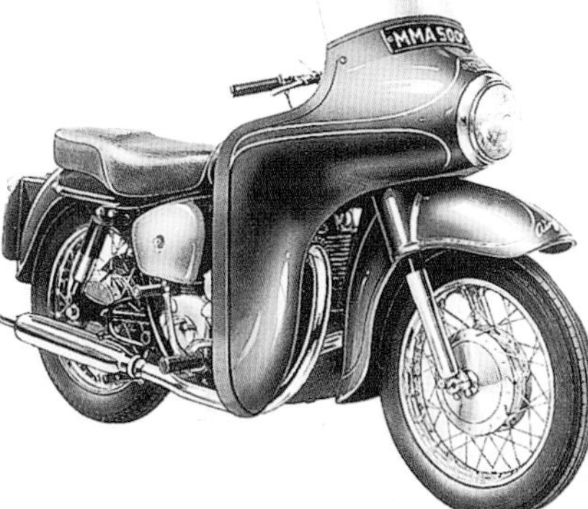

BELOW: The Bullet was attractive in a cobby sort of way

Royal Enfield's Continental GT was the ultimate 250cc road bike of its time

offer in Britain. Unlike the more sporting 650s, this one was aimed more at the sidecar market. Like the other Enfields, it soon developed a reputation for oil leaks (hence the old 'Royal Oilfield' gag) and produced fearsome vibration at speed. Despite this, like its single-cylinder progenitor, the Meteor was quite tuneable, and did well in Production Endurance Racing, notably when ridden by Syd Lawton.

The company was certainly keeping busy as 1956 saw the launch of the new Crusader. This was different from previous cut-price 250s. Of unit-construction and with a four-speed gearbox, its oversquare cylinder dimensions made it revvy and eager. With only a little tuning it turned into the 127km/h (79mph) Crusader Sports, and culminated in the five-speed Continental GT. Arriving in time to take advantage of a new 250cc limit for learners, the little Royal Enfield became the coffee-bar cowboy's favourite, faster than a BSA C15 and, in red liveried, fly-screened GT form, flashier too. It even formed the basis of a new 500 twin, the Meteor Minor. Unusually, it could be had with a big factory-fitted fairing, which no other manufacturer offered at the time. This 'Sportsflow' was actually a smaller version of the Airflow, which Enfield offered as an option on all the bigger bikes. Wind-tunnel developed, the glassfibre fairing allowed more speed, better fuel consumption and, of course, excellent weather protection. Once again, Royal Enfield was out in front.

Sadly, none of this was enough to stem the inevitable decline. The Bullets

ABOVE: The Indian Enfield Bullet – still in production

BELOW: 1965 Royal Enfield Interceptor

ABOVE: Royal Enfield Turbo Twin Sports

were dropped in 1962, due to falling demand, but there seemed nothing suitable to replace them. The company was taken over by the Smith Group, and much money was spent on the promising GP5 250cc (15cu in) racer, while the Villiers-engined Turbo was a short-lived attempt to broaden its 250 market. Meanwhile, the Meteor had ended up as the 736cc (45cu in) Interceptor which by 1968 was Enfield's sole motorcycle. In its final Series II form, this bike was seen by some as one of the better British big twins, being both fast and oil-tight, but in 1970 Enfield Precision (as it now was) decided to concentrate on military contracts. The final batch of engines were built into Rickman frames. But it wasn't the end of the Royal Enfield story by any means. When the Bullet was dropped, all the tooling was sold to an Indian company and, ever since, a factory just outside Madras has been churning out Bullet 350s and 500s in far greater numbers than the one in Redditch ever did. The quality may not be up to Royal Enfield standards, but the rugged Bullet has proved ideal for conditions in India. Optional diesel conversions, and modern 12-volt electrics were among the minimal changes made, but otherwise, it is still possible to buy a brand-new Enfield Bullet in 1999!

ROYAL-MOTO *France 1923–33*
98–244cc (6–15cu in) Massardin two-strokes, plus four-strokes to 498cc (30cu in).

ROYAL NORD *Belgium 1950–early 1960s*
Various lightweights to 248cc (15cu in), plus mopeds.

ROYAL-RUBY *England 1909–32*
Mostly used its own sv singles, though Villiers and JAP engines were offered later on.

ROYAL SCOT *Scotland 1922–24*
This was an assembly job, with engine from Barr & Stroud and frame from Victoria.

ROYAL SOVEREIGN *England c.1902–03*
Used the ubiquitous (at the time) 211cc (13cu in) Minerva engine.

ROYAL STANDARD *Switzerland 1928–32*
Unit-construction 398cc (24cu in) twin powered by Zurcher.

ROYAL SUPER *Italy 1923–28*
A rebadged 132cc (8cu in) Royal.

ROYAL WELLINGTON *England c.1901*
Used a 211cc (13cu in) Minerva.

R&P *England 1902–c.1906*
A 346cc (21cu in) single.

RS *Germany 1925–28*
Tried and abandoned a 380cc (23cu in) unit-construction two-stroke twin in favour of a bought-in BMW flat twin.

RTV *Australia 1998–*
An updated Vincent V-twin with electric start, five-speed gearbox and 1200cc (73cu in) power, it is backed up by a throughly modern frame, brakes and suspension. The maker claimed 90bhp at the rear wheel, and promised fuel injection on production machines. Unfortunately, teething troubles meant that only three were built and in early 1999 the company was being offered for sale.

RUBINELLI *Italy 1921–27*
Built own 123/173cc (7.5/11cu in) two-strokes and also sold to others.

RUCHE *France 1952–54*
Produced 123/173cc (7.5/11cu in) two-strokes.

RUD *Germany 1927–30*
Used Kühne, MAG and JAP units to 748cc (46cu in).

RUDGE *England 1910–39*
Rudge came relatively late to the motorcycle industry and failed to survive World War II, yet it still managed to make a significant contribution during its 29-year involvement, thanks to two things which we now take for granted: multi-speed gears and multi-valve heads.

There was nothing particularly radical about Rudge's first machine, a 499cc (30cu in) ioe single which went on sale in 1911. It was no slug, though, and Victor Surridge rode one round the Brooklands circuit at 107km/h (66.47mph), making it

ABOVE: Sales brochure for the RTV range

OPPOSITE and PAGE 332: A 1929 499cc (30cu in) Rudge four-valve single

the first 500 to achieve a mile a minute. A breakthrough came later that year when John V. Pugh developed a gearing system in which the overall ratio was changed by moving the outer face of the engine pulley inwards, thus effectively increasing its diameter while, at the same time, a system of linkages opened out the rear pulley's flange. Consequently, drive-belt tension remained constant but the ratio between the pulleys changed, and the lever actually had 20 notches between the lowest and highest ratios. This was the Rudge Multi (similar in part to Zenith's Gradua system) which gave Rudges a huge advantage over single-speed competitors. However, its period of glory was brief (though it encompassed a second place in the 1913 TT, and a first in 1914), as gearboxes and all-chain drive made it obsolete after World War I.

Rudge introduced a three-speed gearbox and chain-drive in 1920, and applied it to the existing range of bikes: the original 499cc single, the 750cc (46cu in) version (launched in 1913 in response to sidecar demands) and a 998cc (61cu in) V-twin. But, by now, the ioe engine was itself outmoded, belonging more to the pioneer era than the 1920s. Rudge's response was to leapfrog the sidevalve and ohv opposition with another innovation, the Rudge Four. It had four valves to its single 350cc (21cu in) cylinder, not to mention a four-speed gearbox. The public loved this exotic specification, and sales soared, while a 500cc version was soon on offer as well.

Rudge-Whitworth
Four Valve Four Speed
RUDGE-FOUR

YB 7794

ABOVE and ABOVE RIGHT: A 1938 four-valve Rudge Special single of 495cc (30cu in)

The success encouraged Rudge to return to racing in 1927. At the TT, all three works bikes produced 28bhp at 5,200rpm, and could touch 161km/h (100mph) and, though they failed to finish that year, came second in 1928 (ridden by Graham Walker, who doubled up as Rudge's sales manager) and scored a famous win in the Ulster GP. Not only did Walker win by just 200 yards over Charlie Dodson's Sunbeam, but he also averaged over 129km/h (80mph), the fastest for any road race at the time. Henceforth, Rudge's race replicas were known as Rudge 'Ulsters'. More wins came the following year and in the 1930 TT Rudges came first, second and third. (This was part of a calculated gamble by race team chief George Hack that the latest four-valve singles would hold together, despite cracked pistons in practice, and they did, just.)

Naturally enough, Rudge took advantage of all this with 250, 350 and 500 versions of the four-valve racers, though the Depression meant that it was forced to sell the engines to other manufacturers to make ends meet. Cotton, AJW, Grindlay-Peerless, *et al*, bought the four-valve singles in under the Python name. Unfortunately, it wasn't enough to prevent bankruptcy, and Rudge spent the next couple of years in the hands of a receiver. It was eventually bought by HMV (later to become music giant EMI) and refinements continued, including positive-stop foot gearchange and enclosed valvegear. Sales began to recover, and there were plans for an overhead-camshaft 350, while a two-valve ohv 250 was undergoing trials with the Army. Then came war, and the factory was requisitioned to build radios. There would be no more Rudge motorcycles, though a Villiers-powered autocycle (actually designed in 1939) was passed on to Norman to build. Meanwhile, cycle maker Raleigh bought the rights to the name, and EMI did build the Cyclemaster power wheel under contract. And that was that.

RUEDER *Germany late 1910s to early 1920s*
348cc (21cu in) Kühne ohv singles.

RULLIERS *Czechoslovakia 1924–29*
Powered by 147–346cc (9–21cu in) Villiers engines.

RUMI *Italy 1949–62*
Best seller was an 129km/h (80mph) 124cc (8cu in) two-stroke sports twin, but the company later lost its way with the short-lived 175cc (11cu in) ohv single and range of small V-twins that failed to make it to production. The name reappeared on racers in 1991.

An early belt-drive Rudge

RUNGE *Germany 1923–26*
197cc (12cu in) sv machines with only limited production.

RUPP *Germany 1928–32*
Produced its own 198cc (12cu in) single and a Küchen-powered 298cc (18cu in) three-valve machine.

RUPPE *Germany 1927–30*
The ex-Bekamo Hugo Ruppe made 98cc (6cu in) clip-ons.

RUSH *Belgium 1921–34*
Used Blackburnes to 1927, then its own 397–597cc (24–36cu in) units.

RUSPA *Italy 1925–29*
Made a 124cc (8cu in) two-stroke, a 174cc (11cu in) ohv, plus an ohc 347cc (21cu in).

RUSSELL *England 1913*
Short-lived manufacturer of 172/492cc (10.5/30cu in) machines.

RUT *Germany 1923–24*
A 124cc (8cu in) two-stroke.

RUTER *Spain 1957–60*
Used Hispano-Villiers 123/197cc (7.5/12cu in) engines.

RUWISCH *Germany 1948–49*
A 38cc (2.3cu in) scooter, Victoria-powered.

RWC *Austria 1954–60*
98cc (6cu in) Rotax-engined lightweights.

RW SCOUT *England 1919–21*
A range of Villiers-powered two-strokes of 147–269cc (9–16cu in) plus some with 499cc (30cu in) sv Blackburnes.

S

SACI *Brazil 1959–mid-1960s*
A 174cc (11cu in) scooter.

SADEM *France 1951–54*
Lightweights to 98cc (6cu in).

SADRIAN Spain 1956–63
Used 123–198cc (7.5–12cu in) Hispano-Villiers units.

SAGITTA *Czechoslovakia 1928–30*
Imported Villiers' 247cc (15cu in) unit.

SALIRA *Belgium 1955–early 1960s*
Used 98–197cc (6–12cu in) Villiers engines.

SALTLEY *England 1919–24*
Choice of 197cc (12cu in) Villiers, 347cc (21cu in) Vulcanus or 497cc (30cu in) Blackburne power.

SALVE *Italy 1925–26*
A unit-construction 496cc (30cu in) sv.

SANCHOC *France 1922–24*
Produced two-strokes to 246cc (15cu in) and an sv to 346cc (21cu in).

SAN CRISTOFORO *Italy 1951–54*
A 124cc (8cu in) two-stroke.

SANGLAS *Spain 1952–81*
Sanglas started with its own unit-construction singles of 295–497cc (18–30cu in), most of which were sold to the Spanish police. Added two-stroke lightweights (49–325cc/3–20cu inch Zündapp and Hispano-Villiers-powered) in 1962, under the Rovena brand name. In its last six years Sanglas reverted to its own four-stroke single, up to 500cc (31cu in). Had links with Yamaha from 1978 with a bike powered by the Japanese firm's 392cc (24cu in) twin. However, Yamaha took the company over in 1981, and the Sanglas name was no more.

SAN-SOU-PAP *France 1923–36*
Range of Train-powered two-strokes and JAP and MAG four-stroke singles. Taken over by Rovin in 1929.

SANTAMARIA *Italy 1951–63*
Mopeds/lightweights to 147cc (9cu in), all with bought-in engines.

SAN YANG *Taiwan 1962–*
Builds Hondas under licence.

SANYO *Japan 1958–62*
Used an in-house 248cc (15cu in) ohv single.

SAR *Italy 1920–25*
A 498cc (30cu in) flat twin with sv or ohv.

The Sanglas 500-S2 utilized the Spanish company's own four-stroke single

SAR *Germany 1923–30*
Made its own three-port two-strokes of 122–198cc (7–12cu in).

SARENKA *Poland c.1960s*
This brand name was used by WSK for its DKW-based 123cc (7.5cu in) two-stroke.

SARKANA-SWAIGSNE *Latvia c.1960s*
49cc (3cu in) mopeds.

SAROLEA *Belgium 1901–57*
Belgium's leading make, and a real pioneer. Made complete machines with its own singles and V-twins from 1901, and sold engines to many other manufacturers. Concentrated on sv and ohv singles after 1918, and added two-strokes in 1932. After 1945 it resumed making 350/600cc (21/37cu in) four-strokes, adding a 125cc (8cu in) two-stroke in 1950 plus a 498cc (30cu in) parallel twin, and 500cc motocrossers later in the fifties. Produced an Ilo-engined moped from 1955, and merged with Gillet in 1960, production ceasing three years later.

SARTORIUS *Germany 1924–26*
Used Kühne 195/348cc (12/21cu in) singles.

SATAN *Czechoslovakia 1929*
Produced own 548cc (33cu in) sv sloper single.

SATURN *Germany 1921–27*
A 149cc (9cu in) clip-on, progressing to a 497cc (30cu in) V-twin.

SATURN *England 1925–26*
Used own 346cc (21cu in) two-stroke single.

SAUND *India c.1962–88*
Based its machines on DKW designs (originally the 98cc/6cu inch two-stroke).

SBD *Germany 1923–24*
Used the 293cc (18cu in) Bosch-Douglas flat twin.

SCARAB *Italy 1967–85*
Brand name used by Ancilotti, a maker of lightweights.

SCHEIBERT *Austria 1911–13*
A 197cc (12cu in) sv mounted above the front wheel.

SCHICKEL *U.S.A. 1912–c.15*
An unusual 648cc (40cu in) two-stroke single in a light alloy frame.

SCHLIHA *Germany 1924–33*
A two-stroke with poppet inlet valve, up to 596cc (36cu in).

SCHLIMME *Germany 1924–25*
142/173cc (9/11cu in) DKW two-strokes.

SCHMIDT *Germany 1921–24*
Built own clip-ons and 196cc (12cu in) lightweights.

SCHNEIDER *Germany 1924–26*
Used bought-in 142–206cc (9–13cu in) DKW two-strokes.

SCHROFF-RECORD *Germany 1923–25*
A 148cc (9cu in) sloping single two-stroke.

SCHÜRHOFF *Germany 1949–53*
Produced a variety of mopeds and lightweights with bought-in engines.

SCHÜTT *Germany 1933–34*
A duralumin frame was notable in this 196cc (12cu in) two-stroke.

A 1929 two-speed Scott Super Squirrel

SCHWALBE *Switzerland 1901–05*
A 2.75hp Zedel single was used in the usual strengthened cycle frame.

SCHWALBE *Germany 1922–24*
124/198cc (8/12cu in) flat-twin engines.

SCHWEPPE *Germany 1949–50*
Used Ilo two-strokes to 184cc (11cu in) and was later sold as the Pirol scooter.

SCK *Germany 1924–25*
JAP or MAG-powered singles to 498cc (30cu in).

SCOOTAVIA *France 1951–56*
An AMC-powered 173cc (11cu in) scooter.

SCORPION *England 1951–56*
Utilized 197/246cc (12/15cu in) Villiers engines in a pressed steel frame, principally in off-road trials machines.

SCOTO *France 1949–50*
A scooter with the Garelli Mosquito 38cc (2.3cu in) engine.

SCOTT *England 1908–mid 1960s*
Scott, 'the yowling two-stroke', was unique, and remained so during the entire span of its production. No other manufacturer, British or otherwise, dared to emulate Alfred Scott's formula of a water-cooled high-performance two-stroke. Suzuki was to produce a liquid-cooled two-stroke for the road in the 1970s, and the format has become dominant in track racing. But in the 1920s, two-strokes were nasty, cheap, smelly little things, confined to commuters. Real enthusiasts rode big, air-cooled four-stroke singles, and anything else was not to be trusted. Consequently, after an early Scott humiliated the big bikes at a hillclimb, other manufacturers persuaded the ACU (the sport's governing

body) to slap a handicap on water-cooled two-strokes.

Alfred Scott developed his unusual engine for use on boats as well as two-wheelers, though the first Scott motorcycle was completed in 1908. The motor itself was a 180-degree vertical twin of 333cc (20cu in) and even as a two-stroke it was innovative, with a three-port crankcase and deflector pistons. The large central flywheel spun between two separate crankcases and undoubtedly contributed to the Scott's smoothness and flexibility. At first, just the cylinder-heads were water-cooled, though the barrels soon followed.

As if all this avant-garde thinking were not enough, the engine was housed in a bike which positively bristled with fresh ideas. The frame was an open or 'ladies model', in the language of the day (what might be described as a 'step-through' now). Built of straight tubes and with the motor mounted low down for a low centre of gravity, it provided excellent handling. All-chain drive was only just trickling onto the market at the time, but the Scott had it, not to mention the first kickstart (no tiresome pedalling to start). And with the first foot pedal gearchange as well, not to mention rotary valves in 1911, there seemed no end to Alfred Scott's capacity for 'firsts'.

The competition handicap was withdrawn in 1912 when a Scott promptly won the TT, and again in the following year. Eventually, the Scott's lack of outright speed (the road machines produced around 30bhp) saw them overtaken by larger bikes, but their acceleration more than made up for that for a time. In 1914, Alfred Scott gave his bike drip-lubrication, gear-drive for the rotary valves and built engine and gearbox into a unit. But after this, he seemed to lose interest in the thing, having developed the concept as far as his fertile imagination could take it. He died in 1923, having worked on some very diverse (non-motorcycle) projects in the meantime.

But the Scott motorcycle lived on, only ever produced in small numbers as the tiny firm, dependent on outside suppliers, was never stable financially. Of necessity, the price was high, and Scotts tended to sell to the select few. A few improvements were made, but most of the changes appeared to be counter-productive, as if Alfred Scott's original vision had been fundamentally right to begin with. The more conventional-looking Squirrel was launched in 1922, and three years later the engine was expanded into 498 and 586cc (30 and 36cu in) versions. Power increased, but so did weight, and the pricey Scott began to look increasingly uncompetitive.

The production rights were bought by Matt Holder of the Aero Jig and Tool Company in 1950, who kept production going, albeit erratically. From 1956, the latest Flying Squirrels had a swinging-arm frame, full-width drum brakes and telescopic forks (Scott's original had prototypical telescopics in 1908), though the 596cc engine remained largely unchanged. Production finally petered out in the early sixties, though Matt Holder did build one final bike for a very persistent buyer in 1978! But in a way, one can understand that persistence. For all their foibles, Scotts of whatever age provided a very different riding experience, whether burbling quietly through country lanes or yowling (there's no better word) up to peak revs.

A 1929 two-speed Scott Super Squirrel

SCOTTA *France 1952–55*
Small-wheeled lightweight with 123cc (7.5cu in) Ilo engine.

SCOTT-CYC-AUTO *England 1934–50*
Another name for the Cyc-Auto.

SCYLLA *France 1931–37*
Lightweights of 98 and 123cc (6 and 7.5cu in), Aubier-Dunne-powered.

SEAL *England 1912–23*
A sidecar outfit which was actually ridden and controlled from the sidecar and powered by a 98cc (6cu in) JAP V-twin.

SEARS *U.S.A. 1912–16*
Sears, Roebuck, the Chicago, Illinois-based department store, sold motorcycles branded as Sears that were made by other

Sears

OPPOSITE and ABOVE: This 1910 Sears single is possibly the only surviving example of the machine

concerns at different times in its history. The first time this happened was in 1910 when single-cylinder machines were listed in the company's catalogue. They were designed to be sold by mail order through the catalogue, one of many diverse items which were sold including cars and gravestones. After 1912 the simple single-cylinder machines featured Spake single-cylinder inlet-over-exhaust engines with Bosch magnetos and chain transmission, based around an Excelsior-manufactured loop frame and with leaf-sprung trailing-link forks. Sears also offered a V-twin-engined machine and both were dropped in 1916. Sears then sold Austrian Puchs and Italian Gileras as Allstate and Sears brands.

SEEGARD *Germany 1924–25*
Produced own sv singles to 197cc (12cu in).

SENIOR *Italy 1913–14*
Moser-powered 296/330cc (18/20cu in) singles.

SERVETA *Spain 1973–*
Began with 49cc (3cu in) mopeds and now builds Lambrettas under licence.

SERVICE *England c.1900–1912*
Rebadged Connaught motorcyles.

SESSA *Italy 1950–56*
47cc (3cu in) Ilo-engined lightweights.

SETTER *Spain 1954–56*
Used its own 60cc (4cu in) power unit.

SEWÜT *Germany 1924–26*
DKW-powered 147–206cc (9–12.6cu in) two-strokes.

SFM *Poland 1956–64*
Sold as the Junak, the two-strokes were powered to 348cc (21cu in).

S-FORTIS *Czechoslovakia 1929–31*
Powered by Sarolea's 598cc (36cu in) ohv single.

SFW *Germany 1924–26*
A 2.5hp two-stroke.

S&G *Germany 1926–32*
Produced four-strokes to 596cc (36cu in), and later two-strokes to 198cc (12cu in). Had links with AJS.

SGS *England 1926–33*
Utilized Villiers or JAP power, to 490cc (30cu in).

SHARRATT *England 1920–30*
Used full range of JAP engines from 193–996cc (12–61cu in).

SHAW *England 1904–22*
Used Kelecom and Minerva bought-in engines and later imported a 115cc (7cu in) American clip-on.

SHAW *U.S.A. 1909–23*
2.5/3.5 hp models with own sv single.

SHEFFIELD-HENDERSON *England 1919–23*
The company's main business was sidecars, but it also produced Blackburne-engined bikes to 498cc (30cu in).

SHIN-MEIWA *Japan 1950s–1960s*
Two-strokes to 153cc (9cu in) with pressed steel frames.

SHL *Poland 1935–*
Produced Villiers-engined bikes before the war, and survived nationalization with its own two-strokes to 174cc (11cu in).

SHOWA *Japan 1948–60*
Made clip-ons from 1948, then graduated to 250cc (15cu in) two- and four-strokes. It was taken over by Yamaha. No connection with Showa suspension components.

SIAMT *Italy 1907–14*
Singles to 344cc (21cu in), V-twins to 731cc (45cu in).

SIAT *Italy 1924–26*
Two- and four-stroke engines to 198cc (12cu in).

SIC *France 1921–25*
Used bought-in engines of 98–346cc (12–21cu in).

SICRAF *France 1947–53*
Used Ydral and AMC power units to 246cc (15cu in).

SIEG *Germany 1922–30*
Used a vast variety of bought-in engines of 110–598cc (7–36cu in).

SIEGFRIED *Germany 1925*
A 142cc (9cu in) DKW-powered lightweight.

SIGNORELLI *Italy 1928–30*
A 173cc (11cu in) two-stroke.

SIL *India 1978–*
With minor updates, Lambretta scooters are still made by this company, the Indian government having acquired Lambretta tooling when Innocenti ceased making scooters in 1971.

ABOVE and BELOW: A Silk 700S, a 1970s update on the water-cooled two-stroke Scott theme

SILK *England 1972–79*
When Matt Holder built the last-ever Scott in 1978, its replacement was already in production. George Silk was a Scott enthusiast, not to mention a good practical engineer, whose dream it was to build a modern-day Scott. After five years with Scott specialist Tom Ward, Silk proved his abilities with his very fast Scott Vintage Racer which could broach 161km/h (100mph). In short, if anyone was qualified to produce a modern Scott, it was George, as he knew their every weakness intimately.

So he went into business with Maurice Patey, and set about designing the first Scott Silk Specials. The Scott twin came in for major changes, for Silk knew that the bottom-end couldn't stand hard use, so the crank was strengthened and roller-bearing mains and big-ends were used. A proper throttle-controlled oil pump (always a problem on Scotts) gave a good, reliable oil supply. Power was boosted by taking the engine out to 636cc/39cu inches (later 653cc) and increasing the compression ratio. The frame was made by Spondon Engineering (based like Silk Engineering in Derby), which also built its own forks and made up the front disc brakes from Lockheed components. This was by no means a home-built special. Two-stroke specialist Dr. Gordon Blair of Queens University, Belfast advised on the bore/stroke and scavenge cycle, while Southampton University supervised the silencers and rubber mounting.

By 1975, a combination of gradual development and small-scale production (20 Silk Scott Specials had been built in around three years) saw the Silk 700S ready for full production. George Silk and his collaborators could be rightly proud of the result; the 700S was flexible, just as the Scott had been, but capable of over 100mph, not to mention economical, with fuel consumption at 19.5km per litre (55mpg). It was also remarkably light, and the claimed 140kg (309lb) was less than many Japanese 250s then on sale. Unfortunately, it inherited something else that could be attributed to the original Scott – price. When it was launched in late 1975 the 700S was listed at £1,350, or £500 more than a Triumph Bonneville.

For Scott enthusiasts, this really was the original, but better than ever, with all the major weaknesses thoroughly addressed. But if the Silk did have a problem, apart from price, it was the availability of minor components. Producing bikes on such a tiny scale (30 machines were built in 1976) meant it was very difficult to get reliable supplies from outside component manufacturers. To make matters worse, the British motorcycle industry was rapidly winding down, and manufacturers like Lucas were thinking twice as to the viability of supplying Triumph or Norton, let alone a fledgling company that required a couple of alternators a month. At such small quantities and even when components could be bought, they were expensive and Silk Engineering just didn't have the capacity to order parts in bulk.

ABOVE: Silver Prince

Eventually, the parent company called a halt (Silk had been taken over by its largest shareholder in 1976), and just before Christmas 1979 the last Silk was completed.

SILVA *England 1919–20*
An early scooter with a 117cc (7cu in) four-stroke.

SILVER PIGEON *Japan early 1946–64*
A big player in the early Japanese scooter market, with engines of up to 210cc (13cu in), it was first inspired by the American Salsbury scooter, later by the Lambretta.

SILVER PRINCE *England 1919–24*
Used Villiers or Blackburne power units to 346cc (21cu in).

SILVER STAR *Japan 1953–58*
Used own 123/147cc (7.5/9cu in) ohv engines.

SIM *Italy 1953–1955*
Produced Puch-powered scooters and Ilo-engined lightweights.

SIMARD *France 1951–54*
Used a 174cc (11cu in) Ydral engine and was similar to a Lambretta.

SIMONETTA *Italy 1951–54*
Built by San Cristoforo.

SIMPLEX *U.S.A. 1906–09*
Peugeot-engined V-twins.

BELOW: An American Simplex V-twin

SIMPLEX *England 1919–22*
A 105cc (6.4cu in) clip-on.

SIMPLEX *U.S.A. 1935–75*
A 125cc (8cu in) Servi-Cycle lightweight, later with automatic transmission, and a scooter version from the late 1950s. Minibikes were produced from 1960.

SIMSON *East Germany 1950–*
Produced a BMW-based shaft-driven single at first, then 49/74cc (3/4.5cu in) lightweights.

SINGER *England 1900–15*
Started with 208cc (13cu in) engines in cycle frames, followed by machines of up to 535cc (33cu in).

SIPHAX *France 1951–56*
Used a 98cc (6cu in) AMC two-stroke.

SIROCCO *Czechoslovakia 1925–28*
Used Villiers power of 147–346cc (9–21cu in).

SIRRAH *England 1922–25*
Used a variety of two- and four-stroke proprietory enignes, from a 211cc (13cu in) Wisemann to a 490cc (30cu in) JAP.

SIS *Portugal 1950–*
Producer of Sachs-powered mopeds and lightweights to 98cc (6cu in).

SISSY *Austria 1957*
A 98 or 123cc (6–7.5cu in) Rotax-powered mini-scooter.

SITTA *Germany 1950–55*
A range of Ilo-engined mopeds, scooters and lightweights.

SJK *Japan 1956–early 1960s*
Made mopeds and lightweights to 249cc (15cu in) and its own two-stroke engines.

SKO *Czechoslovakia 1924–26*
A 498cc (30cu in) three-port two-stroke single.

SKOOTAMOTOR *England 1919–22*
One of the first scooters with a 123cc (7.5cu in) ABC ohv engine.

SL *England 1924–25*
An interesting three-valve single of 345cc (21cu in).

SLADE-JAP *England 1920–23*
Utilized a 346cc (21cu in) sv JAP engine.

A rare Sparkbrook on display at the National Motorcycle Museum, England

SLANEY *England 1921–22*
A 688cc (42cu in) flat twin.

SM *Poland 1935*
Limited production of a unit-construction 346cc (21cu in) single with shaft-drive.

SMART *France 1922–27*
Produced 198cc (12cu in) sv lightweights.

SMART *Austria 1925–27*
Used JAP engines to 596cc (36cu in).

SMS *England 1913–14*
A 211cc (13cu in) two-stroke with an extra inlet port between carburettor and crankcase.

SMW *Germany 1923–33*
Apart from its own 198cc (12cu in) two-stroke, it used Bosch-Douglas and BMW flat twins, plus various English singles.

S&N *Germany 1901–08*
A licence-built Laurin & Klement, badged Germania or Slavia.

SNOB *Germany 1921–1925*
Used own 154cc (9cu in) ioe single.

SOCOVEL *Belgium 1947–55*
Made Villiers-engined lightweights with enclosed engines and later used power units from Jawa, Sachs and others.

SOK *Sweden 1925–28*
Used mainly JAP engines.

SOKOL *Poland 1936–39*
A 598cc (36cu in) sloper sv single.

SOLO *Germany 1949–82*
Produced mopeds and lightweights with own 49cc (3cu in) two-stroke.

SOS *England 1927–39*
Machines were almost entirely Villiers-powered, to 347cc (21cu in).

SOUPLEX *Belgium 1947–53*
Used a 123cc (7.5cu in) Villiers, later a 296cc (18cu in) Coventry-Victor flat twin.

SOUTHEY *England 1905–25*
Used Villiers and Blackburne engines from 246–346cc (15–21cu in).

SOYER *France 1920–35*
Used a variety of bought-in engines from Chaise, Sturmey-Archer and JAP.

SPA-JAP *England 1921–23*
Used 246 or 293cc (15 or 18cu in) sv JAP engines.

SPAKE *U.S.A. 1911–14*
Sold its ioe engines (550cc/34cu inch singles and 980cc/60cu inch V-twins) to other manufacturers, as well as producing complete machines under its own name.

SPARK *England 1903–04*
Used a 2hp engine with surface carburettor.

SPARKBROOK *England 1912–25*
Used various bought-in engines, ranging from a 269cc (16cu in) Villiers to 980cc (60cu in) JAP.

SPARTA *The Netherlands 1931–*
Sachs, Ilo and Villiers-engined mopeds and lightweights. Since 1982, it has produced a 30cc (1.8cu in) clip-on only.

SPARTAN *England 1920–22*
Used a Broler 349cc (21cu in) three-port two-stroke.

SPAVIERO *Italy 1954–55*
98cc (6cu in) four-stroke twins.

SPÉCIAL-MONNERET *France 1952–58*
A 49cc (3cu in) lightweight, VAP or Sachs-engined.

SPEED *France 1951–56*
A scooter with 60, 115 and 124cc (4, 7 and 7.5cu in) engines.

SPEED-KING-JAP *England 1913–14*
Made JAP-engined utilities for sale by a chain store.

SPHINX *Belgium 1923–26*
Used JAP engines to 490cc (30cu in).

SPIEGLER *Germany 1923–32*
Used JAP and MAG engines from 198–598cc (12–36cu in).

SPIESS *Germany 1903–05*
Utilized 2/2.75hp engines from Minerva, Zedel and Fafnir.

SPINDLER *Germany 1922–25*
Bekamo-engined 149cc (9cu in) two-strokes.

SPIRIDITIS *Latvia early 1950s–*
123/246cc (7.5/15cu in) two-strokes.

SPRING *Belgium 1910–40*
Began with a four-cylinder machine (with rear suspension) and later produced transverse V-twins to 996cc (61cu in).

STABIL *Belgium 1931–33*
Produced Villiers-engined 98/123cc (6/7.5cu in) lightweights.

STADION *Czechoslovakia 1958–66*
49cc (3cu in) mopeds, Jawa-powered.

STAFFETT *Norway 1953–63*
49cc (3cu in) mopeds.

STAG *England 1912–14*
Used 4.5–6hp Precision engines.

STAHL *U.S.A. 1910–14*
Used own 4.5 and 7hp V-twins.

STANDARD *Germany 1922–24*
132 and 148cc (8 and 9cu in) two-strokes.

STANDARD *Switzerland 1931–52*
Initially used JAP, then MAG bought-in engines plus others, and later produced its own ohv singles.

STANGER *England 1921–23*
A 538cc (33cu in) V-twin two-stroke of 'square' bore and stroke dimensions. It was an unusual design, but in practice overheated and fouled its plugs.

STANLEY *England c.1902*
2.5hp powered cycles with friction-drive.

STAR *England 1898–1914*
Used De Dion engines first, later JAP 625cc (38cu in) singles and 770cc (47cu in) V-twins.

STAR *Germany 1895–c.1900*
A licence-built Werner, the 1.5hp engine was mounted above the front wheel.

STAR *England 1919–21*
269cc (16cu in) Villiers-powered.

STAR *Germany 1920–22*
Using its own 393cc (24cu in) flat twin, it became the D-Rad.

STAR-GEM *Belgium 1930–33*
Used in-house and Sachs two-strokes to 123cc (7.5cu in).

STEFFEY *U.S.A. c.1902–10*
Own 1.25/3hp singles, air- or water-cooled.

STEIDINGER *Germany 1925–27*
199cc (12cu in) two-stroke engine.

STELLA *Belgium 1921–36*
Used 98cc (6cu in) two-strokes to 490cc (30cu in) four-strokes, all licence-built JAPs from Staub of France.

STELLAR *England 1912–14*
A water-cooled, vertical-twin two-stroke of 784cc (48cu in) with shaft-drive.

STERLING *France 1952–54*
Used a 123cc (7.5cu in) Ydral, fully enclosed.

STERNA *Germany 1922–24*
A water-cooled 614cc (37cu in) flat twin, similar to the Aristos.

STERVA *France 1953–56*
Sabb-powered scooter of 98–123cc (6–7.5cu in).

STEVENS *England 1934–37*
Built by the Stevens brothers after they sold AJS to the Colliers (Matchless).

STICHERLING *Germany 1923–26*
Used DKW engines to 206cc (13cu in).

STIMULA *France 1902–c.1939*
Used in-house and bought-in engines to 492cc (30cu in).

STOCK *Germany 1924–33*
Used own advanced three-port two-strokes to 298cc (18cu in).

STOEWER *Germany 1904–05*
Powered by a 2.75hp Fafnir.

STOLCO *Germany 1922–24*
Used bought-in 144cc (9cu in) Grade two-strokes.

STROLCH *Germany 1950–58*
Sachs-engined scooters to 198cc (12cu in), later renamed Progress.

STRUCO *Germany 1922–25*
Used own two- and four-strokes to 198cc (12cu in).

STUART *England 1911–12*
A 298cc (18cu in) two-stroke.

STUCCHI *Italy 1901–27*
Built three- and four-wheelers as well as bikes.

STURM *Germany 1923–25*
Used 147cc (9cu in) Alba engines.

STYLSON *France 1919–34*
Used both original and licence-built JAPs from Staub.

STYRIA *Austria 1905–08*
Used Fafnir singles and V-twins.

SUDBRACK *Germany 1949–51*
Ilo-engined 98/123cc (6/7.5cu in) lightweights.

ABOVE, BELOW and OPPOSITE: A 1927 Sunbeam S9 displaying all the hallmarks of 'The Gentleman's Motorcycle'

SUDBROOK *England 1919–20*
269cc (16cu in) and Villiers-powered.

SUECIA *Sweden 1928–40*
Used JAP engines to 490cc (30cu in), plus two-strokes built by Sparta.

SULKY *France 1954–57*
To our ears, not a happy name for a user-friendly scooter. It had AMC power from 98–124cc (6–8cu in).

SUMITA *Japan 1951–55*
Producer of 123cc and 148cc (7.5 and 9cu in) motorcycles with Sumita's own engines.

SUN *England 1911–61*
Began and ended with utility two-strokes, but also used Blackburne and JAP engines. Post-1945 bikes (including the Sunwasp scooter) were exclusively Villiers-powered.

SUNBEAM *England 1912–57*
The Sunbeam (and it always was *The* Sunbeam) was 'The Gentleman's Motor Cycle'. With its glossy black finish, enclosed chain and attention to detail, it was a true quality product. It was not always at the cutting edge of technology, but was solid and well made if a little expensive. All of which could equally describe Sunbeam cycles ('The Gentleman's Bicycle'). Like many motorcycle makers of the time, Sunbeam grew out of cycle manufacture, though the company claimed to have been in business since 1790 as Marston Ltd. Indeed a Marston (John, with son Roland ready to succeed him) was not only holding the reins, but made the decision to tackle the motorcycle market.

It was a relatively late decision as the first Sunbeam bike did not go on sale until 1912, though in the same black livery as the bicycles. In fact, that weatherproof finish became almost legendary, said to stem from Marston's pioneering of a baked gloss finish on kitchen utensils. It is said that it took nine coats of paint to achieve, and old John Marston never allowed visitors to the enamelling shop for fear they might upset the process.

The new bike's engine was right first time. Designed by John Greenwood, it was a 347cc (21cu in) sidevalve single which had the unusual feature of eccentric internal flywheels, these being to balance the crankshaft. The already outmoded belt was eschewed in favour of all-chain drive (with of course the Sunbeam oil bath enclosure), two-speed gearbox and multi-plate clutch. It was soon joined by a V-twin, albeit powered by a bought-in JAP 770cc (47cu in) engine, driving through Sunbeam's own three-speed gearbox. A 500cc (30.5cu in) version of the single was unveiled in late 1913 and actually finished equal second in the following year's TT, the first of many Sunbeam competition successes. It was also built in quantity during World War I for the French army who, much to the disgust of Mr. Marston, insisted on a crude belt-drive.

A whole string of race wins followed in the early 1920s (including two Senior TTs) which perhaps encouraged Sunbeam to produce new ohv singles in both 350 and 500 sizes in 1923. The respected rider, Graham Walker, joined as competitions manager the following year, and began entering Sunbeams for European races. The ohv 493cc Model 90 continued to win races after an overhead-camshaft design gave disappointing results. This Sunbeam was the last two-valve ohv engine to win the Senior TT, in 1929.

In fact, this reflected a certain reluctance to innovate, and Sunbeam road bikes hung on to flat fuel tanks and Druid front forks when most rivals had switched to modern-looking saddle tanks and girder forks. But it managed to survive the Depression, thanks in part to ownership by the mighty ICI empire (the Marston family had sold out soon after the war) and to a pruned range of simple reliable bikes, notably the Lion (which was the old 492cc (30cu in) sidevalve single) and a cheaper 344cc (21cu in) ohv machine. Slowly, the bikes were updated with saddle tanks and a positive-stop foot change, while a couple of 250s joined the range. Dropping the faithful oil bath chain was a recognition of fashion rather than a desire for improvement.

In 1936, Sunbeam was again taken over, this time by Matchless, which was forming Associated Motor Cycles together with AJS and Sunbeam. Production was moved from Sunbeam's native Wolverhampton to Plumstead in London. After a couple of years, the old Sunbeams were replaced with a new range of high-camshaft singles of 250, 350 and 500. They were hardly established before war intervened, which was the end of Sunbeam for a while.

When a Sunbeam motorcycle reappeared in 1947, it was not only under a new owner (BSA had bought the name) but with a startlingly avant-garde design that shared only its name with the old Sunbeams. In fact, the all-new S7 showed little resemblance to any other rival. The twin-cylinder all-alloy engine was mounted longitudinally, had an overhead camshaft and used shaft-drive. Big valanced mudguards and fat 5-inch section tyres gave it a comfortable, civilized appearance, and interest in the new Sunbeam was huge. Sadly, this didn't translate into mass sales as the S7 produced only 25bhp and was not a fast machine; even if the engine had been capable of much more power, the final-drive would not have been able to stand it. The lighter-looking S8 looked more conventional, but the public were not convinced, and the BSA-designed Sunbeams died a death in 1957. A BSA Sunbeam scooter was to follow briefly, otherwise, another famous British name had disappeared.

SUPERBA *Italy 1928–35*
Small sportsters with 173cc (11cu in) Piazza and JAP engines.

SUPERB-FOUR *England 1920–21*
Advanced sohc in-line four of 998cc (61cu in) and unit-construction, with three-speed gearbox.

SUPÉRIA *Belgium 1957–70s*
Used a variety of bought-in 49cc (3cu in) two-strokes.

SUPER-X *U.S.A. 1924–30*
Successor to the American-X, it was powered by ioe V-twins of 746 and 996cc (45.5 and 61cu in).

SUPPLEXA *France 1922–32*
JAP-powered singles and V-twins.

SUPREMOCO *England 1921–23*
Used various bought-in engines to 346cc (21cu in). Also assembled Defy-All and Supermoco brands.

ABOVE and OPPOSITE: The BSA-designed Sunbeam S7 and S8, though certainly gentlemanly, were unfortunately unsuccessful

SUNBEAM
KCD 451

ABOVE, RIGHT and OPPOSITE: Suzuki concentrated on small two-strokes throughout the 1960s

SUZUKI *Japan 1952–*
If World War II had never occurred, Suzuki might well have beaten all its major home-grown rivals to first place in the motorcycle industry. In 1937, Soichiro Honda was concentrating on piston rings, Yamaha on making musical instruments and Kawasaki was still 23 years away from its first motorcycle. Yet in that year, Suzuki had built a prototype motorcycle engine, so it is clear that the company was contemplating the two-wheel market long before its contemporaries. That all four ended up building bikes were for the same pragmatic reasons: that they had seen their traditional markets disrupted or decimated because of war, and that post-war Japan was seeing an unprecedented demand for cheap two-wheeled transport.

Like its contemporaries, Suzuki did not start out as a motorcycle manufacturer at all. Michio Suzuki was born in February 1887, in the village of Hamamatsu, where the company is based to this day, though now it is a general part of Japan's coastal industrial sprawl. Like Soichiro Honda, Michio was as much an entrepreneur as an engineer, and in 1909 at the age of 22 went into business on his own account, building silk looms.

The silk industry was important to Japan, being so widespread, so the new Suzuki company grew fast, even though its founder was seeking other diversifications, hence that prototype engine in 1937, and an agreement the same year to build the Austin Seven car under licence. But the war, and Japan's rearmament programme which preceded it, put a stop to any thoughts in that direction. Obliged to commit itself to the military machine, Suzuki was granted permission to recommence loom production by the American occupying forces in September 1945. Unfortunately, raw silk was by now very difficult to come by, and Suzuki's only means of survival was to look to other markets, which it did in the form of heaters, farm machinery and various other

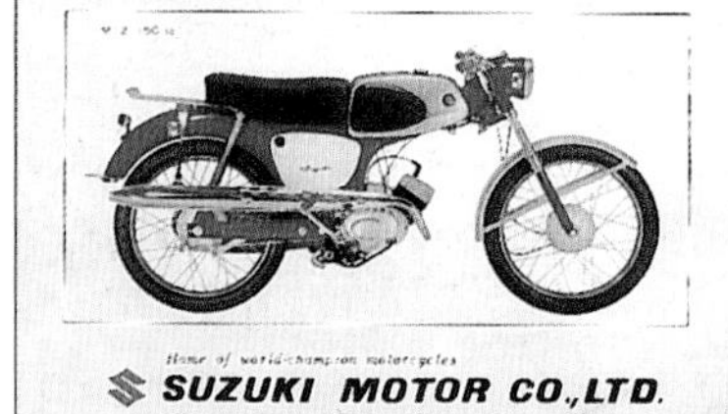

SPECIFICATIONS

ENGINE	Type	Air-cooled, 2-stroke, single cylinder
	Bore and stroke	41 mm × 38 mm ⟨45 × 50⟩
	Displacement	50 cc ⟨79⟩
	Compression ratio	6.7
	Lubrication	Gas 15 : oil 1 mixture
	Carburetor	VM 15 SC ⟨VM 17 SC⟩
	Starting system	Kick
	Ignition system	Flywheel high tension ignition
PERFORMANCE	Maximum output	4.5 hp/8000 r.p.m. ⟨7.3/7000⟩
	Maximum speed	85 km/h (53.2 m.p.h.) ⟨95 (59.5)⟩
	Maximum torque	0.42 kgm/7000 r.p.m. ⟨0.75/6000⟩
	Climbing ability	14°30' ⟨16°⟩
	Fuel consumption	65 km/liter (153 miles/U.S. gallon)
TRANSMISSION	Type	4-speed foot operated with constant mesh, return change type
	Primary ratio	Gear 4.40 ⟨3.84⟩
	Secondary ratio	Chain 2.46 ⟨2.31⟩
	Clutch	Multiple wet disk
OVERALL DIMENSIONS	Length	1815 mm (71.5") ⟨1830⟩
	Width	613 mm (24.2")
	Height	930 mm (36.6") ⟨935⟩
	Wheel base	1160 mm (45.7")
	Ground clearance	130 mm (5.1") ⟨135⟩
	Dry weight	60 kgs (132.3 lbs) ⟨70⟩
OTHERS	Frame	Pressed steel, back-bone type
	Brakes, front	Internal expanding hand brake
	rear	Internal expanding foot brake
	Tires (front and rear)	2.25" - 17" - 4 PR ⟨2.50⟩
	Suspension system, front	Telescopic oil damper
	rear	Pivot swing oil damper
	Fuel tank capacity	6 liter (1.6 U.S. gallon) ⟨6.5⟩

Blue figures are the data of "MODEL K11"

products which kept the company afloat for the next few years.

Michio Suzuki was well into his 60s when he decided upon the final solution that would set the seal on his company's fortunes. He was a keen fisherman and was accustomed to cycling to his favourite fishing haunts; but he could also see the attraction of a motorized bicycle, designed to take the effort out of such trips. More importantly, he was also able to recognize the crucial connection with this and the country's rapidly growing demand for such transport. Perhaps, like the men behind Lambretta, the Vespa and Harley-Davidson, he was simply there at the right time.

Work began on the first prototype in November 1951, a 36cc (2cu in) two-stroke clip-on unit which could be fitted to any bicycle. It went on sale seven months later, under the name of Power Free. Significantly, it was all made in-house by Suzuki itself, which underlined the company's serious intent; this was no short-term attempt at making money on the back of the clip-on boom. Suzuki clearly intended to stay with the two-wheel market, and grow with it. The original Power Free was soon followed by the 60cc (4cu in) Diamond Free in March 1953. But the Diamond Free wasn't just a clip-on, and as a complete bike won its class in the 1953 Mount Fuji hillclimb.

This success (both in the marketplace and in racing) encouraged the company to produce its first complete road bike, and the Colleda ('This is it') was announced in May 1954. Now some say this was Suzuki's first four-stroke, others that it was a two-stroke. Whoever is right, it is certain that the 90cc (5.5cu in) single won the Mount Fuji hillclimb in its debut year. A bigger 125cc (8cu in) two-stroke, the Colleda ST, followed in 1955. By now, the clip-on engines had been dropped and Suzuki was becoming a mass-producer of small motorcycles. Two years later, a new plant and increased capacity made it second only to Honda in the Japanese market.

Just as significant at the time was Michio's son Shunzo's trip to North America, which convinced him that here was another huge market ripe for exploitation. Also, the Colleda's early competition success led to Suzuki's long (and still successful) association with racing. A special 125cc racer was built in 1955, though met with little success and it was another four years before a purpose-built racer (another 125, with 10bhp, a four-speed gearbox, telescopic forks and swinging-arm frame) ventured onto the tracks. The Colleda RB could only manage fifth in the 1959 Asama races (Honda was unassailable that year), but afterwards Soichiro Honda was to casually ask Shunzo Suzuki why they didn't race such a fast machine abroad. The following year, Suzuki was in the Isle of Man.

The RV125 was Suzuki"s answer to the Honda Monkey Bike

Pumps & Bloops

Although racing was important to Suzuki, just like its rivals it relied on small, simple commuter bikes as its mainstay. Typical were the K- and M-series machines of the early sixties, two-stroke singles which were made in huge numbers (Suzuki built over half a million of the K10 and K11 alone). Not that they were unsophisticated – all these bikes shared the attraction of oil injection. Instead of the usual petroil system, where the rider had to manually add the correct amount of two-stroke oil when filling up, the little Suzukis had separate oil tanks which automatically pumped lubricant directly to where it was needed, according to engine revs and throttle opening; the harder the engine worked, the more oil it got. With petroil, lubrication was a more haphazard affair where the petrol/oil mixture was sucked in

ABOVE: Suzuki DR400 trail bike

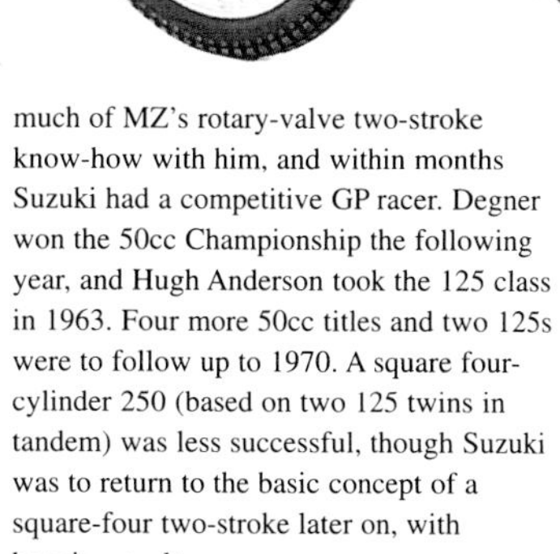

ABOVE RIGHT: The 100cc (6cu in) commuter with trail overtones

together and it was fingers crossed that sufficient oil reached the right parts! It may seem like an esoteric technical point, but Suzuki's CCI system (Controlled Crankshaft Injection) was really a huge step forward for non-enthusiasts, who could now fill up with pure petrol just as with any car.

The K- and M-series were replaced by the B100P of 1964. Nicknamed the 'Bloop', this 119cc (7.3cu in) two-stroke (with CCI of course) proved a long-running hit, and remained on sale until 1970. It was even revived in the mid-1970s as the B120 Student. Similarly long-lived was the smaller A100 of 1967, which survived right into the 1980s, while slightly bigger was the 246cc (15cu in) T10, which was a development of the 1956 Colleda TT (Suzuki's first twin-cylinder bike) and the Twinace models of 1960. Although mechanically similar, the 1963 T10 was evidence of a new attack on export markets, with the electric start and indicators with which Japanese lightweights were making their mark. Surprisingly, considering Suzuki's imminent association with fearsome performance two-stroke twins, the T10 was mild-mannered, with a flat, gentle power curve and four-speed gearbox. With its pressed steel frame and Germanic styling, the T10 had all the appearance of the early Japanese bike that it was. However, something very different was to come.

Meanwhile, Suzuki had been making its mark in the West, not with mass-market sales, but in racing. Entries to the 1960 and '61 Isle of Man TTs had brought a best of 15 place. But it was Ernst Degner's controversial defection from MZ and East Germany to Suzuki in late 1961 that provided the real breakthrough; he brought much of MZ's rotary-valve two-stroke know-how with him, and within months Suzuki had a competitive GP racer. Degner won the 50cc Championship the following year, and Hugh Anderson took the 125 class in 1963. Four more 50cc titles and two 125s were to follow up to 1970. A square four-cylinder 250 (based on two 125 twins in tandem) was less successful, though Suzuki was to return to the basic concept of a square-four two-stroke later on, with happier results.

While all this was going on, Suzuki's road bike range was basically non-sporting, but 1966 saw the launch of its first true sportsbike, which was also designed with an eye on export markets. The T20 Super Six (named the X6 in America) was much more than a tuned-up T10. In fact, it was completely different. Although it too was a 247cc two-stroke twin, the engine was completely new, with alloy barrels, 24mm carburettors and a six-speed gearbox. To save weight, the electric start was omitted and the pressed steel frame was dispensed with in favour of 'proper' tubular steel. With 29bhp at its disposal, the Super Six could easily top 145km/h (90mph), and contemporary road tests waxed lyrical about a bike that set new standards in the 250 class. More than any other bike, the Super Six brought Suzuki to the attention of the European and American markets. It was evidently a success, for the company followed it up with the smaller T200 and larger T500 only a year later. The 500, in particular, won many friends, although it

didn't handle as well as the lighter 250, but 46bhp at 7,000rpm gave it a 177km/h (110mph) performance, so it was almost as fast but less frenetic than Kawasaki's manic two-stroke triple. The T500 (known as Titan in the United States, Cobra in Britain) enjoyed a long life, and survived until 1977 as the GT500 with front disc brake and electronic ignition.

There were also updates in the 250 twin theme (plus enlarged 305cc and 316cc/19cu inch inversions up to 1973) in the early/mid 1970s, culminating in the GT250X7, which claimed to be the first-ever 100mph production 250. (Ducati had actually claimed the same for its Mach 3 a few year earlier, but no doubt the arguments will rag for years to come.) To supplement the popular 500 twin, Suzuki produced two-stroke triples of its own, the GT380 and GT550 from 1972; both were smoother and faster than the older bike and the six-speed 380 was something of a classic of its time, one of the last air-cooled performance two-strokes. They came complete with 'Ram Air', which sounded mighty impressive but was merely squared-off cylinder cowling. The thirstier 550 was dropped in 1977, its smaller brother a couple of years later. At the same time, and in the same style, there were GT125 and GT185 twins.

The early 1970s also saw Suzuki's first real trail bike. Like its rivals, it had already sold street scramblers (road bikes with high level exhausts) but the all-new TS125 of 1971 was a true dual-purpose machine, and designed as such. It could reach 113km/h (70mph) on tarmac, but was easy to ride of it, and was so successful that it led to a whole family of TS trail bikes. Smaller TS50 and TS100 variants came first, both c them (unlike the 125) with rotary-valve induction. A TS250 followed which, with 23bhp at 6,500rpm, gave useful on-road performance, while the later TS185 and TS400s completed the family. The biggest TS was later dropped, but the smaller ones were gradually updated in the eighties and nineties, notably with water-cooling. Suzuk carried on making the bikes that were to be its mainstay, notably, of course, the two-stroke GP100/125 from 1978, which replaced the venerable B120 and was capable of 70mph, as well as a succession of step-thrus. The latter were clearly inspired by the success of Honda's Cub, an

ABOVE and BELOW: Different generations of two-stroke twins, the 1960s T10 and the late'70s GTX7

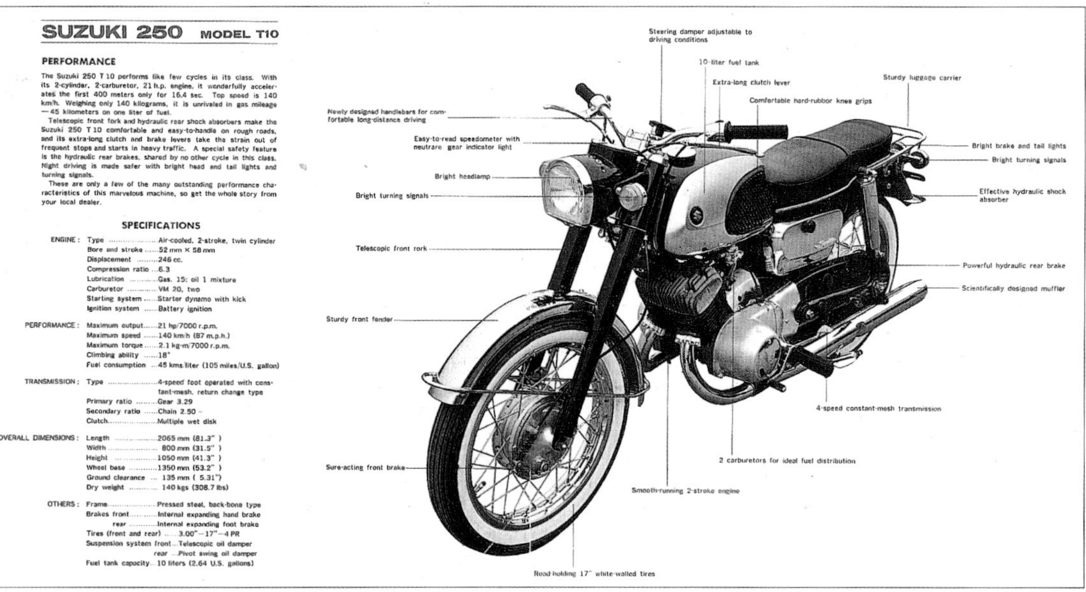

SUZUKI 250 MODEL T10

PERFORMANCE

The Suzuki 250 T 10 performs like few cycles in its class. With its 2-cylinder, 2-carburetor, 21 h.p. engine, it wonderfully accelerates the first 400 meters only for 16.4 sec. Top speed is 140 km/h. Weighing only 140 kilograms, it is unrivaled in gas mileage —45 kilometers on one liter of fuel.

Telescopic front fork and hydraulic rear shock absorbers make the Suzuki 250 T 10 comfortable and easy-to-handle on rough roads, and its extra-long clutch and brake levers take the strain out of frequent stops and starts in heavy traffic. A special safety feature is the hydraulic rear brakes, shared by no other cycle in this class. Night driving is made safer with bright head and tail lights and turning signals.

These are only a few of the many outstanding performance characteristics of this marvelous machine, so get the whole story from your local dealer.

SPECIFICATIONS

ENGINE:	Type	Air-cooled, 2-stroke, twin cylinder
	Bore and stroke	52 mm × 58 mm
	Displacement	246 cc.
	Compression ratio	6.3
	Lubrication	Gas. 15: oil 1 mixture
	Carburetor	VM 20, two
	Starting system	Starter dynamo with kick
	Ignition system	Battery ignition
PERFORMANCE:	Maximum output	21 hp/7000 r.p.m.
	Maximum speed	140 km/h (87 m.p.h.)
	Maximum torque	2.1 kg-m/7000 r.p.m.
	Climbing ability	18°
	Fuel consumption	45 kms/liter (105 miles/U.S. gallon)
TRANSMISSION:	Type	4-speed foot operated with constant-mesh, return change type
	Primary ratio	Gear 3.29
	Secondary ratio	Chain 2.50
	Clutch	Multiple wet disk
OVERALL DIMENSIONS:	Length	2065 mm (81.3")
	Width	800 mm (31.5")
	Height	1050 mm (41.3")
	Wheel base	1350 mm (53.2")
	Ground clearance	135 mm (5.31")
	Dry weight	140 kgs (308.7 lbs)
OTHERS:	Frame	Pressed steel, back-bone type
	Brakes front	Internal expanding hand brake
	rear	Internal expanding foot brake
	Tires (front and rear)	3.00"—17"—4 PR
	Suspension system front	Telescopic oil damper
	rear	Pivot swing oil damper
	Fuel tank capacity	10 liters (2.64 U.S. gallons)

A 1978 GN250, the archetypal factory custom

looked very similar, the important difference being a two-stroke engine rather than the unfamiliar (to Suzuki) four-stroke, and 50cc and 70cc variants were offered.

Rotary, Big Four-Strokes

The story of Suzuki in the early/mid-1970s was of a search for alternatives to the air-cooled two-stroke, for big bikes at least. The success of Honda's CB750 and Kawasaki's Z1, not to mention the first fuel crisis and tighter emissions regulations, were making big, thirsty two-strokes untenable. This presented Suzuki with a problem, wedded as it was to the two-stroke principle, and it wasn't until 1976 that it bowed to the inevitable and produced a big four-stroke of its own. In the meantime, there was the GT750 of 1969, Suzuki's immediate response to the 750cc (46cu in) Hondas and Kawasakis. Although a two-stroke triple, Suzuki's entrant was very different to the hair-raising Kawasaki H1. It was water-cooled, quiet and well-mannered, not over-tuned, but it still equalled the four-stroke Honda with 67bhp. Despite the 'GT' tag, the 750 (or 'Kettle' as it was known in Britain) was more of a smooth, comfortable tourer, being too heavy to rival sportier machines for handling. It lasted seven years. Shorter-lived, but more radical, was Suzuki's rotary-engined RE5, which was unveiled at the Cologne Motorcycle Show in 1974. Unlike the simpler air-cooled rotaries being developed by DKW and Norton, the water-cooled RE5 looked monstrously complicated. It was heavy (245kg/540lb), produced less power than the GT750 and drank more fuel. It was not a success.

Fortunately for Suzuki (which lost a great deal of money with the RE5) better was to come. The GS750, launched in 1976, couldn't have been more different from the brave but flawed RE5. Instead, it was a thorough reworking of the big air-cooled four-cylinder concept popularized by Honda and Kawasaki. It was inevitable that the Suzuki GS750 would be a little faster than the Honda at 201km/h/125mph (thanks to twin overhead camshafts and a shorter stroke, power was 68bhp at 8,500rpm, with 44lb ft of torque at 7,000rpm). What set it apart was respectable handling. Until then, it was almost a truism that you couldn't have a high-horsepower Japanese four and good handling as well, but the GS750 broke this 'rule' with a relatively stiff frame that placed it well ahead of Honda. The result was a success for Suzuki, who followed it up with the 997cc (61cu in) GS1000 the year after. Suzuki's biggest bike yet produced 87bhp and could manage 217km/h (135mph), but it too handled well by the standards of the day and had adjustable suspension. It was no wonder that Suzuki's copywriters came up with the line, 'The lightweight heavyweight'. All sorts of variations on the GS1000 theme followed, notably the shaft-driven G version, and it lasted until 1981 when both it and the 750 were replaced by the four-valve GSX series.

Both GS750 and 1000 were the big sportsters of their day, but the GS850 was different. It was Suzuki's first purpose-designed tourer, and an attempt to grasp a slice of the touring market so successfully exploited by Honda with the Gold Wing. The 850 (it was announced in 1979) owed much to the 750, but was bored out to 843cc (51.4cu in) to produce 79bhp at 8,500rpm. The extra power was there to cope with the 850's extra weight (40kg/88lb more than the 750), much of which was down to the adoption of shaft-drive. Gas and rubber dampers were added to the transmission to minimize the clunky gearchange then associated with shaft-drive. The 850 was replaced by the GS1000G in 1980 which in turn became the 1100G in 1983. Suzuki was evidently getting the hang of four-stroke design, replacing all its mid-range two-strokes with fours in the mid/late 1970s. Alongside the GS750 it had unveiled a GS400 twin, with gear-driven balance- shaft. It looked little different from the rival CB/Z/XS400 twins but evolved into a long-lived line of reliable, ride-to-work bikes. The 400 soon became a 425 (in 1979) then a 450 (1980) and returned as the GS500 in 1989. Now with a more modern chassis, but the same basic two-valve air-cooled twin-cylinder motor, it offered cheap, basic motorcycling with reasonable performance. The four-cylinder GS550 from 1977 acquired a similar reputation for toughness, due to the use of roller bearings in the engine and a gear primary-drive. Like many Suzukis, its cosmetic qualities didn't always match up to its mechanics, but that didn't deter the buyers. Suzuki's four-stroke conversion affected its trail bikes as well.

ABOVE: GT125

ABOVE: The GSX400 was Suzuki's second-generation four-stroke twin

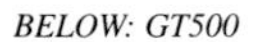

BELOW: GT500

BELOW RIGHT: GT550

The SP370 of 1978 led the change, perhaps in part inspired by Yamaha's XT500, and had 25bhp at 7,500rpm. It was soon enlarged into the SP400, but far bigger trail bikes were to come, starting with the DR600 in 1984. This was far in advance of the SP, with a twin-plug four-valve head, and 44bhp. If that wasn't enough, a DR750 was unveiled three years later, which eventually became the 780cc (48cu in) DR800, and the biggest single on sale, though it failed to deliver its early promise.

What made far more sense was the DR350 of 1991. Now here was a genuine dual-purpose bike, big enough to give useful on-road performance, but light and sufficiently wieldy to be rideable on dirt. Like Yamaha's XT350, the mid-range DR (there was also a 125 and 650) proved for many riders to be the best compromise

GS550 (this one with Dunstall extras) extended the four-cylinder range

GT380 gave smooth two-stroke performance

between power, weight, road and off-road use, which is what trail bikes are all about. By then, Suzuki had already proved it was well able to design sohc four-stroke singles for the road, with the custom-styled GN250/400 and the neat GS125 commuter.

16-Valve Debut

If the GS-series represented Suzuki's four-stroke revolution, then the GSX was the second generation that took it through the 1980s. It began in 1980 with the launch of the GSX1100 and 750. Their main innovation was the four-valve TSCC ('Twin Swirl Combustion Chamber') head, with a square-profiled combustion chamber designed to maximize swirl and thus combustion. The result was 100bhp for the 1100, which seemed impressive at the time. This was backed up by adjustable air damping for the telescopic forks, and lumpy, angular styling with a rectangular headlamp. Not everyone liked the way the new bikes looked, and Suzuki responded with the more radical-looking Katanas in 1981. With low bars and small pointed fairings, they certainly transformed the looks of the GSX, and were available with a number of different four-cylinder engines over the years, from 250 to 1100cc (15 to 67cu in).

The 550 four also got the GSX 16-valve treatment in 1983, with power up to 65bhp, enough for a claimed 201km/h (125mph). It also acquired a new alloy square section frame, a half-fairing, monoshock rear suspension and anti-dive front forks. At the same time, the 750 and 1100 were sold in updated ES form, with 83 and 111bhp respectively. Naturally, four-valve heads made their way into the twins as well as the GSX250 and 400, along with (again) more angular styling, and 177km/h (110mph) was claimed for the 400. The mid-1980s was also the time when a few manufacturers flirted with the idea of turbocharging, to give big bike power in a smaller, lighter package. Suzuki's offering was the XN85 Turbo, based on the existing air-cooled four which, in practice, produced 85bhp at the cost of extra complication, which wasn't enough. But really, the Turbo disclosed the fact that Suzuki's air-cooled four was nearing the end of its development life. The final 123bhp GSX1100E was certainly fast, but times had moved on, and Suzuki had another new generation to satisfy; it was the oil/air-cooled GSXR.

The GSXR Milestone

The 'race replica' as we understand it today (a powerful four-cylinder motor hung from an alloy perimeter frame, with a lean-forward race-style riding position) originated in the mid-1980s, and it is arguable that Suzuki was there first with the GSXR series. Although some might say that Yamaha's FZ750 has much of the same elements, the Suzuki GSXR750 was much more of a true race replica, being very close to the company's works endurance racers of the early eighties. By this time, Suzuki had established an enviable racing record, notably with the square-four RG500, which did so well in Grand Prix racing in the late 1970s/early '80s. Riders like Barry Sheene, Keith Heuwen, Graeme Crosby and Franco Uncini (and later Kevin Schwantz on the V4 RGV500) brought many race wins. In 1983,

Water-cooling was tried on Suzuki's GT750 to compete with the big four-strokes. It was smooth but heavy

Like its rivals, Suzuki's custom bikes took the V-twin route

the company won the World Endurance Championship and the GSXR, unveiled in September 1984, was simply a means of capitalizing on the fact.

What marked it out from all previous Suzukis was the use of oil-cooling. The four-cylinder engine was still partly air-cooled, but oil played the bigger role. It used two oil pumps to double the flow rate, while the underside of each piston crown was cooled by an oil jet, and there was of course a large oil cooler. Thin, tightly-packed cylinder fins further helped heat dissipation, as did a magnesium cam cover. The result of all this was a compact, relatively light engine (Suzuki said water-cooling would have added 5kg/11lb) that produced 100bhp at 10,500rpm. Coupled with a remarkably low all-up weight (175.5kg/387lb) – partly due to the new frame, which weighed half as much as the old steel one – this gave the new bike stunning performance.

Not that it was perfect. In fact, the early GSXR750 suffered from a peaky power delivery that offered little urge below 7,000rpm and everything thereafter – torque peaked at 10,000rpm! Nor was the handling all that it should have been, with some riders complaining of a high speed weave despite that state-of-the-art frame and suspension. Still, none of that mattered to the buyers. Here was a bike that offered real excitement, seemed genuinely new and to all intents and purposes looked like a road-going version of the endurance racer. It sold well, and established a new class – the race replica.

A more acceptable form of GSXR was the 1100 of 1987, with the same oil-cooled concept, but with its 1052cc (64cu in) four in a less frenetic state of tune. In practice, with its much broader spread of power, the bigger bike was easier to ride in traffic. And of course it was fast, with its much broader spread of power and 249km/h (155mph) was a genuine top speed. But the 750 did succeed as a clubman's racer, which was part of the original intention. The addition of factory racing parts made it competitive in Superbike and Superstock racing. In fact, so popular was the GSXR concept that 250, 400 and 600cc (15, 24 and 37cu in) versions followed, the smaller bikes being mainly for the restricted Japanese market. However, the 600 did well in the burgeoning European Supersports 600 arena. As with the 750, the Suzuki GSXR soon earned a reputation as wild boy of the 600 bunch – the uncompromising race replica to Honda's more civilized CBR600. All the GSXRs were gradually improved over the years, and by 1998 the 750 had gained fuel injection, water cooling and 135bhp.

Just as Suzuki based the GSXR's appeal on endurance racers, so the RG250 owed something to the two-stroke GP bikes. The company had been campaigning the V-twin two-strokes in 250 and 500 GP racing for some time, so road-going equivalents made some sense. Naturally, the RG250 and 500 were very light and fearsomely fast, the 250

GSX1100, which used four valves per cylinder

ABOVE: *GSX1100G offered shaft-drive, but no fairing*

LEFT: The Bandit 600 was a huge success

ABOVE: Burgman 250 super-scooter

Gamma claiming 177km/h (110mph) from its 45bhp and the 500 225km/h (140mph) from around twice the power. The V-twin RGV250 followed in 1990, with 60bhp and 217km/h (135mph) or so. If you could live with the thirst, the noise and the expense, these bikes offered the closest it was possible to get to a Grand Prix racer on the road.

But among all the race replicas, Suzuki took care to cater for the more sensible end of the market as well. The GSX600F and an equivalent 750 were fairly basic sports tourers, using a development of the air-cooled four and aiming at a budget-priced alternative to bikes like the Honda CBR600. Announced in 1989, they had a substantial revamp in 1998. Also from 1993 there was an upgraded, more powerful RF600F, still in the sports tourer mode but with a higher specification (a similar 900cc/55cu inch version ran alongside it, and both are still on sale). A new top-of-the-range tourer was announced in 1988, the GSX1100F. Notable for its electrically adjustable screen, the 1100 also represented the first use of Suzuki's oil-cooled four outside the GSXR sportsters. A slight capacity increase to 1127cc (69cu in) and much detuning saw 120bhp and a claimed 241km/h (150mph), but unfortunately the handling suffered from 16-inch wheels, and this GSX failed to have the impact of rivals such as Kawasaki's ZZR1100. There was also an unfaired GSX1100G, in the old 1000G tradition. Also, and of limited impact, was the VX800, using Suzuki's 800cc (49cu in) air-cooled V-twin from the cruiser range (750 and 1400cc/46 and 85cu inch versions of which were sold in the late 1980s) which added shaft-drive and conservative styling with a long wheelbase. Some traditionalists quite liked it.

An All-Round Winner

But if its tourers didn't always hit the mark, Suzuki did better in other areas. By the early 1990s, the 600cc class had become dominated by the super sportsters – bikes like the GSXR, in fact. But exciting as these machines were, they were hard work and uncomfortable to ride in traffic and difficult for those starting (or returning to) motorcycling late in life, of which there were increasing numbers. What was needed was a simpler, more accessible all-rounder, and Suzuki hit the nail on the head with the Bandit 600 in 1995. The Bandit used a detuned version of the GSXR600's oil-cooled engine, housed in a steel tubular frame. The rider sat upright on a naked, almost traditional-looking bike with no hint of race pretensions. It was easy to ride and with 80-odd bhp, was still fast enough for many riders. It went straight to the top of the sales charts. Part of the Bandit's success was that it actually looked very good, particularly in non-faired form, as the close-finned oil-cooled engine made an attractive lump. The Bandit was soon joined by a part-faired version, and the 1157cc (71cu in) Bandit 1200 was again in naked and part-faired guise. Such was the

The RF-series (both 600 and 900) was Suzuki's stab at the sports-touring market

Pat Hennan racing a 1978 Suzuki 500 at the Isle of Man TT

Bandit's success that it encouraged Honda (with the Hornet) and Yamaha (the Fazer) to produce their own equivalents.

But Suzuki's heart evidently lay in sportsbikes, as illustrated by the TL1000 V-twin sportster of late 1997. It was really an attempt to beat Ducati at its own game. The Italian marque had been riding the crest of a wave through the 1990s, thanks to racing success and new owners, and here was a chance for the Japanese to produce a cheaper, more user-friendly sports V-twin. The twin-cam, fuel-injected eight-valve V-twin produced 125bhp, weighed 187kg (412lb) and promised to be a Ducati with convenience. It was certainly exciting to ride, but perhaps too much so, and Honda's version – the VTR1000 Firestorm – was certainly less demanding. A slightly more powerful, but very different under the skin TL1000R followed in 1998, intended to form the basis of Suzuki's new V-twin Superbike contender. Introduced that year was also something very different, the 250cc (15.3cu in) Burgman superscooter. In the same mould as the Yamaha Majesty, it offered better handling and slightly more performance, while its bigger all-round build pointed towards the 400cc (24.4cu in) version, which was launched the following year. The Burgman 400 is currently the biggest scooter on sale, and with a claimed 100mph top speed offers true motorcycle performance.

The Burgman might claim to be the fastest scooter of all, but another new Suzuki did the same for motorcycles in 1999. It certainly had more power than anything else, and talk of it dominated the motorcycle press for months, the Hayabusa GSXR1300R hinting at a top speed of

ABOVE: GSX1300R Hayabusa – 200mph?

BELOW: V650S V-twin

Suzuki's TL1000S V-twin got off to a shaky start, but was soon supplemented by the 1000R

ABOVE: *GSXR750 – the first of the real race replicas*

BELOW: *A 1991 Suzuki RGV250*

322km/h (200mph). The figures alone said all that was necessary: 173bhp, 102lb ft, 0–60mph in 2.75 seconds, to 225km/h (140mph) in 10 seconds. Would it reach the 200mph mark? That seemed to be the question on everyone's lips in the spring of 1999, and at the time of writing no one has managed to find out either way. Still, the Hayabusa (a Japanese falcon that allegedly reaches that speed when diving) showed not only that the horsepower race was not yet over, but that Suzuki was also out there in front.

But just as everyone was getting over the Hayabusa, Suzuki launched a bike that was undeniably less spectacular, but probably more relevant to more riders. By the late 1990s, the Bandit 600 was increasingly coming under fire from younger competition, and Suzuki's answer was an all-new all-rounder, the SV650. It was a V-twin, slim and lightweight, that came in naked guise and with a more sporting half-fairing and lower bars. The first promised to be a lighter, handier Bandit, with added V-twin character; the second a mini-TL1000.

SUZY *France 1932–33*
A fully-enclosed 498cc (30cu in) ohc Chaise single, unit-constructed.

SWAN *England 1911–13*
Similar to the Neracar, it used a 499cc Precision single and had leaf-sprung rear suspension.

SYMPLEX *England 1913–22*
Used 311cc (19cu in) Dalm two-strokes.

SYPHAX *France 1952–53*
Produced 98–174cc (6-11cu in) two- and four-strokes with AMC or Aubier-Dunne engines.

T

TANDON *England 1948–57*
Used a large range of Villiers engines up to the 322cc (20cu in) twin.

TAPELLA-FUCHS *Italy 1953–57*
Fuchs-powered mopeds.

TAS *Germany 1924–31*
Produced 173cc (11cu in) two-strokes to 498cc (30cu in) four-strokes, with a variety of bought-in engines.

TAURA *Italy 1927–30*
Used JAP and Blackburne power units.

TAURUS *Italy 1933–66*
Made various singles of 173cc–496cc (11–30cu in) before the war, including a dohc racer, with more utilitarian two-strokes and ohv singles after 1945.

TAUTZ *Germany 1921–23*
A DKW-powered 118cc (7.2cu in) scooter.

TAVERNIER *France 1921–23*
Utilized a range of bought-in engines from Zurcher, JAP, and Blackburne.

TECO *Germany 1920–26*
Used Alba and Kühne engines to 346cc (21cu in).

TEDDY *France 1922–24*
203cc (12.4cu in) lightweights.

TEE-BEE *England 1908–11*
Used own and JAP's 293cc (18cu in) sv.

TEHUELCHE *Argentina 1958–62*
A 75cc (4.6cu in) ohv, many parts being imported from Italy.

TEMPLE *England 1924–28*
Part of the OEC range.

TEMPO *Norway 1949–*
Bought-in two-strokes of up to 123cc (7.5cu in). Now distributes mopeds.

TERRA *Germany 1922–24*
Own two-stroke of 127–172cc (8–10.5cu in).

TERROT *France 1901–61*
France's leading manufacturer for some time, it used various bought-in four-strokes in the early years, plus its own 175–250cc (11–15cu in) two-strokes after World War I. Then came its own four-strokes from 1927, including a 750cc (46cu in) V-twin from 1930. After 1945 it continued its pre-war 498cc (30cu in) single, but most production lay in two-stroke lightweights up to 175cc, including a scooter. It had increasingly strong links with Automoto (part of Peugeot) in the late 1950s until Peugeot took over altogether in 1961.

TERROT *Czechoslovakia 1933–35*
Subsidiary of the French Terrot, with a 346cc (21cu in) sv.

TESTI *Italy 1951–83*
Used bought-in 49cc (3cu in) two-strokes on mopeds and small sportsters. Also exported with Horex or Gitane badges and had limited production alongside OMC from 1987.

TETGE *Germany 1923–26*
Produced 148/172cc (9/10.5cu in) singles, and a MAG-powered V-twin.

THIEM *U.S.A. 1903–14*
Typically offered American 550cc (34cu in) ioe singles and 890 or 996cc (54 or 61cu in) V-twins.

THOMANN *France 1912–39*
Made two-strokes from 98–248cc (6–15cu in).

THOMAS *U.S.A. 1900–08*
A 3hp 'sloper' single.

THOMAS *England 1904*
Used Minerva and Sarolea units.

THOR *U.S.A. 1903–16*
Produced its own 6 and 9hp machines, but mainly sold its ioe V-twins to other manufacturers.

THOROUGH *England 1903*
Used MMC and Coronet engines.

THREE-SPIRES *England 1931–32*
A 147cc (9cu in) two-stroke for 18 guineas – cheap at the price, no doubt.

THUMANN *Germany 1925–26*
Built own 246/346cc (15/21cu in) sv singles.

THUNDER *Italy 1952–54*
An advanced but expensive 127cc (8cu in)

Thor made its own engines and sold most of them to other manufacturers

twin with unit-construction, swinging-arm rear suspension and four-speed gearbox.

TIGER *U.S.A. 1915–16*
Used a 241cc (15cu in) two-stroke.

TIKA *Germany 1921–24*
Used a bought-in 145/195cc (9/12cu in) Herko sv.

TILBROOK *Australia 1950–53*
Made Villiers-engined lightweights to 198cc (12cu in).

TILSTON *England 1919*
A short-lived 225cc (14cu in) Precision-engined two-stroke.

TITAN *Austria 1927–33*
Produced both two- and four-strokes, notably a 144cc (9cu in) twin.

TIZ-AM *Russia 1913–40*
596cc (36cu in) sv singles.

TM *Italy 1968–92*
Made lightweights to 123cc (7.5cu in), first with Franco-Morini and Zündapp engines, later with its own.

TOHATSU *Japan 1935–66*
48–248cc (3–15cu in) disc-valved two-strokes.

TOMASELLI *Italy 1931–39*
173–490cc (11–30cu in) JAP-engined singles.

TOMMASI *Italy 1926–27*
Used Della Ferrera two-strokes, the 246cc (15cu in) version being two singles coupled together.

TOMOS *Slovenia 1954–*
Began with licence-built Puchs and later developed its own mopeds, plus a few larger bikes of up to 175cc (11cu in).

TOREADOR *England 1924–26*
Used bought-in engines from Bradshaw, JAP and MAG.

TORNAX *Germany 1926–55*
Pre-war, utilized a range of bought-in four-strokes up to a 996cc (30cu in) JAP, plus the Columbus 598/698cc (36/43cu in) ohc vertical twin. After 1945, produced mostly Ilo-engined two-strokes.

TORPADO *Italy 1950–62*
38–74cc (2.3–4.5cu in) Mosquito and Minarelli-engined two-strokes.

TORPEDO *Germany 1901–07*
Used Zedel and Fafnir engines.

TORPEDO *Czechoslovakia 1903–12*
Nearly everything was built in-house for this range of singles and V-twins up to 8hp.

TORPEDO *England 1910–20*
Precision singles and V-twins up to 499cc (30cu in).

TORPEDO *Germany 1928–56*
Used bought-in Blackburne, Sachs and Ilo power units.

TORROT *Spain 1960–85*
Began as a Terrot subsidiary and went on to build its own mopeds and lightweights.

TOWNEND *England 1901–04*
2/2.5hp engines.

TOYOMOTOR *Japan 1949–59*
Initially produced a motorized bicycle which was actually Japan's third best-seller by 1952. Later, an Adler-inspired two-stroke twin failed to save it.

TRAFALGAR *England 1902–05*
Used MMC and Minerva engines.

TRAFFORD *England 1919–22*
Used 269cc (16cu in) Villiers engines.

TRAIN *France 1913–39*
Built a complete range of engines, from a 173cc (11cu in) two-stroke to a 996cc (30cu in) V-twin, and supplied countless small assemblers (mostly in France and Italy) with ready-made power units. Also built an ohc in-line four in 1930, and was an early user of unit-construction.

TREBLOC *England 1922–25*
Built its own 63cc/3.8cu inch-engined lightweight.

TREMO *Germany 1925–28*
Own 308cc (19cu in) single with sv or ohv.

TRENT *England 1902–c.1906*
A 207cc (13cu in) engine in a strengthened cycle frame.

TRESPEDI *Italy 1926–30*
Own 173/246cc (11/15cu in) three-port two-strokes.

TRIANON *Germany 1922–26*
Own 232cc (14cu in) two-stroke.

TRIBUNE *U.S.A. 1903–c.1914*
Little is known, but Aster and Thor engines were possibly used.

TRIPLE-H *England 1921–23*
246cc (15cu in) two-strokes.

TRIPLETTE *England 1923–25*
A 147cc (9cu in) Villiers-powered utility.

TRIPOL *Czechoslovakia 1925–26*
Utilized a 246cc (15cu in) Villiers engine.

TRIUMPH *England 1903–*
It is odd that Triumph, who produced that most British of bikes, should have actually been established by two Germans, Mauritz Schulte and Siegfried Bettmann who, emigrating to England from their home town of Nuremberg, ended up in Coventry. Bettmann teamed up with Schulte in 1897 to make bicycles, and it was only five years before the fledgling Triumph produced its first motorized cycle. Whether their original intention was to set up as motorcycle manufacturers, history does not record, but they couldn't have chosen a better location in which to do so. With its long history of light engineering and central position in Britain's industrial West Midlands, Coventry offered several generations of craftsmen with the right skills and know-how useful to the nascent motorcycle industry.

Schulte and Bettmann's first effort resembled a bicycle rather than a motorbike, but this was no different from countless others. There was good reason for this: it was no more nor less than an adapted bicycle frame with an engine bolted on, though strengthened with a vertical brace on the front forks. Like many rivals, the Triumph founders chose to buy in an engine, in this case a Belgian-made Minerva of 239cc (14.6cu in) and 2.25bhp.

Early manufacturers tried various positions for these little bolt-on power units, but Triumph's was close to the standard motorcycle position, fixed to the frame's downtube. A slim tank inside the frame held fuel, oil and a battery. Transmission was by direct belt-drive, so to start it was necessary to pedal up to speed until the engine fired. Once running, the Minerva-engined Triumph would top about 40km/h (25mph).

Other proprietory engines followed, notably from JAP and Fafnir, before Schulte produced Triumph's first in-house design. It was an unremarkable sidevalve single of 3.5hp which was however to power Triumphs for some time. It started out at 499cc (30cu in), though a longer-stroke 547cc (33cu in) version later became available. Success in the TT (Jack Marshall won the 1908 single-cylinder class) underlined Triumph's arrival as one of the major manufacturers, as did World War I, when despatch riders learned to love their 'Trusty Triumphs'.

Other models followed, notably the two-stroke 225cc (13.7cu in) Baby, and the company demonstrated that it wasn't averse to innovation when a 496cc vertical twin was produced in prototype form as early as 1913 (20 years before Val Page's first production twin) and the early twenties saw a 346cc (21cu in) single with unit-construction. Perhaps most famous was the 'Riccy', the four-valve 499cc single designed by Harry Ricardo, a classic sports machine of its time which lasted until 1926 and was succeeded by a simpler two-valve 500.

It is often forgotten that there were close links between the British and German Triumph factories in those days. Coventry supplied many components, including engines, to Nuremburg until 1929 when the two finally went their separate ways.

Triumph motorcycles very nearly died a death in the 1930s. The parent company was more interested in four wheels than two, and had already sold off the bicycle side of the business to Raleigh. It was a golden opportunity to pick up a well established company for a song, and here two men were to become crucial to Triumph's existence. Jack Sangster was an astute businessman who had bought the bike side of Ariel from the receiver a few years earlier. His forward design engineer was someone who would be central to the Triumph story for the next 30 years – Edward Turner.

Much has been written of Turner, not all of it complimentary. He was the classic flawed genius, at times brilliant and far-sighted, at other times difficult, irascible and impatient. Although he had designed several significant bikes, notably the Triumph Speed Twin and the Ariel Square Four, he was more of an ideas man than an engineer. He was lacking in formal engineering training and Bert Hopwood (his protégé and a qualified engineer) suspected him of often preferring gut feeling to science, liable to dismiss anyone using a slide rule as an 'academic'. It became the norm at Triumph, Hopwood was later to report, to have two sets of drawings for every part – Turner's, and a set which had been painstakingly corrected and were the ones which were used in actual production. Turner, of course, knew nothing of this, which was probably just as well. On the other hand, he had tremendous energy and enthusiasm and a well developed aesthetic sense, together with a genuine feel for what the riding public really wanted.

ABOVE and OPPOSITE: An early belt-drive Triumph, the kind used by despatch riders in World War I

127
139
OA 7823

'Trusty Triumphs' were (and are) simple and easy to ride

ABOVE and BELOW: In order to help sales, Edward Turner spruced up Triumph's singles

In short, he was the right man arriving at the right time to revive the ailing Triumph concern and at the age of 35 was placed in charge of the new Triumph Engineering Company. His first job was to revamp Triumph's well-engineered but lacklustre range. The singles were given the Turner treatment, with a little more power, a curvaceous silver-and-chrome tank, and high-level exhausts. There were new names, too: the 250, 350 and 500 singles were now the Tiger 70, 80 and 90 respectively, the numbers suggesting their top speeds which was decidedly optimistic. But that didn't matter, as they fitted in with Triumph's new sporting image, which Turner was particularly adept at encouraging. Not surprisingly, Val Page's solid but slow 6/1 was dropped and even the Triumph logo was given the Turner touch. Aided by a general recovery in the motorcycle market, Triumph sales grew apace.

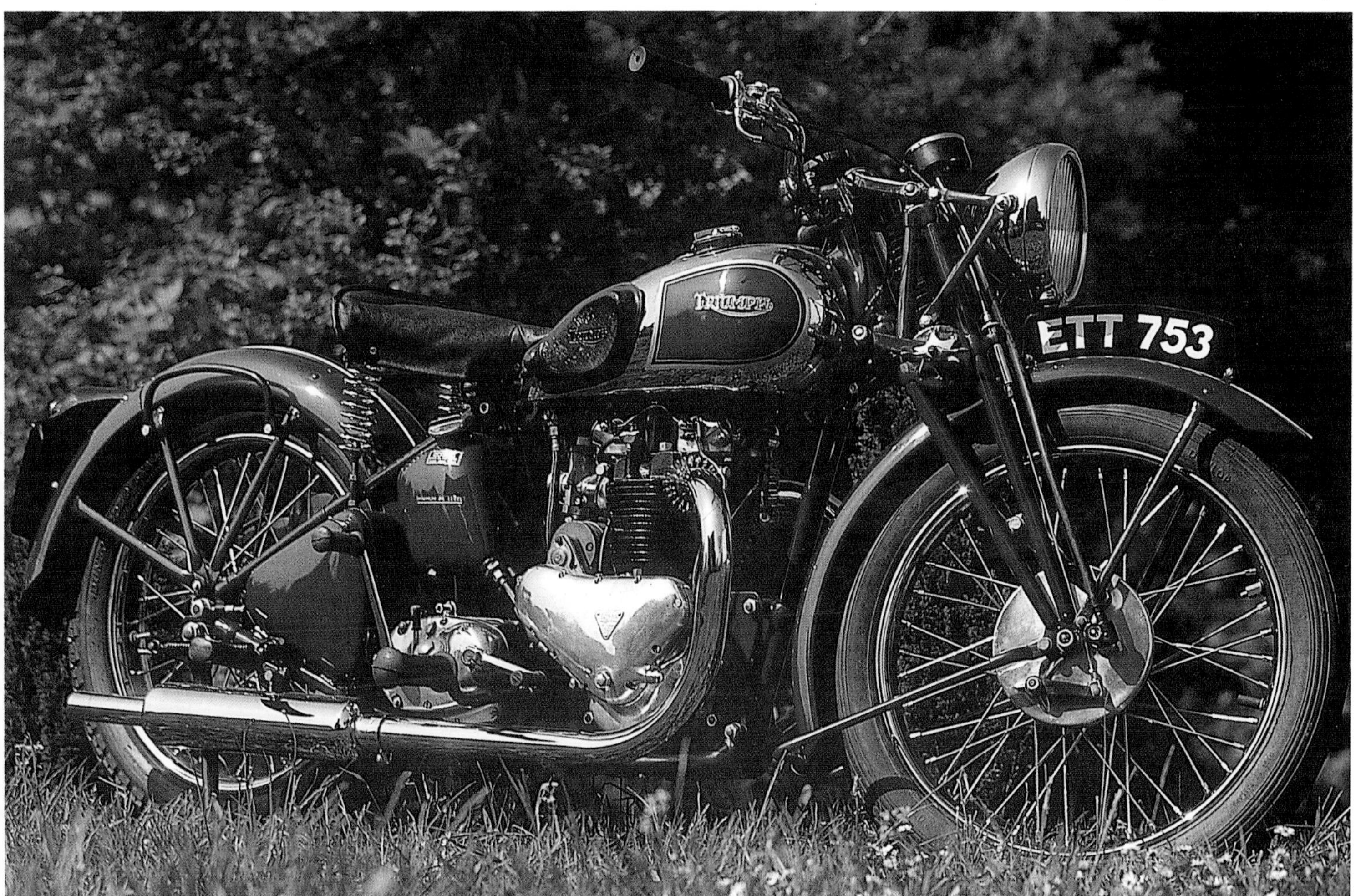

Triumph's milestone machine, the 1937 Speed Twin, transformed the company's fortunes and every major rival followed suit

The Twin

All this, however, was more of a holding operation before Turner's Big Idea for Triumph was ready, the Speed Twin, which was unveiled in July 1937. There had been twins before, but nothing like this; most were big, lumbering sidecar tugs with zero sporting potential. The Speed Twin weighed only 2.3kg (5lb) more than Triumph's existing Tiger 90 single; it was revvy and quick off the mark in a way that no other sporting single had been and, in its

The 1971 Bandit was meant to be a new-generation twin. It never made it

TR5 in ISDT trim

The late-model Sports Cub introduced many to motorcycling

LEFT: A 1965 Bonneville and one from 1971 (RIGHT)

original mild tune (a small carburettor and 7.2:1 compression), relatively smooth as well. Despite the mild tune, it produced 29bhp at 6,000rpm, enough for a top speed of 137–145km/h (85–90mph).

Even the conservative buying public liked it, attracted by the price (only £5 more than the Tiger 90) and, paradoxically, the fact that it looked very much like a single. Whether intentional or not, Turner's characteristically compact design resulted in an engine that was no wider than a contemporary single, and from certain angles even looked like one. Part of this was necessity: in order to get the Speed Twin into production as quickly and as cheaply as possible, it used the Tiger 90 chassis and 63mm x 80mm bore and stroke from the Tiger 70 single. The initial idea for an overhead-cam twin was rejected on cost grounds, but the basic layout of the Triumph twin was born. It was a 360-degree vertical twin with big central flywheel, two high, gear-driven camshafts, plunger oil pump and cast-iron barrel. So although Turner's twin was a new concept, there was much about it that was very familiar to a whole generation of riders, which lessened its revolutionary impact and paved the way for its acceptance. What also helped were the clean, symmetrical looks with the classy Aramanth Red finish, plus chrome highlights. Knowingly or not, Edward Turner had established a 'Triumph look' that was to stand the company in good stead for the next 30 years.

It was an instant success, and the company followed it in 1938 with the more sporting Tiger 100, which really did have 100mph potential. Unfortunately, its 33bhp also proved too much for the basic engine, and snapped con-rods and broken cranks were not uncommon until the company got to grips with the problems.

War interrupted Triumph's new-found success, though it is instructive to know that BSA was aiming to introduce a rival 500cc (30.5cu in) twin in 1940, which showed just how far Triumph had leapt ahead of its rivals. For the moment, though, the Speed Twin had to give way to a 350cc (21cu in) version, the 3TW, which needed some adaptation for army use, plus the 3SW and 3HW 350 singles (sidevalve

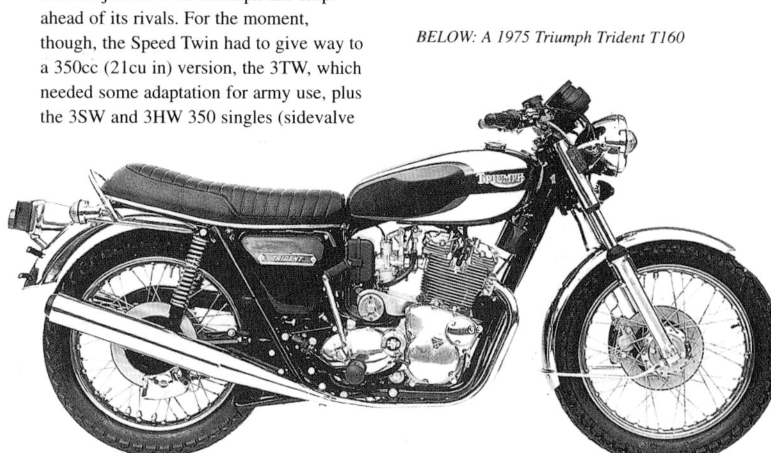

BELOW: A 1975 Triumph Trident T160

The 1952 Triumph Thunderbird 650 was produced in response to demand from the American market

ABOVE: Neat and clean, the TZ1350 introduced unit-construction

and ohv, respectively). But Bettmann and Schulte's factory in Priory Street was destroyed in the Coventry blitz in November 1940. As a temporary measure, the works were moved to some unused buildings in Warwick (an ex-Methodist chapel held the design team) before an all-new factory was built at Meriden, a village just a few miles south-west of Coventry. Meriden became synonymous with Triumph, and the company benefited from this green-field site and very quickly had production up and running again. But as Triumph grew after the war, the Meriden factory had to be expanded again and again. Although Triumph is often seen as the archetype of all that was wrong with the old-school British motorcycle industry, it musn't be forgotten that in the two decades after the war it was a tremendous success story, producing thousands of bikes a year, and profitably too. Much of the success was down to simplicity of production, with Turner determined to streamline Triumph's production to twins only, and promote the popularity of the Meriden bikes in North America. By the late sixties, over 90 per cent of production was exported.

In fact, it was demand from the U.S.A. that encouraged Triumph's first big model launch after the war. It was a market demanding more performance, and Triumph responded with the 649cc (40cu in) Thunderbird in 1949. Again, it stole a march on the opposition, which had only recently come up with its own 500 twins. The 650 produced little more power than the Tiger 100 (34bhp) but it was in a more relaxed way, and was not lacking in stamina. In a superb piece of public relations, three Thunderbirds were raced around the Montlhéry race track in northern France for 500 miles at an average 148km/h (92mph) with a final flying lap of 100. (No one, of course, mentioned the 'practice' run shortly before, where a crankcase was holed.)

The Thunderbirds continued the same Triumph look established by the Speed Twin, with the addition of the headlamp nacelle, which greatly tidied up the handlebar area. It spread to the rest of the range, and lasted right through the fifties. The nacelle was really a forerunner of the brief vogue for bodywork in the 1950s; perhaps it was the scooter influence that encouraged Triumph to half-enclose the rear wheel in what became known as the 'Bathtub'(because it looked like one). The aim was to make motorcycling a cleaner and more civilized activity, which was laudable enough, but an increasingly sports-obsessed market derided this excess metal which often found itself relegated to the back of the garage.

A more enduring model was the TR5 Trophy, a dual-purpose on/off-road bike that used an all-alloy version of the twin. This alloy engine had an interesting history, with its origins in war surplus generator units which allowed post-war racers a better-cooled Triumph twin. Meriden's experimental department got to work on one (unofficially, as Edward Turner saw most racing as a waste of money) and with twin carburettors, power was up to 47bhp at 7,000rpm. Ernie Lyons

BELOW: The 1981 Thunderbird revived the old name for a year or two

To cut costs, the 1967 Tiger Cub now shared parts with the BSA Bantam

won the 1946 Manx Grand Prix on one (despite breaking the bike's downtubes on the fifth lap). In the face of such success, Turner relented, and GP replicas were offered. The TR5 was a successful competitor in the ISDT but, being sold with lights, was a genuine dual-purpose bike.

Meanwhile, despite Edward Turner's post-war determination to build only twins, he could not ignore the rapidly growing market for lightweight bikes and scooters. Triumph's answer came in 1953 with the 149cc (9cu in) Terrier. Billed as a 'Real Triumph in Miniature', it certainly looked that way, with its headlamp nacelle and familiar tank badge. The ohv single itself was of unit-construction with a four-speed gearbox and, although it suffered from teething troubles (which went on longer than such troubles should), it developed into a highly popular bike for learners. The Terrier was joined by the 199cc (12cu in) Tiger Cub in 1954 and over 100,000 were made before it was finally dropped in the late sixties, by which time it had been far outclassed by the faster, stronger Japanese opposition. But the Tiger Cub was only part of Triumph's answer to the imports. By now taken over by BSA (though a smaller company than the BSA conglomerate, Triumph sold more bikes), it unveiled the Triumph Tigress scooters (also sold as the BSA Sunbeam). Designed by Turner, these were offered in a choice of a 175cc (11cu in) BSA Bantam-powered version, or a 250cc (15cu in) four-stroke twin. The 250, in particular, was fast but lacked a Vespa's convenience and style. In any case, the scooter boom had passed its peak when the Tigress appeared in 1959, and sales were disappointing.

The Bonneville

Triumph had happier experiences with bigger bikes. American dealers were complaining that even the Thunderbird now wasn't fast enough, and in 1954 the T110 gave them their answer. As well as bigger valves and higher compression, it had a swinging-arm rear suspension, alternator electrics and improved braking. It could also manage 183km/h (114mph), according to contemporary road tests, and Johnny Allen took a tuned T110 in a cigar-shaped shell to 214mph on Bonneville salt flats, Utah. It was a new world speed record for motorcycles.

Allen's record was to lend its name to perhaps the most famous Triumph of all – the Bonneville. This was really no more nor less than a tuned, twin-carburettor T110 but somehow, as the fastest machine of its type (and from the early 1960s, with good handling as well), it captured the public's imagination. Although unable to achieve the 120mph its T120 name implied, it was still faster than most things on the road as well as being reasonably tractable and easy to ride through town. The Bonnie was the Honda FireBlade of its day and as the decade progressed it was modernized in some ways, acquiring unit-construction in 1963 and 12-volt electrics shortly afterwards. But as the horsepower race continued, so did the pressure to increase power year on year, from what was now an elderly basic design. Certainly

The T160 Trident offered electric start and a five-speed gearbox, but still didn't manage to save the company

Meriden managed to squeeze out a little more power each year, but the price to be paid soon became evident in increased vibration and reduced tractability. In a futile attempt to keep ahead of the growing Japanese opposition, the Bonneville was becoming overtuned. On the other hand, many believed the very last 'real' Bonnevilles of 1969/70 represented the peak of the bike's career, with a heavier flywheel to partially quell the vibration and various measures taken to combat oil leaks. Still, others thought that the single-carburettor TR6 650 was a much nicer machine, being nearly as fast without being overstressed. It was the TR6 that became a police force favourite as the Triumph Saint, which allegedly stood for **S**top **A**nything **I**n **N**o **T**ime!

With all this emphasis on the big twins, it might be thought that Triumph was forgetting its roots, but in 1957 a small twin arrived with very different priorities. The 3TA was an up-to-date (at the time) 350cc (21cu in) unit-construction machine, aimed as much at America as the U.K. where 250s were thought too small, even for learners. In layout, it followed the familiar Turner vertical-twin pattern, with two high-mounted camshafts and hemispherical combustion chambers, the real change being to unit-construction of the gearbox with the engine, which made for a more rigid structure. Incidentally, the 3TA was also known as the '21', both because 350cc equalled 21 cubic inches (more familiar to Americans) and the year 1957 marked the 21st anniversary of the Triumph Engineering Company. The 3TA was relatively light so that its 18.5bhp was enough for 129km/h (80mph), easy to ride and very economical. In short, the 3TA was also a return to the less stressed Speed Twin days. Its safe-and-sensible ethos was marked by the peak of Edward Turner's enclosure period, with optional leg guards and screen to make a practical, all-year-round motorcycle. Of course, as noted above, that wasn't what the growing youth market required, a fact which Triumph's smaller twins were soon to reflect.

A 500cc (31cu in) version soon followed in 1959, using the same 65.5mm stroke as the 350, which meant it actually had oversquare (69mm x 65.5mm) dimensions. No doubt Bert Hopwood (by then in a senior position at Meriden) had a hand in this, as he had long been keen on a modular range where different bikes shared the same components, thus saving costs and simplifying spares supply. Still, the new 500 showed no signs of being compromised; it was a likeable, free-revving bike, with significantly more power than the 3TA but little more weight. The 5TA Speed Twin produced 27bhp at 6,500rpm and, like the 350, had the rear panelling as standard. Inevitably, sports versions soon followed. First was the T100A Tiger in 1960 which used a 9:1 compression and different camshafts for 32bhp at 7,000rpm. It also had Energy Transfer ignition, which allowed a quick conversion to running without battery or lights. This was for competition, where the smaller Triumph twins were building up a good record in trials and the ISDT, while the 650s were out track racing.

Bonnie's final years: the 1981 T140 (ABOVE) and (BELOW) the 1977 Silver Jubilee

'A whole range of 350s and 500s was to follow through the sixties, underlining the fact that Triumph twins outsold their rival BSAs by five to one. This created tensions in the BSA-Triumph amalgamation in that Triumph was ostensibly the junior partner while being more successful in the motorcycle market. (BSA, of course, was a huge company with many more strings to its bow than motorcycles, but tension existed just the same.) So 1962 saw another sports 500, the T100SS which used 650 influence to produce 34bhp at 7,000rpm, while the following year there was a sporting 350 (marking the return of the Tiger 90 name) with 27bhp at 7,500rpm. The ultimate small twin (in terms of power) was the Daytona of 1967 which used twin carburettors, bigger valves and a high compression of 9.75:1 (these were the days of high-octane five-star petrol). The Daytona could manage 182km/h (113mph) from its 39bhp at 7,400rpm, though like the Bonneville was showing signs of being overtuned. Also like the Bonnie, it was named after an American sporting achievement. A works 500 won the Daytona Production Race in 1967 when Doug Hele's attention had boosted the bike's power to 50bhp at 8,800rpm. Meanwhile, Bonnevilles were doing well in production racing at home with victories in the Production TT in 1967 and '69, while Bonnies filled five of the first seven places in the 1969 Thruxton 500 and also won the Barcelona 24-hour race that year.

The Triple

However fast the racing Bonnevilles were, a new breed of bike was about to overtake them. Bert Hopwood and Doug Hele had worked together on a 750cc (46cu in) triple as early as 1963, and even had a running prototype on the road the following year. But Triumph's board failed to share their enthusiasm, and it only got the go-ahead once they learned of Honda's imminent four-cylinder CB750. Even then, it was another two years before the new Trident (also sold in virtually identical BSA Rocket Three form) actually went on sale. Much of this was down to the infamous Umberslade Hall, BSA/Triumph's massive design centre that consumed much but produced little. Umberslade (nicknamed Slumberglade) restyled the Trident, but in a way that actually lost them buyers, so it didn't reach the market until September 1968, the same year as Honda's CB750. It was tragic that a bike that could have gone on sale at least two years earlier was inevitably compared to the CB750, which offered electric start, overhead camshaft and front disc brake, yet at no greater cost.

Still, the Trident certainly made an impact. It was one of the new breed of superbikes, and testers wrote breathlessly of 80mph in second, 110 in third and having to hang on desperately as this 'big, fast groundshaker of a machine' (*Cycle World*) leapt forward. Compared to the twins that everyone was familiar with, the Trident came over as incredibly fast, very smooth and revvy, if a little heavy as well (which it was, at 212kg/468lb). Fifty-eight bhp doesn't sound much now, but in 1969 it made the Trident one of the fastest bikes one could buy. It made a successful racer too, albeit in modified form, coming just in time to take over from the Bonneville; in 1971, Tridents won the Bol d'Or, both Production and F750TTs and scored a 1-2-3 at Daytona. It was a brief blaze of glory,

The Tiger Cub's characteristic low weight and four-stroke power made it a popular basis for a trials bike

Triumph would do anything for publicity. Here are 807 Squadron R.N.A.S. and a fleet of Triumph Tigress scooters

though impressive nonetheless, and of course one particular Trident (nicknamed 'Slippery Sam' after a mid-race oil leak) won the Production TT five times. It was quite an achievement for a bike that owed much to the elderly twins and was originally intended as a stopgap.

There were a few changes in its six-year life. The Umberslade slab-side styling was soon dropped (for the U.S. market) in favour of a more traditional look, while 1973 saw a front disc brake and five-speed gearbox. There was also the X-75 Hurricane, with transformed styling by American Craig Vetter. Finally, the T160 of 1974 was NVT's last gasp with the Trident. It actually included over 200 changes from the old bike, including an electric start, and longer, lower styling and some think it was the best-looking Trident of all. Sadly, a price of £1,215 was too much to ask (£200 more than the CB750), and the Trident's brief, but glorious career was soon over.

Meanwhile, twins were still the mainstay of Meriden's production, and it was the final 750cc version which was to keep the factory going right up to the end in 1983. The 650s had been substantially updated in 1971, shoehorned into the new oil-in-frame cycle parts, which themselves were a less than total success, another of the problems being 34-inch seat height! It was also planned to launch an all-new dohc 350cc twin at the same time – the Triumph Bandit. This actually got quite close to production, and several prototypes were built and tested, but the BSA/Triumph group's parlous financial state put paid to it.

Much of the company's problems stemmed from over-dependence on the huge American market with its short selling season. U.S. dealers had pressurized Triumph to produce the 650cc (40cu in) twin, then the Bonneville. Now they insisted on a 750cc version of the twin. There was some resistance at Meriden, where they knew that yet another capacity increase was too much to ask of the venerable vertical twin. But in the end they relented, and the Bonneville 750 was launched in late 1972. In practice, it was no faster than the 650 (prototypes had to be detuned when it was found that crankshafts were breaking on a regular basis), but the vibration (as the Meriden men could have told them) was worse. It has to be said that the 750's *raison d'être* was more a marketing exercise than any real advantage, though it did bring a five-speed gearbox and front disc brake as well. The company's fortunes continued down the slippery slope, with many redundancies at the BSA end, and although Lord Shawcross (brought in as a caretaker chairman) had managed to reduce the deficit, he was forced to approach the Government for financial aid. Finance was agreed with the proviso of a merger with Norton to form Norton Villiers Triumph (NVT). After some wrangling, this went ahead, but it soon became clear that Norton, under Dennis Poore, was to be the senior partner; one of Poore's first actions was to announce the closure of Meriden. However, Triumph's factory was probably the most cohesive of all the British plants, and the workforce promptly staged a sit-in, which was to last 18 months. It wasn't until early 1975 that a settlement was finally reached whereby Meriden was able to go it alone as a workers' co-operative, and probably the most famed in Britain!

At first, the 750cc twin was its sole product, in single carburettor Tiger twin-carb Bonneville form (in practice the Tiger was almost as fast, and probably pleasanter to ride as well), but a number of variants on the same theme were to follow over the years. The Meriden co-op's real problem was that it was always short of cash, there never being enough to develop the all-new machine it needed, so the Bonneville had to struggle on. For all that, it sold in respectable numbers in the late 1970s. Although out of the performance game, it was still well liked in both Britain and the United States, and was actually the best-selling 750 in Britain for a while. There were all sorts of special editions to keep interest alive, as well as some more fundamental changes. An electric start arrived in 1980, and there was the Tiger Trail dual-purpose version. More ambitious was the eight-valve TSS of 1982 and the 'AV' (Anti-Vibration) frame. Alas, teething troubles and Meriden's endemic problems put paid to both of them. A happier swan-song was the TR65 Thunderbird, a short-stroke, cut-price 650 which was smooth

BELOW: Tigress missed the scooter boom

ABOVE: An odd, articulated Tina-based one-off

T150 was a stunning performer, but should have been launched several years earlier

ABOVE: The Trident's three-cylinder engine owed much to Triumph twins

ABOVE: The Craig Vetter-styled Hurricane showed just how important the U.S.A. was to Triumph

and free-revving compared to the 750. And there were plans for the future when, at the 1983 Motorcycle Show in Birmingham, Triumph exhibited a new 600cc (37cu in) version of the twin, plus the prototype T2000 Phoenix. The latter was a 900cc (55cu in) liquid-cooled twin which Triumph hoped would take it to the end of the century. Sadly, none of this was to happen and the co-operative, which had struggled on for nearly ten years, finally went into liquidation in August 1983.

There is, however, a postscript. Millionaire John Bloor, who had made his fortune from house building, bought the Triumph name and sold a five-year rights deal to former spares maker Les Harris. The Harris Bonnevilles, as they became known, went into production in a south Devon factory, and were built until 1988. So this was not the end of the Triumph story. In fact, it was the prelude to a new chapter.

Hinckley

In the 1990s, 'Hinckley' was to become as much a byword for Triumph as Meriden had been. In a way that would have seemed unbelievable not so long ago, John Bloor funded the development of a range of all-new, thoroughly modern British motorcycles. He built a factory to make them, launched them on time and to media acclaim, and has gone on selling them ever since.

When Meriden collapsed in 1983, many thought this would be the final end of the British motorcycle industry. The difference between the new Triumph and the earlier attempts to revive the British industry (which had been labelled as such by an over-eager motorcycle press) was proper funding by a sole backer. This time, there would be no shareholders pressing for short-term profits, and no scratching around for money.

So it wasn't until early 1990, after six years of development, that the new range of Triumphs was announced. The press loved them and everyone seemed genuinely surprised (and perhaps a little relieved) that this time a British motorcycle maker had got it right first time. The new range was a whole family of bikes sharing the same steel spine frame chassis and three- or four-cylinder liquid-cooled engines of 750–1200cc (46–73cu in). It was really

TRIUMPH
900
TRIUMPH
Daytona

OPPOSITE: The 1994 Daytona 900 was still a little too tall and heavy to be a sportster

ABOVE: 1997 Thunderbird Sport

ABOVE: Meanwhile, older twins were competing in classic events

Bert Hopwood's modular philosophy put into practice at last; the new family shared many components and allowed Triumph to launch a complete range of big bikes at one go and at a relatively low price.

There were the basic unfaired 750 and 900cc three-cylinder Tridents (John Bloor knew the value of these old-established names); 750-3 and 1000-4 Daytona sports versions; and the Trophy sports tourers, with 900-3 or 1200-4 engines. The 900cc triple seemed to be most testers' favourite, with a distinctive howling exhaust note and plenty of torque, and it seemed that the new Triumphs had character as well. Even more surprising, there were no horror stories; these Triumphs were at least as dependable as the Japanese competition.

Variations on the theme soon appeared. The Speed Triple was really the later Daytona 900 without its fairing, and a lighter, more powerful Daytona Super III sought to catch the Japanese race replicas (though it wasn't fast or light enough). A bigger change was the Tiger 900, basically the now familiar 900 triple dressed up in off-road clothing. It followed the style of big 'dual purpose' bikes like the BMW GS, though was even less likely to get its tyres muddy.

More of a pointer to the future was the return of the Thunderbird name in late 1994, designed to spearhead a return to the American market. It was an unashamededly nostalgic machine, with old-style Triumph tank, badge and silencers, more chrome and spoked wheels. It also (to sighs of relief from the shorter-legged) had a lower seat height than the other Hinckley Triumphs. The 900cc triple

FOWLERS
Daytona
TRIPLE FUEL INJECTION

OPPOSITE: *The 1997 Daytona T595 was the fastest Hinckley Triumph yet*

ABOVE: *An early Trident 900*

was detuned to suit the character of this retro cruiser (a real growth market in the nineties) though a sharper Thunderbird Sport was to appear in 1997.

More significant that year was the launch of the substantially new Daytona T595. If any of the new Triumphs had lagged behind the opposition, it was the supposedly sporting Daytonas, which were really too tall and heavy to compete. The new bike cured that with an alloy frame, far more nimble handling and a new fuel-injected 955cc (58cu in) version of the triple, with 130bhp and a top speed of around 257km/h (160mph). It was a success, and soon became Triumph's best-selling bike. At the other end of the scale, the Trophies moved further towards being true tourers (though their lack of shaft-drive was a bar to success). The T595 was followed in late 1998 by a sports touring version, the Sprint ST, which was substantially all-new. (It wasn't before time, as eight years on, the original spine frame was starting to look very dated indeed.) Moreover, riders of early STs found them smooth, civilized and deceptively fast. Triumph was back.

TRIUMPH *Germany 1903–57*
This was a subsidiary of the better-known English Triumph, which split from Coventry in 1930. Until then, it built own versions of Coventry bikes, afterwards developing its own two-strokes to 350cc and used Sachs and MAG engines. It resumed production in 1948 with a range of utility two-stroke split-singles of 125–350cc (8–21cu in), powering lightweights and the 200cc (12cu in) Contessa scooter. The company was taken over by Grundig in 1957.

TRIUMPH *U.S.A. 1912*
A subsidiary of the English Triumph, building singles from imported parts.

TROPFEN *Germany 1923–24*
Another attempt (there were a few) by an airship maker to attempt a motorcycle with airship-like full enclosure on a 248/308cc (15/19cu in) two-stroke.

TRUMP (TRUMP-JAP) *England 1906–23*
Utilized a full range of JAP engines of 248–996cc (15–61cu in), as well as the British-Anzani V-twin and 269cc (16cu in) Peco two-stroke.

TSUBASA *Japan 1955–60*
Own 246/345cc (15/21cu in) ohv singles, later a 125cc (8cu in) two-stroke.

TÜRKHEIMER *Italy 1902–05*
There were 1.25hp lightweights from this motorcycle importer.

TVS *India 1976–*
Produced licence-built Batavus mopeds, then entered a licencing agreement with Suzuki in the 1980s. Produced its own 60cc/3.7cu inch scooter (the Scooty) from 1993 and is now the Indian market leader in mopeds.

TX *Germany 1924–26*
Had an unusual frame using the big top tube as a fuel tank. Powered by 132/174cc (8/11cu in) Bekamo two-strokes.

TYLER *England 1913–23*
Made lightweights powered by four-stroke Precision and two-stroke Villiers or in-house engines.

TYPHOON *Sweden 1949–51*
An advanced 198cc (12cu in) two-stroke.

TYPHOON *The Netherlands 1952–68*
Concentrated on mopeds, later importing the Italian Giulietta moped under its own name.

U

UDE *Germany 1924–25*
A 249cc (15cu in) three-port two-stroke.

ULTIMA *France 1908–58*
Used bought-in engines from Aubier-Dunne, JAP and Zurcher, among others. Like most French and German factories, it concentrated on small two-strokes after 1945.

UNIBUS *England 1920–22*
A fully enclosed scooter with leaf-sprung suspension, a 269cc (16cu in) two-stroke and 16-inch wheels.

UNION *Sweden 1943–52*
Only used JAP ohv singles, from 348–498cc (21–30cu in).

UNIVERSAL *Switzerland 1928–64*
Used bought-in engines from a variety of suppliers, including Ilo, JAP and Anzani, but also built its own 676/990cc (41/60cu in) sv V-twins for the Swiss Army. After 1945, went on making in-house engines, notably a 578cc (35cu in) flat twin and a 248cc (15cu in) single, both with unit-construction and shaft-drive.

UNIVERSELLE *Germany 1925–29*
Ioe four-stroke singles of 183–247cc (11–15cu in), with unit-construction.

ABOVE: The Ural Cossack 650D, of which not many were exported

ABOVE: The Jupiter 350 was another product of the former U.S.S.R.

BELOW: To Western eyes, the Ural simply looked odd

URAL *Former U.S.S.R. 1945–*
Ural was a product of the Soviet Union's pragmatic if ruthless post-war policy of seizing any valuable plant in occupied Germany and taking it back to the Motherland. So it was with BMW's production equipment which was transferred from the Eisenach factory into Russia. There, the flat twin was faithfully reproduced, and was even passed on (third-hand, you might say) to China.

Several factories in the U.S.S.R. built the ex-BMW, but the Kiev, Irbit, Cossack, Dneiper and Neval were all basically the same machine. It first surfaced as the Ural Mars M63 (even retaining a BMW model name) and turned out to be a combination of an R66 and wartime R75. There were updates from time to time, notably swinging-arm suspension and a capacity increase to 650cc (40cu in), but there was much of the original still in place. Even the R75's driven sidecar wheel and auxiliary gearchange were retained which, according to the maker, made gearchanging easier when towing a plough!

URANIA *Germany 1934–39*
Made Sachs and Ilo-engined two-strokes to 123cc (7.5cu in).

UT *Germany 1922–59*
Used many different bought-in engines prior to 1939 (Bekamo, Blackburne, JAP, Küchen and Bark) but concentrated on Sachs and Ilo-engined lightweights after the war.

UTILIA *France 1929–36*
A large variety of engines were used, from 98cc (6cu in) two-strokes to 498cc (30cu in) four-strokes, all bought-in.

V

VAGA *Italy 1925–35*
Produced 124cc (8cu in) two-strokes initially, followed by bought-in four-strokes including units from JAP and Sturmey-Archer.

VAL *England 1913–24*
Used JAP sv singles of 488cc (30cu in).

VALIANT *U.S.A. c.1964–65*
Made a 197cc (12cu in) Villiers-engined version of the Simplex minibike.

VAN VEEN *Germany 1978–81*
Henk van Veen distributed Kreider mopeds in Holland, but is best known for his rotary-engined OCR1000. The heavy 295kg (650lb) machine used a water-cooled Wankel engine and shaft-drive. Claimed top speed was 150mph. Limited numbers made.

VAP *France 1951–early 1970s*
Built moped engines, later complete lightweights.

VAREL *Germany 1952–53*
Produced 43cc (2.6cu in) mopeds and 99cc (6cu in) Moto-engined scooters.

VASCO *England 1921–23*
Used 261cc (16cu in) Orbit power, then 349cc (21cu in) Broler two-stroke singles.

VASSENA *Italy 1926–29*
A 124cc (8cu in) two-stroke with horizontal cylinder.

VATERLAND *Germany 1933–39*
Sachs-engined lightweights of 98 and 120cc (6 and 7.3cu in).

VECCHIETTI *Italy 1954–57*
Mopeds using 49cc (3cu in) Victoria engines.

VELAMOS *Czechoslovakia 1927–30*
Used its own three-port two-strokes of 246–496cc (15–30cu in), designed by Gustav Heinz.

VELOCETTE *England 1904–71*
From the beginning and right to the end, Velocette was a family concern and three generations of the Goodman family ran it: John Goodman set the firm up, his sons Percy and Eugene (both talented engineers) took care of it between the wars, while their sister Ethel acted as buyer and her husband, George Denly, was sales manager. In the last 20 years, *their* sons Bertie and Peter took charge of the company.

Although such continuity was one of Velocette's strengths, it is arguable that it also held the seeds of its destruction, for while Percy Goodman was interested in building racing singles, his brother Eugene was set on that other, probably more elusive goal – the practical motorcycle for the man in the street. There is no evidence of any friction between the two brothers as

The rotary-engined Van Veen was only made in small numbers

The all-French Velo-Solex is now made in Hungary

a result of their conflicting interests, but it did mean that the small firm's resources (Velocette never employed more than 400 people) were often over-stretched by ambitious new projects it could ill afford.

Being so small, Velocette could not afford to mass-produce its utility bikes, so these cost more than they should have done, and none was successful. In fact, when the company was wound up, it cited the Viceroy scooter as instrumental in its downfall. On the other hand, Veloce Ltd. had a talent for sporting four-stroke singles, and its high quality, high performance 350s and 500s, in their classic black and gold livery, are seen by many as the definitive British singles.

John Goodman began life in Germany as Johannes Gujtemann, but anglicized his name when he emigrated to England. His fledgling company experimented in all sorts of fields, including roller skates, a car, and even rickshaws, until the success of an advanced little 276cc (17cu in) unit-construction bike and a more conventional 500cc (30.5cu in) machine convinced him that this was the way to go. There were 250cc two-stroke 'Velocettes' (the name stuck) from 1913, which helped give the company a firmer footing.

Percy and Eugene soon proved themselves fine design engineers, and it was the former who succeeded, where established companies like Sunbeam and Norton were still struggling, in designing a reliable overhead-camshaft racing single. Using an early strobe light in the early 1920s, Percy discovered the correct cam profiles to use, and also solved the problem of lubrication. The result was the 350cc (21cu in) K-series racer which won the

ABOVE and BELOW: Classic Velocette singles, of which the 1934 KSS (above) was one, formed the basis of the company's reputation

Junior TT in 1926. Suddenly, Velocette wa[s] high-profile, and orders flowed in so fast that it was forced to move to a larger factory. More TT successes followed, aide[d] by the first production foot gearchange, wi[th] a positive stop lever. (Every manual-transmission motorcycle uses this now, but Velocette was first.) Another Velocette first was the combined dual seat, and that too was soon adopted by everyone else. Both [of] these stemmed from a designer named Harold Willis, who was prolific in his inventiveness and responsible for many of Velocette's innovations.

Although, by 1930, Velocette's main production consisted of the road- and race-going K-series (with the lovely black and gold finish already a feature), Eugene was keen to produce a cheaper bike which wou[ld] appeal to non-enthusiasts which, after all, had been the Velocette's original intention. The result was the GTP250, a two-stroke single in the now traditional black and gol[d] in addition to a few innovations of its own notably the use of the engine as a stress-bearing member of the chassis, and coil ignition. A throttle-controlled oil pump wa[s] added in another few years. But like the more glamorous Velocettes, the GTP was built up to a standard of quality, rather tha[n] down to a price.

Meanwhile, that very philosphy was undermining the K-series. Popular as it wa[s] the ohc single needed skilful assembly (especially the cam's bevel-drive). Eugene came up with the answer, and it was to prove Velocette's mainstay for the rest of t[he] firm's life. The overhead camshaft was too expensive, but a conventional ohv set-up, with long, whippy pushrods would limit

The 1935 GTP250 was an attempt to reach the ride-to-work market

engine revs and thus power. His solution was to mount the camshaft high up (driven by intermediate gears), which allowed the use of relatively short, stiff pushrods, not quite as powerful as the K-series, but not far off, and much easier and cheaper to build. Ironically enough, although cost was the new M-series' *raison d'être*, its advantage was severely compromised by the use of costly helical teeth for the timing gears. Once again, Velocette had chosen the fundamentally correct engineering solution with little heed to the expense.

In production form, the first M-series was the 250cc (15cu in) MOV of 1933. At around 97km/h (60mph), it was fast for its capacity, sweet and relatively smooth, no doubt helped by the almost square cylinder dimensions of 68mm x 68.25mm. The following year, a longer-stroke 350cc (21cu in) version, the MAC, was unveiled, which used the same chassis as the 250 and weighed only 4.5kg (10lb) more. It could top 121km/h (75mph) and, like the MOV, was a deserved success. The range was completed in 1935 with the 500cc (30.5cu in) MSS ('Super Sports') with a near-80mph top speed little lower than that of the K-series. It also introduced automatic ignition control in 1936 – yet another Velocette first. The M-series bikes were not perfect: they could leak oil, used Velocette's unusual single plate clutch and it needed a knack to start them. But it sold well, and kept the company profitable right through to the mid-1950s.

Supercharged

The very inventiveness that produced Velocette's many firsts also led to other projects that failed to make it. There were various attempts at twin overhead camshafts, and Harold Willis experimented with rotary valves, while Phil Irving (on a brief sojourn away from Vincent) designed a 600cc (37cu in) vertical twin with shaft-drive and rear suspension. More promising was the famous 'Roarer', a supercharged 500cc twin-cylinder racer. It was certainly advanced for its time, being rear-sprung, shaft-driven and with full-width hubs. Unfortunately, it was only once run competitively, in the 1938 TT, when Stanley Woods failed to make much of an impression with it (though he won the Junior TT on a 350 single and was second in the Senior). After the war, the FIM's ban on supercharged racers was enough to put paid to the project.

Unlike the larger British factories, Velocette did not produce endless ranks of motorcycles for wartime despatch riders, lacking the mass-production facilities to do so, and although there was a military-specification MAF, most of the company's wartime work was in the form of sub-contracts for such things as gun components. But even while war was still

Thruxton in a rare silver finish. Note the adjustment slot for the rear damper

being waged, Eugene Goodman's thoughts kept returning to his motorcycle for everyman – simple, reliable and well-built.

The result (also worked on by Phil Irving, and finalized by Charles Udall, who had also productionized the M-series) was the LE. It was unusual in many ways, chiefly for its flat-twin layout, shaft-drive and water-cooling. A prototype of the 150cc (9cu in) machine was running in 1945 but it was four years before it finally entered production. It was an ambitious project which swallowed much of Velocette's slender resources when it could have been concentrating on the popular, profitable MAC. Sadly, the LE was expensive for a utility bike, and sales were disappointing. Eugene had predicted sales of 14,500 for 1950, but in fact less than 3,000 bikes found homes. The LE was certainly quiet, docile and easy to ride, providing a measure of weather protection from its legshields, and it was very comfortable. But it was also heavy and underpowered (despite a bigger 192cc/11.7cu inch engine in 1951) and only the police really took to it. Meanwhile the 350cc MAC had been gradually updated with telescopic forks in 1948, an alloy engine in 1951 and a swinging-arm frame two years later. But like Triumph and other British manufacturers, Velocette was faced with a demand for more capacity from its American customers, and responded by bringing back the 500cc MSS in 1954. Both were updated a few years later into the 350 Viper and 500 Venom, with more racing success (Bertie Goodman was a noted rider) bolstering the Velocette heritage.

Coffin Nails

But Eugene hadn't given up on the utility end of the market, and Velocette's response to criticisms of the underpowered sidevalve LE was the overhead-valved Valiant of 1956. On paper, this seemed just the thing, with a four-speed gearbox, air-cooling to reduce weight, conventional motorcycle styling (though still with the practical shaft-drive) and twice as much power as the LE. Unfortunately, it was based on the LE's bottom-end, which couldn't cope with 12bhp, and engine failure often resulted. The Valiant remained available until 1963, by which time sales had reduced to a trickle.

But even with the Valiant, there was still time for Velocette to turn itself around. What really set the company on the slippery slope was the Viceroy scooter. Like BSA/Triumph, Velocette woke up late to the scooter boom with a bike that was too big, heavy and expensive to compete. It was yet another variation on the flat twin theme, this time a two-stroke version of the 247cc (15cu in). In theory, it handled better than a Vespa, with its tubular frame, big 12-inch wheels and good weight distribution, but it also weighed a lot more and was expensive. Once again, predictions of mass sales proved hopelessly optimistic; the aim was 5,000 in 1962, but a mere 300 had been sold when the scooter was dropped in 1964. There were other attempts to find alternative outlets for the LE flat twin: its quiet operation gave it potential as a stationary power plant, though that came to nothing. Instead, Velocette went ahead with the Vogue, a fully-panelled, twin-headlamped luxury commuter in the mould of the Ariel Leader. It was no match for the younger Ariel, though, and not many were sold.

ABOVE: The Venom Thruxton of 1965 was the final development

BELOW: A 1956 500cc (31.5cu in) Venom

While money was being spent and lost on the various lightweight projects, the Viper and Venom went on selling steadily, though even these were beginning to look increasingly outdated against home-built twins and, as the 1960s progressed, new rivals from Honda and Kawasaki. There was one final development in 1965 with the Venom Thruxton. Its inspiration was a squish-type cylinder-head produced by Velocette's U.S. importer, Lou Branch, which the factory adopted for its ultimate big single. Around a thousand Thruxtons were built over the last few years, and one even won the first Production TT in 1967. But from that year onwards, the company was being kept afloat only by the relatively lucrative spares production for Royal Enfield, which had recently collapsed. Production gradually slowed, although one of the final contracts was for 194 500cc engines for the Italian-built Indian 500. This was the idea of American entrepreneur Floyd Clymer, who wished to sell a combination of Italian styling and British engineering. It was not a success. So Velocette finally went into liquidation in February 1971, and yet another famous British name went under. Sadly, if Velocette had concentrated on what it was good at, it might possibly have still been around today.

VELO-SOLEX *France 1946–91*
With its 49cc (3cu in) two-stroke mounted on top of the front wheel the bike, like the Citroën 2cv, was part of the French landscape, and no French rural family would have been complete without one. It was really a cross between a clip-on engine and a conventional moped. Taken over by Motobécane in 1974, it is now made in Hungary. To date, over 6 million have been produced.

VELOX *Czechoslovakia 1923–26*
First used a 147cc (9cu in) Villiers, later 123/147cc (7.5/9cu in) Bekamo two-strokes.

VENUS *England 1920–22*
Used a 318cc (19.4cu in) Dalm engine.

VENUS *Germany 1920–22*
A Sachs-engined scooter of 98–174cc (6–11cu in).

VERGA *Italy 1951–54*
A 73cc (4.5cu in) two-stroke, with swinging-arm rear suspension.

VERLOR *France 1930–38*
Produced 98–120cc (6–7.3cu in) lightweights with Aubier-Dunne or Stainless engines.

VEROS *Italy 1922–24*
A rebadged Verus (see below) for export to Italy.

VERUS *England 1919–25*
Choice of own two-strokes to 269cc (16cu in) or larger Blackburne four-strokes.

VESPA
See Piaggio.

VESUV *Germany 1924–26*
Own 246cc (15cu in) two-stroke in step-through frame.

VIATKA *Russia 1957–79*
Copy of the Vespa scooter in 150/175cc (9/11cu in) versions.

VIBERTI *Italy 1955–late 1960s*
Produced mopeds and 123cc (7.5cu in) lightweights.

VICTA *England 1912–13*
Used a Precision 499cc (30cu in) single.

VICTORIA *Scotland 1902–26*
No connection with the German Victoria, it used a variety of bought-in engines from 127–688cc (8–42cu in). Built in Glasgow.

VICTORIA *Germany 1899–1966*
Founded in 1886 and originally a bicycle maker, it built a prototype motorcycle in 1899 but it was another six years before full production of Zedel and Fafnir-engined machines appeared. After World War I it briefly used BMW's fore-aft flat twin before designing its own, and introduced a new range of singles in 1928 with bought-in engines (the 198–499cc/12–30cu inch Horex and the licence-built Sturmey-Archer). After 1945, it initially produced clip-ons only, then two-strokes up to 247cc (15cu in). Attempted to return upmarket with the shaft-driven 347cc (21cu in) V-twin Bergmeister in 1951, but a falling market caused it to concentrate on lightweights only, some with Italian Parilla engines. Merged with DKW and Express to form Zweirad Union in 1958, and the name finally disappeared in 1966.

ABOVE: 1938 Victoria Aero 250cc (15cu in)

BELOW and OPPOSITE: 1954 Victoria Bergmeister 350cc (21cu in)

ABOVE: Sales brochure for the Victory. Inspired by Harley-Davidson's success, Polaris designed and built an all-new rival

VICTORY *Italy 1950–55*
Made Villiers-engined lightweights of 98–123cc (6–7.5cu in).

VICTORY *U.S.A. 1998–*
The 1990s have seen the revival or rebirth of some very famous marques, names such as Ducati, spurred on by racing success and American corporate finance; Triumph rescued by a self-made millionaire; Laverda promising a new three-cylinder bike in the near future. It is part of a general revival of interest in the European industry that is now managing to flourish alongside the Japanese giants. At the time of writing, there is even an all-new marque from France, the Voxan. And let's not forget the non-Japanese manufacturer whose revival began years ago – Harley-Davidson. In little more than a decade, Harley transformed itself from corporate no-hoper to an all-American success story. So successful, that other American entrepreneurs have sat up and taken notice of this newly-profitable field of operation.

One of them was Polaris. Based in Wisconsin, it makes golf carts, ATVs and jet-skis. Always on the look-out for new opportunities, it had noted Harley's success, as well as its inability to keep up with demand. Not only that, but sales in the cruiser market sector were high and profit margins generous. It was also a sector where being an American manufacturer was a positive bonus. A survey discovered that many existing Polaris customers already rode bikes so, for a manufacturer like Polaris, it was a golden marketing opportunity. Consequently, in 1993 the big decision was made to proceed.

The first thing to do was to go out and buy a Harley (an FXRS), plus a Honda Shadow. Each was stripped down and painstakingly costed, part by part, the aim being to determine which components Polaris should make in-house and which should be bought-in. It was decided early on that the V-twin engine (could it really have been anything else?) would have to be made in-house, to give the project credibility. Harley sold on being a genuine all-American motorcycle, and the Polaris could not afford to be anything else.

With the best will in the world, the Polaris design team had little experience of designing bikes, so it sensibly bought up most of the competition, the Honda Valkyrie, Harley Road King – even non-cruisers such as Ducati's Monster, and evaluated all in great detail. Everyone liked the Kawasaki Vulcan V-twin (then the biggest, at 1470cc/90cu inches) so Polaris determined to build something slightly

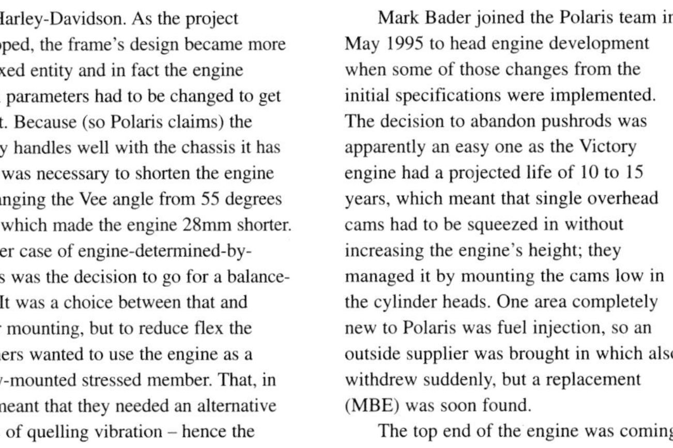

bigger still. It came out at 1507cc (92cu in) and three years on, as this is written, Yamaha has just launched a 1600cc (98cu in) twin. It may be that once this book is published, on the shelves and you are reading it, Polaris or someone else will have come up with something bigger still. One thing that emerged during the evaluation rides was that many of the cruisers had unpleasant, wallowy handling when pressed hard. It's often argued that for the laid-back riding style that cruisers are supposed to provide, this doesn't really matter, but the Polaris team was apparently determined to produce a cruiser that handled well at speed as well as when cruising.

Geoff Burgess was brought in as project leader. A Scotsman by birth, he had worked for Norton-Villiers in the mid-1960s before emigrating to North America and eventually joining Polaris to develop the Victory into a production bike. A 'mule' rolling chassis was built on which critical factors like wheelbase, rake and trail were adjustable. 'Francis' (as it was called) was taken out on the road, and everything was adjusted until it was deemed to be just so. Polaris' own engine wasn't ready at this stage, so Francis was powered by a Harley Sportster engine, which had the additional benefit of being able to fool onlookers that this secret prototype was really no more than a well-used Harley-Davidson. As the project developed, the frame's design became more of a fixed entity and in fact the engine design parameters had to be changed to get it to fit. Because (so Polaris claims) the Victory handles well with the chassis it has got, it was necessary to shorten the engine by changing the Vee angle from 55 degrees to 50, which made the engine 28mm shorter. Another case of engine-determined-by-chassis was the decision to go for a balance-shaft. It was a choice between that and rubber mounting, but to reduce flex the designers wanted to use the engine as a solidly-mounted stressed member. That, in turn, meant that they needed an alternative means of quelling vibration – hence the balance-shaft. One more apocryphal story concerning the Victory's handling development. The test riders decided something wasn't quite right, but couldn't work out what it was. Someone (history does not record who) remembered that the Norton Manx's superlative handling stemmed partly from having both wheel spindles in line with the crankshaft; so they dropped the Victory's crank by an inch, and all was apparently well.

Engine Design

In fact, the Victory's engine ended up significantly different from the original outline specification, which envisaged an air-cooled, pushrod ohv twin with rubber mounting, carburettors and no balancer shaft. The production engine uses more sophisticated technology, with fuel injection, oil cooling and overhead cams. It was an interesting departure from Harley-Davidson's philosophy of keeping its power unit deliberately low-tech.

Mark Bader joined the Polaris team in May 1995 to head engine development when some of those changes from the initial specifications were implemented. The decision to abandon pushrods was apparently an easy one as the Victory engine had a projected life of 10 to 15 years, which meant that single overhead cams had to be squeezed in without increasing the engine's height; they managed it by mounting the cams low in the cylinder heads. One area completely new to Polaris was fuel injection, so an outside supplier was brought in which also withdrew suddenly, but a replacement (MBE) was soon found.

The top end of the engine was coming together nicely, but the crankcases weren't ready, being a month behind schedule. So for bench testing, the team took a 159kg (350lb) block of aluminium, and carved it to accept the heads and barrels. Nicknamed the Hammer, it was bulky and block-like, but it served its purpose. There were undoubtedly a lot of crossed fingers on a Friday in September 1996 when the first Victory top-end was finally installed into the Hammer, everything hooked up and ready to go. The key was turned and ... it wouldn't start. They purged air from the fuel system, tried again, and the Victory V-twin roared into life for the first time.

After that first excitement, the donkey work began; fuel mapping for the injection had to be done through a long and laborious process of calculating the engine's fuel needs at every combination of speed and load. The basics were done on the bench, but final tweaks had to be made on the road. So a running Victory was hitched up to a sidecar, and Jeff Moore of MBE sat in the chair, tapping away at his laptop, which was hooked into all the engine's essential points. Geoff Burgess later recalled that the fuel mapping and fine tuning took about six months to complete. Yet more road testing ensued on what was now a pre-production prototype. As with anything all-new, the priority was to accumulate some miles in the hope that if anything broke, it would break then. All the time, work was progressing on styling details, and of course the launch.

The first public unveiling was at the Planet Hollywood restaurant in Bloomington, Minnesota in June 1997; then it was time to start the show circuit, and two Victory V92Cs, the '92' referring to the engine capacity in cubic inches, went on display at Sturgis that August. And at Daytona, a lot more people had the opportunity to ride the Victory for the first time. Among them was journalist Ian Kerr, who wrote about it for *Motorcycle Sport & Leisure*: 'The 1507cc twin certainly delivers its claimed 85lb ft of torque – open the throttle and it goes; in no uncertain terms. It's an instantaneous response too, thanks to the electronic fuel injection and engine management. Roll-on in any gear was excellent, and if you want to brave both Florida radar traps and the wind, three-figure speeds are easily obtained ...' He also remarked that it had a clunky gearchange (which would be changed for production), felt well balanced, was stable through bends, though ground clearance was inevitably compromised, and exuded quality. He was also convinced that people would be queuing up to buy it. Whether this all-new motorcycle fulfills its early promise remains to be seen, but it's a good start.

The final Vincent was the enclosed Black Prince

VILLA *Italy 1968–88*
Concentrated on two-stroke lightweights, mostly with bought-in engines, but used its own engines in successful motocross bikes. Master-minded by ex-racers, Francesco and Walter Villa.

VILLOF *Spain 1951–61*
75–123cc (4.6–7.5cu in) two-strokes, both Hispano-Villiers-powered and with in-house engines.

VINCENT-HRD *England 1927–55*
Today, a one-litre V-twin with a cruising speed of 100mph, able to top 120 and with great attention given to rider comfort, would be a respectable sports-tourer. Little more than half a century ago, the Vincent-HRD V-twin must have seemed like something from outer space. It was faster than any contemporary racer (let alone road bike), yet behaved like a well-mannered tourer. It had cantilevered rear suspension (25 years before most motorcycles adopted rear suspension of any type) and was built of the finest materials. It was, to put it mildly, a milestone machine.

Philip Conrad Vincent was something of a visionary and many of his ideas were literally years ahead of their time. That cantilever suspension, a hydraulic clutch, even a front-wheel-drive car, were all established through the Vincent decades before becoming common currency. Perhaps it was just as well that his inventive mind contained an entrepreneurial streak. If Vincent had not decided to set up on his own and join the British motorcycle industry, it is likely that his free-ranging ideas would have been quickly diluted, if not stifled altogether.

He certainly had an unconventional upbringing; his father was English but owned a ranch in Argentina, where Philip was born in 1908. In the manner of the time, he was sent away to England for his education, and it was at Harrow that he developed an interest in motorcycles that was to dominate the rest of his life. He outlined his cantilever rear suspension at the age of 17, went to Cambridge to study engineering, but soon decided that he needed to be in the trade as soon as possible. So he persuaded his father to put up the money to buy HRD.

HRD had been a short-lived success. Howard R. Davies (hence the name) was himself something of a character. Apprenticed at AJS, he rode in the TT, was a pilot during World War I, was shot down and was taken prisoner. There was more TT success after the war before Davies decided, in a Vincent-like manner, that contemporary machines simply weren't up to the job, to build his own bike around a JAP single. Unveiled at the 1924 Motorcycle Show at Olympia in London, the first HRD was admired for its quality and looks. Davies rode it at the TT the

Fast, expensive and long-lived, many Vincents are still in active use

following year, coming second in the Junior race and winning the Senior. Sadly, he was less successful as a businessman; the HRD's high price was enough to stifle sales, and the company went into liquidation.

It was bought by one Ernie Humphries, who seems to have done little with it, for in 1927 Philip Vincent came along with £400 and bought the name and its illustrious, albeit brief history.

Irving Arrives

The new Vincent-HRD company set up shop on the Great North Road in Stevenage, and went to work. Its first products used JAP engines (as had HRD), ohv singles of 350, 500 and 600cc (21, 30.5 and 37cu in). Of course, its unique point was Vincent's rear suspension system, which used a pivoting triangular rear frame, with the spring units almost horizontal under the seat. They failed to meet with immediate success, one reason being that, amazing as it might seem now, rear suspension was viewed with suspicion. The company almost collapsed, but fortunately an enthusiastic customer named Bill Clarke persuaded his father to step in and save it and Captain Clarke became chairman. (Sadly, Vincent's own father had lost the ranch to an unreliable partner, so wasn't in a position to help.)

Help of a different kind arrived in 1931. Phil Irving's name has become as associated with the company as that of Vincent himself. An Australian engineer, Irving came to join Vincent-HRD by chance. Jack Gill had ridden a Vincent and sidecar from England to Australia in 1929/30. At Melbourne, his passenger decided to quit, and Irving (presumably on a whim) took his place, returning to England with Gill and joining the company forthwith. Phil Irving was a wonderful production engineer, and much has been written concerning his place in the Vincent company: 'PCV' the engineering idealist, down-to-earth Irving who turned his visions into reality. What is clear is that both men contributed hugely to Vincent-HRD and the company and its motorcycles would not have been the same without either of them.

Over the next few years, the two Phils designed and produced a number of different bikes, still with JAP engines, which began to win acceptance through competition success, while Vincent continued to experiment with new ideas. One such was the balance beam braking system which used two drum brakes on each wheel controlled by a single cable via a balance beam. They also entered three JAP-powered bikes for the 1934 TT but, when all three broke down, thoughts turned to producing their own engine.

The Comet 499cc single was the result. It had a relatively short stroke for the time, with high-mounted camshaft (to allow shorter, stiffer pushrods) and a 6.8 or 7.3:1 compression ratio. Set in a frame with Vincent's rear suspension, it produced 26bhp at 5,600rpm in higher Comet tune and could push the bike to 145km/h (90mph), while a more highly tuned TT Replica broached 100mph. It was less well known than the V-twin, but the 500 single remained a part of the Vincent range almost to the end.

There is more than one story of how the Meteor single became a V-twin, the most attractive of which was that two drawings of the single were blown together by a breeze, noticed by Phil Irving, and the rest is history. Whatever the truth, Philip Vincent was equally enthusiastic about the idea (one of his visions had been a gentleman's high-speed motorcycle, a kind of two-wheeled Bentley), and in just three months they had a bike ready for the1936 Motorcycle Show. The Series A Rapide produced 45bhp, which doesn't sound much now but was enough for a 174km/h (108mph) top speed and an effortless, loping cruise on the high gearing. Also enough, in any case, to make the 998cc (61cu in) twin the fastest production motorcycle of its day. However, only 78 were sold before war broke out, simply because Vincent-HRD was still a very small company that could not afford to spend much on expanding production.

Oddly enough, it was the war that

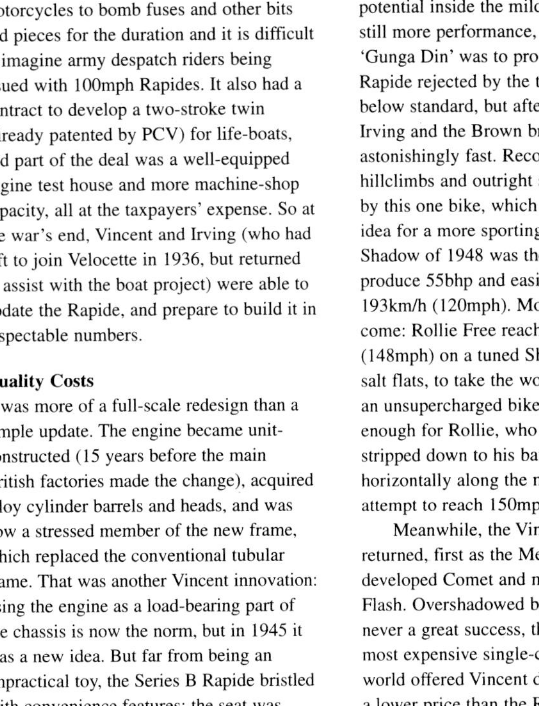

OPPOSITE and ABOVE: Black Prince with and without modern add-ons

changed all that. Vincent switched from motorcycles to bomb fuses and other bits and pieces for the duration and it is difficult to imagine army despatch riders being issued with 100mph Rapides. It also had a contract to develop a two-stroke twin (already patented by PCV) for life-boats, and part of the deal was a well-equipped engine test house and more machine-shop capacity, all at the taxpayers' expense. So at the war's end, Vincent and Irving (who had left to join Velocette in 1936, but returned to assist with the boat project) were able to update the Rapide, and prepare to build it in respectable numbers.

Quality Costs

It was more of a full-scale redesign than a simple update. The engine became unit-constructed (15 years before the main British factories made the change), acquired alloy cylinder barrels and heads, and was now a stressed member of the new frame, which replaced the conventional tubular frame. That was another Vincent innovation: using the engine as a load-bearing part of the chassis is now the norm, but in 1945 it was a new idea. But far from being an impractical toy, the Series B Rapide bristled with convenience features: the seat was height-adjustable (how many machines offer that now?); the rear wheel could be removed in less than a minute; all controls were adjustable; an optional rear wheel for sidecar users could be reversed, with a sidecar-geared sprocket on the other side. None of this was cheap, of course, and the Series B cost twice as much as a big BSA or Triumph. But it was beautifully made, long-lived and well-mannered, not to mention faster than anything else on the road.

Faster perhaps, but there was plenty of potential inside the mildly tuned V-twin for still more performance, as the famous 'Gunga Din' was to prove. This was a 1947 Rapide rejected by the test department as below standard, but after attention from Irving and the Brown brothers, proved astonishingly fast. Records for tracks, hillclimbs and outright speed were broken by this one bike, which gave Vincent the idea for a more sporting Rapide. The Black Shadow of 1948 was the result, tuned to produce 55bhp and easily capable of 193km/h (120mph). More speed was to come: Rollie Free reached 238km/h (148mph) on a tuned Shadow at Bonneville salt flats, to take the world speed record for an unsupercharged bike. It wasn't quite enough for Rollie, who immediately stripped down to his bathing trunks and lay horizontally along the machine in an attempt to reach 150mph! He did it.

Meanwhile, the Vincent single had returned, first as the Meteor, then as the developed Comet and more sporting Grey Flash. Overshadowed by the twins, it was never a great success, though even this the most expensive single-cylinder bike in the world offered Vincent design and quality at a lower price than the Rapide. In 1949, the latter was updated into Series C form, notably with the addition of Girdraulic forks. It was a time when other manufacturers were switching to the new hydraulically-damped telescopic forks, but typically, Irving and Vincent knew they could do better. The Girdraulics used two strong blades of aircraft quality L64 alloy, with forged steel yokes and long enclosed springs. Far stronger and more rigid than conventional forks, but just as soft in action,

ABOVE: Egli–Vincent at Daytona

RIGHT: Vincent-HRD 500 Comet single

they kept the wheelbase constant and did not dive under braking. They were (inevitably) more costly than telescopics and needed to be properly maintained, but the Girdraulics were a typically advanced Vincent solution. (There are some similarities to BMW's Telelever system, introduced in the early 1990s.)

In 1949, with the Series C seen into production, Phil Irving decided to return to Australia and, according to some, development then entered a quiet phase until the Series D of 1955. By now, the Vincent twin was beginning to look a little elderly, despite its still-advanced features, though it was selling well and remained the fastest bike you could buy at any price. Philip Vincent was quite in favour of diversification, however, taking over the Firefly cyclemotor from Miller (a company which had long supplied Vincent's electrical equipment) and built 3,000 of them. There was also an agreement with the importer of the NSU Quickly to sell this little German moped and assemble 98/125cc (6/8cu in) NSUs at Stevenage. Alas, the Quickly was so successful that the U.K. importer lost no time in taking the concession back.

The time was nearing for Vincent's swansong, the Series D. Although some long-standing complaints were addressed (notably through more reliable coil ignition, and a steering damper) the Series D's main feature couldn't be missed – it had all-enclosing bodywork. PCV had been keen on this idea for years, and had offered it on some pre-war machines, but with other British factories making tentative moves in this direction, he decided the time was right. A large black fibreglass fairing protected the rider, with side panels hiding most of the mechanics from view. The Black Knight (in Rapide tune) and Black Shadow (Shadow) certainly gave more protection than the naked bikes, and were more economical at speed, though ultimately not quite as fast. Once again, Vincent proved himself far ahead of his time, for now most high-speed sports-tourers are similarly enclosed.

Sadly, it was not enough. Despite full order books in 1955, Philip Vincent decided to cease production altogether. Costs continued to spiral upwards, and the company was now losing money on every machine. Motorcycle sales were declining at home, while vital U.S. exports were controlled by businessman Joe Berliner, who was said to drive a very hard bargain indeed. Vincent the company was taken over in 1959, while Philip was beset by illness and financial problems: he died in 1979. But his bikes lived on, and the efforts of the Vincent Owners Club to again manufacture spares has ensured that Vincent V-twins (the 'Snarling Beasts') will be roaring over our roads for yet a while.

VINCO *England 1903–05*
Used the 211cc (13cu in) Minerva favoured by many pioneers.

VINDEC *England 1902–29*
Produced a range, often of JAP-engined bikes of 172–490cc (10.5–30cu in), under its proprietors the Brown brothers.

VINDEC-SPECIAL *England 1903–14*
A rebadged Allright for the English market, built in Germany.

VIPER *England 1919–22*
A step-through frame and 293cc (18cu in) JAP sv.

VIRATELLE *France 1907–24*
Produced a variety of models with bought-in engines.

VIS *Germany 1923–25*
249cc (15cu in) single or 496cc (30cu in) fore-aft flat-twin two-strokes.

VITTORIA *Italy 1931–80*
Brand name used by Carnielli. Used Sachs, JAP, Küchen or Python power units, but mostly 98cc (6cu in) two-strokes after 1945.

VOLLBLUT *Germany 1925–27*
Utilized 248/348cc (15/21cu in) Blackburne ohv singles.

VORAN *Germany 1921–24*
A 143cc (9cu in) three-port two-stroke lightweight.

VOSKHOD *Former U.S.S.R. 1966–*
Brand name used on a 174cc (11cu in) two-stroke, which owes something to DKW and Jawa.

VOXAN *France 1999–*
In the 1990s, the European motorcycle industry, not to mention Harley-Davidson and its new home-grown rivals, seemed to be undergoing a true renaissance. Triumph had returned, BMW prospered, Ducati was reaching new heights, and a rapidly expanding Cagiva was restoring MV Agusta to life. Only France, of the once-major motorcycle producers, seemed to be the odd one out.

Jacques Gardette had other plans. A successful businessman, who happened to ride a Ducati 916, he was frustrated by the lack of a home-grown French industry and decided to follow John Bloor's example and set some up. From 1995, he began to attract finance from government agencies and Michelin, not to mention his own investment. Chassis designer Alain Chevallier was taken on to produce the first major new French motorcycle for 50 years, and in late 1998 it was revealed.

Its basis was a 72-degree one-litre V-twin with fuel injection, dohc and eight valves. While not as overtly sporting as the Italian opposition, the new bike was certainly up-to-the-minute, with a light (9kg/20lb) twin tubular frame that used the engine as a stressed member. One interesting point was that the head angle could easily be changed by swapping the chassis' headstock casting. Fuel was carried low down behind the V-twin with a dummy fuel tank actually housing the airbox. Rear suspension was by monoshock, mounted Buell-style underneath the engine, but working in compression rather than extension. In standard form, the new engine produced 108bhp at 9,000rpm and 80lb ft at 7,000rpm, though it was also destined for the half-faired Café Racer Voxan, which promised 120bhp. A more relaxed 1240cc (76cu in) version was planned for a cruiser and fully-faired tourer.

ABOVE: The German-made VS lasted only a few years

Alan Cathcart was one of the first journalists to ride the Voxan in October 1998, and was duly impressed. 'What Voxan has done,' he wrote in *Motorcycle Sport & Leisure*, 'is build the bike that Ducati has so far opted out of making. This is the first fuel-injected, eight-valve European V-twin sports roadster with superbike performance and a chassis package to suit.' And if in early 1999 the initial orders were anything to go by, the French buying public certainly agreed.

VOYAGER *Britain c.1990*
The Voyager was another attempt at producing a large feet-forward machine. Like the earlier Quasar, it used the Reliant four-cylinder car engine of 747cc (46cu in). With built-in luggage space and a car-type seat, it was a serious attempt at a practical all-round bike, and early road tests suggested that the Voyager had much promise. Sadly, the production versions were both heavier and slower, and only a few were sold.

BELOW: Voyager promised a new style of motorcycling

VS *Germany 1922–24*
The VS was only made in limited numbers.

VULCAAN *The Netherlands 1911–27*
Built own singles and V-twins, possibly with help from the Zedel factory.

VULCAN *Czechoslovakia 1904–24*
Connected to Perun, it only manufactured spares after World War I.

VULCAN *England 1922–24*
Used mostly 248cc (15cu in) two-strokes, except for a 293cc (18cu in) sv JAP.

W

WACKWITZ *Germany 1920–22*
A 108cc (6.6cu in) clip-on.

WADDINGTON *England 1902–06*
Single-cylinder motorcycles with a variety of engines which included Minerva, MMC and other products.

WAG *England 1924–25*
A two-stroke V-twin of 496cc (30cu in) with limited production.

WAGNER *Czechoslovakia 1930–35*
Produced two- and four-strokes from 98–499cc (6–30cu in).

WAKEFIELD *England c.1902*
Utilized Minerva or MMC engines in cycle frames.

WALBA *Germany 1949–52*
Ilo-engined scooters of 98–173cc (6–11cu in).

WALLIS *England 1925–26*
Notable for its hub-centre-steering. Engines were JAP ohv singles.

WALMET *Germany 1924–26*
Used its own 246cc (15cu in) two-stroke or a Kühne ohv 346cc (21cu in) unit.

WALTER *Germany 1903–42*
Used Fafnir engines first, later Villiers two-strokes, and finally a 98cc (6cu in) Sachs.

WALTER *Czechoslovakia 1900–49*
Josef Walter built his own singles and V-twins, leaving the company to set up another (below), and building a 496cc (30cu in) sv single and some racing ohc singles. Taken over by CZ in 1949.

WALTER *Czechoslovakia 1923–26*
A 746cc (45.5cu in) transverse V-twin, mainly for the Czech Army.

WANDERER *Germany 1902–29*
Well-respected maker of singles (327/387cc/20/24cu in) and V-twins (408/616cc/25/38cu in) before World War I, adding a 184cc (11cu in) ohv after 1918, plus unit-construction V-twins to 749cc/46cu inches (some eight-valved). A new 498cc (30cu in) unit-construction ohv single was on the drawing board in 1927, but was sold to Jawa before it reached production.

WARD *England 1915–16*
298cc (18cu in) two-strokes.

WARDILL *England 1924–26*
An unusual 346cc (21cu in) two-stroke single, with separate charging cylinder.

WARRIOR *England 1921–23*
Utilized a 247cc (15cu in) Villiers engine.

WATNEY *England 1922–23*
Used Villiers, JAP or Blackburne engines to 345cc (21cu in).

WAVERLEY *England 1921–23*
Used 269cc (16cu in) Peco two-strokes or 346/496cc (21/30cu in) Blackburne sv power units.

WD England 1911–13
An ioe 496cc (30cu in) single.

WEARWELL *England 1901–c.1906*
2.5/3.25hp engines from the Stevens brothers (pre-AJS days). Also built Wolfruna and Wolf machines and sold frames to others.

WEATHERELL *England 1922–23*
Used ohv Blackburne engines only, from 248–676cc (15–41cu in).

WEAVER *England 1922–25*
Began with a 142cc (9cu in) ohv single and was soon offering two-strokes as well.

WEBER-MAG *Germany 1926–27*
Used MAG engines of up to 746cc (45.5cu in).

WEBER & REICHMANN
Czechoslovakia 1923–26
Licence-built DKW frames with two-stroke engines direct from DKW.

WECOOB *Germany 1925–30*
Had a small production but large range, with power from the 142cc (9cu in) Rinne to 996cc (61cu in) JAP.

WEE McGREGOR *England 1922–25*
Not Scottish, but a 170cc (10cu in) two-stroke made in Coventry.

WEGRO *Germany 1922–23*
A 452cc (28cu in) two-stroke twin with long wheelbase.

WELA *Germany 1925–27*
Used a 348cc (21cu in) Kühne ohv engine.

WELLER *England 1902–05*
Used its own 1.75/2.25hp power units.

WELS *Germany 1925–26*
Used 348cc (21cu in) Kühne and 490cc (30cu in) JAP engines.

WELT-RAD *Germany 1901–07*
A 3.5hp single and 6hp V-twin.

WERNER *Germany 1897–1908*
The Werner brothers were first to place the engine at the base of the frame, a huge step forward away from the motorized bicycle and towards the true motorcycle. Built both singles and vertical twins, and sold their engines to other manufacturers.

WERNER-MAG *Austria 1928–30*
Used MAG engines in a 498cc (30cu in) single and V-twins up to 996cc (61cu in).

WERNO *Germany 1925–30*
Choice of a 143cc (9cu in) two-stroke or 154cc (9.4cu in) four-stroke.

WESPE *Austria 1937–38*
A Villiers-engined 122cc (7.4cu in) lightweight.

WESTFALIA *Germany 1901–06*
Mostly used De Dion and Fafnir engines.

WESTFIELD *England c.1903*
2.75hp MMC power units.

WESTOVIAN *England 1914–16*
Used bought-in engines (including JAPs and Villiers) from 197–498cc (12–30cu in).

WFM *Poland 1947–*
123–173cc (7.5–11cu in) two-strokes.

W&G *England 1927–28*
A two-stroke flat twin of 490cc (30cu in).

WHEATCROFT *England 1924*
Offered a two-stroke, the 318cc (19cu in) Dalm, and the four-stroke 546cc (33cu in) Blackburne sv.

WHIPPET *England 1903–c.1906*
Used 1.75–3hp engines and Aster and FN units among others.

WHIPPET *England 1920–59*
A 180cc (11cu in) ohv single scooter with 16-inch wheels.

WHIPPET *England 1957–59*
Part scooter, part moped, with 49–64cc (3–4cu in) power.

WHIRLWIND *England 1901–03*
A 1.5hp clip-on and 2/2.5hp machines.

WHITE & POPPE *England 1902–22*
Sold its engines to both car and motorcycle manufacturers, as well as producing complete machines which included 498cc (30cu in) vertical twins, and 347cc (21cu in) two-strokes.

WHITLEY *England 1902–c.1906*
Produced 2.75/3.5hp singles and sold its engines to others.

WHITWOOD *England 1934–36*
A motorcycle with a car-like body like the earlier German-made Mauser, with 248–490cc (15–30cu in) JAP engines.

ABOVE: A 1950 199cc (12cu in) Whizzer

WHIZZER *U.S.A. 1947–54*
A 199cc (12cu in) sv single scooter.

WIGA *Germany 1928–32*
Utilized 198–498cc (12–30cu in) JAP and ohc Küchen power units.

WIGAN-BARLOW *England 1921*
Used 293cc (18cu in) sv JAP and 346 (21cu in) Barr & Stroud sleeve-valved singles.

WIKRO *Germany 1924–26*
Used Precision and Blackburne engines.

WILBEE *England 1902–c.1906*
Used 2hp Minerva engines.

WILHELMINA *The Netherlands 1903–15*
A 2.5hp Precision single.

ABOVE: A 1914 Williamson

WILIER *Italy 1962–c.1970*
Made 49cc (3cu in) mopeds and lightweights.

WILKIN *England 1919–23*
Used 346/499cc (21/30cu in) sv Blackburne engines in sprung frames.

WILKINSON-ANTOINE *England 1903–06*
Bought-in Belgian Antoine singles of 2.25 and 2.75hp.

WILKINSON-TAC (WILKINSON TMC) *England 1909–16*
The same Wilkinson that still makes razor-blades, it then offered an air-cooled four of 676cc/41cu inches (later 844cc/51.5cu in) with rear suspension and a bucket seat.

BELOW: Four-cylinder Wilkinson

WILLIAMS *U.S.A. 1912–20*
Built its single-cylinder engine into the rear wheel.

WILLIAMSON *England 1912–20*
Early bikes used an air/water-cooled 996cc (61cu in) flat twin, later a 770cc (47cu in) JAP V-twin.

WILLOW *England 1920*
A 269cc (16cu in) Villiers-powered scooter.

WIMMER *Germany 1921–39*
Made a 134cc (8cu in) clip-on, and a variety of lightweight and mid-sized bikes up to 497cc (30cu in), both water- and air-cooled

WIN *England 1908–14*
Used 499 and 599cc (30 and 37cu in) Precision singles.

WINCO *England 1920–22*
Used a 261cc (16cu in) Orbit two-stroke.

WINDHOFF *Germany 1924–33*
An interesting range of bikes, including water-cooled two-strokes of 122/173cc (7.4/11cu in). Also an oil-cooled ohc 746cc (45.5cu in) four which was used as a stressed member and was shaft-driven as well. Produced a prototype 996cc (61cu in) flat twin later. Last bikes were quite conventional Villiers-powered lightweights.

WITTEKIND *Germany 1952–54*
Produced mopeds with 40cc (2.4cu in) Komet engines.

WITTLER Germany 1924–53
Used own 249cc (15cu in) two-stroke before the war, and resumed in 1949 with Sachs or Zündapp-powered mopeds.

WIZARD *Wales 1920–22*
A 269cc (16cu in) Liberty two-stroke.

WK *Germany 1920–22*
A 249cc (15cu in) sv for bicycles, for building into the wheel.

WKB *Austria 1923–24*
A 183cc (11cu in) three-port two-stroke.

WMB *Germany 1924–26*
Built own 1.8hp sv engine.

WOLF *England 1901–39*
All engines were bought in from Moto-Rêve in early years, with Villiers, Blackburnes and JAPs later on, to 678cc (41cu in).

WOOLER *England 1911–55*
All of John Wooler's designs were unusual, notably the 344cc (21cu in) double-ended piston two-stroke (one end acted as compressor) and the 346/496cc (21/30cu in) flat twins with side-mounted (but ohv) valves. After 1945, a small number of shaft-driven flat fours were sold.

The unusual two-stroke Wooler remained unique

WOTAN *Germany 1923–25*
A 170cc (10.4cu in) three-port two-stroke.

WSE *Germany 1924–25*
Built own 249cc (15cu in) sv.

WSK *Poland 1946–*
123–240cc (7.5–14.6cu in) two-strokes, the 125 being the longest-lived derivative of DKW's RT125.

WSM *Germany 1919–23*
Built a few complete bikes, and sold 496cc (30 cu in) flat twins to Victoria.

WUCO *Germany 1925*
Offered own 174cc (11cu in) sv, and bigger JAPs up to 490cc (30cu in).

WURRING *Germany 1921–59*
Also sold as the AWD and used a large variety of bought-in engines of 142–596cc (9–36cu in).

WÜRTTEMBERGIA *Germany 1925–33*
Used only Blackburne engines from 198–596cc (12–36cu in).

W&W *Austria 1925–27*
Mostly used MAG 498cc (30cu in) singles, but V-twins were made to order.

X

XL *England 1921–23*
Used JAP or Blackburne sv singles to 538cc (33cu in).

XL-ALL *England 1902–c.1906*
Built own small 90-degree V-twins of 2 and 4hp.

Y

YALE *U.S.A. 1902–1915*
A big, typically American V-twin of 950cc (58cu in), with early use of chain-drive.

YAMAGUCHI *Japan 1941–64*
Produced mostly 49cc (3cu in) mopeds, plus a 123cc (7.5cu in) two-stroke twin.

YAMAHA *Japan 1953–*
Torakusu Yamaha, whose name graces the sides of millions of motorcycles did not, as far as we know, ride one himself. In fact, as he died in 1916, he may never have even seen a motorcycle, for which an explanation is required.

Yamaha was born in Nagasaki in 1851 and was first apprenticed to a clock maker

ABOVE: Sales brochure for Yamaha V50, very similar to the Honda Cub

then to a manufacturer of medical equipment. He moved to Hamamatsu in 1883, then working as a self-employed engineer, where he was asked to repair the organ at the local primary school. Yamaha evidently found this interesting as he decided to go into the musical instrument business himself. Nippon Gakki, it was called, and it thrived and was soon a major force in the market, which is why the Yamaha logo to this day consists of three tuning forks. But after Yamaha's death, the company acquired an apparently dictatorial head named Chiymanu Amano, who was present during a number of strikes, not to mention the Kano earthquake of 1923. Order was restored by Kaichi Kawakami, who took over as president in 1926. His team-building approach paid dividends and Nippon Gakki recovered, though during the war production of musical instruments was subsumed by military work.

In 1948, sufficient normality was restored to allow for the manufacture of instruments to begin once more, though only two years later Kawakami passed the presidency to his son, Genichi. One of his first acts as president was to utilize the wartime machinery which was lying idle, and one of the best uses was to build a small motorcycle for Japan's rapidly growing home market. With no experience of bikes, the company sensibly based its design on an existing one, namely the DKW RT125, which was the same DKW copied by BSA for the Bantam and Harley-Davidson for the Hummer, though there were others. Being well-established with capital behind it, Nippon Gakki could afford to take its time perfecting the new

BELOW: The DS two-stroke twin survived until 1973

Yamaha always sold as many commuters as sportsbikes

bike while building a brand new factory for it at Hamamatsu. And the name of the new motorcycle division? In honour of the company's founder, it would be 'Yamaha'.

That first machine, the 125cc YA1, did much for Yamaha's image by winning national races and, by the end of 1955, the company was building 200 a month. A larger 175cc (11cu in) version, still DKW-based, went on sale for 1956 and the YA series continued until the early 1970s. A 250 was the next step, and the obvious thing was to base it on an existing bike. The DKW 250 was rejected as being a single, and an Adler MB250 twin was bought instead. But once it was there, the design head considered their own 250 could do better. This was agreed, and Yamaha's YD1 was the result, sharing nothing with the Adler apart from basic layout and dimensions. A successful road bike with a period pressed steel frame, it gave 17bhp.

Encouraged by its early race successes, the company built a works racing version of the YD1, with a lighter, stronger tubular frame and even a short-stroke version of the motor. It was rewarded with a 1-2-3 in the Asama races in 1957, plus first and second in the 125cc race. Rival Honda had been conclusively beaten, and orders for the YD1 began to flow in. It is illuminating that, so early on, Yamaha had discovered the sales advantage that competition success could bring. Maybe this was why racing of all kinds has been so central to the company's activities ever since. Thus it was the first Japanese company to race in America, and plunged into European Grand Prix racing in 1961, scoring 7th in both 125 and 250 French GPs.

Racing Pays Off

So not long after its very first motorcycle (based on a pre-war DKW) went on sale, Yamaha was competitive in international racing. It had a slight headstart by taking over the Showa marque in 1959, whose 125cc racer was very fast and taught Yamaha much about disc valves. Unlike Honda, Yamaha at the time was still wedded to the two-stroke engine, whether for its racers or for a simple commuter like the 80cc (5cu in) YG1, which was launched in the early sixties, but was still on sale as the YB100 30 years later. Although those early Japanese machines might look a little basic nowadays, they were actually quite advanced, the YB100 having automatic oiling (no tiresome pre-mix) and a disc valve (the racing influence), plus an impressive 10bhp. Practical and reliable as well as nippy, it is no wonder they sold so well.

A twin-cylinder 100, the YL1, appeared in 1966, though this one only lasted five years. It could manage 113km/h (70mph) in standard guise (not far behind some European 250s) and true to form, Yamaha offered a race kit which nearly doubled the power. The YDS series were 250 twins, starting with the YDS1 in 1959, updated into the YDS2 (1962) and YDS3 (1964). All were 246cc (15cu in) piston-ported twins, with 28bhp at 8,000rpm. There was also a 305cc (19cu in) YM1. They eventually developed into the DS7, which itself was the immediate precursor of the long-running RD-series. All these were road bikes, but just as important to Yamaha were the TD-series of off-the-shelf racers, starting with the 250cc (15cu in) TD1 in 1962, plus the 350cc (21cu in) TR-series, which was to become the liquid-cooled TZ from 1969. That Yamaha was able to sell these racers was down to its own success. Remember the European debut in 1961? Yamaha couldn't afford to race in Europe in 1962, but the year after saw a determined assault with the 250cc RD56, now with 45bhp at 11,000rpm. Yamaha was rewarded with its first GP win on the Spa circuit in Belgium, plus second places in Holland and the Isle of Man. The following year, Phil Read won the 250cc World Championship for Yamaha, and again in 1965. They couldn't match the Hailwood/Honda combination in 1966/67, but won both 125 and 250 titles in 1968, though both Honda and Suzuki had pulled out at the end of the previous season.

That same year, Yamaha announced something new. It was now exporting successfully to the United States where, by

ABOVE: *1976 Trail 50*

BELOW: *The Yamaha 350 autolube, with late sixties performance*

the late sixties, the market for dual-purpose trail bikes, as happy off the road as on it, was growing rapidly. Yamaha's importer persuaded the factory that what was needed was something close to the off-road ability of a Greeves or Bultaco, but with more civilized on-road manners. The DT1 was the result, and it was truly a new type of bike. The 175cc (11cu in) two-stroke single was relatively comfortable and easy to ride; it was well silenced, had good lights, and cruised happily at 97km/h (60mph), yet it could also take to the dirt if you so wished. (DT stood for 'Dirt Trail'.) It was a hit, and Yamaha's competitors soon came out with trail bikes of their own. So successful was the DT that a whole range of bikes grew up around it, from a DT50 to the relatively short-lived DT400. It was said that, like luxury 4x4 vehicles, some of these trail bikes never got their tyres muddy – it was the suggestion of trailing that riders wanted.

Although the DT opened up a new market, it wasn't that difficult for Yamaha to produce, being a two-stroke. The XS1, unveiled the following year, couldn't have been more different. It was the largest bike Yamaha had ever built, and it was a four-stroke. The basic idea was a sound one: take the highly popular (but increasingly outmoded) British vertical-twin concept and update it to take up where the Bonneville had left off. The XS certainly looked good on paper, being a 653cc (40cu in) twin with overhead cam, five-speed gearbox and electric start, plus Japanese reliability. It wasn't an instant success, for at the time Japanese manufacturers had yet to master the art of motorcycle roadholding and handling, especially with the larger bikes. However, Yamaha persevered, and the revamped, renamed XS650 was developed into quite a decent bike, acquiring a following of its own. The torquey engine was to prove adept at sidecar motocross and American flat-track racing. A measure of its eventual success is that Yamaha went on making it until the early 1980s.

However, one development didn't get that far. The TX750 was a bored out version of the 650, though as Triumph was finding out at the same time (this was 1972), 750cc (46cu in) was really too much for an unbalanced vertical twin. Yamaha accepted this, and designed a balancer system (two counter-rotating weights in the rear of the crankcase) to counteract the vibration. It worked, and the 750 was certainly smoother than the 650. Unfortunately, the crankshaft-driven balancer sapped so much power that the TX was actually slower than the smaller bike, struggling to even reach 161km/h (100mph). It was ignominiously dropped, just a few months after launch.

Two-Stroke Days

Meanwhile, Yamaha was having a happier time with what it knew best – small two-strokes. The company had noted the huge success of Honda's Cub and like Suzuki came up with something very similar to meet it though, being a Yamaha, it was a two-stroke. It came in V50 and V80 forms, both having reed-valves. The smaller had a two-speed automatic gearbox (though with manual selection) and the 79cc (4.8cu in) V80 was a three-speeder. Naturally, the two-stroke oil was mixed automatically, while drive was by enclosed chain. These two were later replaced by the four-stroke T50 and T80, both of which boasted the sophistication of shaft-drive. The earlier step-thrus offered no real advantage over the Honda, though that wasn't really the point – they gave Yamaha something to sell in this fiercely competitive market.

A more obvious class leader was the FS1 sports moped, which first appeared in 1972 and is actually still being made, though in restricted, sanitized form only. With its disc-valved engine and motorcycle looks, the FS1E was the bike for 16-year-olds to be seen on in 1970s Britain. There were daring tales of 52, even 53mph on the right downhill stretch, when the author's Puch could barely manage 61km/h (38mph) on a good day! However, laws changed and these sports mopeds were restricted back to a maximum of 30mph. But it is still on sale, 20 years later, in drum-braked (FS1) or disc-braked (FS1DX) forms.

If our sports moped rider survived the FS1E, he (and they usually were, though not exclusively male) would often graduate to a DT175. Of all Yamaha's DT trail bike series, the 175 was possibly the best compromise. It had enough performance to be exciting, yet was light enough to take off-road easily, and much cheaper on fuel and insurance than the 250 and 400. No wonder it enjoyed a production run of 12 years (1973–1985).

Among certain generations of riders, the letters 'FS1E' and 'DT' have a certain resonance, but none can compete with the magical 'RD' (apart perhaps from its successor, the 'LC'). RD in this case stood for 'Race Developed' which in Yamaha's case had more than an element of truth in it, rooted as the company was in racing air-cooled two-stroke twins. The RD-series replaced the long-running YDS in 1973, and its main advance was the use of reed-valve induction in place of conventional piston ports. Reed valves were not a new concept, and the basic idea is simple. Instead of relying on the passing piston to open and close off each port, the reed is a flap valve, sucked open by the vacuum under a rising piston, and closing as the piston descends. A key advantage is that ports are less compromised in shape and the power band is wider. But Yamaha's version used an innovation of its own, an extra transfer port above the inlet port, which drew in an extra helping of charge after the main one and improved scavenging as well. Perfect scavenging (the evacuation of all exhaust gases from the cylinder to allow a full fresh charge to come in) is the object of every two-stroke. In practical terms, this meant that the new RD250's power band now started at 4,000rpm instead of the previous 6,000rpm, with obvious benefits in rideability and fuel consumption.

Yamaha Tenere, a 660cc (40cu in) five-valve single, was inspired by Paris–Dakar racers

Yamaha demonstrated its faith in the new system (which rejoiced in the marketing-friendly term of 'Torque Induction') by launching a whole range of RDs within a couple of months of one another. There was an RD125 (124cc/8cu in), RD200 (196cc/12cu in), RD250 (247cc/15cu in) and RD350 (347cc/21cu in). The two larger bikes had a six-speed

Competition success has been important to Yamaha. This is a 250cc (15cu in) enduro bike

ABOVE: 1980s XJ650

ABOVE: A straightforward XJ550

BELOW: 750 Super Tenere

gearbox which, according to author Mick Walker, was merely a convenient means of homologating the TZ racer's gearbox. Those early RDs looked very similar to the older YDS, but all had a comprehensive restyle in 1975, with squared-off tank and seat and block-style graphics that became the RD trademark. At the same time, the RD125 and 200 acquired front disc brakes. A year later, the RD350 became the RD400, due to an 8mm longer stroke, with 40bhp and a stronger bottom-end to suit. After that, there were just minor changes, though electronic ignition was a worthwhile advance in 1978. However, the RD two-strokes, for all their power, were simply unable to meet imminent U.S. emissions limits, and the whole range was dropped in 1980.

XS & LC

It is odd that while Yamaha was producing such class-leading and popular two-strokes, its four-strokes should still be relatively lacklustre. At first glance, the XS500 twin announced in 1975 looked promising: twin overhead camshafts, four valves per cylinder, and a balancer shaft to dampen the vibration. The all-new engine produced a claimed 48bhp at 8,500rpm for a top speed of 175km/h (109mph). Unfortunately, the 500 was a weighty old thing at over 200kg (441lb) with disappointing acceleration and no real get up and go. The lighter, simpler XS twins sold rather better. First was the XS360 of 1976, with single overhead cam and 180-degree crankshaft. An XS250 followed, while the 360 was later bored out to 399cc/24cu inches, all three bikes

The TZ750 two-stroke did well in circuit racing, but is shown here adapted for the American dirt track

The shaft-drive, three-cylinder XS750

ABOVE and OPPOSITE: XS850 was an update of the XS750

sharing the same 52.4mm stroke. The 400 actually lasted up to 1983, by which time it had a new backbone frame, twin overhead-cam cylinder head and monoshock rear suspension. It is still not remembered with quite the same affection as the RD.

There was a lot more anticipation when the XT500 trail bike was launched in 1977. Although rather heavy for serious off-road use, it echoed the DT in opening up a new market for trail bikes, in this case for big four-stroke singles which, until then, Japanese manufacturers had ignored. The 499cc (30cu in) single overhead-cam engine looked simple in the extreme with just two valves, one carburettor and no electric start. Indeed, some thought this was the long-awaited return of the simple, torquey big single. But it put out confusing messages, with the ground clearance, suspension travel and seat height of a proper off-roader, together with that 138kg (304lb) mass.

Perhaps the SR500, a pure road bike, was a more honest use of the 499cc single. The engine was basically similar, but had larger valves and carburettor, and various parts strengthened to cope with high-speed cruising. There were also decent 12-volt electrics (the XT was 6-volt) and a disc front brake. Some were sold, but the SR wasn't really a modern BSA Gold Star.

But in the same year that the XT appeared, Yamaha also came up with its first truly successful four-stroke. The XS750 was its belated Superbike competitor, and it was right first time. The 747cc (46cu in) dohc triple wasn't an out-and-out sportster; it was too heavy for that, and in any case the shaft-drive indicated that this was a bike with touring pretensions. Nor was it quite as fast, at 177km/h (110mph) as some other 750s, but it was smooth and comfortable. Performance was improved by an increase in capacity to 826cc (50cu in) in 1980, which took power up to 79bhp at 8,500rpm and top speed to 201km/h (125mph). And despite the weight it handled reasonably well, due to fully adjustable suspension at both ends. It was superseded by the four-cylinder XJ900 in 1983.

Despite its determination to break into the big four-stroke market, Yamaha's two-strokes were still doing well on the track, especially the twin-cylinder production racers. It won the 250cc World Championship four times in the 1970s (1970–73) and the 350 class in the following three years, plus two 125cc titles. The 500 class came Yamaha's way in 1973, then (thanks to Kenny Roberts) from 1978–'80 as well. It was also developing a presence in off-road sport, winning motocross GPs by the middle of the decade.

Meanwhile, although the air-cooled RD had been killed off by U.S. regulations, the bike had been so successful in Europe that Yamaha decided to launch a replacement aimed specifically at the Europeans. Still a two-stroke twin, the big news was that it was liquid-cooled, which gave a more even-

POWERFUL AND SMOOTH, THE GRAND TOURER WITH THE SPORTING EDGE

The best in engineering is said to be a compromise. Perhaps so. But the only compromise Yamaha are prepared to make in our pursuit of perfection is the compromise between sheer inspiration and ceaseless development. That compromise, and no other, has produced the XS850.

The inspiration that produced the XS750 and led to its undisputed reign as the world's finest tourer lies at the heart of the new 850. The double-overhead-camshaft three-cylinder engine was perfect for its purpose. Powerful and smooth, it gave the grand tourer a sporting edge and a character that won it instant favour the world over. Now, we have given the 850 just a little more power, a little more torque, and perhaps still greater character.

The XS850 retains the features that gave the 750 its reputation — the shaft drive, the ultra-comfortable seat, and the Teflon-lined heavy-duty forks, while incorporating vital improvements. The 850 features new, upswept exhausts for extra ground clearance, a larger tank for still longer distances between fuel stops, and new 200mm halogen headlight. It also carries an oil cooler for enhanced reliability and still longer engine life.

The XS850 is the result of the only kind of compromise that Yamaha recognise: the compromise that seeks nothing short of perfection.

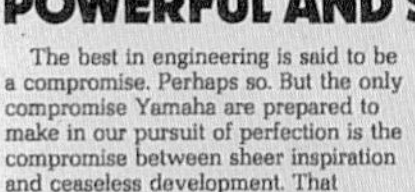

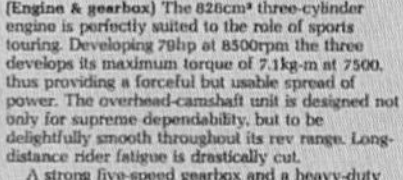

(Frame & suspension) The 850 employs the same superbly balanced double-loop cradle frame that gave the 750 its legendary handling. The Teflon-lined long-travel forks and the adjustable rear suspension ensure a balance of handling and comfort under all conditions, whatever the load. The 850 features a redesigned seat and newly styled exhausts to provide extra ground clearance.

To further extend the safety margin of the XS850, a more powerful 200mm halogen headlight has been fitted. Indicators are of Yamaha's self-cancelling design. Wheels are cast alloy in black and silver trim. There are two disc brakes on the front wheel, with rear-mounted calipers; the rear brake is a single disc.

(Engine & gearbox) The 826cm³ three-cylinder engine is perfectly suited to the role of sports touring. Developing 79hp at 8500rpm the three develops its maximum torque of 7.1kg-m at 7500, thus providing a forceful but usable spread of power. The overhead-camshaft unit is designed not only for supreme dependability, but to be delightfully smooth throughout its rev range. Long-distance rider fatigue is drastically cut.

A strong five-speed gearbox and a heavy-duty multiplate clutch are connected to the rear wheel by Yamaha's famous shaft-drive system. Completely free of drive-train snatch and torque reaction, the shaft is the most efficient and least demanding transmission system that can be fitted to a tourer. Maintenance is minimal and reliability is total.

BELOW: The V-twin XV1000, shown here in Midnight Special' guise

BELOW: A TZ750 racer

running temperature (both over time and over different parts of the engine) and less noise. Although it looked completely different to the old RD, with the squared-off shape giving way to a pleasing rounded form, the LC owed much to its predecessor. Reed-valve induction was still there, and the six-speed gearbox was familiar as well, but there was a new monoshock rear suspension (derived from the YZ motocrossers) and anti-vibration rubber mounting for the engine. Predictably, the LC (known as 'Elsie' to U.K. enthusiasts) became the bike to have in Production Racing, winning 250 and 500 classes in its first TT. The only big development of the bike was the Yamaha Power Valve System (YPVS) which was unveiled in 1982. Its impressive 59bhp at 9,000rpm was made

INNOVATIONS
1981
YAMAHA

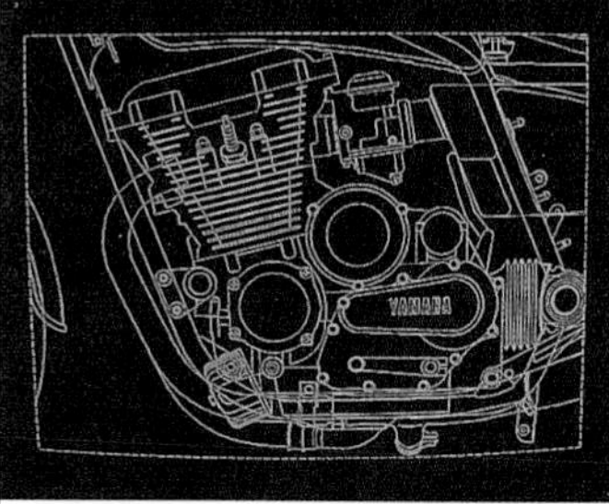

YAMAHA

YAMAHA – ALWAYS LEADERS IN MOTORCYCLE DEVELOPMENT

It was in 1955, over a quarter of a century ago, that the first Yamaha motorcycle made its public debut.

That machine was a simple, single-cylinder 125cc two-stroke but, ever since that time, Yamaha has been in the forefront of motorcycling development.

Waterproof brakes, rotary valves, automatic oiling for two-strokes, reed valves, direct chrome plating of alloy cylinder bores, multiple transfer ports, omniphase crankshaft balancing, air-damped forks and monoshock suspension, eight-valve cylinder heads for four-stroke twins, curved-spoke cast wheels .... Yamaha were responsible for the introduction of all these important technical advances to mass production motorcycling.

Now the innovations continue into the nineteen-eighties with six important developments this year in the fields of fuel consumption, suspension, transmission and general engine efficiency.

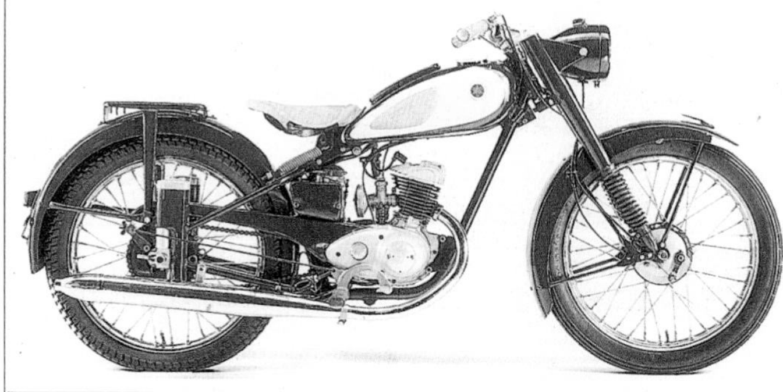

Yamaha's first bike (TOP RIGHT) was worlds apart from the bulky XS1100 (BELOW)

ABOVE: RD350 YPVS

BELOW: Special fairing option for XS1100

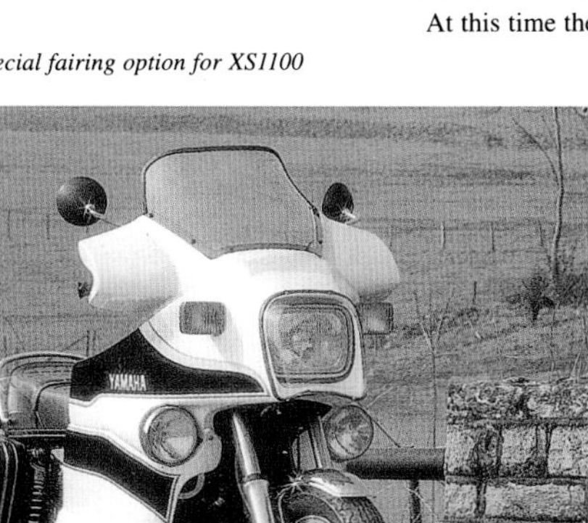

possible by a variable exhaust port, whose size and position changed automatically according to engine revs.

YPVS was also fitted to the ultimate RD, the 499cc (30cu in) V4 of 1984. The RD500LC was built to capitalize on Grand Prix success, but owed more to the LC than Kenny Roberts' racer. The cleverly-designed motor used two crankshafts and four carburettors, while the four YPVS valves were mechanically linked, operated by a single servo motor. Not for the faint-hearted, this ultimate road-going two-stroke could run up 217km/h (135mph) on its 80bhp. At the other end of the scale there were also liquid-cooled RD80s and RD125LCs, plus an air-cooled RD50 (Yamaha seemed determined to make the most of that 'Race Developed' prefix!)

At this time there were less exciting tiddlers from Hamamatsu as well. The SR500 had been followed by an SR250 and 125, though these were in a different mould being mild-mannered commuters with custom styling. And all this time Yamaha was selling a full range of tiddlers, examples being the Passola 50 and scooter-style 79cc (4.8cu in) Beluga.

It took Yamaha some time to follow the four-cylinder four-stroke route along which its Japanese rivals had already ventured. After vertical twins and triples, its next attempt at an alternative big four-stroke was the TR1. Launched in late 1980, this was a 981cc (60cu in) roadster in European style. To appeal to its chosen market, the TR1 was relatively simple: the 75-degree V-twin had single overhead cams and two valves per cylinder; there was an enclosed chain-drive, vertically-split crankcases and five-speed gearbox. The only newer elements were electronic advance for the ignition timing and monoshock rear suspension, which Yamaha had now been using for seven years. Alongside the TR1 was the basically similar but smaller-engined 740cc (45cu in) Virago, with shaft-drive and custom styling. Both used steel backbone frames.

If the TR1/Virago showed a traditionalist approach to the V-twin, the XZ550 announced a couple of years later couldn't have been more different, proving that Yamaha was nothing if not eclectic. This 70-degree 552cc (34cu in) V-twin was liquid-cooled, with dohc four-valve cylinder-heads, each with twin exhaust ports. The engine had a balance shaft and was unusually hung from the downtubes of the cradle-type frame. There was shaft-drive, trailing-axle front forks and

The Virage 1100 was a popular factory custom

SRX600, a good-looking sporting single

unpleasant squared-off styling. In fact, the XZ550 resembled one of those concept bikes where every idea the R&D boys can come up with is thrown together on one machine in order to gauge reaction. In this case, all the gizmos added up to less than their sum, and performance was disappointing and problematic. Buyers could not be tempted, and the XZ was soon dropped.

Fours & Fives

But simultaneously with the XZ550, Yamaha was also selling a range of perfectly straightforward dohc fours. The XJ series began with a 550 before growing into the shaft-driven 650 and 750. None made a huge impact apart from the XJ650 Turbo, which along with Honda's CX Turbo marked a brief flirtation with turbos as an alternative to big engines, neither being successful. What did succeed was the bigger XJ900, which was unveiled in 1983. It was a strong, torquey, fairly simple touring machine, with an 853cc (52cu in) dohc air-cooled four-cylinder engine and shaft-drive. The capacity was soon increased to 891cc (now with 91bhp) and the FJ900 was quite a success, still selling 16 years on. In much the same mould was the FJ1100 of 1984, still an air-cooled shaft-driven four, but with far more power, monoshock rear suspenson and an alloy frame. It could break the 241km/h (150mph) barrier and dawdle through town at minimal revs, winning the big FJ many friends. It also had a capacity increase in 1986 to 1188cc (72.5cu in), as the FJ1200. There were more minor changes in 1988, but perhaps more significant was the ABS option launched in 1991. Like the XJ900, the FJ is still in production.

Maybe this success with the bigger fours gave Yamaha more confidence with the smaller ones. The Diversion 600 of 1991 certainly suggested this. There was nothing very radical about it, but it was a very good seller where the old XJ600 was not. Its 600cc (37cu in) four was a much simplified version of the Genesis concept (see below), still with a slant-forward block, but with air-cooling and just two valves per cylinder. Despite, or perhaps because of the modest specification, the Diversion proved to be an excellent all-rounder, which is what many people still want from a bike. Available in naked and half-faired forms, it was good value and a deserved success. The 600cc class has moved on so fast in the nineties that the Diversion is now very much the budget option, the 95bhp Fazer 600 from 1998 being more contemporary, but it goes on selling nonetheless.

The V-Max, on the other hand, could never be described as a sensible all-rounder. Launched in 1985, it was an unashamed performance muscle machine, with sheer acceleration and speed (in a straight line) its single-purpose goal. It looked like nothing else, with the surprisingly compact liquid-cooled 1198cc (73cu in) V4 filling the frame completely. It was based on the V4 of the Gold Wing-style XVZ12, but with larger carburettors and valves, not to mention higher compression, stronger valve-springs and toughened bottom-end. It is hardly surprising that the V-Max became something of a cult bike.

Yamaha hadn't forgotten the trail bike market that it had pioneered, though it was now applying four-stroke technology. The XT500 wasn't perfect, but it persevered with the four-valve, twin-carburettor 558cc (34cu in) XT550 (and a smaller XT400), which in turn was superseded by the XT600 and XT600Z Tenere. The latter came about due to the popularity of desert rallies such as the Paris–Dakar, where huge fuel tanks and long, tall suspension was part of the required look. An electric-start version followed in 1990, all part of the thorough updating of the XT concept which kept it selling. The road-going single wasn't neglected either, with the SR500 transformed into the SRX600, using the same four-valve 608cc (37cu in) single as the XT. The SRX was a good-looking bike too, less traditionalist than the SR but with the big single on full display and it was through it that many found their way into single-cylinder racing. A new XT350 was already part of the range by then, with an all-new dohc four-valve 346cc (21cu in) single. It was a winner, and perhaps underlined the fact that for genuine on/off-road use, a 350 was more manageable than a 600.

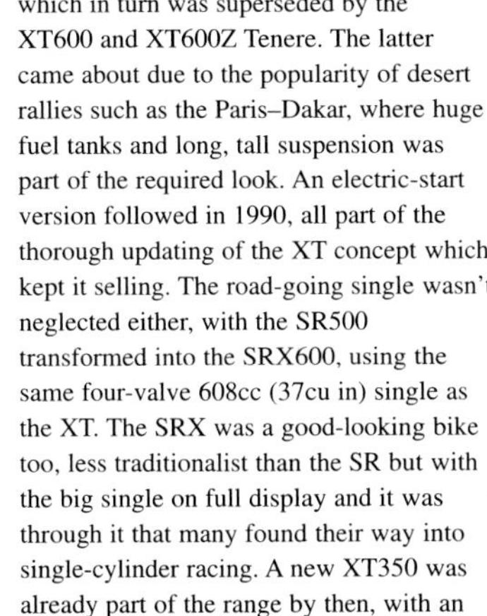

By the early 1980s, Yamaha had built successful four-stroke singles and tourers, but had yet to really take the sportsbike market by storm. That came in 1985 with the FZ750. There was much new about the FZ, specifically its liquid-cooled 749cc (46cu in) four, with five valves per cylinder. Over a long development period, Yamaha engineers had experimented with six- and even seven-valve heads before settling on five as the best compromise between power and reliability. The cylinder-block was slanted forward at 45 degrees (the Genesis concept) to lower the centre of gravity and allow good, straight inlet and exhaust ports, not to mention space for the four down-draught carburettors. It all added up to a very efficient and powerful engine (106bhp, plus a good flat torque curve) that gave Yamaha class leadership for a while. It was followed up in 1987 with the FZR1000 Genesis, whose main innovation was an alloy box section frame known as Deltabox. The latter was a big step forward, giving a lower seat height and far better handling than the steel-framed FZ750. The engine was simply an enlarged 750, though with great attention paid to weight and space saving. Power was 135bhp, with a 266km/h (165mph) top speed.

The addition of EXUP (Exhaust

The 1988 brochure showing part of the XT trail-bike range

Ultimate Power Valve) in 1989 gave even more power, with a valve in the exhaust collector box to control the gas pressure wave. That same year saw the 750 updated with the alloy frame, plus a new FZR600 to contest the up-and-coming supersports 600 class. It was sobering to realize that the 600 produced 90bhp at 10,500rpm, not much less than the 750 had just four years earlier, and with a mere four valves per cylinder. An FZR400R, to comply with Japanese licencing laws, was another addition to the range. The 600 and 1000 models were updated in 1996 into the fully-faired Thundercat and Thunderace, but here Yamaha seemed to have lost its sporting edge. Where the FZ/FZR were genuinely innovative with strong race influences, the new bikes looked and rode more like softer sports tourers.

New Sport, New Standards

Meanwhile, Yamaha had not forgotten its smaller bikes, and still favoured the two-stroke. The TZR125 of 1988 used a reed-valved two-stroke single together with the latest Deltabox frame. It came with or without a fairing, and was a great success. More intriguing was the TDR250, an attempt at mirroring the big TDM850 with a trail bike style but with road tyres and road performance. The twin-cylinder two-stroke gave an amazing 172km/h (107mph) maximum speed, and the TDR certainly provided an alternative to race replicas. We musn't forget to mention the TDM, which was launched in 1990. It had elements of the sportsbikes, notably the Deltabox, and its 849cc/52cu inch twin-cylinder engine, based around the Genesis five-valve layout, with vaguely trail bike styling. Yamaha called it a 'New Sport' concept, and it is

1998 Drag Star Classic

ABOVE: FZ750

BELOW: The FJ1100 (and 1200) were reliable tourers

The TDM850; not sports, touring or trail, but 'New Sport'

Kenny Roberts on a 1980 TZ750 at Daytona

ABOVE: 1984 500cc (31.5cu in) Grand Prix racer

successful enough to be still on sale at the end of the decade. It also led to the TRX850 offshoot, more of a traditional café racer using the same mechanics. Custom bikes, meanwhile, were becoming more specialized. In the 1970s and early '80s it had been enough to fit high bars and extra chrome to existing twins and fours, but Yamaha's XV535 Virago did much to change this. It managed to look like a big V-twin, but was in fact a simple, cheap-to-run 535cc (32.6cu in) unit, producing a moderate 47bhp, and shaft-drive reduced maintenance as well. Light, low-seated and easy to ride, the Virago was an instant hit. So successful, that it spawned 125, 250, 750 and 1100 versions. And as the 1990s draws to a close, a new market is appearing for luxury scooters. Pioneered by Honda, this has taken off to such an extent that Yamaha and Suzuki have both responded with versions of their own. Yamaha's Majesty is typical, the 250cc (15cu in) four-stroke allowing main road performance, with added weather protection and lockable luggage built-in.

But for Yamaha, two bikes stand out in the 1990s, and neither are scooters. We've mentioned how the FZR series seemed to lose its way as the Thundercat and Thunderace. The bikes that changed all that were the R1 in 1998, and the R6 of 1999. The R1 is a milestone bike, setting new standards in the one-litre supersports class. It is lighter, smaller and more powerful than any of its rivals, and great play is made of the 'three figures': 150bhp, 177kg and 1,395mm (shortest wheelbase). As Alan Cathcart wrote in *Motorcycle Sport & Leisure*: 'The face of sportbiking has just changed: the new look is red and white (or blue, if you insist) with snake-eye

YAMAHA FZR600R

RIGHT: Sales brochure for the FZR600

The FZR Genesis, with Yamaha's 'Genesis' box-section alloy frame on clear display

headlights and works Superbike performance on the road. No compromises.' In fact, the R1 is the first of a new family of supersports bikes, including a 750cc R7 for Superbike racing and a 599cc (36.5cu in) R6. With the R6, Yamaha has done it again. More power (120bhp at 13,000rpm) than any other 600, and it is marginally lighter than them all as well, its top speed being over 274km/h (170mph). For a 'mere' 600, it gives an astonishing performance, and underlines the fact that Yamaha intends to hold tight to its sportsbike market leadership. One just wonders what organ repairer Torakusu Yamaha would have made of all this.

BELOW: The 1998 R1, which set new standards for one-litre sportsbikes

YANKEE *U.S.A. 1970–74*
An interesting 488cc (30cu in) machine made by coupling two 244cc Ossa two-strokes together, the idea of Ossa's American importer.

YORK *Austria 1927–30*
Jap-powered and made by Omega in England, to a design by Robert Sturm.

YOUNG *England 1919–23*
A 269cc (16cu in) engine for bicycles and a 130cc (8cu in) replacement design sold to Walton Engineering.

YVEL *France 1921–24*
Used own 174/233cc (11/14cu in) engines.

OPPOSITE: Yamaha GTS1000. Note single-sided front suspension

Z

ZANELLA *Argentina 1957–*
Produced mopeds, lightweights and scooters, first built under licence from Ceccato of Italy. Its own designs appeared from 1960, and there were increasing links with Yamaha in the 1990s.

ZEDEL *France 1902–15*
A range of singles and V-twins of 2–3.5hp.

ZEGEMO *Germany 1924–25*
Used bought-in 248cc (15cu in) two-stroke Baumi engines.

ZEHNDER *Switzerland 1923–39*
Various two-strokes up to 248cc (15cu in). The factory was moved to Switzerland by its new owner in the early 1930s.

ZEHNER *Germany 1924–26*
A 197cc (12cu in) sv utility.

ZENIT *Italy 1945–56*
Used 123/174cc (7.5/11cu in) AMC engines.

ZENITH *England 1907–49*
First used a 482cc (29cu in) sv single, but the big breakthrough came with Gradua gear from 1908, giving a variable-gear ratio when most machines had fixed single-speed. This gave it a huge advantage in competition from which the Zenith Gradua was notoriously banned. Used mostly V-twin JAPs from 1914, and 1922 saw more conventional chain-drive bikes with JAP, Bradshaw and Blackburne engines. Production ceased in 1931 when Zenith changed hands, followed by limited production which finally ceased for good in 1949.

ABOVE and OPPOSITE: 1914 Zenith 550cc (34cu in) V-twin. The engine is a JAP

AJ 2396
ZENITH
ZENITH
JAP

ZEPHYR *England 1922–23*
A 131cc (8cu in) two-stroke clip-on.

ZETA *Italy 1948–54*
A small-wheeled scooter type, with bought-in 48/60cc (3/4cu in) engines.

ZETGE *Germany 1922–25*
Used both DKW two-strokes to 173cc (11cu in) and its own of similar capacity.

ZEUGNER *Germany 1903–06*
Used a wide variety of bought-in engines, including units from FN and Peugeot.

ZEUS *Czechoslovakia 1902–12*
Produced singles (3–3.5hp) and V-twins (4–4.5hp) and also sold under the Linser brand name.

ZEUS *Germany 1925–27*
Used Küchen three-valve ohc singles to 498cc (30cu in).

ZIEJANÜ *Germany 1924–26*
211/246cc (13/15cu in) two-strokes and 348/498cc (21/30cu in) sv and ohv JAP four-strokes.

ZIRO *Germany 1919–24*
Disc-valved two-strokes of 148 and 346cc (9 and 21cu in).

ZÜNDAPP *Germany 1921–84*
The company began relatively late with a copy of the 211cc (13cu in) two-stroke Levis, but at one time came to be the leading German manufacturer. By 1930 it was building its own range of two-strokes of up to 300cc (18cu in) and had built 100,000 machines by 1933. The first four-

1939 Zündapp KS750 746cc (45.5cu in) flat twin with Stoppa Sidecar

A beautifully restored 1958 600cc (37cu in) Zündapp, with swinging arm frame and high-rise bars

stroke used the Rudge Python four-valve single but it introduced its own four-strokes in 1933, flat twins of 398/498cc (24/30cu in) and 598/797cc (36/49cu in) flat fours. Designed by Richard and Xavier Küchen, all had pressed steel frames and shaft-drive. There were new 198/348cc (12/21cu in) unit-construction two-strokes, also with pressed steel frames and shaft-driven and the KS750 flat twin was built during the war (during which time the 250,000th Zündapp was made). After the war it resumed with the 198cc two-stroke and 597cc flat twin. New post-war products were a 48cc (3cu in) clip-on and the 147cc (9cu in) Bella scooter in 1953, as well as lightweight two-strokes expanded up to 247cc (15cu in). A wide range of air- and water-cooled two-strokes (road and off-road) continued into the 1980s, but Zündapp was unable to survive, and closed in 1984.

Zündapp KS175 on display: smart but not enough to keep the company going

ZÜRTZ-REKORD *Germany 1922–26*
A variety of power units were used, from the 142cc (9cu in) DKW to 490cc (30cu in) JAP, all using a wide top-tube frame which acted as a fuel tank.

ZWEIRAD-UNION *Germany 1958–74*
Faced with a declining market, a number of German manufacturers (DKW, Express, Victoria and later Hercules) merged to form Zweirad-Union. Despite rationalization, the combine itself eventually succumbed to takeover by Fichtel & Sachs in 1969.

ZWERG *Germany 1924–25*
Used own 147/187cc (9/11cu in) two-strokes.

ZWI *Israel 1952–55*
Produced 123cc (7.5cu in) Villiers or JAP-engined machines.

ZZR *Poland 1960–*
Produces mopeds only, under the Komar brand name.

BELOW and RIGHT: Zündapp's shaft-driven flat twins were remarkably similar to contemporary BMWs, the only difference being that, from the 1950s, Zündapp tried selling smaller, cheaper machines

Bibliography

An encyclopedia can never be more than a collection of summaries. For fuller details of the better-known marques, it is worth tracking down the books listed below, all of which were referred to when preparing this work.

Aermacchi, by Mick Walker (Transport Source Books)

Benelli, by Mick Walker (Transport Source Books)

BSA Singles Gold Portfolio (Brooklands Books)

BSA Competition History, by Norman Vanhouse (Haynes Publishing)

BSA: The Complete Story, by Owen Wright (Crowood Press)

Ducati Supersport, by Ian Falloon (Haynes Publishing)

The Ducati Story, by Ian Falloon (Haynes Publishing)

Gilera Road Racers, by Raymond Ainscoe (Osprey)

Harley-Davidson Classics 1903–65, by Jerry Hatfield (Motorbooks International)

Inside Harley-Davidson, by Jerry Hatfield (Motorbooks International)

The Harley-Davidson Motor Company, by David Wright (Motorbooks International)

Honda: The Early Classic Motorcycles, by Roy Bacon (Niton Publishing)

The Humber Story, by A.B. Demaus & T.C. Tarring (Sutton Publishing)

The Indian, by Tod Rafferty (Bramley Books)

Kawasaki, by Mick Walker (Osprey)

Kawasaki Fours, by Mick Walker (Crowood Press)

Lambretta: An Illustrated History, by Nigel Cox (Haynes Publishing)

Laverda Gold Portfolio (Brooklands Books)

Moto Guzzi, by Mick Walker (Osprey)

Moto Guzzi V-twins, by Mick Walker (Crowood Press)

MZ, by Mick Walker (Transport Source Books)

Norton Rotaries, by Kris Perkins (Osprey)

Norton, by Mick Woollett

Royal Enfield, by Anne Bradford (Amulree Publications)

Suzuki, by Roy Bacon (Chartwell Books)

Suzuki, by Mick Walker (Osprey)

Triumph Triples, by Andrew Morland & Peter Henshaw (Osprey)

Vespa: An Illustrated History, by Eric Brockway (Haynes Publishing)

The Victory Motorcycle, by Michael Dapper & Lee Klancher (Motobooks International)

Vincent, by Duncan Wherret (Osprey)

Yamaha, by Mick Walker (Osprey)

British Motorcycles of the 1940s & 1950s, by Roy Bacon (Osprey)

British Motorcycles of the 1960s, by Roy Bacon (Osprey)

The Encyclopedia of Motorcycles, by Roland Brown (Lorenz Books)

Whatever Happened to the British Motorcycle Industry? by Bert Hopwood (Haynes Publishing)

Well Made in America, by Peter Reid (McGraw Hill)

Motorcycle Milestones Vol 1, by Richard Renstrom (Classics Unlimited)

Motor Scooters Colour Family Album, by Andrea & David Sparrow (Veloce Publishing)

The Illustrated Encyclopedia of Motorcycles, by Erwin Tragatsch (Hamlyn)

Superbike Specials of the 1970s, by Mick Walker (Windrow & Greene)

The History of Motorcycles, by Mick Walker (Hamlyn)

Great British Bikes, by Ian Ward & Laurie Caddell (Tiger Books International)

The Encyclopedia of the Motorcycle, by Hugo Wilson (Dorling Kindersley)

British Motorcycles since 1950 (Vols 1–6), by Steve Wilson (Haynes Publishing)

A 1948 customized Harley-Davidson 747cc (46cu in) WLC

HARLEY